# The Search for Meaning in Psychotherapy

If, when a patient enters therapy, there is an underlying yearning to discover a deeper sense of meaning, how might a therapist rise to such a challenge? As both Carl Jung and Wilfred Bion observed, the patient may be seeking something that has a spiritual as well as psychotherapeutic dimension. Presented in two parts, *The Search for Meaning in Psychotherapy* is a profound inquiry into the contemplative, mystical and apophatic dimensions of psychoanalysis.

What are some of the qualities that may inspire processes of growth, healing and transformation in a patient? Part One, The listening cure: psychotherapy as spiritual practice, considers the confluence between psychotherapy, spirituality, mysticism, meditation and contemplation. The book explores qualities such as presence, awareness, attention, mindfulness, calm abiding, reverie, patience, compassion, insight and wisdom, as well as showing how they may be enhanced by meditative and spiritual practice.

Part Two, A ray of divine darkness: psychotherapy and the apophatic way, explores the relevance of apophatic mysticism to psychoanalysis, particularly showing its inspiration through the work of Wilfred Bion. Paradoxically using language to unsay itself, the apophatic points towards absolute reality as ineffable and unnameable. So too, Bion observed, psychoanalysis requires the ability to dwell in mystery while awaiting intimations of ultimate truth, O, which cannot be known, only realised. Pickering reflects on the works of key apophatic mystics including Dionysius, Meister Eckhart and St John of the Cross; Buddhist teachings on meditation; *śūnyatā* and Dzogchen; and Lévinas' ethics of alterity.

*The Search for Meaning in Psychotherapy* will be of great interest to both trainees and accomplished practitioners in psychoanalysis, analytical psychology, psychotherapy and counselling, as well as scholars of religious studies, those in religious orders, spiritual directors, priests and meditation teachers.

**Judith Pickering** is a psychoanalytic psychotherapist, analytical psychologist, couple therapist and scholar of religious studies working in private practice in Sydney, Australia. She is the author of *Being in Love: Therapeutic Pathways Through Psychological Obstacles to Love* (Routledge, 2008) and has over forty years' experience in meditation, prayer and contemplation.

# The Search for Meaning in Psychotherapy

## Spiritual Practice, the Apophatic Way and Bion

Judith Pickering

Routledge
Taylor & Francis Group

LONDON AND NEW YORK

First published 2019
by Routledge
2 Park Square, Milton Park, Abingdon, Oxon OX14 4RN

and by Routledge
52 Vanderbilt Avenue, New York, NY 10017

*Routledge is an imprint of the Taylor & Francis Group, an informa business*

© 2019 Judith Pickering

*British Library Cataloguing-in-Publication Data*
A catalogue record for this book is available from the British Library

*Library of Congress Cataloging-in-Publication Data*
Names: Pickering, Judith, 1959– author.
Title: The search for meaning in psychotherapy : spiritual practice,
   the apophatic way and Bion / Judith Pickering.
Description: Abingdon, Oxon ; New York, NY : Routledge, 2019. |
   Includes bibliographical references and index.
Identifiers: LCCN 2018052134 (print) | LCCN 2018053046 (ebook) |
   ISBN 9781315639581 (Master) | ISBN 9781317274469 (ePub) |
   ISBN 9781317274452 (Mobipocket) | ISBN 9781317274476 (Pdf) |
   ISBN 9781138193062 (hbk : alk. paper) | ISBN 9781138193079
   (pbk. : alk. paper) | ISBN 9781315639581 (ebk)
Subjects: MESH: Psychotherapy—methods | Spirituality | Psychoanalytic
   Theory | Religion and Psychology
Classification: LCC RC480.5 (ebook) | LCC RC480.5 (print) | NLM WM
   427 | DDC 616.89/14—dc23
LC record available at https://lccn.loc.gov/2018052134

ISBN: 978-1-138-19306-2 (hbk)
ISBN: 978-1-138-19307-9 (pbk)
ISBN: 978-1-315-63958-1 (ebk)

Typeset in Times
by Apex CoVantage, LLC

MIX
Paper from
responsible sources
FSC
www.fsc.org    FSC® C013056

Printed and bound in Great Britain by
TJ International Ltd, Padstow, Cornwall

# Contents

# Acknowledgements

Writing a book is an experience of interdependence. It is not only a labour of love, but without the wisdom of the mystics quoted and labours and insight of others to inspire, read, edit and comment, there would be no book. I am profoundly grateful to Anne Morris Bannerman, Doug Bannerman, Giles Clark, Jason McFarland, Peter Oldmeadow, Geoffrey Samuel, Neville Symington, Francis Tiso, Ian and Ruth Gawler, Brian Macauley and Megan Makinson who all served as thoughtful readers. Andrew Leon, ANZAP librarian, was most helpful. Miriam Parkinson gave technical support, Naomi Parkinson offered on-going editorial advice and Ann Pickering moral support. I am grateful to my teachers and guides along the path, who shall remain anonymous. As ever, I am grateful to my editors at Routledge for their patience and encouragement. Here Susannah Frearson, Kate Hawes and Charles Bath are to be lauded as are editors at Pre-Press Solutions: Marie Roberts, Samantha Mitchell and Caroline Lalley.

I gratefully acknowledge the permission to quote from the following:

The Marsh Agency to quote from Bion, W. (1965). *Transformations*. London: Karnac (Reproduced by permission of The Marsh Agency Ltd. on behalf of the Estate of W.R. Bion).

Taylor and Francis, LLC for permission to quote from Bion, W. (1970). *Attention and interpretation*. London: Tavistock.

John Wiley and Sons, Inc. for permission to reprint Pickering, J. (2012). 'Bearing the unbearable: Ancestral transmission through dreams and moving metaphors in the analytic field', *Journal of Analytical Psychology*.

Susan Pickering and Stephen Brown for permission to use as the cover image *Disappearing Voices, Fourteenth Elegy*, etching and aquatint, Susan Pickering, 2016.

# Abbreviations

## Dionysius

*CH*  *The Celestial Hierarchy*
*DN*  *The Divine Names*
*EH*  *The Ecclesiastical Hierarchy*
*Ep*  *Letters*
*MT*  *The Mystical Theology*

## John of the Cross

*A*   *Ascent of Mount Carmel*
*CA*  *Spiritual Canticle – Redaction A*
*CB*  *Spiritual Canticle – Redaction B*
*DN*  *Dark Night of the Soul*
*LF*  *Living Flame of Love*

## Lévinas

*BV*  *Beyond the Verse*
*DF*  *Difficult Freedom*
*EI*  *Ethics and Infinity*
*OB*  *Otherwise than Being or Beyond Essence*
*TI*  *Totality and Infinity*
*TO*  *Time and the Other*

# Preface

I am singing in a concert entitled *Songs of Farewell*. The music circles around themes of remembrance, paying homage to all who have lived on our common earth, those close to us and those far away; those who died in war and those who died in peace; those who have died of cancer, accident or old age; and all those who have departed life unknown and unsung.

We begin with a minute's silence. A minute is a long time in our hurried world. Silence, like rising mist, gradually envelops us in a sense of communion, audience and choir partaking in the same memorial rite. In honouring those who have died, we confront the ephemerality and mutability of life. Yet there is hope in the possibility of some form of continuity beyond the grave.

What is a life? When a person dies, what continues? The uniqueness of a human being can never be replaced, but they continue to inspire and so accompany us. Who that person was continues, and so still is, in our hearts, our minds and our memory.

We sing of 'countries far beyond the stars', 'above noise and danger', of the 'flower of peace', the 'Rose that cannot wither', and of 'One who never changes'.[1] There are hauntingly poignant themes, soaring melodic lines, changes in mood from terrible desolation, grief and mourning to a realm of peace beyond understanding.

We sing a setting by Charles Parry (1848–1918) of a poem by John Gibson Lockhart (1794–1854):

> There is an old belief, that on some solemn shore, beyond the sphere of grief dear friends shall meet once more, beyond the sphere of time and sin and fate's control, serene in changeless prime of body and of soul . . . Eternal be the sleep, if not to waken so
>
> (in Quiller-Couch, 1968, p. 25)

I remember my grandfather who, when he went to war, wore a gold medallion with a picture of his beloved wife and a lock of her hair in a locket. She gave it to him as a keepsake to keep him alive, praying that awareness of her love would sustain him through ghastly horror. He was shot in the leg and taken to an army hospital in England. My grandmother set sail on the S.S. *Arabia* to be at his bedside, but the ship was torpedoed off the shore of Gibraltar. She survived to tell the tale, writing of her war experiences under a pseudonym, Max Arthur. You can read her war correspondence in the National Library Archives.

We sing the setting by William Harris (1883–1973) of a prayer by John Donne (1572–1631) in the spirit of apophatic mystery:

> Bring us O Lord God, at our last awakening
> into the house and gate of heav'n
> to enter into that gate and dwell in that house
> where there shall be no noise, nor silence, but one equal music
> no fears nor hopes
> but one equal possession
> no ends nor beginnings, but one equal eternity
> in the habitation of thy glory and dominion
> world without end.
>
> (in Counsell, 1999, p. 237)

Our singing makes one instrument of so many diverse voices, and diverse personalities, beliefs and different motivations for singing. I am reminded of John Donne's Sermon CIX:

> Man is but a voice, but a sound, but a noise, he begins the noise himself, when he comes crying into the world, and when he goes out; perchance friends celebrate, perchance enemies calumniate him, with a diverse voice, a diverse noise.[2]

We sing but for fleeting moments, then the sound dies away and the rest is silence. For two hours, everyone puts aside worldly concerns. We are together in the same atmosphere of deep contemplation, remembering those who have died – audience, conductor, each singer, all part of a greater whole.

Although we are singing religious music, the majority of those singing are not religious *per se*. Some members of the choir are 'believers', whether Jewish, Christian, Buddhist, Hindu or Muslim, but most, as with the audience, would probably describe themselves as agnostic, atheist or areligious, part of the post-faith, secular twenty-first-century society. Nevertheless, there is a sense of being inspired by some unnamed source, taking us into a subliminal realm of transcendence.

As singers, despite our best intentions, despite hours of crafting the formation and rhythmic placement of each vowel, diphthong and consonant, expressing every sentiment with both precision and passion, we make mistakes.

One small passage terrifies me: it is so poignant, so exposed, so sublime, so pure that I am afraid I will not be able to sing it without my voice cracking. Who can dare sing:

> And you whose eyes shall behold God
> And never taste death's woe.

My mother did taste death's woe. Her dying was woefully unendurable. Right now I have to sing as if my life depends upon it, as if to God herself. As I sing the first note, fear and trembling passes away as my voice is carried across the divide between life and death on a gentle breath of sound, like a feather on the breath of God, as Saint Hildegard would say. Entering a timeless yet totally present realm I am freed from black despair concerning my mother's final agony. In this utterly ephemeral, mutable moment there is a presentiment of immutability. Like a mother reassuring her infant with the most primordial sound, a mother's voice, I sing to God and through God to her, beholding God and so never tasting death's woe.

This is why people come to sit and listen to music in a disused church on a Saturday afternoon, taking time out from the hurry and worry, the greed and grasp of the modern, urban world. They come to be transported beyond immediate quotidian concerns. Even in a post-religious age, we still face the big questions: death, old age, sickness, loss, war, loneliness, alienation, the search for the reason we are alive.

This is why composers compose music, poets write poetry, conductors conduct, artists paint. This is why we sing this concert, and this is why I wrote this book. It matters not whether we are religious or simply have a spiritual bone left in our body, for all of us in our finitude are touched by that which is infinite, yet also infinitely full of pathos and gentleness of spirit. This indefinable sense of mystery beyond comprehension is what inspires this book. I will not label it or seek to define it, but only hope to allow it to course its way through what I write, and try not to get in its way. It is an offering, full of mistakes, imperfect, repetitive and incomplete, but hopefully conveying something of meaning.

## Notes

1  Parry's setting of Peace, by Henry Vaughan (1621–1695) in Quiller-Couch (1953, pp. 407–408).
2  John Donne, Sermon CIX, Alford edition, pp. 505–506.

**In memoriam**

Chögyal Namkhai Norbu, Maxine Pickering and Susan Pickering, whose apophatic vision continues to inspire in aeternam

# Introduction

## The meaning of life

'Jenny'[1] says, 'I am sorry, it's a tall order, but what I'm really asking you is, what is the meaning of my life?' I answer gently, 'Perhaps this is something we may discover, slowly, together'.

A voice wells up within 'James' as he leaves the consulting room after his first session. 'There is only one place that this will lead, and that is to God'. This is highly disturbing, as, reacting against his 'bible-bashing, fundamentalist upbringing', James is an avowed atheist. He firmly dismisses the voice, yet it gnaws away at him at a subliminal level, emerging from time to time in dream imagery. Two years later he sheepishly says to me, 'Look, I have been thinking. Perhaps I just need to give in to this voice and see where it will lead me'. James begins to explore the spiritual dimension of his personality, but on his terms, not those of his parents. Three years later, he does a short retreat at a contemplative monastery. Four years later he ends therapy to enter a Trappist monastery.

'Arvind' and 'Damayanti' are a Hindu couple who ask me to teach them 'anger management strategies'. As well as analysing the explosive interlocking conflicts threatening their marriage, I wonder how they 'manage' their anger at home. Damayanti says that 'when it's really bad, I go into my bedroom and pray before a statue of Vishnu that my mother gave me as a child'. Surprised, Arvind responds, 'I love the *ślokas* of Vishnu; my grandfather taught me how to recite them when I was a child! Maybe we could chant them together?' Arvind and Damayanti begin each day in a new way, chanting the *ślokas* of Vishnu. Gradually they notice a lessening of conflict.

'Sally' describes herself as a 'self-confessed arch-atheist, rationalist and materialist. If it cannot be proved scientifically, it doesn't exist'. Engaged as an international medical aid worker, she wants to help others, yet a restless uneasiness pervades her life. 'I just want to do all I can to help those most in need. But why is that not enough? I feel so discontent. What am I *really* meant to be doing with my life?' Sally is adamant that she will find no answers in religion. Although trained in mindfulness meditation, she is highly suspicious lest hidden religious elements lurk behind meditation techniques. Yet the quest to find the meaning of her life eats away at her. Sally is in good company:

> The meaning of my existence is that life has addressed a question to me. Or, conversely, I myself am a question which is addressed to the world, and I must communicate my answer.
>
> (Jung, 1963, p. 350)

This book takes this question as a starting point. The question has no ready-made answers. Here question and quest are linked, the quest for truth, meaning, purpose, truth, being. Jung believed that 'psychoneurosis must be understood, ultimately, as the suffering of a soul which has not discovered its meaning' (1932, para. 497).

Underneath the presenting problems propelling a person into therapy – longing for love, a failed relationship, depression, anxiety, family feuds, a work crisis, grief and loss – some also experience an inchoate sense of emptiness and futility. They suffer existential loneliness and feel disconnected from the core of themselves, from others, from life itself. All the usual avenues to fill the void – affluence, possessions, ambition – have somehow failed to deliver. The Buddhists call such dissatisfaction *duḥkha*. The original Sanskrit for *duḥkha* referred to an axle hole that was off-centre, leading to a bumpy ride. Dissatisfaction is a condition of life that is unbalanced, stuck in ceaseless spirals of repetition compulsion and destructive behaviour: a life that has not found its true meaning.

Among his patients aged over 35, Jung observed that

> there has not been one whose problem in the last resort was not that of finding a religious outlook on life. It is safe to say that every one of them fell ill because he had lost that which the living religions of every age have given to their followers, and none of them has been really healed who did not regain his religious outlook.
>
> (Jung, 1933, p. 229)

The psychoanalyst Wilfred Bion also held that an individual is born with an instinct predisposed to experience 'reverence and awe' (Bion, 1992, p. 285). Quoting John of the Cross, Bion argues that the goal of analysis is cure of the soul: 'The soul is now, as it were, undergoing a cure in order that it may regain its health – its health being God himself' (1968/2014, *CWXV*, p. 64). He felt that 'psychoanalysts have been peculiarly blind to the topic of religion'. Such a glaring omission was like saying a human being had 'no alimentary canal' (1990, p. 6). Bion lamented the tendency among psychoanalysts to reduce belief in God to no more than a glorified father figure.

Yet for atheists such as Sally, it would be as disrespectful to say that their discontent is a displaced religious issue as it would be to say that a religious person is merely suffering a disowned psychological complex.

The search for meaning manifests in myriad ways: as simple *joie de vivre*, a passionate engagement with the world, or wanting to do good, be engaged in humanitarian or political concerns, or lead the ethical life. It may be a love of nature or pursuit of physical prowess. One's *raison d'être* may take creative, philosophical or metaphysical forms. It might appear as a concern for being well, living well, wholeness, integration, balance or self-realisation. The quest for meaning may take a different direction, through a narrow gate, along a path less travelled, towards realisation, an intimation of ultimate truth, the path of the mystics.

## Psychotherapy and spiritual direction: a human relationship

If, when a person enters psychotherapy, underneath the ostensible presenting problems, there is an underlying yearning for a deeper dimension to life, how might the therapist rise to the occasion? The person coming to see the therapist may be asking something of the therapist that is intrinsically spiritual. The contemporary psychotherapist could be seen to inherit the role of the traditional healer: the medicine man or woman, shaman, staretz, priest, rabbi or spiritual guide. Jung found that patients often 'force the psychotherapist into the role of a priest, and expect and demand of him that he shall free them from their distress. That is why we psychotherapists must occupy ourselves with problems which, strictly speaking, belong to the theologian' (Jung, 1933, p. 278). Conversely, spiritual directors often need to attend to the psychological as well as spiritual disposition of the person seeking their help, being 'actively concerned in aspects of the soul in a "therapeutic" sense' (Bion, 1968/2014, *CWXV*, p. 68). Psychotherapy may help a practitioner gain insight into and so resolve, dissolve and heal old wounds and so remove psychological obstacles to their spiritual path.

## Meditation and psychotherapy

It is said that Buddha observed there were over 84,000 forms of emotional and psychological disease; consequently, he taught over 84,000 forms of meditation as psychological medicine, to be applied judiciously according to need. Although the application of mindfulness to psychotherapy has recently become popular, numerous techniques of meditation, as well as methods of prayer and practices of contemplation are to be found in a variety of forms in all religious traditions. Just as good doctors know their patients well and so can prescribe the right treatment for a given condition, the teacher-student relationship is a critical factor. The teacher has to know the disposition, condition and capacity of the student in order to know which methods will be suitable. Certain practices are contraindicated for certain mental conditions. Cultural and religious background needs consideration. With Arvand and Damayanti it was more appropriate to encourage them to apply their own Hindu-inspired practices they had already discovered for themselves than suggest mindfulness meditation or Western psychological anger management strategies.

Under what conditions might meditation have a place in the consulting room? Is it ever appropriate to include meditation as part of therapy? In specific situations I may suggest a particular meditation practice that is appropriate for those who come to see me, given that I am trained to do so and knowing full well that some people find it too daunting to attend meditation courses. This enables the careful selection of meditations to fit the world view, culture and disposition of the person in question: finding authentic Christian practices for the Christian, Buddhist practices for those open to Buddhism, non-religious meditations for those seeking to be free of anxiety but not wanting anything ostensibly spiritual. There are many other important considerations, such as whether the person suffers anxiety, depression, ADHD, psychosis, PTSD or autism, as well as typology and predilection. Meditation should not ever be 'one-size fits all' any more than medicine or psychotherapy is.

## Psychotherapy as spiritual practice: the therapist

'Physician heal thyself'. Nietzsche's Zarathustra, thus quoting from Luke's Gospel, adds, 'Then wilt thou also heal thy patient. Let it be his best cure to see with his eyes him who maketh himself whole' (Nietzsche, 1908, p. 102). Central to this book is the issue of the spiritual practice of the psychotherapist, its form and degree, or perhaps its absence. As well as intensive vocational training and ongoing professional development, might some form of meditative or contemplative practice help a therapist? Could psychotherapy be considered as a form of spiritual practice? There are many parallels. The therapy session is a demarcated time and space, just as a meditation session is time put aside for meditation. The therapist undertakes the disciplined practice of paying free-floating as well as undivided attention, cultivating analytic reverie, empathic attunement, equanimity and patience in the face of turbulence, frustration, doubt and uncertainty, listening out for promptings of a still quiet voice of intuition.

What are the particular transformational qualities that, in the sanctuary of therapy, aid processes of psychological healing? First of all the therapist should not get in the way of a given person's innate capacity for self-healing. But the therapist's own state of being is vital as well. The patient comes to understand, work through and heal developmental lacks, losses, relational traumas and other psychological obstacles to their well-being, through a deeply personal, committed therapeutic relationship. This relationship is imbued with certain 'psychotherapeutic virtues'. Among these are free-floating attention, pure presence, reverie, contemplation, attunement, resonance, equanimity, calm, reflective capacity, compassion, loving kindness, patience, understanding, open-mindedness, generosity and gentleness of spirit, discernment, intuition, courage, and truthfulness. There are qualities related to the therapist's training and technique such as an analytic attitude, a capacity to work symbolically and interpretively in and with transference and countertransference. There is the importance of what the therapist should avoid: being overly advice-giving or directive, let alone exploitative, seductive, revengeful, violent or retaliatory. The therapist needs to be constantly on the lookout for hidden agendas and mixed motives. There needs to be finely attuned, yet rigorous ethical awareness, honest self-reflection and examination of conscience. Such psychotherapeutic virtues are some of the most powerful factors in the healing process, inspiring the patient to enhance their own nascent capacity for transformation. But even if any such virtues are vital aspects of the therapeutic relationship, they are not givens. How might a therapist actively cultivate them? There is a range of meditation and contemplative practices that are aimed at increasing awareness, concentration and the capacity to be fully present, to listen deeply, as well as to develop loving kindness, altruism, compassion, equanimity, generosity of spirit, ethical discipline, patience, diligence, and wisdom. A therapist could do well to consider what spiritual or meditative practices may benefit their own work, to which we might add a life creatively lived and other sources of inspiration according to the unique interests of the therapist, such as artistic pursuits, love of nature, physical activities, dancing, singing, music, poetry, reading, friendships, close relationships, time for stillness and deep reflection.

## Care of the soul: psychological, spiritual and mystical dimensions

What is the relationship between psychotherapy and spirituality? They are etymologically related since both derive from words meaning to breathe. To breathe is to be alive; breath is the basis of communication and mediates inner and outer. Among the many meanings of 'psyche', from the Greek *psyxō*, meaning to breathe and to blow, is the breath of life which animates the body, the life principle, life itself. This life principle has also come to be related, equated or conflated in different ways with soul, spirit, intellect, mind, self and consciousness.

'Spiritual' derives from the Latin noun *spiritus* meaning 'breath', *spiriare* meaning to breathe and to blow and the adjectives *spiritalis* or *spiritualis*. The spirit is the principle that inspires us, stirs things, moves matter and perhaps is the movement of matter. For some, it is matter that moves spirit into action. 'A wind from God (*ruah elohim*) swept over the face of the waters' (Genesis 1:2). God breathes into Adam's nostrils the breath of life (Hebrew *n'shama*, Greek *psyche*, Latin *anima*) and so Adam becomes animate, a living soul (Genesis 2:7).

In the history of Western thought, the word 'spirit' has been used to refer to the spirit of life, the human spirit, the Spirit of God, the Holy Spirit and spirits in the sense of disembodied souls or ghosts. Spirit is sometimes equated with the soul and sometimes seen as in between, mediating between body and soul. For many, including Descartes, spirit was seen as the breath of life which was a fine vapour that animates living beings.

A distinction is often made between soul and spirit. In Greek thought this is reflected in the two words *psychē* and *pneuma*, in Latin between *anima* and *spiritus*, in Hebrew between *ruah* and *nephesh*, in German between *Seele* and *Geist*. To distinguish is not necessarily to separate: sometimes *psychē* was seen to consist of *pneuma* or spirit. This distinction lead to a tripartite view of the human being. For the Stoics the person consists of body, soul and mind. For many Christian theologians it was body, soul and spirit, as propounded by St Paul and taken up by Justin Martyr, Clement of Alexandria, Origen, Irenaeus and Eusebius. In the earlier Greek context, further distinctions between related terms abound: such as between *psychē* as life and *autos* (the 'person'), *nous* (mind or intellect) and *phrenes* (thought), and their respective relationships to the body or *sōma*. *Psychē* as 'life' also has a combination of many other aspects such as mind, thought, emotions and virtues such as courage and justice.

For the German psychologist Von Schubert (1780–1860) the three-fold division of human nature consisted of living body (*Lieb*), soul and spirit. This trio is in a constant process of self-becoming (*Selbst bewusstein*) or self-consciousness. An original state of harmony with nature is severed due to self-love (*Ich-Sucht*). The purpose of life is to regain this original state in a perfected form (Ellenberger, 1970, p. 205).

Troxler (1780–1866) added a fourth to comprise the *Tetraktys*: *Körper, Leib*, soul and spirit. He distinguished two 'bodies'. *Körper* is the anatomical body and *Leib* is the soma or body as meaning. He also posited two polarities within the *Letraktys*: soma-soul and spirit-body. All are held together by the *Gemüt* which is 'the true individuality of man by means of which he is himself most authentically, the hearth of his self-hood, the most alive central point of his existence' (Ellenberger, 1970, p. 206).

William James (1842–1910) linked breath with consciousness and the stream of thinking:

> The stream of thinking . . . is only a careless name for what, when scrutinized, reveals itself to consist chiefly of the stream of my breathing. The 'I think' . . . is the 'I breathe' . . . breath, which was ever the original of 'spirit' . . . is, I am persuaded, the essence out of which philosophers have constructed the entity known to them as consciousness.
>
> (James, 1904, p. 491)

What is the difference between spirit and soul? 'Soul' is the word most often chosen to translate either psyche or anima into English. The word 'soul' is derived from Old Gothic. Wulfila (311–382 CE), a Cappadocian who evangelised the Goths, devised a Gothic alphabet primarily out of Greek, and to a lesser extent Latin. In coining Gothic Christian terminology, he drew on existing Gothic words but gave them new meanings, such as *ahma* 'spirit'. He used the word *saiwala* to translate the Greek psychē. However, *\*saiwala* was originally used to denote the spirit of a dead person, whereas *\*ferh* denoted 'the spark of life, the animating spirit in a living being' (Green, 1995, p. 148). When translating anima/psychē the difficulty was to extend the meaning to refer to both the immortality of the soul after death and the essence of a person during life (Falluomini, 2015). The Gothic version of the Magnificat differentiates soul (*saiwala*) and spirit (*ahma*):

*Mikileid saiwala meina fraujan, jah swegneid ahma meins du guda nasjand meinamma.*

My soul magnifies the Lord, and my spirit rejoices in God my saviour.

(Luke 1:4, 46–47 in Mendez, 2013, p. 99)

Soul was used by Tyndale in the first Bible in English to translate the Hebrew *nephesh*. The KJB translated *nephesh* variously depending on the context, attributing a range of meanings: soul, life, person, mind, heart, creature, body, himself, yourselves, dead, will, desire, man, themselves, any, appetite.

The common etymology of psyche and spirit underlies the common tasks of both psychotherapy and spirituality: care of psyche, healing of the soul, freeing it from entanglement in neurotic, defensive and destructive constraints. Many spiritual traditions hold that ultimate reality is something that we discover and realise, not create or develop. In such traditions, one's true self, the spark of divinity, godliness, primordial purity, enlightenment, is always there behind all that occludes, entraps and contaminates it. The Greek word *alétheia*, unconcealment, has this sense. The implication is that at the ultimate level, the myriad forms of psychological disease are accidental, not substantial or inherent. The pursuit of truth is a process of removing all that is false to reveal the primordial purity and spontaneous presence of one's true nature. Dionysius suggests that we should be 'sculptors who set out to carve a statue. They remove every obstacle to the pure view of the hidden image, and simply by this act of clearing away (*aphaeresis*) they show up the beauty which is hidden' (*MT* 2 1025B).

This raises a question debated in many religious traditions concerning primordial godliness or original sin. Are we made in the image of God (*imago dei*) or inherently flawed from conception? Is enlightenment a potential or a latency? Is Buddhahood like a seed, that may be realised, or is our fundamental nature already one of primordial purity, although covered over by the obscuring grime of ignorance?

Not only are spiritual traditions divided on this point, so is psychotherapy. For example, Klein saw the infant as innately destructive whereas Jung emphasised a teleological dimension, suggesting that we have an inbuilt impetus towards individuation, becoming who we truly are. Myriad psychological disorders may thwart and distort our lives, yet they are also opportune, for without them we would never be called forth to work things through and thus flower into the fullness of whom we might be.

A 'teleological stance' is clinically helpful. No matter how ferociously and destructively a patient may behave and despite tendencies to revert back to the neurotic gains of familiar defence systems, it may help to be reminded of the possibility of an underlying fundamental ground of being which, like sky behind clouds, is always present. This is not to sentimentally avoid confronting the reality of human destructiveness, greed, envy, hate, apathy and selfishness. A borderline patient's envy, resentment, angry frustration and self-harm can be seen as a defence against (and so covering over) a developmental lack, a basic wound, desperate loneliness, depressive defeat and primitive anxiety or fear. To remember this in the heat of borderline attacks, one needs reason, clinical understanding and heteropathic empathy.

Psychotherapy is the handmaiden of spiritual practice, in that psychotherapy may uncover the specificity of one's habitual destructive tendencies, traumatic complexes and defence mechanisms which impede one from realising psychological and spiritual health and well-being. The Greek word *eudemonia* has the sense of flourishing and well-being, for to live in accordance with ultimate truth naturally brings a sense of contentment, serenity and grace as well as compassion for others, harmony with one's environment, a sense of aliveness.

Therapy, from the Greek *therapeia*, relates to care of the psyche. It is based on the root *dher*, to 'carry, support, hold'. This is the same root *dhṛ* for Dharma in Sanskrit, which has a wealth of meanings, but one of them is 'that which upholds, supports, or sustains'. Dharma is a word that is almost impossible to translate, meaning many different things in different schools of Hindu and Buddhist thought. On the absolute level dharma refers to absolute truth itself (*dharmatā*).

*Therapeia* derives from *therapōn* and has etymological meanings related to servant, attendant, ritual substitute and curing. It also relates to Indo-European words meaning 'dwelling' or 'house'. Therapy has spatial, temporal and relational dimensions. The therapeutic space provides a 'dwelling' to safely house, contain and thereby ameliorate psychological disorder, fragmentation, rage, grief, yearning, terror, shame, mourning, doubt, confusion, bewilderment and perplexity. Therapy is a path that patient and therapist take together, unfolding over time. The therapist serves, cares for and supports the patient on this journey of deconstruction, reconstruction and discovery. Therapy is an intrinsically relational process. Following Jung, not only does each patient make of the therapy a different theory; patient and therapist are both transformed by the process.

Gregory Nagy argues that *therapōn* derives from a Hittite word *tarpalli* meaning 'ritual substitute' or scapegoat where pollution is transferred from the one being purified into another who serves as a ritual substitute and who is 'identified as another self, *un autre soi-même*' (Nagy, 2013, p. 149). There are parallels here with Jung's descriptions of psychic contagion, Freud and Jung's unconscious-to-unconscious communication, and Bion's observation that the therapist takes in the analysand's confusion, psychically metabolising and then returning it as detoxified 'food for thought'.

In *The Contemplative Life*, Philo of Alexandria described contemplative ascetics, philosophers and hermits as *therapeutae* and *therapeutrides* because they

> heal souls which are under the mastery of terrible and almost incurable diseases, which pleasures and appetites, fears and griefs, and covetousness, and follies, and injustice, and all the rest of the innumerable multitude of other passions and vices, have inflicted upon them.
>
> (1981, p. 42)

They had a two-fold task of healing souls and serving God, thus combining the spiritual and psychotherapeutic dimensions together. Could a psychotherapist be considered as a form of modern-day *therapeutae*? Hillman suggests that the 'psychotherapist is literally the *attendant of the soul*' and 'by carrying, by paying careful attention to and devotedly caring for the psyche, the analyst translates into life, the meaning of the word *psychotherapy*' (1989, p. 73).

In order to retain the ancient Greek idea of *therapeia* as care or cure of psyche, this book uses 'psychotherapy' as an inclusive term, encompassing psychoanalysis, analytical psychology, psychotherapy, psychology and spiritual care.

## Psychotherapy, spirituality, religion and mysticism

What are the relationships between psychotherapy, spirituality, mysticism and religion? In contemporary society spirituality is often differentiated from religion, with its attendant belief systems, moral codes and formalised rituals and practices. Spirituality can denote a deep inwardness and a search for transcendence that may not involve adherence to any formal belief system.

What is the relationship between psychotherapy and mysticism? The adjective 'mystical' derives from the Greek *mysterion* (mystery) and *mystikos* (mystical). From the second century CE *mustikes* referred to the mysteriousness of God. Mystical theology for Pseudo-Dionysius, Thomas Aquinas, St John of the Cross and other Christian mystics referred to experiential realisation of the hiddenness and mysteriousness of God, infused into the soul through mystical contemplation.

In the psychoanalytic context, according to Bion, mystical experience involves direct encounters with ultimate reality. For Bion, it is more than an encounter with the absolute or seeing ultimate truth. It is about *being* ultimate reality, absolute truth. The paradox is that, for apophatic mystics and Bion, such 'being' is not realised through knowing but through unknowing. Studstill's definition is inclusive of monotheistic, polytheistic and non-theistic traditions:

> In all of the world's major religions certain individuals experience – directly and vividly – what they believe is ultimate reality. Depending on the religion, they seem to perceive/know (in some cases, merge with) God, Viṣṇu, *śūnyatā*, *gzhi*, the Tao, the (Neoplatonic) One, Brahman, etc. These individuals are referred to as 'mystics,' and their apparent encounters with ultimate reality are 'mystical experiences.' The term 'mysticism' encompasses the experiences, traditions, practices, rituals, doctrines, etc. comprising and associated with their various religious paths.
>
> (2005, p. 1)

## The apophatic way

The project of psychoanalysis is related to the epistemological aim 'know thyself'. Through analysis one seeks greater self-knowledge, self-awareness and self-realisation, to bring consciousness to what was unconscious. Yet for the followers of the apophatic way, ultimate reality cannot be realised through ordinary ways of knowing.

*Apophatic* comes from the Greek *apophasis*, where *phasis* comes from *phemi* meaning to 'assert' or 'say', and *apo* means 'away' (from). *Apophatic* could be translated as 'unsaying', 'non-assertion' or 'negation' but also 'revelation'.

The apophatic is related to 'negative theology' or the *via negativa*, based on the recognition that through negating concepts, names, formulations and ideas about ultimate reality, we clear space for direct realisation of the utter mystery of the Godhead or absolute.

The apophatic is contrasted with affirmative strands of mysticism known as the kataphatic.[2] The apophatic and kataphatic are interdependent: one cannot 'unsay' except by saying. Affirmation followed by negation is a process of clearing away attributes to uncover and reveal the hidden mystery of the One.

The apophatic can be discovered in Plato and in Neoplatonic writers such as Plotinus (205–270 CE), the Alexandrian Jewish philosopher Philo (15/10 BCE–45/50 CE) and the Neoplatonist Proclus (412–485 CE). In the early Christian tradition it is associated with Clement of Alexandria (150–211/215 CE), Basil of Caesarea (329–379 CE), Gregory of Nyssa (335–394 CE) and the sixth-century Pseudo-Dionysius the Areopagite.[3] Later Christian apophatic mystics include Meister Eckhart (1260–1327/1328), Marguerite Porete (d. 1310), John Tauler (1300–1361), John Ruysbroeck (1293–1381) and Julian of Norwich (1342– after 1416). There is also the fourteenth-century anonymous author of *The Cloud of Unknowing* and John of the Cross (1542–1591). Judaism, permeated with the recognition that God is ineffable and unnameable, also has the *Ein Sof*, or 'infinite beyond description' in the Kabbalah. Maimonides (1138–1204) was a major Jewish proponent of apophatic philosophy. In Islam, we not only find negative theology in Sufism but also in the Kalam schools. In Arabic two terms for the apophatic are *lahoot salbi* or *nizaam al lahoot*. In Hinduism there is the apophatic non-dualism of Advaita Vedānta.

In the Western philosophical tradition, the apophatic is found in Lévinas, Deleuze, Derrida, Merleau-Ponty and Wittgenstein. In psychoanalysis Jung, Lacan and Bion are important exponents.

In the Buddhist context, we find it in the Zen, Chan and Dzogchen traditions as well as the *Prāsaṅgika Mādhyamika* of Nāgārjuna (150–250 CE). *Prāsaṅgika Mādhyamika* uses a *reductio ad absurdum* technique through which all ideological conceptualisation of reality are dissolved in order to open the mind to a numinous realm of absolute truth beyond concepts.

Dzogchen has both apophatic and kataphatic elements. Although associated with Tibetan Buddhism, Dzogchen is seen to both predate and transcend any school. Dzogchen means total (*chen*) perfection (*dzog*). Dzogchen relates to the discovery and 'awareness (*rig pa*)[4] of the true nature of reality in its ultimate purity and perfection' (Samuel, 1993, p. 550) that, underneath all obscuration and defilement, is self-perfected, primordially pure, empty and free of limitations.

The 'path' towards realising such perfection is the state of contemplation in which there is a 'simplicity of immediate awareness, unconditioned by any concept, symbol, practice' (Studstill, 2005, p. 126).

A core element of this book involves the application of the apophatic way to psychotherapy. The apophatic dimension has much to offer psychotherapy because in seeking to avoid false certitudes and stale presumptions of knowledge, the apophatic also avoids dogmatism, essentialism and reification. Apophatic approaches to the question 'what is the meaning of life' may also transcend dual-istic divisions between schools of thought, even within psychotherapy. This is not to create false dichotomies where apophatic approaches are posited as superior to the 'kataphatic' richness of archetypal images, symbols, personal and universal myths. As we shall see, the kataphatic and apophatic condition each other.

This book celebrates both the richness of diversity and the fundamental unity behind all spiritual paths. Like spokes on a hub, different formulations of truth may be based on different cultural world-views, historical epochs and typologi-cal differences. The apophatic way has the potential to transcend limitations of a particular cultural or ideological viewpoint, without collapsing into a spurious syncretism. Alterity, diversity, transcendence, mystery and ineffability are orna-ments of the apophatic. As psychotherapists sitting with patients of different back-grounds and beliefs, the apophatic approach aids us in the search for truth, a truth which is utterly unique for each patient. An apophatic approach enables us to embrace the quest for the meaning of life of our patients beyond any denomina-tion or even psychoanalytic school of thought. The apophatic lends itself to ecu-menism, both religious and psychoanalytic. As Bion observed:

> Verbal expressions intended to represent the ultimate object often appear to be contradictory within themselves, but there is a surprising degree of agree-ment, despite differences of background, time and space, in the descriptions offered by mystics who feel they have experienced the ultimate reality.
>
> (Bion, 1965, p. 151)

## Bion, mysticism, ultimate reality and O

The apophatic mystics were a major inspiration for Bion. Bion sought to find lan-guage capable of gesturing towards the indescribable nature of absolute truth, language that undid itself, opening one out to a domain beyond thought and beyond understanding. He used the sign O to refer to absolute reality, ultimate truth, the Godhead. O as symbol is unsaturated with preconceptions, ideas or theories which obscure rather than reveal ultimate reality. O, like a thing-in-itself, cannot be known but O can be realised through processes of transformation in O.

Tracing Bion's original sources for O in the apophatic mystical tradition leads to a radical implication. Psychoanalysts, if they are seekers of truth, are invited to enter through the narrow gate to follow the path taken by the apophatic mystics who seek union with the unknowable Godhead, realisation of their inner divinity, or enlightenment. According to Bion, becoming O is the same fundamental goal for the patient, although the patient may well resist this aim. For Bion, 'Resistance operates because it is feared that the reality [of O] is imminent' (Bion, 1965, p. 147).

## Know thyself and un-know thyself: apophatic epistemology and anthropology

The apophatic tradition is radical in seeing the meaning of life to be found, not in the search for self-knowledge, but through unknowing, in *agnōsia*. Related to such apophatic epistemology is what Stang and others call apophatic anthropology. The search for one's true self is a *via negativa*, clearing away all that is false, distorted or contorted. For Dionysius, the goal of all self-development is apophasis of the self. To un-know the unknown God, one must un-know oneself.

As it is for apophatic mystics, a central theme for Bion is that of unknowing as an analytic discipline: 'What we are concerned with is not only what we know and understand, but what we do not know and do not understand' (Bion, 1991, p. 264). Absolute reality cannot be known, only realised. In psychoanalysis 'there is more at stake than an exhortation to "know thyself, accept thyself, be thyself". . . . The point at issue is how to pass from "knowing" "phenomena" to "being" that which is "real"' (Bion, 1965, p. 148).

Inspired by *The Ascent of Mount Carmel*, Bion advises therapists to cultivate a state of mind involving the suspension of memory, desire, understanding and sense impressions. This is the state of mind that is necessary if there is to be 'restoration of god (the Mother) and the evolution of god (the formless, infinite, ineffable, non-existent)' (Bion, 1970, p. 129).

Bion also quotes Freud who, in a letter to Lou Andreas-Salome on 25 May 1916, describes a meditative discipline in which one blinds oneself artificially 'in order to focus all the light on one dark spot'. Freud writes:

> I have to blind myself artificially in order to focus all the light on one dark spot, renouncing cohesion, harmony, rhetoric and everything which you call symbolic.
>
> (in E. L. Freud, 1961)

Although Freud did not apply such a principle to a spiritual end, this statement places Freud in the tradition of Dionysius who describes plunging into a 'truly mysterious darkness of unknowing' in order to be 'borne up to the ray of divine darkness that surpasseth all being' (Dionysius, *MT* I, 1, in Johnston, 1967, p. 33).

This book will draw out the apophatic strain in the psychoanalytic tradition, particularly Bion's writings on O as ultimate reality beyond knowledge and understanding. I explicate Bion's apophatic epistemology. I seek out Bion's sources in the apophatic mysticism of Dionysius, John of the Cross, the author of *The Cloud of Unknowing* and Meister Eckhart. Bion suggested that while all are at some level religious, 'the expression of religious forces in the individual is coloured by each person's character and mental quality' (1991, p. 286) as well as by culture and history. As psychotherapists sitting with patients of different backgrounds and beliefs, Bion's apophatic approach may aid us in the search for truth: even if it is also indescribable and incomprehensible (although not for Bion, inconceivable).

## Qualifications

This book is full of questions, contradictions and paradoxes. I shall not attempt to either answer or reconcile them. A simple example is the rather ambitious title of this book: *The Search for Meaning in Psychotherapy*. This book has been written by way of a response to the implicit question posed by many patients, 'What is the meaning of my life?' However, when confronting a terrible crisis, we may defensively manufacture false or sentimental meaning. Indeed, sometimes courage is needed to accept the pain of not finding true meaning. A given 'meaning' may be merely provisional, needing to be led go so that a deeper meaning might emerge.

Many patients are not concerned with spiritual questions. They may be seeking financial and physical security, a good job, good home, good relationship, good family and good health. They may be motivated by a passion for art, music, literature, film, poetry, drama, nature, physical culture, bushwalking or sport. I do not wish to suggest that spiritual concerns are 'better', 'deeper' or more lofty. There are potentially spiritual dimensions to all life's passions. It is vital to remain deeply respectful of the myriad different motivations inspiring a life.

Patients who do not ordinarily talk about the meaning of life, might, in a crisis, wonder 'What's it all about really?' The inspiration may be something joyful, an intimation of some mysterious presence or beauty that moves and inspires. A patient described feeling this when swimming in the ocean, of being one with the water and the powerful surging currents. Another felt a sense of the sublime listening to a Bach cello concerto. For some a sense of unease has been gnawing away at them, life has not worked out according to plan, something vital is missing. In other words, perhaps questions concerning the meaning of life impact more people than may meet the eye.

## Structure of the book

The book falls into two major sections. The first part considers the relationships between the practice of psychotherapy, spirituality, meditation, contemplation and reverie. The second part explores the relevance of apophatic mysticism in the work of Bion and psychoanalysis.

## Part One: the listening cure: psychotherapy as spiritual practice

Chapter 1 concerns the relationships between spirituality, religion, mysticism and psychotherapy. Chapter 2 elaborates on an ethic of analytic hospitality. Chapter 3 argues for the benefits of a regular practice of meditation reflection and contemplation, as well as cultivating presence, awareness and attention in general. The focus of Chapter 4 is the healing potential of the analyst's state of mind, including the role of contemplation, reverie and Freud's free-floating attention. It outlines Bion's theory of thinking, container/contained and thoughts without a thinker. Chapter 5 considers the relevance of Buddhist teachings on meditation to psychotherapy. Chapter 6 presents an outline of the teachings of Dzogchen. Using a clinical vignette, Chapter 7 warns of the dangers when Western meditators suffering depersonalisation and derealisation draw on misunderstandings of Buddhist teachings on non-self or *anātman* and emptiness or *śūnyatā*. Chapter 8 explores the role of analytic reverie, containment and compassionate witness in situations involving intergenerational transmission of trauma.

## Part Two: a ray of divine darkness: psychotherapy and the apophatic way

Part Two considers the clinical relevance of the apophatic way. Chapter 9 represents the ethics of alterity of Emmanuel Lévinas. It is followed by four chapters on the history and core elements of the apophatic way: Chapter 10 provides a brief history of early apophatic writers; Chapter 11 outlines key themes in the works of Dionysius; Chapter 12 refers to the contributions of John the Scot Erigena, Moses Maimonides, Thomas Gallus, Nicholas of Cusa and Meister Eckhart; and Chapter 13 is devoted to John of the Cross.

Chapter 14 recounts the practice of apophatic contemplation in the tradition of Christian contemplative prayer. Chapter 15 engages with negative epistemology in Bion including his writings on the K link, faith (F), Keats' concept of negative capability, Henri Poincaré's selected fact and the Language of Achievement. Chapter 16 locates the original source for Bion's admonition that analyst should eschew memory, desire and understanding in John of the Cross, who taught that annihilation of the understanding, the memory and the will was necessary for those seeking union with God. Chapter 17 takes the reader into the depths of Bion's writings on O as a numinous, ineffable realm of pure being, absolute truth and ultimate reality.

A common thread woven throughout the book is the apophatic way of unknowing. The search for meaning is found through uncovering our true nature, a primordially pure ground of being in Dzogchen; through divinisation and union of the unknown self in the unknowable Godhead for Christian apophatic mystics; and through realising our true nature in at-one-ment in O for Bion. In all three traditions such realisation takes place through a cloud of unknowing beyond all understanding.

There is a sense of a mystical core through which one partakes in that which is incomprehensible and transcendent. There is a goalless goal of becoming who we already are, but cannot fully know, in communion with all beings. There is a presentiment of an immanent eternity, in every moment, in every meeting, if we can but be open to that which is:

> Beyond words, beyond thought, beyond description,
> Unborn, unceasing, the very essence of space
> Yet it can be experienced as the wisdom of our own awareness:
> Homage to the mother of the buddhas of past, present and future!
>
> Prajñāpāramitā

## Notes

1 Clinical vignettes draw on clinical material, but all identities are fictional.
2 Sometimes transliterated as 'cataphatic'.
3 Pseudonymously named after Dionysius the Areopagite, the Athenian convert mentioned in *The Acts of the Apostles* 17, but thought to be a late-fifth- or early-sixth-century Syriac writer. Hereafter I will simply refer to him as Dionysius.
4 Sanskrit *vidyā*, Tibetan *rig pa*, has been translated as intrinsic awareness, knowledge, intellect, pristine cognition, pure presence, the realised mind of enlightenment.

# Part One

# The listening cure

## Psychotherapy as spiritual practice

# Chapter 1

# Spirituality and psychotherapy

## Spiritual but not religious

'Layla' sits cross-legged on the couch and arranges her voluminous, flowing skirts around her slight frame, her arms jangling with silver bracelets. She sits in contemplation for a moment before beginning to speak:

> I am not religious, but I am spiritual. I came to see you because unresolved childhood issues are interfering with my spiritual practice. I hope you won't be dismissive of my spirituality.

Layla is representative of a number of people who describe themselves as 'deeply spiritual' but 'not religious'.[1] Institutional religion is associated with a number of negative features, such as patriarchy, clericalism, dogmatism, authoritarianism, fundamentalism and sexism, if not corruption and abuse, especially after the sexual abuse scandals rocking many religious institutions. Organised religion is seen to have lost vital connections with original sources of revelation, becoming an empty, constrictive shell, opposing the inspiration of freedom.

People such as Layla take their search for authentic spirituality seriously. They may seek out religious traditions that they feel are living sources of inspiration such as Hindu or Buddhist teachings, Zen, *Vipaśyanā* Kabbala, Sufism or Taoism. Alternatively they could be attracted to an array of other possibilities including rebirthing, shamanism, reiki, chakra balancing, astrology, or occultism. Some are interested in spiritual practices not requiring any form of religious belief, such as mind-body therapies. Others simply have an attitude of openness to a spiritual dimension, found in contemplation of nature, poetry, music, creativity or in contemplation itself.

Spirituality is often associated with a personal experience of mystery, transcendence, a sense of the sacred, that which is beyond mundane material concerns. In September 1928 Virginia Woolf wrote in her diary of finding:

> a consciousness of what I call 'reality': a thing I see before me: something abstract but residing in the downs or sky; beside which nothing matters; in

which I shall rest and continue to exist. Reality I call it. And I fancy sometimes this is the most necessary thing to me – that which we seek.

(1980, p. 196)

When can such consciousness of 'reality' be considered to be a religious or
spiritual experience? For Santayana it is only truly spiritual when it is intuition of
essences of reality, without motivation or intent, goal-seeking or false meaning-
making. To be spiritual, is to be absolutely pure, living in the eternity of the immanent moment, an immanent eternity which is temporary, for other emotional and
bodily forces intervene.

William James, in his *Varieties of Religious Experience* (1902), argues that
the goal of religion is 'union with the spiritual domain'. Rather than replacing
the word religion with spirituality, he makes a distinction between 'personal religion pure and simple' on one hand and institutional religion, ecclesiasticisms and
systematic theology on the other (1902, p. 26). James views 'personal religion'
as 'more fundamental than either theology or ecclesiasticism' because the prove-
nance of any genuine religion is direct revelation. The founders of religion 'owed
their power originally to the fact of their direct personal communion with the
divine' (1902, p. 27). According to James, religion refers to the 'feelings, acts,
and experiences' of individuals 'in their solitude' in relation to the divine (1902,
p. 26). 'The divine' includes the atheism of Buddhism, transcendental idealism, as
well as the 'immanent divinity in things' (1902, p. 27).

Given the intricate relationship between religion and spirituality I will consider
the etymological derivation of the word 'religion' before turning our attention to
spirituality.

## Etymology of religion

Religion was used to translate the Greek *thrēskeia* or Latin *religio*. Yet the etymological derivation of the word 'religion' is unclear. Different derivations include:
from *religare* meaning to re-bind, to re-tie, fasten or restrain; from *legere* meaning
to gather and collect; from *relegere* meaning to re-read, retrace, re-choose or go
through again. Others relate the etymology of religion to the Greek word *alegein*,
meaning to heed or to have a care for, to be careful about. *Relegere* has been
opposed to *neglegere* which stands for 'neglect' of one's duties and observances,
to 'not observe, not heed, not attend to, be remiss in attention or duty toward a
thing'. Here, the inference is that religion is 'akin to *diligence*, and opposed to
*negligence*' (Hoyt, 1912, p. 128).

Cicero (106–43 BCE) derives *religio* from *relegere*, meaning to re-read, retrace,
consider again or 'to treat carefully, or to go through or over again in reading,
speech and thought'. Cicero held that the act of 're-choosing' God and the capacity to read and re-read scriptures over and over made one 'religious' (*De Natura
Deorum*, 2. 28, 72 in Wynne, 2008, p. 123).

Lactantius (240–320 CD) suggested that *religo* comes from *re-ligare*, 'to tie back' or 'bind together' and means 'the bond of piety by which we are joined and "linked back" to God' (DI 4.28.3, in Schott, 2008, p. 105).

In contemporary society, the word 'religion' sometimes means 'observant, conscientious, strict, practicing'. We use the word to denote someone who is conscientiously abiding by the teachings, ritual practices and moral obligations of their religion. A 'practicing Catholic' is someone who regularly attends mass and follows the dictates of the church. Another distinction often made is between religious or cultural identity. Mira explains how 'I am culturally Jewish but not religious. However our family does observe shabbat'. Maslow argued in the 1960s that religion is in danger of becoming redefined as 'a set of habits, behaviours, dogmas, forms' if not 'entirely legalistic and bureaucratic, conventional, empty, and in the true meaning of the word, antireligious' (1964, p. viii). He saw this as leading to the emphasis on personal spirituality rather than organised religion.

## History of the term spirituality

The popularising of 'spirituality' in the English-speaking world is relatively recent. Prior to the twentieth century the word 'spirituality' as such was rarely used in English contexts and it meant very different things.

The Latin *spiritualitas* derives from the noun *spiritus* and adjective *spiritalis* or *spiritualis* (Principe, 1983, p. 130). *Spiritus* and *spiritualis* were originally used to translate into Latin the Greek *pneuma* and *pneumatikos* in the Pauline letters. The distinction is neither between immateriality and materiality, nor between the incorporeal and corporeal. Rather, to be spiritual is to live a life guided by the Holy Spirit.

The first citation of the word *spiritualitas* is said to date from the fifth century. In an anonymous letter, the person addressed is urged to *Age ut in spiritualitate proficias*, to 'act as to advance in spirituality' (in Principe, 1983, p. 130), that is, to live one's life in accordance with the Spirit of God.

*Spiritualitas* as referring to living a life inspired by the Spirit is found in Christian authors from the ninth to thirteenth centuries. But from the time of the Scholastics in the twelfth century, an additional meaning accrued as referring to the non-material as opposed to materiality (*materialitas* or *corporalitas*), or the rational against the non-rational.

In monastic contexts *spiritualitas* continued to be related to transformation in the Spirit. There are the Spiritual Exercises (*Exercitia Spiritualia*) of Ignatius of Loyola published in 1548, consisting of meditations, contemplations and prayers designed to better enable discernment of God's will. Spirituality was allied to mystical theology and the interior life of those whose goal was a 'life of perfection', through the three-fold way of purification, illumination and mystical union.

In seventeenth-century France *espiritualité* was used to refer to the devout life and a form of interiority and piety in terms of a personal devotion to God. With growing interest in Eastern religions in the nineteenth century, spirituality came to be used in contexts of inter-religious dialogue. Eastern 'spirituality' was often contrasted with Western 'materialism' for example.

However, it was only from the 1960s that spirituality entered common parlance. It was the same period that witnessed the growth of the counter-culture in the Western world. Many counter-cultural or New Age seekers sought inspiration from Eastern spiritualities including neo-Hindu movements, Transcendental Meditation, Rajneesh, Maharishi Mahesh Yogi, Baba Ram Dass, Zen and Tibetan Buddhism.

There has been cross-fertilisation from alternative forms of spirituality in Christianity as well as in popular culture. The Catholic Church witnessed internal reforms arising from a recognition that the church had to take more account of the spiritual needs of the laity and interest in Eastern religion. Since Vatican II there has been an explosion of terms relating to Christian Spirituality. As well as more traditional forms such as Trinitarian Spirituality, Patristic Spirituality, Benedictine Spirituality and Franciscan Spirituality, attention is being given to Lay Spirituality, Feminist Spirituality, Liberation Spirituality and Ecological Spirituality.

Certain Christian contemplatives have sought spiritual renewal from Hindu, Buddhist and Taoist traditions. Henry le Saux (Abhishktananda), Bede Griffiths, Raimond Pannikar, Thomas Merton, William Johnston, Anthony de Mello and more recently James Finley, John Main, Henri Nouwen, Thomas Keating and Wayne Teasdale are among those who have found revivification from Eastern spiritual traditions.

There is growing interest in inter-religious dialogue. According to Abhishiktananda, such dialogue needs to be grounded in 'real spiritual experience at depth and when each one understands that *diversity does not mean disunity, once the Centre of all has been reached*' (in Oldmeadow, 2008, pp. 19–20). At the mystical level relative forms and religious divides are transcended, whilst still respecting alterity, pluralism and diversity. This also opens the way for recognition of the transcendent unity of all religions.

## Spirituality and psychotherapy

There is a correlation between the popularisation of spirituality and psychotherapy. In addition to interest in a wide variety of meditative practices, spiritual seekers sometimes sought psychotherapy for the psychological component of their spiritual search. Just as Westerners interested in Eastern religion might look for a suitable guru, so they might also seek a psychotherapist in order to work through psycho-spiritual problems. Jungian analysis, Assagioli's psychosynthesis, the human potential movement, humanistic psychology and transpersonal psychology are examples of therapies sympathetic to spirituality.

## A psychoanalytic split

Psychotherapists are inheritors of an ancestral split regarding the validity and origin of spiritual experience. Jung and Freud fell apart over this issue. Jung felt that

Freud over-emphasised the sexual aspects of libido at the expense of a more gen-eralised understanding of libido as life-force, including spirituality, creativity and the imagination. Jung viewed Freud's scientific outlook as a 'materialist preju-dice'. Having failed to co-opt Jung in the fight against 'the black tide of mud – of occultism' (Jung, 1963, p. 173), Freud accused Jung of having had a religious conversion. Freud felt that Jung's wider definition of *erōs* to include life-force and spiritual forms of love was a defensive manoeuvre.

How do therapists respond to a patient who wishes to explore an inner world of imagination, creativity and spirituality? Do we write spiritual experience off as merely magical thinking, a manic defence or even bordering on psychosis? Do we reduce belief in God, Goddesses, Buddhas, saints, prophets etc. to inter-nalised parental object relations and magical thinking? Or do we show respect for a patient's belief systems while at the same time acknowledging how traumatic memories, neurotic complexes and psychological defence systems may distort perceptions and contaminate relationships when in their grip.

> A young university student disturbed by her experiences during an ayawaska ceremony came to see me. She found resonance between her psychedelic visions and the archetypal world of the collective unconscious described by Jung. Initially concerned that she might slip into psychosis, therapy enabled her to gradually integrate her visions in a more symbolic, grounded way, leading to a flowering of her creativity as an artist, albeit without the ayawaska!

## Defining, redefining and undefining spirituality

The term spirituality is often used to denote experience that is trans-denominational, trans-cultural, trans-historical and even at times trans-religion. From this perspec-tive there is not 'one spirituality' but a diversity of spiritualities, and it has come to be seen as a universal human quest, connected to the human search for mean-ing, purpose and transcendence. The philosopher John Cottingham suggests that the 'spiritual dimension of life' is 'inseparable from a search for self-understanding and moral growth, in the context of an asceticism of the spirit' (Waaijman, 2005, p. 24).

## Mysticism, contemplation, mystical theology

'Mysticism' is as elusive as 'spirituality'. 'Mystical' as an adjective derives from the Greek *mystikos* and has an ancient history such as in the Greek mys-tery religions. The nominalisation derives from the seventeenth century. The French *la mystique* as a noun emerged from the adjective *mystique*. From the second century CE *mustikes* referred to the hiddenness and mysteriousness of God. In the sixth century, Pseudo-Dionysius wrote *Peri mustikes theologias* (*De mystica theologia* in Latin), coining the term 'mystical theology'. Yet, just as we have seen with the word 'spirituality', translating *mustikos* as *mystica* is misleading if later understandings of mysticism are projected backward (Rorem, 1993, p. 183). McGinn points out, 'the term "mystical theology" antedated the coining of the term "mysticism" by over a millennium' (1991, p. xiv). For Dionysius *mustikes* is more a sense of something mysterious, invisible and hidden, 'but revealed to those initiated into the mysteries' (Rorem, 1993, pp. 183–184).

One of the major aspects of mystical experience is that of direct, unmediated experience of 'ultimate reality'. Outer forms such as meditation, prayer, ritual and even inner formulations, visualisations, theology, faith and belief are supportive means to an end. Signs, symbols and practices designed to point towards reality are not reality itself but signify something beyond. The signpost should not be mistaken for what it points towards.

From the apophatic dimension mystical realisation transcends thought, sense perception and conceptualisation, and is beyond any ordinary way of knowing.

## Spirituality, mysticism, religion and freedom

When people say, 'I am spiritual but not religious', it may express concern with how a direct unmediated mystical experience is mediated through religious forms, or how a personal spiritual belief becomes a belief system, formulation becomes formulaic, dogma becomes dogmatic, lived reality becomes institutionalised. Here one of the etymological derivations for religion, to re-bind, is apposite. When one feels bound in the sense of coerced, confined or constricted, the sense of spaciousness, vastness, limitlessness, formlessness, eternity, infinite freedom, all qualities of mystical experience are in danger of being limited if not lost. It also has to do with the process of codification itself. What might have been an original revelation or genuine mystical experience can lose some of its inspiration in the very process of being codified.

Many individuals do not wish to risk having their personal freedom curtailed and see institutional religion as too restrictive. They also seek to find their own answers to questions of meaning, personal destiny and the spiritual dimension of life, rather than being told what to think, feel and believe, and be bound by the dictates of religious institutions.

How is genuine revelation to be preserved and shared? Can a second-hand vessel of transmission, whether a text, icon, ritual practice or mediation technique, give rise to first-hand experience for future practitioners? In Dzogchen for example, it is not so much the written text as the living process of transmission of a realisation from master to disciple that enables the disciple to enter the same experience as the master who has realisation. Texts serve as a means of transmitting transformational insight and primordial wisdom, but the teachings are a living tradition and one needs to have person-to-person direct introduction and transmission from a realised master, as well as the assiduous application of the methods of meditation that have been taught. So too, one does not become psychoanalysed through a self-help book but through psychoanalysis which involves both a dedicated analytic relationship and process unfolding over time.

Religion can and often does serve as a way to codify and transmit authentic spiritual experience. In this sense religion could be seen as a wider framework within which to contain spiritual experience. Yet codification is also the means by which a living, experiential, personal spiritual or mystical experience runs into the dangers of becoming ossified, concretised, thereby losing its living inspiration. Bion addressed such matters in his writings on the Mystic and the Group.

> The mystic makes direct contact with, or . . . is 'at one' with, God. This capacity is not attributed to the ordinary member of the group. The Establishment must pronounce dogmatically, make laws or rules, so that the advantages of the mystic's communion with God or ultimate truth or reality may be shared with one remove by the ordinary members.
>
> (1970, p. 111)

However, the Establishment 'may fail' to share such direct communion 'through lack of discrimination, leading to the furtherance of false views, or through rigid adherence to an existing framework' such that the 'life is then squeezed out of the mystic or messianic idea' (Bion, 1970, p. 111). The mystic's oneness with the Godhead is felt as threatening to the status quo. One way to avoid such disruption is to attempt to incorporate the mystic in such a way that the truth he or she conveys is watered down through conformity or expulsion. The Christian Establishment coped by 'delineation of the borders of the group, selection and training, and stabilization of the hierarchy' (Bion, 1970, pp. 112–113).

In the context of psychotherapy, originators such as Jung, Freud, Winnicott, Klein and Bion had vital first-hand insights into the human condition. Their writings enabled others to benefit from their psychological observations. However, difficulties arise when an established school of psychotherapy becomes so codified that it loses the freshness of a new vision based on direct clinical experience. The requirement for dogmatic adherence to the psychoanalytic 'model' and 'techniques' of therapy can become stultifying and constricting, losing touch with living inspiration, fresh discovery and freedom of expression.

## Problems with spirituality

Spirituality is often contrasted with materialism and consumerism. This can lead to an 'otherworldly' disconnection from the environment, from one's physical surroundings and from one's body. If spirituality is dualistically contrasted with the physical domain it can lead to a disembodied view of spirituality, an opposition between psyche and soma, mind and body, and spirit and matter. Likewise, over-emphasis on inwardness may lead to individualistic and non-relational rather than inter-subjective forms of spirituality. Sheldrake fears that spirituality as part of the popular psychology movement can run the danger of perpetuating 'a theologically lightweight, individualistic, self-help approach to the spiritual quest' (2013, p. 169).

Psychotherapists need to address possible neurotic or psychotic elements accompanying spiritual experience, without being reductively dismissive. Yet some patients use spirituality defensively. There is the danger of etherealising, magical thinking and schizoid splitting between mind and body, idea and matter, let alone a deep confusion of inner and outer. There may be an over-focus on the inner realm of fantasy, images, dreams and spiritual flights of imagination as forms of denial, avoidance or disconnection from the difficulties of the physical, practical domain.

The psychotherapeutic setting functions as a potential space for old wounds to be uncovered, understood and worked through, freeing the spirit from its cell. Psychotherapy is an arduous and courageous process involving clearing away all that hinders, handicaps, distorts and obscures the true self, which may be akin to primordial reality, absolute truth. It also enables the possibility of opening out in the cave of the heart to grace, unbidden dawning of new insights, new ways of being in which there is a freedom, an openness of heart and openness of mind.

## Note

1  This sentiment has become something of a cultural movement, as studied by Erlandson (2000), Fuller (2001) and others.

# Chapter 2

# An open heart and an open hearth

## Towards an ethic of analytic hospitality

The patient knocks. We open the door. Bidding them welcome with a kindly gesture, we usher them into the consulting room. We welcome them as a revered, yet unknowable guest. Sitting together in a receptive stillness, tranquillity envelops us, allowing us to settle and draw breath. Even if the atmosphere is loaded with foreboding, we try to maintain serenity in the midst of uncertainty, chaos and confusion. As patients begin to talk in their own time and their own way, we listen, seeking to hear with the 'ear of our heart' (St Benedict). Or we sit in silence, a silence that enfolds us in a spirit of peace.

With an attitude of open-heartedness and open-mindedness, the therapist becomes a suitable vessel to receive and contain the deepest being of the person.

We do not assume we can see what is invisible and unknowable. We lay aside judgements based on how people presented themselves in the past and avoid overlaying the bare immediacy of our encounter with theoretical formulations or models. Such assumptions merely create a veil of obscuration clouding our ability to be fully present to the mystery of this unique person sitting before us. However long a given person has come to see us, we do not know what will emerge during this meeting, or what will remain unbidden and hidden.

An open heart and an open mind that is not filled with memories of the person based on previous sessions, anticipations of the future, a mind that is uncontaminated by subtle possessiveness, unconscious antipathy, ulterior motives, intellectual theory, such a state of mind functions as a psychological and spiritual sanctuary ready to receive our guest. The patient depends upon on our ethical attitude of care, compassion and commitment to their well-being. They depend on our hospitality.

## Towards an ethic of analytic hospitality

> All guests who present themselves are to be welcomed as Christ, for he himself will say: I was a stranger and you welcomed me (Matt 25:35).
>
> The Rule of St Benedict

Genesis describes how Abraham was sitting by the entrance to his tent at the Oak of Mamre during the hottest part of the day. He looked up and saw three men standing near him. He ran from the entrance of his tent to greet them and bowed to the ground, crying,

> My lord, if I find favour with you, please do not pass your servant by. Let me have a little water brought, and you can wash your feet and have a rest under the tree. Let me fetch a little bread and you can refresh yourselves before going a little further, now that you have come across my path.
>
> (Genesis 18:1–8, paraphrased)

Abraham and Sarah did not know, at first, that they had been entertaining angels.

I use this story as an inspiration for an ethics of analytic hospitality. It contains essential elements of the ethic of hospitality: welcoming the weary traveller, inviting the guest into one's midst, tending to the stranger's physical needs, providing shelter and nourishment, venerating the unknowable alterity, inherent godliness and divinity of the stranger.

Hospitality as a concept is multivalent and gives rise to a rich tapestry of anthropological, cultural, religious, metaphysical, ethical, interpersonal, political and philosophical perspectives. I will be drawing pertinent elements of many of these perspectives towards developing an ethos of analytic hospitality.

The ethics of analytic hospitality is inclusive of physical, spiritual, emotional, intellectual, inter-personal, philosophical, political, cultural and collegial hospitality. Analytic hospitality is physical, about the place and space of therapy. The most basic principle is that the patient is offered a physical place of sanctuary and safety, a quiet, clean, comfortable room, an outer container for healing and transformation to take place.

Analytic hospitality is a state of heart and mind, a mind that is receptive, not filled with stale memories and assumptions but open to the epiphany of each analytic encounter in a given moment. Holding the person in mind creates a psychological space of sanctuary. The analyst is also open to the change that the analytic encounter will involve for both parties. The analyst's hospitality and the intersubjective dwelling enables the patient to develop a capacity to host new realisations, to come alive within the context of a highly personal and unique relationship, a meeting of embodied minds and hearts.

Philosophically and politically, hospitality is linked to self-other relations, insider and outsider, identity and difference, familiarity and strangeness, ownership and dispossession, citizenship and alienation. It is related to nationalism and ideas of the 'homeland', issues connected to migration, refugees, racism, language, politics and power.

## Hospitality: themes

Although the ethics of hospitality vary historically and culturally, those relevant for the topic of analytic hospitality may be summarised as follows:

- Although taking many forms, the ethics of hospitality can be seen to be universal, the basis of culture.
- The word hospitality itself contains paradox, contradiction and ambiguity pointing to the ambivalence between host and hostility, guest and dangerous stranger.
- The law of hospitality as an unconditional law or principle is compromised by conditional practices of hospitality.
- There are intimate relationships between ethics, ethos and hospitality.
- Hospitality rituals serve as initiation rites transforming the outsider from stranger to guest. The offer of hospitality is a means to disarm the potential threat of a stranger. The host has a responsibility to offer hospitality to the unknown stranger.
- There are many customary rules governing the roles of host and guest based on mutual respect. These involve implied if not explicit rules that the guest is to follow, duties to follow the example set by the host.
- Hospitality involves spatial and temporal aspects. Spatially hospitality means giving shelter, sustenance and sanctuary. Temporally hospitality has a time-span that may or may not be extended.
- There is a zone of protection surrounding the guest who enters this sphere.
- Hospitality involves the crossing of a threshold into the zone of hospitality as a place to rest, and then once more out into the world.
- The greeting of welcome is an essential aspect of hospitality.
- Guests are aware they are on the territory of the host. Territoriality impacts hospitality.
- Hospitality governs potentially dualistic demarcations between insider and outsider, belonging and exclusion.
- Hospitality usually includes the provision of shelter, asylum and sustenance in the form of food and drink.
- The guest remains under the personal protection of the host until he or she leaves the zone of protection.
- The guest is not explicitly expected to reciprocate but may do so with a gift or in kind.
- Hospitality operates around the circumstances of nomad and settler. The guest is a traveller who is not in his or her own territory, a sojourner, pilgrim, exile or refugee. The host is one located in their own territory, space, home or dwelling.
- Hospitality is extended not just to strangers but even to enemies as well.
- Hospitality as a conditioned principle involves power relations, ownership, possessiveness and, in many cases, judicial and political elements. There are national and global parameters of hospitality such as how to offer hospitality to refugees. Individual hospitality may be conditioned by social and state parameters.
- Hospitality relates to group identity and therefore how outsiders are admitted to the group as temporary members.

- Hospitality often relates to language: the 'guest' speaks a different language from the host.
- Hospitality relates to self-other relationships, otherness and alterity.
- Hospitality is a disturbance to the status quo of the solitude of the one at home, an 'interruption' to the sovereign self (Derrida, Lévinas).
- Hospitality relates to the principle of alterity, the unknown, the unfamiliar.
- Gestation is a form of hospitality: the mother as host, the womb as dwelling.
- The metaphysical theme of hospitality is often depicted in the motif of the stranger who knocks as God, Zeus, the unknown stranger or the beggar who is divine.
- Hospitality relates to the capacity to 'host' a new realisation.

## Hospitality: etymological considerations

Ambivalence, ambiguity and paradox are embedded in the word 'hospitality'. The late Latin word *hospitalis* means 'hospice', 'shelter' or 'guesthouse', and derives from the Latin words *hostis* and *hospes*. *Hospes* can mean 'host', 'guest or visitor', and 'stranger or foreigner'. *Hostis* can mean 'an enemy of the state' or 'the enemy'. The shelter or guesthouse could well prove to be a hostile environment. The therapist is in a position of power, and the patient, as guest, is dependent upon the provision of benign hospitality.

Derrida's (2000a) neologism 'hospitality' is based on *hosti* and the root *pet*. He uses it to highlight the aporia, the inherent unresolvable contradictions between absolute hospitality and conditional hospitality.

In French, the word for guest and host (*hôte*) is interchangeable (Derrida, 1999). This single word reminds one that to be the host is to receive as well as to give, to be the guest is to give as well as receive. The host is in turn hosted by their house, the land they live in. They rely on having a guest to be hospitable, such as Abraham who was waiting for a guest to appear so he could offer hospitality. This points to the reciprocal mutuality of therapist and patient, who both give of themselves, both receive something vital from their encounter.

## Hospitality conditional and unconditional

The ethic of hospitality as an unconditioned principle entails welcoming the one who comes seeking our help without conditions. Such an ethic is compromised by conditional practices of hospitality. For Derrida, there is tension between the law (singular) of absolute, unconditional hospitality and conditioned laws (plural) of hospitality which, 'in marking limits, powers, rights, and duties, consist in challenging and transgressing *the* law of hospitality, the one which would command that the "new arrival" be offered an unconditioned welcome' (2000b, p. 76).

Conditional hospitality refers to particular laws, policies, guidelines and codes governing the practice of hospitality. On one level both the unconditional law of hospitality and conditioned laws of hospitality are interdependent. Conditioned forms of hospitality are informed by the law of unconditioned hospitality. Yet unconditioned hospitality needs the laws of conditioned hospitality to prevent it from being too abstract (Derrida, 1999).

The absolute law of hospitality is related to the apophatic dimension, because it requires opening one's metaphysical as well as physical 'home' to the unknowable absolute, to the ever strange and mysterious.

## Ethos, ethic, mores of a group and hospitality

The word 'hospitality' is often accompanied by words such as 'laws', 'principles', 'ethics', 'protocols', 'customs' and so forth, each of which have different connotations. Ethos derives from the Greek *ēthos* which originally meant 'an accustomed place', and came to mean nature, disposition and customs.

Hospitality and ethos are intimately connected, for the ethic of hospitality governs how to ethically accommodate and incorporate a stranger-guest who enters a place with its particular ethos.

For both Lévinas and Derrida, hospitality is 'ethnicity itself, the whole and the principle of ethics' (Derrida, 1999, p. 50):

> Hospitality is culture itself and not simply one ethic amongst others. Insofar as it has to do with the *ethos*, that is, the residence, one's home, the familiar place of dwelling, inasmuch as it is a manner of being there, the manner in which we relate to ourselves and to others, to others as our own or as foreigners, *ethics is hospitality*; ethics is so thoroughly coextensive with the experience of hospitality.
>
> (Derrida, 2001, pp. 16–17)

For Lévinas, the other who comes before me issues an implicit ethical responsibility to respond to their inviolable vulnerability and unknowable mystery. To respond is to 'give the bread from one's mouth'. In the presence of the other who comes before me face to face, the avidity of my gaze turns into generosity. I am 'incapable of approaching the Other with empty hands' (*TI*, 50).

## The rite of hospitality

When a patient arrives for their session and the therapist bids them welcome, a rite of hospitality is being enacted. Rituals have the purpose of enshrining principles, ethics and truths, and are thereby ways to transmit and realise such principles in the here and now.

The inspiration for the rite of hospitality could be seen to be foundational. 'There is no culture or social bond without a principle of hospitality' (Derrida, 2005, p. 6). Hospitality as an ethic recognises the vulnerability of the guest and the principle of responding to the call of the sojourner who comes to one's home. Psychotherapy too is such an interpersonal social bond bound by such ethical principles. The patient can be seen to be on a life journey and they come to us for help and companionship on that journey. They are as vulnerable and dependent on the therapist's hospitality as the nomad.

A patient, Amy, continually dreams of being in a waiting room, hotel foyer, at a train-station or bus stop, an in-between-place. Life feels like something not yet begun, yet at the same time is slipping away, out of grasp. Amy longs for a room in which she can stay put, be safe and simply be. She finds this in the therapy room and so hates leaving. She takes a long time to gather up her belongings and I become concerned lest the next patient arrives disturbing her session. I am aware of the paradox of analytic hospitality. We offer a hospitable space only to demarcate it in terms of both space and time. I bid her welcome at the start of her session. After 50 minutes, I show her the door. The act of hospitality has a limitation and Amy is acutely aware of this.

The rite of hospitality is a form of initiation rite signalling a change of status from stranger to guest. The stranger is unknown and unpredictable. The stranger may be hostile, and may not know or abide by the 'rules of the house'. Rules concerning hospitality often involve a form of testing of the outsider, which serves as a 'rite of incorporation' such that the status of stranger is superseded by that of guest (Pitt-Rivers, 2012, p. 503). Such transformation is also related to how the host negotiates alterity, how the otherness of the stranger is 'domesticated' by becoming a guest.

## The frame of therapy in the light of laws of hospitality

Hospitality customs frame the respective behaviour expected of host and guest so as to make certain elements concerning the principles of non-harm and protection reliable. Both guest and host have their respective obligations that have cultural variations. The host has duties of care such as offering sanctuary and refreshment, both physical and emotional. The guest also has an implied etiquette to follow.

So too, both therapist and patient have respective expectations in regard to the frames of analytic hospitality. The patient can expect to be made welcome, be given physical safety and a clean, quiet space of sanctuary, a comfortable chair to sit on or couch to lie on. The therapist undertakes to do no harm, to care for the patient's well-being, to keep their confidence, to abide by ethical principles. The patient can expect that the therapist will give emotional sustenance in the form of compassion, undivided and unsaturated attention and 'food' in the form of 'well-cooked' interpretations. The patient also agrees to abide by the frames of analysis, such as paying the fee. We can see here the tension between conditional and unconditional hospitality.

The analytic frame was originally conceived by Marion Milner who, as well as being a psychoanalyst, was also a painter. She reflected on how paintings, poems, plays, rituals, dreams and the analytic process all tend to have surrounds that both contain and frame them. She applied the metaphor of a picture frame to the outer surround of therapy, as 'marking off a different kind of reality that is within it from that which is outside it' as well as 'a temporal spatial frame [that] also marks off the special kind of reality of the psychoanalytic session' (1952, p. 183).

A central element of the analytic frame is that it demarcates what is within as being perceived in symbolic rather than literal terms. Drawing the boundaries of the frame also helps contain chaotic, harmful or explosive emotional matters, so that they can be reflected upon and understood symbolically rather than enacted upon and taken literally.

## Spatial and temporal dimensions of hospitality

Analytic hospitality has spatial and temporal dimensions. Spatially the analytic frame includes both the physical and symbolic setting that encloses therapy. Temporally analytic hospitality has a time frame—the fifty minute session, the number of sessions per week, the duration of the whole analysis.

Hospitality requires a dwelling in which to offer it. As Derrida observes, hospitality is always about 'answering for a dwelling place, for one's identity, one's space, one's limits, for the *ethos* as abode, habitation, house, hearth, family, home' (2000b, pp. 149–150). The space of therapy can be seen as a *temenos*, the analyst as a host who welcomes the patient into both the outer *temenos* of the consulting room and inner *temenos* of the analyst's heart and mind. The spacious mind of the analyst is a 'dwelling place' to receive and contain the patient's psychological matters. The consulting room serves as a physical sanctuary, sheltering and supporting the analytic couple. Winnicott described what was required to create a hospitable environment:

> This work was to be done in a room, not a passage, a room that was quiet and not liable to sudden unpredictable sounds, yet not dead quiet and not free from ordinary house noises. This room would be lit properly, but not by a light staring in the face, and not by a variable light. The room would certainly not be dark and it would be comfortably warm. The patient would be lying on a couch, that is to say, comfortable, if able to be comfortable, and probably a rug and some water would be available.
>
> (Winnicott, 1954/2013, p. 285)

For Lévinas the dwelling is a refuge of inwardness (*intimité*), a habitation which actualises recollection, as well as intimacy and warmth (*TI*, 152–154). Such warmth manifests as loving kindness and caritas for 'the intimacy which familiarity already presupposes is an *intimacy with someone*. The interiority of recollection is a solitude in a world already human. Recollection refers to a welcome' (*TI*, 155, emphasis in the original).

## Temporal dimensions of hospitality

In Bedouin culture hospitality is limited to 'three days and a third' (Shryock, 2012, p. S30). So too in analysis the frames of therapy encompass a temporal limit to analytic hospitality: the patient is allocated a given set of weekly times for their sessions, the sessions will end after 50 minutes, the patient is expected to know not to over-stay their welcome, not to come early and disturb the hospitality given to another patient, nor attempt to engage in extra-therapeutic communication outside their allotted session time.

## Hospitality and the intersubjective third

Hospitality is relational: the relationship between a particular host and a particular guest, who co-create a particular relational space. The relationship of host and guest is interdependent and gives rise to a third overlapping form of intersubjectivity. Who they are in a given encounter is defined by the conditions: the space, the time and the roles they each have. Thomas Ogden writes of an intersubjective analytic third subject of analysis that arises out of a complex, multi-layered dialectic involving an interplay between conscious and unconscious, fantasy and reality within the analytic setting. The 'analyst and analysand come into being in the process of the creation of the analytic subject' (Ogden, 1994, p. 5).

## Thresholds of hospitality

The therapeutic enclosure has an opening, a portal, serving as the point of transition between entry and exit, coming and going, inner and outer, symbolic and literal. When a guest crosses a threshold from the outside world into the zone of hospitality there are rituals concerning how the threshold is crossed. If a patient is left waiting on the doorstep because the therapist doesn't hear their knock, it would be a breach of hospitality and a break in the frame of therapy. It may feel like the x + y + z minutes that Winnicott (1971) describes, of the baby abandoned by its mother, that leads to a break in the sense of the continuity of the world. This will particularly be the case for a patient who has already experienced such a break in life's continuity in the early environment.

'Pat' finds it very hard to get to therapy on time. Yet when she does eventually arrive, her knock is so tentative as to be like a breath drawn in. I hover by the door waiting for the softest of knocks, lest if I miss hearing it, I keep her waiting. Such a break of continuity would catapult her into a black hole of no-thing-ness. Pat's mother, having given birth, was in so much pain she had to be immediately anaesthetised. Her father fainted at the sight of the blood. Pat was not welcomed into the world with loving comforting arms but felt she was falling forever in an alien space. She needed to know that she could depend on my hearing her almost imperceptible indication of her arrival.

In Homer's *Odyssey* Tellemachus was scandalised that a guest should be left waiting at the gate.

> He saw Athene and went straight to the forecourt, the heart within him scandalized that a guest should still be standing at the doors. He stood beside her and took her by the right hand, and relieved her of the bronze spear, and spoke to her and addressed her in winged words: 'Welcome, stranger. You

shall be entertained as a guest among us. Afterward, when you have eaten dinner, you shall tell us what your need is'.

(Hom., Od. 2:118–24, in O'Gorman, 2008, p. 123)

At the end of the guest's sojourn in the host's territory, the host shows them the door and bids them farewell. The moment they step outside, they are no longer a guest, but an outsider once more. Yet it is not out of sight out of mind; our care for a patient continues between sessions.

## Hospitality as interruption

Hospitality is, according to both Derrida and Lévinas, an interruption to the sovereignty of the self. When the stranger knocks and 'disturbs the being at home with oneself' (*TI*, 39), one is confronted not only with the incumbent responsibility of being hospitable, but with their alterity.

> I meet him for the first time in his strangeness face to face. I see his countenance before me nude and bare. He is present in the flesh. [Yet] there is also a sense of distance and even of absence in his questioning glance. He is far from me and other than myself, a stranger, and I cannot be sure of what this strangeness may conceal.
>
> (Wild, 1969, p. 13)

This 'interruption' is also related to the theme of hospitality as welcoming the infinite beyond the self: a form of 'ex-stasis'. The other who comes before me breaks open the cosy confines of egocentrism, disturbing my universe, yet potentially liberating me from its strictures, opening me out to the world of which I am inherently ever a part.

Solitude has a purpose, to collect oneself so one is ready to hospitably welcome the other into that space of solitude. This welcome breaks open the solitude of being and brings about encounter, an encounter that retains the alterity and strangeness of the stranger who is also the welcomed guest. As Lévinas puts it:

> For the intimacy of recollection to be able to be produced in the oecumenia of being, the presence of the Other must not only be revealed in the face . . . but must be revealed, simultaneously with this presence, in its withdrawal and in its absence.
>
> (*TI*, 155)

## The greeting of welcome is an essential aspect of hospitality

For Lévinas the word welcome is almost interchangeable with the word hospitality. To say welcome is to pay homage to the holiness, incomprehensibility and sanctity of the visitation. It signifies a rite of passage where the subject at home enters into relationship with another who comes into this intimate space where neither knows how it will enfold. To welcome is 'to *receive* from the Other beyond the capacity of the I, which means exactly: to have the idea of infinity' (*TI*, 51, emphasis in the original). There is a link between the words 'welcome' and 'ethics'; *ethica* means how to live well with oneself and with each other, and we bid the guest 'well come'.

> The welcome determines the 'receiving,' the receptivity of receiving as the ethical relation.
>
> (Derrida, 1999, p. 25)

## Hospitality: provision of refreshment, sustenance and conviviality

Hospitality often includes the provision of sustenance expressed through a shared meal. Traditional enactments of hospitality often featured conviviality, from the Latin *convīvium* (a feast), combined form of *con* (together) with *vīvō* (to live), by implication meaning to live together well. Although the preparation and offering of food to guests is not part of therapy in a literal sense, the analyst offers an interpretation that has been slowly cooking, giving psychological sustenance to the patient.

## Hospitality operates around the respective circumstances and needs of nomad and settler

Laws, ethics or protocols surrounding hospitality centre around the two categories of settler and nomad/traveller. The guest is a sojourner, pilgrim, exile or refugee. Cultures placing a high value on hospitality often develop such protocols because there is a need to manage the conflict between traveller and settler. The guest may be an exile from their own homeland, homeless, stateless, a nomad or a refugee, and they may speak a different language. Psychotherapists are also called to attend to the traumatic legacies suffered by refugees and descendants of refugees, who, having fled tyranny, torture, war, genocide, persecution, famine or other natural disasters, seek the sanctuary of therapy.

## Hospitality is extended not just to strangers but even to enemies

In most cultural contexts the law of hospitality overcomes demarcations between friend and enemy. In Bedouin Arabic hospitality for example,

> The *ger* [stranger] was a man of another tribe or district, who, coming to sojourn in a place where he was not strengthened by the presence of his own

kin, put himself under the protection of a clan or a powerful chief. From the earliest times of Semitic life the lawlessness of the desert has been tempered by the principle that the guest is inviolable. A man is safe in the midst of his enemies as soon as he enters a tent or touches a rope. To harm a guest or to refuse him hospitality, is an offence against honour, which covers the perpetrator with indelible shame.

(Robertson Smith, 1927, p. 76)

Most ethics statements of analytic societies stipulate that patients will not be discriminated against on the basis of race, ethnicity, religion, gender or sexual preference. In addition, therapists rarely refuse to treat a patient they dislike, but rather apply equanimity to all. However, the patient *has* to be a stranger in order to qualify. It is not appropriate to treat 'familiars' such as family, friends, or the family or friends of patients.

## Hospitality and reciprocity

The stranger who seeks hospitality remains implicitly indebted to the host in terms of reciprocity. Pitt-Rivers elaborates on the theme of grace involved in hospitality:

Grace, then allows of no payment, no explanation, and requires no justification. It is not just illogical, but opposed to logic, a counter-principle, unpredictable as the hand of God. . . . The opposition is clear and applies in every case: grace is opposed to calculation, as chance is to the control of destiny, as the free gift is to the contract, as the heart is to the head, as the total commitment is to the limited responsibility, as thanks are to the stipulated counterpart, as the notion of community is to that of alterity, as *Gemeinschaft* is to *Gesellschaft*, as kinship amity is to political alliance, as the open cheque is to the audited account.

(1992, p. 231)

## Hospitality involves ambivalence

The shadows of hospitality are hostility and power relations. Therapists do well to remember they have the power to unintentionally hurt as well as heal, such as when the therapist fails to understand what the patient is trying to express, and says something off-putting, disturbing the delicate fabric of interconnection.

There are alternating asymmetric relationships between the guest and the host:

The law of hospitality is founded upon ambivalence. It imposes order through an appeal to the sacred, makes the unknown knowable, and replaces conflict by reciprocal honour. It does not eliminate the conflict altogether but places it in abeyance and prohibits its expression.

(Pitt-Rivers, 2012, p. 513)

Although the host is in the position of power and the guest is dependent upon the host's good will and hospitality, the guest also has power and the host is hostage to the guest's compliance. The guest may be unruly, threaten violence or steal. They may overstay their welcome. As therapists, we do not usually 'choose' our patients, they choose us. We have to work with a range of ambivalent feelings towards them, irritation and sometimes fear. We have to set aside the impulse to retaliate against a borderline patient who attempts to enact destructive fantasies by viciously denigrating, belittling if not threatening us physically.

## Hospitality and alterity

Hospitality relates to self-other relationships and alterity. How do I greet the strange and unfamiliar? Do I welcome the inevitable responsibility and change that such an encounter entails or do I defend against it? Kristeva writes that the face of the foreigner 'bears the mark of a crossed threshold' (Kristeva, 1991, p. 4). 'They' have entered 'our' territory. Politically the issue is how to value cultural difference without either seeking to falsely assimilate or eradicate it. The stranger confronts us with our own unfamiliarity and strangeness. Kristeva takes up the relationship between inner alterity and outer alterity:

> To discover our disturbing otherness, for that indeed is what bursts in to confront that 'demon', that threat, that apprehension generated by the projective apparition of the other at the heart of what we persist in maintaining as a proper, solid 'us'. By recognising our uncanny strangeness we shall neither suffer from it nor enjoy it from the outside. The foreigner is within me, hence we are all foreigners.
>
> (1991, p. 192)

The alterity of the stranger is a reminder of the alterity of every being we encounter, however close the proximity we have with those 'near' and those 'far'. The stranger, being someone who 'comes today and leaves tomorrow', represents 'the unity of nearness and remoteness involved in every human relation' (Simmel in Candea and Col, 2012, p. S6).

When a patient knocks and is bade welcome at their first session, it is an encounter with the unknown. We do not know the patient; we do not know what will unfold; we do not know what we are in for. It is a shock of alterity, and ever remains so. We tend to defend against this alterity by arming ourselves with memories of the last session, assumptions about the patient, interpretations and theory, but all this gets in the way of true encounter, of true meeting. Bion suggests that the analyst should feel that the patient he or she is meeting in a given session is someone not met before:

> The psychoanalyst should aim at achieving a state of mind so that at every session he feels he has not seen the patient before. If he feels he has, he is treating the wrong patient.
>
> (Bion, 1967/1992, p. 382)

## Sexual union and maternity as a form of hospitality

Sexual intercourse can be viewed as an enactment of principles pertaining to hospitality. Intercourse, when mutually consensual, is one of the ways we seek to overcome separation and enter an emotional sense of connection, which still involves a paradox of communion but not fusion. If conception follows, the egg as host receives the sperm as guest. The fertilised egg becomes a new guest in the mother's body, being housed in the womb, given protection and nourishment from the mother's body.

At birth the mother creates a hospitable emotional and physical environment and holding space in the way she physically and emotionally cradles her baby, giving rise to a physical and psychological environment that facilitates the baby's development. The mother also welcomes and coaxes the baby into the world with her voice, the 'mother-tongue'.

> First and last, ultimate *as* first: such is the mother tongue, and that is why it is legitimate, even indispensable, to read, in any scene of hospitality, the acting out of what happens around having children and giving birth, and especially around the mother welcoming into 'herself' – but bearing – or its matrix [womb]! – that guest which she puts up, shelters or supports . . . just as she puts up with it, subject to expecting passively, both patiently and impatiently, resisting, more or less in spite of herself, without her knowing, its intrusion. For, we know, the child may be wanted and desired, an invited guest only too awaited and longed for, or as a visitor who insists on coming, without having been invited.
>
> (Michaud, in Still, 2010, p. 130)

## The language of hospitality

For Lévinas, 'The essence of language is friendship and hospitality' (*TI*, p. 305). Yet, just as the word 'hospitality' has its inherent contradictions, language can enhance or inhibit hospitality. For Lévinas, language is hospitality. The 'ethical choice' is 'to welcome the stranger and to share his world by speaking to him', by our welcome. The 'questioning glance' (Wild, 1969, p. 14) of the guest seeks a response, and our capacity to use language to cross the divide is a gift, a form of psychological nourishment.

The guest may speak a different language as well as have a different ethos and behave according to different customs. The guest somehow has to intuit how to behave according to the host's ethos and customs.

Yet such cultural exchange is also a source of richness, and the guest has much to offer the one at home in the solitude of their dwelling. As Kearney writes,

> This ineradicable difference between languages calls in turn for a creative congress of ideas, sentiments, convictions and life-views. And it is very often this very dialogical tension between the translatable and untranslatable which represent what is best in our cultural histories.
>
> (2014)

The encounter between different ways of being and ways of viewing being involves 'interlinguistic hospitality' which can be highly creative for both host and guest. Yet this should not amount to linguistic syncretism, or the reduction of 'host and guest tongues to a single identity of meaning. Good translation seeks to avoid fusion or confusion – the error of reducing the other to the same, the stranger to the familiar. On the contrary, genuine linguistic hospitality can only occur where the unique singularity of each stranger and each host, each author and each reader, is respected' (Kearney, 2014).

In this book we will meet this theme in bringing together the very different world-views and philosophical differences between Western and Eastern, Judaic and Christian thought, together with the implicit theme of inter-religious dialogue.

## Hospitality, inclusion and exclusion, insider and outsider

Hospitality relates to the relationships between insider and outsider and how outsiders may be given temporary admission as 'guest' members. Historically, with the development of nation states, the ethics of hospitality that operated between villages, clans or tribes tended to be replaced by laws governing insider-outsider politics related to the *civitas* (Kearney, 2014).

> What happens to those who are not part of the 'one and indivisible' state – the alien, outsider, emigrant, non-resident, non-conformist? What happens to those who represent a minority – religious, ethnic, linguistic, cultural? Does the State isolate them or send them home? If they are within the nation, do they exist if they are not part of the nation? For Hitler, the Jewish, Gypsy and other non-Aryan communities did not belong and so lost their right to 'exist'.
>
> (Kearney, 2014)

On an intercultural level hospitality involves the ability to engage with others meaningfully outside one's group: across cultures, religious persuasions, ideologies or psychoanalytic lineages without demanding, implicitly or explicitly, conversion. It is an attitude of being open to the other in all their difference, a welcoming of the changes such dialogue will inevitably bring.

## Individual hospitality is often conditioned by social and state parameters

Hospitality operates at micro and macro levels. The individual is bound by conscience to offer hospitality to a wayfarer or a refugee who comes across his or her path. The individual ethic of hospitality may be framed by a wider cultural ethic of hospitality, so that the personal act of hospitality is supported by the cultural ethic. An example would be Albania, where individual families would go to refugee camps for the Kosovars and take a family home and treat them as part of the family. This individual act of hospitality was enshrined in a cultural code of hospitality, as expressed in the word *besa* meaning faith, keeping one's word, word of honour, hospitality. Sometimes individual conscience and state laws are in conflict, such as when an individual wishes to offer sanctuary to a refugee not granted asylum, but is limited by jurisdiction.

A psychotherapist 'Marta' works for a charity organisation that provides therapy via text messaging to asylum seekers forcibly detained in an offshore immigration detention centre. She feels wretched because both as a citizen of Australia and a therapist she has a duty of care to offer sanctuary, both psychological and physical. Her patient, a young teenager, was raped by locals. Marta was, for a time, prohibited by Australian law from bearing witness even though the teenager and her family begged her to report what was going on and to get help. Marta's hands were tied, her mouth gagged. Here, she lamented, she was in danger of breaking United Nations Conventions regarding universal human rights that overrode Australian law, as well as her own moral code of analytic hospitality.

## Hospitality on a national and global scale

The ethic of hospitality begs the question of how we welcome refugees to our shore. It is beyond the scope of this book to enter such a topic, but it is important to remember that the small private world of psychotherapy takes place within (if not against) the backdrop of hospitality on a national and global scale. If hospitality is culture, it is well to remember that culture is connected to, but not co-terminus with, the nation in which it occurs.

Kant, Lévinas and Derrida in their different ways were acutely aware of this question. For Derrida, Lévinas was one to reorient 'our gazes towards what is happening today' across the globe, where

> refugees of every kind, immigrants with or without citizenship, exiled or forced from their homes, whether with or without papers, from the heart of Nazi Europe to the former Yugoslavia, from the Middle East to Rwanda, from Zaire . . . Cambodians, Armenians, Palestinians, Algerians

all whose plight calls for 'an ethical conversion' to respond to:

> the crimes against hospitality endured by the guests [*hôtes*] and hostages of our time, incarcerated or deported day after day, from concentration camp to detention camp, from border to border, close to us or far away.
>
> (Derrida, 1999, p. 71)

This is highly relevant to the practice of analytic hospitality. Many psychotherapists are involved in providing therapy for refugees and asylum seekers. Analysts attend to the traumatic legacies of dispossession, displacement and migration as well as the richness of a multicultural society.

## Collegial hospitality

There are also the principles of collegial and intellectual hospitality. How do we greet our colleagues and share in a spirit of true dialogue, uncontaminated with prejudice, competitiveness, suspicion and in the therapeutic world, not threatened by diversity of psychotherapeutic approach? If we are receptive to entertaining new ideas we might be enriched and our perceptions expanded. Yet all too often analytic societies guard their membership jealously on the basis that to belong, members must fully ascribe to the given ideology or model.

## Hospitality relates to the capacity to 'host' a new realisation

Hospitality as a state of mind includes having the mental conditions necessary to host a new realisation. Bion believed that thoughts exist without a thinker but require a receptive, containing mind for the thought to be incarnated. The mind must act as a container, and this requires the ability to bear absence, the frustration of not knowing, which creates a space for the thought to be conceived (contained).

Just as Bion elaborates on the link between container/contained as an intersubjective and relational principle and as a model of thinking, so too there is a link between intersubjective hospitality and the ability to welcome new insights. How receptive are we to that which is unknown? A close-minded attitude is inhospitable to new ideas, theories and ways of working, whereas open-mindedness enables different perspectives to be entertained and new insights to emerge.

In mystical contexts there is the theme of being a sanctuary for divinity to dwell within us. Here we have the themes of silence, ineffability and the apophatic dimension of mystical hospitality:

> O glorious God who dwells in ineffable silence. You have built for my renewal a tabernacle of love on earth where it is your good pleasure to rest, a temple made of flesh. . . . Then you filled it with your holy presence so that worship might be fulfilled in it . . . an ineffable mystery.
>
> (Isaac in Golitzin, 2013, p. 386)

## Hospitality from the perspective of the absolute

> Recollection in a home open to the Other – hospitality – is the concrete and initial fact of human recollection and separation; it coincides with the Desire for the Other absolutely transcendent.
>
> (*TI*, 172)

The very notion of hospitality is founded on duality, ownership, territoriality, possessiveness and separation. This is a property dualism. Such dualities are constructed by us, and ultimately do not exist. Who is the giver and who given to?

Who is the host and who the guest? In a way hospitality is an ethic aimed at overcoming the self-centric error of viewing the world in terms of oneself and one's selfish needs.

## The beggar at the gate, the unknown divinity

> Do not neglect to show hospitality to strangers, for by doing that some have entertained angels without knowing it.
>
> (Heb. 13:2)

A recurrent trope concerning hospitality is that in offering hospitality we are recognising the divinity within the guest, we are offering hospitality to divinity itself. Abraham and Sarah offered hospitality to the three strangers unaware of their angelic nature. It was only after this offer was carried out that the three strangers conveyed their message to Abraham and Sarah that they were to be with child:

> When hostility is converted into hospitality then fearful strangers can become guests revealing to their hosts the promise they are carrying with them. Then, in fact, the distinction between host and guest proves to be artificial and evaporates in the recognition of the new-found unity.
>
> (Nouwen, 1975, p. 67)

The theme of metaphysical hospitality is often depicted in the motif of the stranger who knocks as God, Zeus, the unknown stranger, the beggar who is divine. Divinity is inherently unknowable. The sacred nature of hospitality is also about our capacity to receive revelation and the confrontation with alterity that this involves.

> The stranger belongs to the 'extra-ordinary' world, and the mystery surrounding him allies him to the sacred and makes him a suitable vehicle for the apparition of the God, the revelation of a mystery.
>
> (Pitt-Rivers, 2012, p. 508)

Hospitality relates to the principle of alterity and mystery involved in incarnation, revelation and metaphysics. The theme of the beggar who is in fact a deity symbolises hospitality as the reception of the holiness of the other, of the Holy itself.

In therapy, there is a possibility of a mysterious process of incarnation taking place. We do what we can to enable the necessary outer and inner conditions for the true nature of the patient to be brought forth, nurtured and supported: for their true self to become incarnate, ever so gradually and imperceptibly over time.

Welcoming the unknown stranger as guest, is to be open to the infinity and ineffability of the other. 'The open door, as a manner of speaking, calls for the opening of an exteriority or of a transcendence of the idea of infinity' (Derrida,

1999, p. 26). Lévinas articulates the theme of that which is finite hosting that which is infinite:

> To metaphysical thought, where a finite has the idea of infinity – where radical separation and relationship with the other are produced simultaneously – we have reserved the term intentionality, consciousness of. . . . It is attention to speech or welcome of the face, hospitality and not thematization.
>
> (*TI*, in Derrida, 1999, p. 46)

Derrida describes metaphysics as opening out to infinity, 'so as to welcome – the irruption of the idea of infinity in the finite' and thus this 'metaphysics is an experience of hospitality':

> Lévinas thereby justifies the arrival of the word *hospitality*; he prepares the threshold for it. The passage *meta ta physika* passes through the hospitality of a finite threshold that opens itself to infinity, but this *meta-physical* passage takes place, it comes to pass and passes through the abyss or the transcendence of separation.
>
> (Derrida, 1999, p. 46)

The ethics of unconditioned hospitality is, for Lévinas, the dimension of metaphysics: 'Metaphysics, or the relation with the other, is accomplished as service and as hospitality. . . . In welcoming the Other I welcome the On High to which my freedom is subordinated' (*TI*, p. 300).

This ultimate ethic of hospitality 'moves' the 'metaphysical relation of the I with the Other . . . into the form of the We' (*TI*, 300).

## Conclusion

How do I put the ethic of analytic hospitality into practice? Before each patient arrives, I make sure that the outer environment is ready for that particular patient, taking into consideration individual needs and, where possible, individual preferences. Then I sit in my chair. I take a moment to examine my conscience, to ensure my motivation is altruistic and not contaminated by hidden ulterior motives. Then I do a simple breathing meditation. Its purpose is to clear my mind to be open, empty and receptive to this particular patient, to be fully present in the here and now.

Like Abraham sitting in the noon-day sun by his tent, I await the arrival of the angelic stranger, the inherent alterity and divinity within every patient. I greet that person with an attitude of hospitality for the unknowable stranger, with the courtesy of *agápē* and motivation of compassion. I seek to avoid prejudging the person based on the last time we met, but instead await the emergence of who and how they are in this given encounter. Every moment is unique, here and now, unprecedented and unrepeatable.

# Chapter 3

# The listening cure

## Presence, awareness, attention

*Obsculta inclina aurem cordis tui*
Listen by inclining the ear of your heart.
                    (St Benedict)

### Under a watchful gaze

A little girl sings to herself, totally absorbed in making mud pies in a park, under the watchful gaze of her father who sits nearby. She is dimly aware of the background sounds of her brothers and sisters playing on swings, joyful chortles mixing in with the steady creak of the rusty swings. Enormously proud of her row of mud pies, she looks up, hoping to catch her father's approving smile. Reassured, she goes back to her pie-making, enjoying the visceral feel of mud on her hands, the sun bathing her body in gentle warmth.

A splash of rain falls on her muddy hands. She notices it has become very quiet. Storm clouds hang ominously over a suddenly deserted park. The only sign of the happy family at play is a swing still moving, whether from the breeze that has blown up, or her brother who was swinging but moments before, she cannot tell.

She has been forgotten. In response to the threatening storm clouds, her family had hurriedly packed up their picnic and set off for home without her. She runs as fast as she can on spindly legs, up the sand dunes, onto the grassy verge, ignoring the pain of bindy-eyes in the grass prickling her bare feet. She reaches the car-park only to see the family car disappearing around the corner. Aghast, then terrified, she begins to cry till she is heaving with sobs. A strange man approaches and asks her if he might offer her a lift home. . . .

This 'creation myth' of a patient 'Jackie' encapsulated, not an isolated incident, but a history of growing up in a large family where there her very existence could be forgotten.

An essential healing element of our work together was an on-going, reliable experience of bathing in my attention throughout her sessions, as well as feeling she was held in mind between sessions. Both elements were vital to being able to let go of rigid hyper-vigilance and terror she would be forgotten. Gradually she regained a sense of interpersonal trust and capacity to play in the presence of another, to muse, imagine and daydream once more.

If psychotherapy is 'the talking cure' then it is also 'the listening cure'. Feeling someone is listening with undivided attention, non-judgmental discernment and intuitive insight is fundamental to fostering the sense that we are deeply 'heard'. We want to feel understood, in all our complexity, even if we also retain sacred areas of privacy.

In the fast-paced, impersonal culture of the atomised individual, psychotherapy offers something rare. The relational element of psychotherapy is a major curative factor. Among other things, it serves to undermine the dualistic separation of self and other that Buddhists identify as the root cause of all mental suffering. We begin to be able to trust in a sense of being neither totally alienated from the world of others, nor totally fused, an aloneness-togetherness (Hobson, 1985, p. 194), a state of non-duality. Psychotherapy is an intimate relationship of close mutuality, infused with compassion and *agápē*, an immersion in a shared realm of experiencing.

What might enable us to truly listen deeply to our patients? Can we actively cultivate a state of mind that brings reassurance and confidence in the healing processes at work in the practice of psychotherapy? The therapist should be fully present, giving their whole attention to the patient, radiating tranquillity, aware and awake yet in a state of reverie and spaciousness. The therapist aims to be open, receptive, fully immersed in the here and now of the session, deeply attuned to the patient, resonating with all that is said, all that is not said and tuning into non-verbal and unconscious channels of communication. The therapist tries to be truthful, compassionate, conscientious and considerate. Such qualities inspire similar states of mind in the patient, helping them tap into their own nascent capacities for wisdom, presence, truthfulness, compassion and love.

How might we distinguish between states of mind that may seem the same but are very different, such as between reverie and trance, or free-floating attention and attention that has freely floated off, a stream of consciousness that is associated with the patient's free associations from a wandering, disengaged mind, acuity of judgement from being harshly judgemental, compassion from sickly sentimentality?

## The spiritual and meditative practice of the therapist

There are innumerable methods of meditation which may enhance a therapist's capacities to attend to their patients. The simple act of beginning one's day with meditation, including setting one's intention to be altruistic, hones the ability to be present and undistracted, integrating the sense of pure awareness experienced during meditation into all one does. You may find your day proceeding a little more smoothly if you have begun with meditation, for you will not only be calmer and more peaceful, but more in tune with your environment. Such awareness allows a gap between perceiving a given situation and reacting to it, enabling more reflective, skilful responsiveness. It may be helpful for an analyst to practise some form of 'chimney sweeping' aimed at cleaning out the mind of extraneous distractions and mental chatter, enabling clarity, tranquillity, lucidity, awareness and attentiveness to manifest more clearly.

The more 'meditative' elements of a therapeutic state of mind consist of a number of overlapping qualities. These include:

- The practice of deep listening
- Presence and awareness, the ability to be fully present with the patient with pure awareness
- Attentiveness, the practice of paying full attention, a state of non-distraction
- Concentration
- Attention with a wide focus, free-floating attention, spaciously abiding in the here and now
- Watchfulness and vigilance
- Resonance
- Attunement
- Contemplation
- Analytic reverie
- Tranquillity, calm, equanimity, equipoise
- Compassion, care, concern, empathy
- Loving kindness
- Intuition
- Discernment, discriminating awareness
- Critical analytical investigation
- Insight
- Ethical awareness, principle of non-harm
- Wisdom and truthfulness

To be fully present requires many of these qualities simultaneously. In a given situation one element may be more important to apply than another and they are to a greater or lesser extent inseparable. In the next four chapters, we will focus on the more contemplative elements of therapy. In this chapter we consider the need to listen with presence, awareness, attention, concentration and watchfulness. Chapter 4 will focus on analytic reverie and contemplative states. Chapter 5 contains a short outline of Buddhist meditation as background for the relevance of meditation and the state of contemplation in the spiritual practice of the psychotherapist. Chapter 6 describes the state of contemplation in Dzogchen and gives an overview of Dzogchen teachings and their relevance to psychotherapy.

## Presence and awareness

> The Buddhas of the past have attained Enlightenment, just as will those of the future, by following the path of continuous presence without distraction. Additionally, those attaining it at this time do so by grounding themselves in presence, because there is no other way of attaining Enlightenment. The recognition

of our true State and the continuation of its presence really are the essence of all the paths, the basis of all meditation the conclusion of all practices, the pith of all the secret methods and the key to all the deepest teachings. This is why we have to try to maintain continuous presence without being distracted.

(Namkhai Norbu, 2005, p. 25)

What do we mean when we say someone has presence? Presence is the opposite of absence: that is, we are not absent-minded, inattentive or disengaged. We spend so much of our lives surrounded by endless external sources of distraction and circling around in internal dialogues, thinking, judging, ruminating if not muttering away under our breath! All such 'noise' drowns out any capacity to be fully present and aware.

Presence has spatial, temporal and interpersonal dimensions. Presence is a mind that is present in the present, and is present to those present. *Being* present is a state of being. *Giving* our presence is interpersonally directed presence. When someone is fully present, a sense of presence communicates itself. We speak of someone radiating presence. Having presence is ethically neutral: a holy man or woman may emanate a tranquil presence, as if we are touched in some indefinable way by their inner spirit of tranquillity and wisdom. But there are also those who radiate a sinister or hostile presence.

Dzogchen teachings describe the capacity to maintain continuous presence, abiding in the state of 'what is', observing but not chasing arising thoughts, images, emotions or sensations (Namkhai Norbu, 1996, p. 114). Continuous presence in the context of psychotherapy means being present on multiple levels, listening deeply, empathically attuned to and resonating with all layers of the patient's psychological, physical and spiritual states of being. One is simultaneously grounded in a deeper state of presence and fully immersed in the present moment with the patient. One is attuned to moment-by-moment fluctuations in the emotional tonality within oneself and the patient. Being present to the patient inspires the patient to be present to themselves.

Being present has temporal dimensions. Meditation teachings frequently enjoin the meditator to abide in the present moment, without being distracted by thoughts of the 'three times', neither following after thoughts of the past, anticipations of the future, nor caught in wandering thoughts arising in the present.

So too, Bion advised the analyst to view every session as a new session, to consider any session as being 'a new session and therefore an unknown situation that must be psycho-analytically investigated'. One needs to avoid being 'obscured by an already over-plentiful fund of pre- and mis-conceptions' (1962, p. 39).

## The presence of God

Another form of presence is that of divine presence. St Teresa of Ávila describes the unbidden experience of 'a consciousness of the presence of God' of 'such a kind that I could not possibly doubt that he was within me or that I was wholly engulfed in him' (in McGinn, 1991, p. xiii). In the tradition of Hesychasm, one seeks through the practice of continuous prayer a continuous awareness of divine presence in the depths of one's being, in the being of others, of the whole world. Bede Griffiths describes presence as laying 'hold of eternity in the present moment . . . in which I am face-to-face with God' (Griffiths, in Du Boulay, 2005, p. 221). He wrote that

> prayer for me is the practice of the presence of God in all situations, in the midst of noise and distractions of all sorts, of pain and suffering and death, as in times of peace and quiet, of joy and friendship, of prayer and silence, the presence is always there.
>
> (1992, p. 498)

Yet for the apophatic mystics, a sense of absence is also mysteriously linked to divine presence. We could say that paradoxically presence is the kataphatic dimension, absence the apophatic.

## *Presence and absence*

Just as a sense of presence is important, so too is a capacity to bear absence, to be able to bear separation, loss, otherness and limitation (Colman, 2010). Symbolic imagination depends on the capacity to negotiate presence and absence. Winnicott spoke of an intermediate or transitional area where creative living occurs in the gaps between the presence and absence of the object. He also observed that many patients are marked by dead or numb spots, if not by a pervasive deadness, that at the deepest levels bear witness to an absence that once seemed endless. This often derives from an absent-minded parent, or from a too-long absence, thus engendering in the baby a primordial break in life's continuity (Winnicott, 1971, p. 114). The infant's ability to symbolise, where the symbol functions as a transcendence of presence and absence, is damaged. Primitive defences in the form of half-aliveness and dissociation may then be organised to defend against a repetition of unbearable absence. An original aliveness is blanked out in the face of this ghastly horror. If any return from such nothingness and absence into aliveness and vitality is continually greeted with the same absent presence, the child may mould itself around the need for self-obliteration (Eigen, 1993). The analyst's presence helps mediate such psychic deadness, enabling new inklings of aliveness to appear, as long as the patient can trust in the analyst's presence of mind.

## Mediation teachings on presence and awareness

What can meditation teachings about presence and awareness have to say that might help therapists develop a capacity to be fully present? Simple breathing meditations cultivate a capacity for presence and awareness. There are many such practices, but they have in common the setting aside of a period of time to do the practice in a quiet space, much like a therapy session is also a time set aside from sources of distraction.

Meditation does not yield instant results, but its benefits are subtle and accumulative. There is a tendency to find innumerable excuses not to meditate and so one is often advised to begin with regular but very simple, short sessions. On the other hand, there are many moments in the day when one could decide to do a short practice. Most teachings on meditation warn that, rather than from a book, it is important to learn from a qualified teacher who can guide you as to the most appropriate practices, and how to do them correctly.

When doing a formal practice of breathing meditation, one begins by setting aside a certain period for meditation. One adopts the meditation posture, the most essential element of which is having a straight back. Breathing is natural, flowing, deep, relaxed. Focusing on the breath, when your attention wanders, you gently bring awareness back to the breath. The key is 'learning to simply rest in a bare awareness of thoughts, feelings, and perceptions as they occur', aware, but not carried away by them (Mingyur and Swanson, 2007, p. 43). Yongey Mingyur gives the following instructions:

> Simply sit up straight, breathe normally, and allow yourself to become aware of your breath coming in and going out. As you relax into simply being aware of your inhalation and exhalation, you'll probably start to notice hundreds of thoughts passing through your mind. Some of them are easy to let go of, while others may lead you down a long avenue of related thoughts. When you find yourself chasing after a thought, simply bring yourself back to focusing on your breath.
>
> (2007, p. 43)

In Tibetan calm abiding practices, (Sanskrit *śamatha*, Tibetan *zhi gnas*) one's eyes are open, the gaze expansive. One either focuses on an object, or the practice may be objectless. The object may involve watching the breath, an image or mantra. These three elements belonging to body, voice and mind can be combined, by simultaneously focusing on an image, chanting a mantra and watching the breath. In regard to an image, the object of support could be an image such as that of a Buddha, saint or holy person, (by extension, an icon of Christ or Hindu deity), a candle, a flower. It need not be a visual image: bodily sensations, breath, sounds, smells, emotions and even thoughts themselves can be used as the object. If using breath, the practice involves lightly focusing awareness on the breath. When breathing in, just know you are breathing in and when breathing out, just notice you are breathing out. There is no commentary, analysis or conceptualisation, just pure awareness and presence. It is about resting in the natural clarity of awareness and presence, without manipulation. This is a very useful simple practice for clearing the mind and resting the mind in the moments before a patient arrives, for cultivating a capacity for free-floating attention, or reverie.

Objectless meditations are also taught, when one effortlessly rests the mind in the present moment, abiding in a state of pure awareness, a state of contemplation. As Longchenpa advises, 'Seek for the Buddha nowhere else than in . . . the pure fact of being aware right now' (in Studstill, 2005, p. 229).

### Pure presence in Dzogchen teachings

Dzogchen is concerned with realising a primordial state of pure presence. To do so, one observes one's mind, leaving it in its natural condition, without judgement or contaminating conceptualisation, simply remaining.

> Those who practice Dzogchen must realize perfect presence and awareness and, to that end, must truly have understood their own mind and succeeded in gaining control of it. Otherwise, explanations about presence and awareness will not get results and will amount to little more than ink on paper or topics for intellectual discussion.
>
> (Namkhai Norbu, 2005, p. 21)

The aim is to maintain continuous presence and awareness without distraction in all situations of daily life. One simple practice helping develop the capacity to be present, aware and non-distracted in ordinary life, is to devote a given period of time to being present and not distracted, whether eating, walking, sitting or sleeping. Such presence may seem difficult at first but it is no different from any new skill. The Tibetan word for meditation, *sgom*, means 'becoming familiar with' and meditation is about becoming familiar with the nature of your mind beneath all the adventitious stains and obscuration that clouds it.

## Paying attention: a state of non-distraction

'Brian' is a psychiatrist in a busy Sydney hospital, training to be a psychotherapist. He finds it hard to pay attention. His mind constantly wanders off to all manner of other preoccupations: what he needs to do after the session, how he must remember to book the car in for a service, what he needs to buy at the shops during his lunch break. He fidgets and takes copious notes to try and harness his mind to what his patient is saying. Supervision is restricted to pulling out the relevant patient's file and reading out his process notes for the last few sessions after which he stops and expectantly awaits my commentary. It is as if the patient exists on paper but not in his heart, that he cannot hold his patient in mind. I suggest he might put aside his notes and just try to describe the raw experience of being with his patient, including all his spontaneous musings. He shifts uneasily in his chair, shuffling through his notes, unable to know where to start. He is used to juggling hundreds of hospital admissions in a busy Sydney public hospital, having to make very quick diagnostic decisions then moving onto the next crisis. Sitting and listening for an hour with one patient several times a week and holding that patient in mind is an entirely new experience.

It may seem a *sine qua non* to suggest that a therapist should be paying attention during sessions. One should not be distracted with thinking about the next patient or the previous one, desires for the session to end, fantasising about the weekend or daydreaming. But how often do therapists actually achieve this? A distracted mind that is unable to focus flits from thought to thought and is never at ease. If a therapist is not paying attention, the patient not only feels disregarded, but the therapist's distracted state of mind engenders a similar state of restlessness, fragmentation and disease in the patient, whereas a tranquil, calm, focused mind tends to engender tranquillity.

### The many facets of attention

For Freud, a cornerstone of analytic technique was *gleichschwebend*, translated as 'free-floating attention' or 'evenly suspended attention', which is linked to the patient's free association. Fliess (1942) recommended 'conditioned daydreaming' while Reik advocated poised attention and 'listening with the third ear' (1949, p. 144). Milner, writing under the pseudonym Joanna Field (1934) used the term 'attention with a wide focus'.

Paying attention combines both focused attention as well as dispersed awareness across the entire situation. There is a delicate balance between alertness and awareness, relaxation and presence, single-pointed concentration and spaciously abiding in the present and non-judgemental empathy with discriminating insight.

An example might be a singer in a choir. The singer's attention is simultaneously concentrating with a wide as well as directed focus on the music, with all its rhythmic and melodic elements, dynamics and phrasing. Another part is directed more narrowly to vocal technique, such as tongue positions, mouth shape, muscular support and breathing technique. Another part of their attention will be engaged with watching the conductor, another tuning in with the other singers, making microtonal adjustments to maintain perfect intonation and harmony. Another part will be aware of the breathing of other singers, co-ordinating or staggering breathing depending on the situation. The chorister will be on guard for unpredictable sources of distraction, such as noticing that the tenors missed an entry, ensuring the singer is not put off making their own entry. If the singer loses the place in the music or is distracted for a moment they know how to find it again and come back in. The singer will also focus on the meaning of the music. Ultimately, inspired by the spirit of the music, all elements of attention converge and unify, the singer enters a state of ecstasy transcending awareness of time, space and individuality, such that the music and singers become all one instrument, one soaring, flowing body of sound.

Paying attention is a form of watchful awareness, where one actively disciplines oneself to avoid sources of distraction, to be alert and keep bringing one's attention back to the task. I am reminded of this when I go to swim at the local pool. There is always an attendant on duty who has the task of watching all swimmers and being ready to jump in if there should be any sign that a swimmer is in difficulty. As I swim up and down, I observe which of these attendants is actually able to hold attention on the entire pool, looking out for signs of distress and danger. You can tell which ones are actually attending, holding the entire area in their field of awareness, as well as tracking for particular potential problems. But many seem lost in a daydream or are easily distracted by someone coming to chat and, when there is nothing else to distract them, obsessively check their mobile phones. The attendant, as 'life-guard', has the primary task of 'attending' yet it is a form of attention that is able to take in a wide field of vision. It is not narrowly focused on any one swimmer but surveys the scene, only turning their focus into a narrow beam when there are signs of distress or danger. Jackie's father was meant to be surveying the scene, and through doing so, keeping her safe, but she slipped off his radar, putting her in grave danger.

## Concentration, spaciously abiding and watchfulness

Of relevance to the analyst's state of mind is a three-fold division between single-pointed concentration, spaciously abiding in the present and watchful vigilance. One part of the mind is focused on the chosen topic. Another part is engaged in abiding spaciously in the present and another portion on watchfulness.

When Jackie sits before me on the couch, there is a sense of being together, resonating, attuning, communing and musing. Part of my attention is devoted to concentrating on all she says as well as all this inspires in me, part is evenly hovering and spacious, and part is watchfully aware of the movements of my mind, allowing them to freely float but not float off. There is a sense of being present in the face of what emerges, as well as a state of quiet expectancy, waiting for a spirit of inspiration, the still quiet voice of the analytic third (if not, at times, a thunderstorm or howling gale).

## Focused attention and concentration

Therapy involves 'evenly hovering attention' rather than single-pointed concentration. Yet a capacity for single-pointed concentration is still helpful. In this age of distraction, many are unable to focus on any one task, their attention scattered, ever-ready to reach for the mobile phone. Being able to concentrate enables one to centre one's attention on the chosen object of cognition and to exclude other objects of attention. Concentration is an art that can be practiced and honed. Here one might remember the original English sense of the word concentrate meaning to bring together, the sense of being totally absorbed in what one is attending to.

Single-pointed concentration is called *samādhi* in Sanskrit, *tingedzin* in Tibetan. 'Right concentration' (*sammā samādhi*) is the eighth of the Eightfold Noble Path of the Theravada school. One-pointedness (*citt'ekaggatā*) enables one to centre on an object of cognition – a sight, sound, smell, thought – and it unifies concomitant mental aspects of cognition in the one act of cognition. As well as unbroken undistracted attention on the object of consciousness, concentration brings inner tranquillity and serenity. This helps the mind to also be incisive and penetrate to the heart of an issue.

## Spaciously abiding

When we allow the mind to naturally settle, we can enter a state of spaciously abiding in the immediacy of here and now, aware of, but not distracted by, thoughts, images, emotions and sensations passing through our mind. Just like a huge spacious ocean, we allow thoughts and images to come and go without following them. Nor do we try to block them. Spaciously abiding has some similarities with Freud's evenly hovering attention and Milner's attention with a wide focus. There is a sense of breadth of vision, as if one were on a high mountain or gazing into space taking in the entire panorama, an all-encompassing field of awareness that has no limits. We can see how single-pointed narrowly focused attention and a more expansive form of spaciousness go hand in hand.

## Watchfulness

Watchfulness or vigilance is the ability to notice when your mind has wandered and to bring attention back to the object of focus. An analogy might be that of a shepherd caring for sheep in a sheepfold. The shepherd's attention spaciously encompasses the entire fold, as well as focuses on each individual sheep. Spaciously abiding is the quality that takes in the entire scene, not focusing on any one element. Single-pointed focus is the quality that focuses on an individual sheep. Watchfulness is like the aspect that guards the entrance to the sheepfold. If one of the sheep wanders out the gate, the shepherd will stretch out his hook and bring it back. Teresa of Ávila describes poetically how the senses and faculties wander off but the king who dwells at the centre of the castle of the soul calls them back once more (2002, p. 240).

So too, with a shepherd's eye of watchfulness, a therapist can notice attention that has floated off and gently hook the meandering mind back into the fold of spacious awareness and focus on the patient.

In therapy one is paying attention to the patient as well as being self-aware. One is also aware that one is aware; there is a self-conscious apperception or a witness. Like the shepherd, it can corral the sheep, direct attention to focus on something, maintain a steady focus. One might be listening intently to a patient's story, but momentarily disturbed by a builder next door. One deliberately continues listening, blocking out the noise next door and showing this through your focus. If you are not distracted, usually the patient will not be either.

## Watchfulness and attentiveness

In Christian contemplative traditions, as well as the practice of stillness, meditation and contemplative prayer, there is the practice of watchfulness and awareness. In the context of the Orthodox practice of continuous prayer, (Hesychasm), St Hesychios has this to say about attentiveness and watchfulness:

> Attentiveness is the heart's stillness, unbroken by any thought. In this stillness the heart breathes and invokes, endlessly and without ceasing, only

Christ who is the Son of God and Himself God . . . through this invocation enfolded continually in Christ, who secretly divines all hearts, the soul does everything it can to keep its sweetness and its inner struggle hidden. . . .

Watchfulness is a continual fixing and halting of thought at the entrance to the heart . . . watchfulness and the Prayer of Jesus Christ, undistracted by thoughts, are the necessary basis for inner vigilance and unfathomable stillness of soul, for the deeps of secret and singular contemplation, for the humility that knows and assesses, for rectitude and love. This watchfulness and this Prayer must be intense, concentrated, and unremitting.

(1983, p. 163)

## Silence and reverie

> *Le silence éternel de ces espaces infinis m'effraie.*
>
> (Blaise Pascal, Pensées, in Bion, 1965, p. 171)

Silence envelops us in a deep sense of peace. 'Celeste' lies on the couch in a state of reverie, remembering playing on the beach as a child, running in and out of the waves, the feel of the sun on her bare skin, the gritty sand beneath her feet. She is able to muse because she is bathing in my presence and being kept safe from harm. I notice the gentle, rhythmical rise and fall of her chest, flickering eyelids, an occasional glance in my direction to check I am still present and attuned.

'Letta' lies on the couch with her back to me, staring at the wall. She does not speak for three weeks. I feel a strong compulsion not to break the silence, yet at the same time I have to feel my way through imagination into what might be going on for her. At the beginning and end of the session, the only time I see her facial expression, there is a look of hurt accusation. I sense that she is punishing me for something I have said. A break is coming up so I dare break the silence to forewarn her. She merely nods then continues to stare sullenly at the wall.

Bion was alert to the need to be comfortable with silences in therapy, as containing a form of presence in itself in the room. As well as not rushing to break the silence out of a sense of uneasiness, there is a need to avoid filling silence with internal dialogues. Bion warns against the temptation to break silence by making noises, including producing an interpretation when you cannot bear the silence.

> I think it is useful to listen to a silence and not to be in too much of a hurry to break it up. I am familiar with this because I know that whenever I am tired I have a spate of interpretations to the mind – all the Freudian, Kleinian, Abrahamian, every blessed interpretation you ever thought of – they all come flocking to my mind. Indeed one could almost say that psycho-analytic training becomes a kind of psychoanalyst's neurosis. . . . Much the same thing can be said to the person who can't listen to silences. I would be surprised if anybody here is unfamiliar with the experience of not being able to tolerate

the silence. 'For goodness sake! Why can't you say something?' But in fact there is a lot to be said for being able to listen to the silence.

(1976/2014, *CWXV*, pp. 42–43)

The analyst enters a deep pool of silence, waiting quietly and simply noting what is heard, such that gradually 'you would be able to hear even things like your heartbeat'. Such silence is a form of attention and is related to the capacity to bear unknowing. But most people find facing the unfamiliar creates a sense of anxiety and that silence is hard to achieve 'because of all the clamour of all the information picked up in the course of life. There is so much noise going on in one's own mind that it is hard to notice any fresh element' (Bion, 1976/2014, *CWXV*, pp. 33–34).

## Applying mindfulness, watchful awareness and spaciously abiding in the present to the analytic session: deep listening

The demarcated time and space devoted to an analytic session could be treated a little like a session of meditation. Before the patient arrives, spend a few moments making sure the outer environment is a hospitable, calm space that won't be unduly disturbed. Take a moment to be fully ready for your patient. Sit in your chair with your back straight. Examine your conscience and set an altruistic intention for this session of therapy. Then focus on your breathing, simply being aware of breathing in, holding for a moment, breathing out, allowing a moment of emptiness before breathing in again. Do not force or manipulate breathing, just allow it to be natural, deep, slow. Simply let your mind settle, mind in body, body on the seat. Then when the patient arrives, welcome them and maintain the same sense of calm tranquillity, compassionate presence and awareness throughout the session. In the analytic session, our field of evenly hovering attention encompasses the patient, the relationship with the patient, the intersubjective analytic field including all the patient is saying, all that is not being said, all that is being indicated with tone of voice, expression, body language, all that you feel emotionally and somatically, images, sounds, feelings, that float into awareness. Mindfulness implies minding the patient. Some of your attention is devoted to a watchful vigilance, noting if your mind is wandering and bringing your attention back to the session so that you are paying full attention to the patient's narrative as well as non-verbal communications. You may take note of what you are thinking and feeling in response, images, links, associations, but without getting too caught up in an internal commentary. The majority of your attention is resting in a state of reverie, abiding in the here and now, deeply immersed in all that unfolds.

At the end of the session as the patient leaves, silently dedicate the session to their well-being and healing.

# Chapter 4

# The state of contemplation and analytic reverie

'May' describes how as a child she had an intimation of eternity, a 'kind of hush, as if the world stood still for an infinite moment'. She was camping with her family in the desert. Clambering out of her tent, bathing in the light of the moon, she looked out at the sandy desert stretching for miles away into the horizon but the horizon seemed to dissolve into the sky and become one continuum with the Milky Way. The stars in the sky shone with a light she had never seen before, and they too stretched into the vastness of space. She saw how small she was and how vast the universe was. It was so still, yet there was a wind blowing the sand into furrows, blowing the sand into the sky where the light of the moon illuminated the grains of sand, so they took on the appearance of stars, the sand becoming one with the Milky Way. She felt that she was infinitesimally small and insignificant, a grain of sand among countless grains of sand, yet also like a star. She tells me how she now longs to regain this sense but the more she grasps after it, the more it eludes her. She does rediscover this sense again, swimming in the sea, where she has the feeling of being at one with the water, the huge surging currents, her body suspended, floating, just being. She begins to paint. And she find that to paint, she needs the freshness of vision of a little girl who could gaze at the sandy desert stretching into the sky, a gaze that floats freely and is at peace.

## Free-floating attention and evenly suspended attention

In 'Recommendations to physicians practicing psychoanalysis' (1912), Freud advocates a state of mind on the part of the analyst which, rather than concentration or directed attention, is 'calm', 'quiet', 'evenly-suspended' and 'free-floating attention'. The 'technique', Freud explains, 'is a very simple one':

> It consists simply in not directing one's notice to anything in particular and in maintaining the same 'evenly-suspended attention' . . . in the face of all that one hears.

> (1912, pp. 110–111)

An analyst 'should simply listen, and not bother about whether' one 'is keeping anything in mind' (p. 111). This is the analytic parallel to the patient's free association. His advice for the practice of free association is as follows:

> For the purpose of self-observation with concentrated attention it is advantageous that the patient should take up a restful position and close his eyes; he must be explicitly instructed to renounce all criticism of the thought formations which he may perceive. He must also be told that the success of the psychoanalysis depends upon his noting and communicating everything that passes through his mind, and that he must not allow himself to suppress one idea because it seems to him unimportant or irrelevant to the subject, or another because it seems nonsensical. He must preserve an absolute impartiality in respect to his ideas.
>
> (Freud, 1900/1913, pp. 109–110)

Free-floating attention is a state of bare attention, alive openness without foreclosing, or going to meet 'sense-impressions half way' (Freud, 1911, p. 220). The analyst has to eschew reliance on all forms of conceptual and sensory information, preconception, memories, judgements, theories or models, in order to attune the capacity for intuition and bare attention. There is a sense of immediacy, aliveness, presence, yet also tranquillity and a state akin to reverie and contemplation.

Yet evenly suspended attention is not easy for many analysts, whose state of mind is cluttered with presuppositions and judgements based on theoretical and diagnostic constructs occluding what is to be observed.

Just as there are similarities between free-floating attention, analytic reverie and calm abiding meditation, there are also similarities between the patient's free association and the practice of meditation. There is the adopting of a 'restful position', taking note of all that passes through one's mind, without supressing, floating freely, letting oneself go (Freud, 1904, p. 251). There are differences regarding posture; in therapy, the couch helps the patient relax into their own inner world of associations, whereas in meditation, the position of being upright with a straight back helps the delicate mixture of clarity, insight and calm presence. Other differences relate to both purpose and process. In analysis the goal of free association is to make the unconscious conscious. In meditation the goal is to achieve a state of mind that is alert, awake, aware and present, if not to have awareness of awareness, penetrating beneath the appearance aspects of the mind to the nature of mind itself. In analysis the patient communicates their free associations without censorship to the analyst. Meditation is usually a solitary, silent process. Yet its motivation is not purely solitary but ideally altruistic, enhancing a capacity for love and compassion towards all beings. There are parallels between a therapy session and a session of meditation. Like watching fish swimming in a lake, the meditator allows the thoughts to appear and disappear, neither suppressing them nor grasping after them. So too, the analyst in the state of evenly suspended attention scans the depths of unconsciousness as well as the surface of consciousness and is 'surprised by glimpses, as it were, of "fish among the weeds under the water"' (Brown, 1977, p. 481).

Freud advises that 'the most successful cases are those in which one proceeds with no aim and allows oneself to be overtaken by surprise' (1912, p. 113). One should not concentrate on one element in particular because to do so means being blind to other elements, selecting 'from among the data offered', seizing 'upon one fragment especially' and following 'our own expectations or inclinations. The danger naturally arises that we may never find anything but what we are prepared to find' and we 'falsify the possible perception' (Reik, 1949, pp. 157–158). Bion reminds us to

> be wide open to what is going on in the session. . . . The unobserved, incomprehensible, inaudible, ineffable part of the session is the material from which will come the future interpretation that you give in so many weeks', or months', or years' time, . . . We must be able to stand the pressure of watching that process.
>
> (1990, p. 127)

As well as 'evenly hovering attention', there is an element of tuning in in a more directed way. The analyst

> must turn his own unconscious like a receptive organ towards the transmitting unconscious of the patient. He must adjust himself to the patient as a telephone receiver is adjusted to the transmitting microphone. Just as the receiver converts back into sound waves the electric oscillations in the telephone lines which were set up by sound waves, so the doctor's unconscious is able, from the derivatives of the unconscious which are communicated to him, to reconstruct the unconscious, which has determined the patient's free associations.
>
> (Freud, 1912, pp. 115–116)

## Reik: listening with the third ear

Reik advocates listening with 'the third ear' and describes how the third ear can 'be turned inward' to 'hear voices from within the self that are otherwise not audible because they are drowned out by the noise of our conscious thought-process' (1949, pp. 146–147).

> The psychoanalyst has to learn how one mind speaks to another beyond words and in silence. He must learn to listen 'with the third ear'. It is not true that you have to shout to make yourself understood. When you wish to be heard, you whisper.
>
> (Reik, 1949, p. 144)

Reik replaced Freud's 'evenly suspended attention' with the term 'freely floating attention', arguing that attention is never evenly suspended but actively roaming.

## Bion on maternal and analytic reverie

Reverie comes from the French 'to dream', but analytic reverie is more than a daydream. In reverie one allows thoughts, images and feelings to rise and fall, come and disappear, without suppressing or trying to lay hold of them, such that one begins to sink to a deeper level of awareness below the surface of thinking. Thoughts and feelings are like butterflies, coming and going at will. One does not try to catch them but notes them as possible sources of unconscious communication and lets them be.

Bion links analytic reverie with Freud's free-floating attention, but suggests that it also involves love and dream-work. For Bion analytic reverie is related to maternal reverie, the mother's willingness to attend to her child, her capacity to take all her baby's being into her loving heart. Without being invasive, evasive or possessive, she ponders it in her heart. Such 'holding in mind' transmutes primitive inchoate anxieties into 'food for thought', and facilitates a capacity to receive, reflect and ponder.

Psychological birth requires a capacity to tolerate no-thing-ness, whilst that which is originally inchoate, unrecognised and unborn is coming into being. The trauma of birth needs to be mediated by certain vital emotional, environmental and interpersonal conditions. We need mother's caring mind to wonder at our existence in a state of reverie. Through her capacity to bear our unthinkable anxieties and unprocessed primitive terrors, she renders them thinkable and bearable. When a baby does not come into the world comforted, cradled and contained, a psychological catastrophe occurs.

For Bion, the mother expresses her love through reverie. When all goes well at the proverbial 'first feed' the mother takes into her heart, unthinkable anxieties such as fear of dying. Retaining a 'comfortable state of mind' (Bion, 1967) in the face of such primitive material, mother shows a capacity to contain, bear and think what is for the infant uncontainable, unbearable and unthinkable. Maternal reverie is the state of mind in which, through what Bion names 'alpha function', primitive unprocessed 'beta elements' projected into the mother by the baby are metabolised, becoming 'alpha elements' or food for thought. Alpha function, which Bion deliberately does not define, refers to the ability to contain, metabolise and transform primitive anxieties, fears of annihilation and destruction. The baby is then able to take back this emotionally digested material and gradually develops its own capacity to contain and think, in other words its own capacity for alpha function.

An example of this communicative process at work is that of a baby who fears it is dying. The baby communicates this fear through body language, facial expression, cries of distress and other non-verbal channels of communication. The baby expels 'feelings of impending disaster into the mother'. Through her compassionate immersion in her baby's reality, she is able to hold her child's existential anxiety in her heart while retaining 'a balanced outlook' (Bion, 1967, p. 106). The mother's calm containing presence detoxifies the baby's 'evacuation' of primitive mental states and modifies it such that the baby can take it in. The mother comforts the baby, 'makes some soothing response' and the baby begins to be able to think the anxiety might just be bearable and thinkable. Unthinkable anxiety has become food for thought and fears of death transmuted 'into vitality and confidence' (Bion, 1963, p. 31).

If, instead, a mother is irritated and perplexed, as if exclaiming 'I don't know what's the matter with the child!', the child 'feels the mother's anxiety and impatience and is compelled to take its own anxiety back again' (Bion, 1990, p. 53) but having been expelled by itself then the mother, the re-introjection of feelings of dreadfulness are exacerbated rather than alleviated. The baby continues to become distressed, crying harder and harder, evoking ever stronger feelings of anxiety in the mother, and so creating a vicious circle (Bion, 1990, p. 53). The baby cannot stand it anymore, shuts up and shuts down, filled with what Bion called 'nameless dread' (Bion, 1967, p. 116).

A breakdown in a mother's capacity for reverie imposes impossible burdens on the infant's developing and hence fragile consciousness. 'The rudimentary consciousness cannot carry the burden placed on it' and, 'instead of an understanding object', the infant internalises 'a wilfully misunderstanding object – with which it is identified' (Bion, 1967, p. 117).

## Container/contained

Maternal reverie is related to containment and container/contained. This has two inter-related applications: an intersubjective container/contained relationship where one person, such as the mother or analyst, functions as a container to contain another's emotional material; and as a model of thinking. The intersubjective dimensions of container/contained and the capacity to contain thoughts are linked. When inchoate psychic beta elements are contained then transformed into alpha elements, they become food for thought. Container/contained is an interdependent function necessary for emotional growth, for learning from experience, for transmutation of nameless dread and of trauma.

> We may deduce from reverie, as the psychological source of supply of the infant's need for love and understanding . . . reverie is that state of mind which is open to the reception of any 'objects' from the loved object and is therefore capable of reception of the infant's projective identifications whether they are felt by the infant to be good or bad. In short reverie is a factor of the mother's alpha-function.
>
> (Bion, 1962, p. 36)

A mother doesn't just take in and digest primitive emotional states transmitted by the baby, then return them processed and hence digestible. What she communicates is her capacity to contain, modelling for the child a capacity to contain and think about difficult emotions. Through such witness, the child has the sense this is something that one can do oneself, to contemplate.

This is precisely the value of analytic reverie in the therapeutic setting. A patient may be in a state of crisis and want instant solutions. The analyst who retains a balanced outlook in the face of suffering brings a sense of calm reflection, the thought that perhaps this terrible situation might just be bearable. It slows things down to allow deeper issues below the surface to be explored.

The analyst through such reverie is providing the existential atmosphere in which the patient, like the infant, feels it has come into a space of feeling alive and real because another human being takes the time, effort and attention to immerse themselves in that patient's reality with all its elusive alterity, its vicissitudes, complexity, depth, flux and change.

## Clinical example: Virginia

'Virginia' came saying that she had a terrible fear of death. She described how when she was aged 3, she was playing in a rock pool by the sea and was washed into the ocean by a large wave and nearly drowned. She survived only because she was scooped out of the sea in the nick of time by a life-saver.

Thereafter Virginia repeatedly fell off a psychological cliff into this traumatic memory system. She found herself perpetually in free fall, with no ground beneath her feet.

This trauma was made worse when she sought comfort from her mother, asking what would have happened if she had drowned. Her mother dismissively evaded the question. 'Don't be silly, you haven't died, you were saved by that nice life-saver'.

Virginia's mother failed to take in the import of her abject, utter terror. Such dismissive failure of imagination intensified the fundamental betrayal of trust in her capacity to care for Virginia and keep her safe in the first place. Virginia felt she was forever drowning. It took years of therapeutic containment before she developed trust that the relational threads we wove together could stitch a fabric of continuity and going on being (Winnicott, 1956, p. 303) across the vast oceans of time. Virginia began to feel real because she was held in my gaze, a gaze of reverie, in which her deepest states of being were being attuned with and amplified.

One day Virginia reflected that 'I don't feel quite so terrified of death anymore. I think it is life I am frightened of'.

## Contemplation, reverie, daydreaming

Reverie in both the maternal or analytic context is very different from being lost in one's own personal daydreaming. If a baby feels that mother is lost in her own private daydream that does not include him, the baby may feel shut out. The mother or the analyst may have a highly refined capacity for reverie. Such reverie, be it spiritual, intellectual, creative, poetic or musical, is related to the capacity for maternal or analytic contemplation. However, the significant element of both maternal and analytic reverie is taking in the child's or patient's emotional, psychological and physical reality without being dismissive or possessive. Such contemplation is highly dynamic as well as relational, involving processes of communication on multiple levels between two people who are in a state of being together.

## Toleration of frustration

Bion links alpha function, reverie, the ability to tolerate frustration and the capacity to suffer mental pain as all facilitating psychological growth whereas intolerance and evasion of suffering pain impedes growth. The crucial word here is 'suffer', since Bion observed that there is a difference between 'feeling' and 'suffering' pain:

> People exist who are so intolerant of pain or frustration (or in whom pain or frustration is so intolerable) that they feel the pain but will not suffer it and so cannot be said to discover it. . . . The patient who will not suffer pain fails to 'suffer' pleasure.
>
> (1970, p. 9)

When one cannot 'suffer' pain, it also denudes the personality of the capacity to 'suffer' a range of other emotional engagements with oneself and with others, such as compassion for another's suffering, or even love for another and emotions such as joy. There is a need to tolerate frustration without seeking to either evade it or modify it.

## Bion's theory of thinking

Maternal reverie is intrinsically linked to Bion's theory of thinking and his reformulation of Klein's concept of projective identification as a normal rather than pathological form of communication. Through a dynamic intersubjective process, mother, in her state of reverie, takes into her heart and bears the baby's primitive fears and other unconscious communications and transforms them. The baby then gradually learns how to bear uncertainty, pain and confusion, to host preconceptions, realisations, thoughts and finally concepts.

Bion argues that 'thinking has to be called into existence to cope with thoughts'. Thinking is 'dependent on the successful outcome of two main mental developments', one being thought and the other being thinking (1967, p. 111). Bion then puts forwards a developmental classification of 'thoughts' as follows: 'preconceptions, conceptions or thought, and finally concepts' (1967, p. 111).

The term 'concept' has a specific meaning for Bion, not to be confused with the negative connotation that conceptual thinking has in Buddhist and apophatic contexts. In Buddhist and apophatic forms of contemplation what is problematic is being carried away by one's thoughts, the preponderance of chaotic, disordered thinking activity as well as clinging to stale, out-dated or fixed rather than dynamic and emergent discoveries. Intellectual concepts, even 'spiritual ones' such as 'enlightenment' or the 'nature of mind' tend to be substituted for direct unmediated experience. What Bion is describing as a concept is a developmental achievement. The 'conception is initiated by the conjunction of a pre-conception with a realization' (1967, p. 111). An example he gives is of a baby who has an innate preconception of a breast. When the preconception of a breast 'mates with awareness of the realization' of a breast, this gives rise to the development of a conception (Bion, 1967, p. 111).

Thinking develops out of absence and 'no-thing'. 'Thought' occurs when there is 'the mating of a preconception with a frustration'. A baby, expecting a breast, when there is no breast available, feels frustrated. The conjunction of the expectation with its absence is experienced as a 'no-breast, or "absent" breast inside' (Bion, 1967, p. 111). If the baby's 'capacity for toleration of frustration is sufficient the "no-breast" inside becomes a thought and an apparatus for "thinking" it develops' (Bion, 1967, p. 112). Thinking enables the baby to cope with absence, gaps, spaces between, emptiness. 'Empty thoughts', when they mate with realisation, give rise to conception. When the baby has sufficient realisation of a positive union of the expectation and the experience, the baby can tolerate the frustration attendant upon the negative realisation of absence. A thought replaces the absence.

In general, an 'inability to tolerate frustration can obstruct the development of thoughts and a capacity to think'. Conversely 'a capacity to think' diminishes 'the sense of frustration intrinsic to appreciation of the gap between a wish and its fulfilment' (Bion, 1967, p. 113).

The experience of the analyst's capacity for reverie not only engenders a growth in a capacity for reverie in the patient as well, but also engenders an increase in the capacity to tolerate frustration of encountering 'no-thing-ness'. Reverie is linked to an apophatic capacity for unknowing, a realm of possibility and openness, yet also a realm open to pathos. This in turn is linked to the capacity to truly 'suffer' painful emotions such as sadness and grief. Although a 'decrease in pain itself' may well be hoped for, the 'analytic experience' should lead to an increase in the capacity for suffering (Bion, 1963, p. 62).

Central to Bion's epistemology is the idea that thoughts exist without a thinker but require a receptive mind for the thought to be incarnated and so instantiated. The mind must act as a container, and this requires the ability to bear emptiness, no-thing-ness, absence and unknowing, which creates a space for the thought to be received, contained and thereby conceived and realised. A mind that is capable of tolerating the emptiness of unknowing creates a space for the hosting of thoughts. A word, symbol or statement can function as a container to convey a meaning: conversely a meaning can convey a word. The growing ability to enable two thoughts to come together with a creative outcome (such as a realisation) is reinforced by emotional environments in which two minds are receptive to each other, who can think (contain) together.

The mystic is one who is able to host thoughts which were once without a thinker. He or she

> becomes aware of these thoughts usually through the medium of what is ordinarily known to him as religious awe, and is variously expressed as incarnation, evolution of Godhead, platonic forms, Krishna, mystic experience, inspiration and the like. Thus the source of emission of the received or evolved thoughts is felt as external, God-given, derived from a particular person or occasion, phrase, book, painting, awareness of a constant conjunction. The fate of the thought and the thinker is to follow one of the paths I have indicated as peculiar to ♂♀, or some variation. In some circumstances the impact is incandescent, growth-producing, and then the individual thinker becomes an emitter.
>
> (Bion, 1992, p. 305)

## Ogden on reverie

Extending Bion's understanding of reverie, Ogden locates reverie as a shared state of mind between analyst and patient. Just as both Freud and Jung observed that in analysis there is unconscious to unconscious communication, analytic reverie is 'an *experience of what is* at an unconscious level in the analytic relationship – the O of the unconscious of the analyst and analysand living in the experience of the unconscious analytic third' (Ogden, 2012, p. 115, emphasis in the original). The implication here is that reverie is the way to incarnate absolute truth, O.

Ogden also includes in what is meant by reverie 'the most mundane, quotidian, unobtrusive thoughts, feelings, fantasies, ruminations, daydreams, bodily sensations, and so on that usually feel utterly disconnected from what the patient is saying and doing at the moment' (Ogden, 2001, p. 21).

For Ogden, reverie is unmediated, not involving self-reflection or self-reflexivity. It is similar to bare attention and pure awareness described in meditation texts. Both analyst and patient, like meditators, develop methods for 'catching the drift' (Freud, 1923, p. 239) through analytic reverie.

## Clinical vignette

'Greg' is a priest working as a chaplain in a nursing home. He is doubting his vocation and fears that he lacks empathy. Greg's parents worked hard all day and spent the evenings aimlessly watching television. He longed to discuss the meaning of life and spiritual matters with his parents but they were not interested. As a teenager he found his way to the church, eventually training to be a priest. However he now found the diocese he was in rigid and fundamentalist. He didn't feel any more at home there than he had in his family.

At the nursing home he finds difficulty dealing with elderly residents facing their mortality. He does not want to offer empty platitudes and many at the home are not religious. Yet situations keep cropping up where he feels he is challenged to be sim-ply be more present to a resident, not necessarily having a solution or pat answer.

Somehow he gradually finds, in an indefinable way, that therapy seems to be increasing his capacity to suffer the anxiety of not having any ready-made answers. He tells me how he was asked to attend an old woman who was dying and at first he didn't know what to do or say and just wanted to run away. What could he say that would in any way be enough to help her face death? But he felt a sense of my presence and how I seemed to be able to sit with him. So too he found that he was able to just sit with the dying woman, simply being present, calm and compassion-ate. In the silence, he entered a state of contemplation, just watching the rise and fall of her chest. He noticed that his breathing and hers had become synchronised, as if he was becoming one continuum with her, breathing with her, being with her.

After a while she gestured with her hand and he sensed that she wanted him to hold it but wasn't quite sure. She gestured again, so he tentatively took her hand. She grasped it. He felt a bit uncomfortable with the raw intimacy of this but reflected that this was what it's all about after all. He didn't have to 'fix' things, which was impossible, as she was clearly on death's doorstep, but being with her, holding her hand, letting her look at him without looking away was all he could do. She cried a little, then eventually squeezed his hand and murmured 'God bless'. As he left the nurse said, 'That's the first time she has spoken in a week'. The next day he was told that she had passed away during the night.

I had the sense that Greg had always been a reflective person with a natural bent for contemplation, but this had been disapproved of in his family and now his church.

The therapy as container helped Greg to feel he could sit with difficult emo-tional situations, uncertainty and not knowing. Greg also found his fundamental-ist church narrow-minded and suspicious of any differing interpretations. Their reading of the Bible had been narrowed into a formula, which disregarded and refused to entertain anything too nebulous or uncertain. His search to find his own answers was seen as mere disobedience. There were implicit accusations that he was not really a proper Christian. In his 'heart of hearts' Greg felt that his propen-sity to seek out a subtler meaning behind dogma, a longing to be in the presence of an unknowable Godhead, was his given nature. We discussed how the local church community gave no sense of resonance with his quest for spiritual experi-ence in his own unique way.

The 'Establishment' (Bion, 1970) as a container was too narrow for Greg's more contemplative experiences. Here, what was to be contained could not fit into such a restrictive doctrinal container, leading Greg to feel profoundly alienated.

## Marion Milner on butterflies and the wide focus of attention

Milner describes drifting and emerging, blindness and illumination. An experi-ence of illumination came about through a process of self-emptying, in which she said to herself, 'I have nothing, I know nothing, I want nothing'. Such an abandonment of desire led to the experience of feeling as if the landscape 'shone with a gleam' as if 'from the first day of creation'. Staring at a faded cyclamen, the words 'I want nothing' came to mind and instantly 'I was so flooded with the crimson of the petals that I thought I had never before known what colour was' (Milner, 1934/2011, p. 79).

> I sat motionless, draining sensation to its depths, wave after wave of delight flowing through every cell in my body. My attention flickered from one delight to the next like a butterfly, effortless, following its pleasure; some-times it rested on a thought, a verbal comment, but these no longer made a chattering barrier between me and what I saw, they were woven into the texture of my seeing. I no longer strove to be doing something, I was deeply content with what was. At other times my senses had often been in conflict, so that I could either look or listen but not both at once. Now hearing and sight and sense of space were all fused into one whole.
>
> (Milner, 1934/2011, p. 55)

Marion Milner observed that there were 'two ways of looking' at the world. One was 'attention with a wide focus', the other 'attention with a narrow focus'. When 'the gesture of wide attention' fails, ideas fall outside the 'narrow beam of atten-tion' (1934/2011, p. xxxv). Milner found that these two different ways of perceiv-ing led to entirely different experiences. A 'wide focus' meant 'knowing with the whole of my body' whereas narrow focus led to 'seeing life as if from blinkers' (1934/2011, p. xxxv). Narrow focus means focusing only on what is of personal concern, blocking out the rest and ignoring it. She also found that 'only a tiny act of will' enabled her to 'pass from one to the other, yet this act seemed sufficient to change the face of the world, to make boredom and weariness blossom into immeasurable contentment' (1934/2011, p. 78).

Marion Milner's writings on attention with a wide focus and a narrow focus parallel the Buddhist practices of spaciously abiding in the present on one hand and single-pointed concentration on the other hand. Milner's description of attention with a wide focus reminds me of Dzogchen practices of contempla-tion without fixation, simply letting the mind rest in natural great peace. As it is experienced by a contemplative, the world is experienced as fresh, new, vibrant, alive.

> Those flickering leaf-shadows playing over the heap of cut grass. It is fresh scythed. . . . Down into the shadows of the gully, across it through glisten-ing space, space that hangs suspended filling the gully, so that little sounds wander there, lose themselves and are drowned; beyond, there's a splash of sunlight leaping out against the darkness of forest, the gold in it flows richly in my eyes, flows through my brain in still pools of light. . . . The air is full of sounds, sighs which fade back into the overhanging silence. A bee passes,

a golden ripple in the quiet air. A chicken at my feet fussily crunches a blade of grass.

(1934/2011, p. 55)

Milner simply allows whatever to be as it is, without manipulating or contriving, fully content in the present moment. Such a sense of eternity in the moment was easily disrupted by 'blind thinking', a chattering, distracted mind. She found a natural way to curb this by relaxing her mind and body, opening herself to whatever emerged. Milner's experience is akin to what many poets, visionaries and mystics describe, the ecstatic experience of non-duality:

a fusion into a never-before-known wholeness; not only were the object and oneself no longer felt to be separate, but neither were thought and sensation and feeling and action. All one's visual perceptions of colour, shape, texture, weight, as well as thought and memory, ideas about the object and action towards it, the movement of one's hand together with the feeling which was different from anything else that had ever happened to me.

(1957, p. 142)

Milner views William Blake as a poet and artist capable of realising that 'perception of the external world itself is a creative act, an act of the imagination; without the imagination we would not in fact see what is there to be seen' (Milner, 1987a, p. 177).

One could also count Milner as an apophatic, aware of a reality beyond images, thought, a letting go:

But I do know that to find the language, gestural, verbal or pictorial, one has recurrently to let everything go, all thoughts of what one loves, all images, and attend to the nothingness, seemingly nothing there – silence.

(Milner, 1987b/2011, p. 126)

## Contemplation, reverie, wonderment, reflection, to muse, ponder, reflect, listen . . .

Contemplation means to ponder, muse and reflect deeply, but for apophatic mystics, it is not contemplation *of* something in an analytical way. It is more a state of primordial awareness, interior awakening, indwelling, deep immersion, open presence, wonderment and reverie, beyond the ordinary mind. In moments of deep quietude, empty of thoughts, undistracted, we brush against intimations of eternity, reality, the absolute. We call this intimation by many names, but it transcends all activity of naming and formulating. This present moment, now, is inherently sacred. In the light of the preciousness of each moment we can become aware of the inherent holiness of life, even in the midst of the unknowns, insecurities and painful vicissitudes of our given circumstances. It is about reaching to a depth of silence, spaciousness and open emptiness within. Thence we may feel filled with unbidden moments of grace, a sense of the spirit, some nameless sense of absolute presence, utterly real, but utterly indefinable.

# Chapter 5

# Some Buddhist teachings on meditation

## Buddhist practices

Buddhist teachings on meditation[1] and mind training are encyclopaedic. There are graded paths to enlightenment based on a vast range of different cultural and historical traditions. Likened to different medicines to treat different illnesses, there are myriad different practices for specific purposes, conditions, personalities and capacities. Some are focused on calming and pacifying the mind, and others work directly with the creative power of strong emotions. Some are single-pointed, others are more discursive or analytical. Some meditations are formless, and other practices involve elaborate visualisations, mudras (hand gestures) and mantras. Some are practised alone, others collectively. Some are silent and motionless, and others involve chanting, ritual and movement.

One way of classifying different meditation techniques differentiates between what are known as open monitoring, focused attention and self-transcending forms. Open monitoring meditations involve simply observing on-going experience. Focused attention involves focusing attention on a particular object, noticing when the mind wanders and bringing attention back to the object of meditation. Self-transcending meditations involve silent recitation of a mantra. These three basic styles are, as we shall see, often combined.

It is beyond the scope of this book to present even a basic overview of the wealth and detail of Buddhist teachings. My purpose will be to give a short description of meditation and contemplation, focusing on Dzogchen. It is important to remind the reader that for certain practices, transmission from a realised master is seen as essential and that it is not sufficient to read about these practices in a book.

A regular practice of meditation is known to have many benefits to mental health, for therapist and patient alike, enhancing tranquillity, alleviating anxiety and depression, overcoming anger and aggression, and gaining a sense of meaning, well-being and equanimity. Certain mediation practices evoke the parasympathetic nervous system, leading to relaxation and low-arousal states (Amihai and Kozhevnikov, 2014, 2015). They lower both diastolic and systolic blood pressure, whilst at the same time increasing alertness and wakefulness. Loving kindness meditations lead to a greater capacity for compassion, love and the flourishing of human relationships. Just as meditation can yield benefits for patients and therapists alike, so psychotherapy can be helpful on the spiritual path, in working with developmental deficits and cutting through the thick brambles of destructive emotional complexes that create obstacles to both spiritual practice as well as life in general.

The ultimate goals of meditation practices in the Buddhist context are not only about relaxation and relieving stress, becoming more calm and healing various forms of mental illness, although all these aims are worthwhile aspects of why we might meditate. The ultimate purpose of practice is to awaken to the true nature of reality, to realise the state of enlightenment, for the sake of all beings. Meditative practice has the purpose of transcending the cage of ego, enabling a sense of interconnection with the world of others, a state of pure being, all-compassing self-arising wisdom, radiating immeasurable love and compassion. Yet, at the same time, it is also 'ordinary' in the sense of natural, an experience that is 'immeasurably peaceful . . . of absolute well-being that radiates through all physical, emotional and mental states' (Mingyur and Swanson, 2007, p. 22).

## *Anātman*, non-self, *śūnyatā*, emptiness

Both psychotherapy and Buddhism are acutely aware of the role of mind in every aspect of our existence. In Buddhism mind is said to be the universal ordering principle, creator of happiness and suffering. Mind turned outwardly lost in its projections is *saṃsāra*, mind turned inwardly contemplating its true nature is *nirvāṇa*. When, like mud settling in a pool of water, the mind rests in natural peace, then tranquillity, insight, clarity and lucidity naturally emerge. But generally speaking one's state of mind is lost in a sea of confusion, delusion, illusion, afflictive emotions and habitual destructive tendencies.

According to Buddhism, the root of all mental suffering and psychological disorder is a fundamental ignorance (*avidyā*) of who we are and the nature of reality. Ignorance is identified as the mistaken belief that one's self or ego or I is autonomous, independent, unchanging. This leads to self-grasping (*ahamkāra/ ātmagraha, ngar/bdag 'dzin*). In turn, this leads to concepts of 'my' and 'mine' (*mamakāra/ātmagraha, nga yi/bdag gir 'dzin pa*). Candrakīrti writes:

> First, [beings] grasp at 'I' thinking 'this is me',
> Then, [they] grasp at things thinking 'this is mine'
> And sway without self-control like a paddlewheel.
> (in Phuntsho, 2005, p. 24)

From the original clinging to ego, dualistic divisions abound between what is I and mine, as well as notions of others as being separate. One arranges the world in a self-centred way, in terms of likes and dislikes, attachment and aversion, greed and hatred. Dharmakīrti warns that 'if self exists' then the concept of 'other is conceived. From discriminating the self and other arise attachment and hatred' and then 'all the defects come into being' (in Phuntsho, 2005, p. 24).

The well-worn neuronal habit of viewing our self as independent, unchanging, unitary and the centre of our world, leads to seeing all that is not self as 'other'. We continually reinforce this basic division of self and other and

> lock ourselves into a dualistic mode of perception, drawing conceptual boundaries between our 'self' and the rest of the world. . . . We begin looking at other people, material objects, and so on as potential sources of happiness and unhappiness, and life becomes a struggle to get what we need in order to be happy before someone else grabs it.
>
> (Mingyur and Swanson, 2007, p. 117)

When we relate to the world from the perspective of self-grasping, we feel attachment towards those who meet our needs, aversion towards those who do not, and apathy towards those who neither help or hinder us. The 'three poisons' of ignorance/delusion,[2] aversion and attachment give rise to innumerable other destructive emotions. Actions based on such poisons in turn create negative karma leading us to spiral in the circle of unhappiness (*samsāra*), a world of dissatisfaction (*duhkha*) (Phuntsho, 2005, p. 24).

Self-grasping is related to the erroneous view of substantiality (*satkāyadarśana/ 'jig tshogs la lta ba*). In traditional Mahāyāna teachings, the antidote, or way to uproot self-grasping, is to realise the view of emptiness.

## *Śūnyatā* and *anātman*

*Śūnyatā* is often translated in the general Mahāyāna context as emptiness, referring to the absence of inherent existence, the negation of all possible constructions of 'reality', and a transcendence of both eternalism and nihilism.[3] Yet *śūnyatā* is difficult to translate accurately. The view of *śūnyatā* does not mean voidness in a nihilistic sense, that all is nothing, or non-existent. Mingyur Rinpoche laments the fact that *śūnyatā* is 'one of the most misunderstood words in Buddhist philosophy'. In Tibetan *śūnyatā* is *stong pa nyid, stong pa* meaning 'empty', in the sense of open, unobstructed. He suggests that a better translation might be 'inconceivable' or 'unnameable'. The word *nyid* when added to another word gives the sense of 'possibility', a 'sense that anything can arise, anything can happen' so *śūnyatā* is closer to meaning 'an unlimited potential for anything to appear, change, or disappear' (Mingyur and Swanson, 2007, pp. 59–60).

Likewise, the Buddhist view of non-self (*anātman*) does not mean that we have no self and do not exist. Teachings on *anātman* point to the absence of a permanent, autonomous, persisting, unchanging, independent, eternal ego.

The basis of both *saṃsāra* and *nirvāṇa* is the same ground that is primordially pure and self-perfected. The person who has realised enlightenment realises phenomena are empty of inherent existence. Although they are empty, like water appearing in a mirage, or rainbows in the sky, they appear. Although they appear, they are empty. A metaphor for the difference between *nirvāṇa* and *saṃsāra* is of water and ice:

> just as water, which exists in a naturally free-flowing state, becomes frozen into ice under the influence of a cold wind, so the ground of being exists in a naturally free state, yet the entire spectrum of cyclic existence is established solely due to the underlying conception of an individual self and a self-nature of phenomena.
>
> (Dudjom Lingpa, in Barron, 1994, pp. 157, 159)

The metaphor of frozen water is evocative when patients find themselves caught up in a traumatic memory system which activates primitive defences; they respond to the world of others in a repetitive, solidified and rigid way. When they are freed from such traumatic complexes they respond more freely, with flow, spontaneity and fluidity.

What are other possible implications of teachings on *anātman* for psychotherapy? In psychotherapy the aim is to find the self. In Buddhism the aim is to un-find the self. Yet these aims are not as divergent as it might seem. What is being questioned in Buddhist teachings on *anātman* is not the self *per se*, but an unchanging, eternal, inherently existing, self-centric and independent ego. For the Buddhists, such self-grasping is a root cause of mental illness and hence realisation of non-self is vital to psychological well-being. Buddhist teachings on *anātman* may help overcome ego-centricity and narcissistic defences of the false self in patients who cling to a rigidly reified view of their existence.

The view of *anātman* is one of continuity, change, interdependence, non-duality and impermanence. The self is fluid and multiple. 'We step and do not step into the same rivers; we are and we are not' as Heraclitus (533–473 BC) observed. William James grappled with the problem of how to reconcile identity and continuity of self with the flux of consciousness as process (James, 1890, p. 239). The stream of consciousness although ever changing, continues, like a river. The same metaphor of a stream of consciousness (*citta-santāna*) is used in Buddhism to explain the paradox of how the self seems to be eternal and unchanging when it is dynamic and impermanent. When we look at a particular river it *appears* to be the same water, although the water we look at is never the same water and what we looked at a moment ago has flowed onwards. We create a construct of something that seems to stay the same and bestow upon our vision of the moving droplets of water the name 'river'. This practice of 'name-making', imputing identity, continuity, cohesion, sameness, permanence and autonomy, is, according to Buddhist teaching, the very basis of the unknowing (*avidyā*) which is seen as the root cause of all suffering and delusion. James avoids this philosophical error by emphasising the continuity of the stream of consciousness as a process, not a fixed entity in itself. Self is an awareness of the movements of an inner life. The 'self' carries feelings of basic unity and continuity, and also a recognition of change, contingency, as well as agency, the sense of freedom of choice. The 'self' is not a static structure, but a process.

A particular clinical issue arises when Western meditators suffering a pervasive sense of unreality and emptiness at their core misunderstand Buddhist teachings on *anātman* and *śūnyatā*. Instead, patients suffering disorders of self may initially need to develop a healthy sense of self before deconstructing the self. This is where it is vital for a psychotherapist to have a sound knowledge of the subtleties of Buddhist philosophy concerning *anātman* on one hand, and for Buddhist masters teaching Westerners to be aware of particularly Western forms of mental illness. In traditional Buddhist contexts there was recognition that one should not teach *anātman* or *śūnyatā* to those who are not ready. A practitioner needed certain psychological prerequisites before undergoing practices aimed at deconstructing the self. Such clinical issues will be explored more fully in Chapter 7.

## Ultimate reality and relative reality

> The dharma that is taught by the buddhas,
> Relies completely on two levels of truth:
> The Worldly conventional level of truth,
> And the ultimate level of truth.
> (Nāgārjuna in the Dalai Lama, 2000,
> pp. 30–31)

Reality in Buddhism is seen to have two perspectives, ultimate and relative or conventional. Conventional reality is the 'ordinary cognition of things as inherently existing' whereas 'ultimate reality' 'refers to the . . . absence of inherent existence' or *śūnyatā*. Studstill points out that while the view is apophatic, there are many kataphatic elements, such as describing *śūnyatā* as 'a radiant presence' that is 'the source of . . . primordial energy that brings all possible forms . . . into manifestation' (Lipman, 1984, p. 8). Although things appear they are empty, although they are empty they appear. According to the *Heart Sutra* 'form is emptiness, emptiness is also form'.

## Modern applications of mindfulness

Mindfulness practices are becoming increasingly prevalent in Western contexts, including psychotherapy. Mindfulness-Based Stress Reduction (MBSR) as a therapeutic modality began in 1979 with Jon Kabat-Zinn. MBSR and related secularised techniques such as Mindfulness-Based Cognitive Therapy (MBCT) have benefitted many Westerners suspicious of meditation methods that are associated with a religious belief system. Mindfulness practices are being used to treat a wide array of mental health issues including depression, anxiety, trauma, addictions and eating disorders. They are taught in prisons, schools, hospitals and workplaces. Mindfulness is presented as an empirical, science-based, non-religious technique. There is a need to consider the possible implications of removing explicit reference to the original Buddhist context, and to the religious, spiritual and ethical content of meditation, in order to make meditation palatable to non-religious patients.

Although the benefits of mindfulness practice are well-attested, it is also important to remember that mindfulness practices may be contraindicated for certain mental conditions. For example, there is evidence suggesting that loving kindness practices are more appropriate for some on the autism spectrum than mindfulness practices (Samuel, 2016). Put simply, bare attention may be simply too bare for them to bear. Complex Vajrayāna deity yoga sometimes exacerbates psychotic tendencies. Here it is important to remember the discernment involved in the original context of Buddhist teachings, where different forms of meditation are compared to different types of medicines, the Buddha to a doctor. A given medicine designed to treat a given condition may be harmful and contraindicated for another condition. It is vital for a teacher to have personal knowledge of the student, so that they can advise the right practice for that student's particular psychospiritual predispositions and circumstances.

## Mindfulness and *sati*

Mindfulness involves a combination of awareness, presence and attention in order to attain awakening. Mindfulness is one English translation for a Buddhist term, called *sati* in Pāli, *smṛti* in Sanskrit and *dran pa* in Tibetan. The difficulty of terms such as *sati* is how to represent the nuances of meaning embedded in the original context. *Sati* is the seventh element in the eightfold noble path to Enlightenment, which comprises Right Understanding, Right Thought, Right Speech, Right Action, Right Livelihood, Right Effort, Right *Sati* and Right Concentration.

Mindfulness is but one of fifty-one mental states delineated in Abhidharma literature. It is one of the 'five object-determining mental states' concerning how mind comprehends an object: interest (Skt. *chanda*), appreciation (Skt. *adhimokṣa*), mindfulness (Skt. *smṛti*), concentration (Skt. *samādhi*) and intelligence (Skt. *prajñā*). In the Tibetan context, *dran pa* refers to attentive inspection, recollection and the ability to continually resettle the mind whenever distracted, until such time as the state of non-distraction is achieved.

The choice of the word 'mindfulness' as a translation for *sati* was made in 1881 by the Pāli scholar Rhys Davids (1843–1922) who translated the Pāli *sammā-sati* as 'Right Mindfulness; the active, watchful mind' (1881, p. 145). In the *Satipaṭṭhāna-sutta*, *sati* has the sense of 'recollecting', 'bearing in mind' and 'taking hold of' the virtuous dharmas in order to apprehend the true nature of phenomena (Sharf, 2015, p. 65). Many mental capacities related to awareness and attention work together. *Sati* involves continual awareness of the mind, returning the focus back to the given object whenever the mind wanders, so it involves moment-to-moment awareness of present events, as well as recollection and awareness of what needs to be attended to and discriminating awareness. In the *Madhyamakahṛdaya* this is expressed as follows:

> As the elephant of the mind wanders,
> It should be bound with the rope of mindfulness,
> Tied to the rooted column of a mental image
> And controlled with the hook of wisdom.
>                                              (in Tashi Namgyal, 2006, p. 45)

## Meditation and the state of contemplation in Dzogchen

Let us now turn to Dzogchen, which is covered in more detail in Chapter 6. Dzogchen teachings distinguish between what is meant by meditation and what is meant by contemplation. To be in the state of contemplation is to be beyond mind, thought, concept, image and even beyond states of meditation. It is a formless, supra-conceptual state of contemplation, a state of pure awareness and instant presence. In the state of contemplation:

> one abides in that continually self-liberating non-dual state which is beyond the limits of the conceptual level of mental activity, and yet which neverthe-less encompasses even the workings of what is called 'ordinary' mind, or rational thinking. Although thought can, and does, arise in contemplation, one is not conditioned by it, and it liberates of itself, just left as it is. In con-templation the mind is not engaged in any mental effort, and there is nothing to be done or not done. What is, is just as it is, self-perfected.
>                                              (Namkhai Norbu, 1986, p. 77)

The teaching of Dzogchen concerns the discovery of our real nature, to realise who one truly is. This primordial ground of being is communicated to the disciple by the master, who always remains in this state of realisation, through what is known as 'direct introduction', which is explained in more detail in Chapter 6. Having had a profound experience of this ground, the task then concerns learning how to remain in this primordial state, such remaining being the state of contem-plation. The 'absolute, spontaneous, non-dual awareness of the primordial state experienced in contemplation, is self-perfected and thus beyond all effort. In this state there is nothing to practice, nothing that must be done, and nothing that can-not be done' (Namkhai Norbu, 2000, p. 142).

## From mind to the nature of mind

One of the major elements of Dzogchen is the need to go beyond ordinary mind to the nature of mind. Ordinary mind (*sems*) is rooted in a state of conceptual igno-rance as to its real nature which continually entraps us in dualism. This ignorance (*avidyā*/*ma rig pa*) is based on the dualistic conception of reality, which is egocentric. The illusory appearance aspect of reality is not to say nothing exists, but that the ordinary mind is contaminated by fundamental ignorance due to pervasive and deep seated misperception of reality. Thoughts and emotions are not the nature of mind, but only appearance. The nature of mind is like the sun; the appearance is like the sun's rays.

## Saṃsāra

What is the cause of mental illness? From the Buddhist perspective the root cause of the delusion and confusion that mires us in ceaseless repetitions of destructive tendencies (*saṃsāra*) is an egocentric clinging to a dualistic view of subject and object that then leads to attachment and aversion. Our ordinary mind is 'shaped by unconscious and conscious beliefs that define an essentially conditional/dualistic relationship to life' (Studstill, 2005, p. 161). We tend to be perpetually caught up in internal narratives which take us away from the bare immediacy of undiluted awareness of the present moment, grasping after passing thoughts and emotions. Our ordinary mind (*sems*) 'through its activities' 'creates the world of illusion' and 'has obscured its own real nature (*sems nyid*) from time immemorial' (Karmay, 2007, p. 175).

## Thoughts and thinking in meditation and psychotherapy

Meditation, when first practiced, can seem as if one has pulled the lid off a hornet's nest of swarming thoughts and emotions. You may feel even less calm, as if meditation has created this swarm. However, all that has occurred is that you have become aware of the chaotic disordered state of your mind. If you continue the meditation practice, thoughts will slowly and gradually abate. Like water that is not stirred, the silt will gradually sink to the bottom and the water become clear. Rather than being carried away by your habitual thoughts, feelings and judgements, their power begins to fade, you 'experience their coming and going as nothing more than the natural function of the mind, in the same way that waves naturally ripple across the surface of a lake or ocean' (Mingyur and Swanson, 2007, p. 43).

Many patients complain of being caught continually in spirals of rumination that bring no peace but only lead to sleepless nights, anxiety and agitation. I suggest that they may not be able to avoid entertaining the initial thought that leads to such rumination, but they don't have to give it a cup of tea let alone a three-course meal! If they just notice thoughts without feeding them, they tend to dissipate.

It is sometimes assumed that the aim of meditation is to suppress thinking and feeling, as if thoughts and emotions are somehow bad. But thinking is also a natural activity of mind, as are emotions. The energy of emotions is linked to the energy of our primordial nature and is also a source of creativity and vitality. Meditation is not a blanked-out state of trance or torpor. One can become fixated on the 'thought of desiring thoughtlessness'. As soon as you try to suppress thinking, 'conflicting thoughts multiply' and in a 'mounting frenzy you run aimlessly hither and thither' (Shabkar Lama, in Dowman, 1994, p. 121). Instead, in Dzogchen teachings one simply lets the mind be, attending to the clear presence of its natural condition, 'without getting distracted, forgetting or letting ourselves get wrapped up in our thoughts'. If the mind is distracted, we simply recognise this and the thoughts 'relax into their own condition' (Namkhai Norbu, 2005, p. 26).

There is a way in which even when thoughts arise there is still the presence of awareness. One finds in the midst of the movement of thinking, there is a background clarity of mind, a space of awareness that is pure, unstained by the thoughts that pass through it, a clarity that is never disturbed or interrupted. One rests in this natural state. Meditation is just allowing the mind to be, open and aware of passing thoughts and emotions. So too, the analyst allows whatever to emerge to be, aware of, but not grasping after, the drift of unconscious current.

## Calm and movement

Sometimes it is thought that meditation is solely about being still. But stillness and motion are both normal aspects of life. The emergence of thoughts is the movement element, their disappearance the emptiness element. When a thought arises and one analyses where it came from, or where it goes, one cannot find it. This is part of the teaching that 'not finding is finding indeed'.

In the state of contemplation, 'one is able to integrate either the moment of calm where there is no thought, or those moments where there is the movement of thought, equally, remaining in full presence and awareness. . . . This pure awareness, this ground of awareness' is what is meant in Dzogchen by *rig pa* (Namkhai Norbu, 1986, pp. 77–78).

Viewing the calm state as positive and movement of thoughts as negative exacerbates the dualism of acceptance and rejection. One simply continues in the state of contemplation, integrating the state of instant presence into any situation we find ourselves in. Whether one is in a calm state or finds oneself carried along by one's train of thought, one retains presence. We do not try to stop movement but see it as like wind stirring over the waters of contemplation. Calm and movement are two aspects of the same reality:

> The truth here is that the calm state is the essence of the mind and movement is its energy: they are two inseparable aspects of the same reality, like the sea and its waves or the sun and its rays.
>
> (Namkhai Norbu, 2005, p. 27)

## Meditation in Dzogchen

There is a treasury of practices of meditation in Dzogchen. There are gradual and non-gradual approaches to be applied as needed to enable one to enter the state of contemplation, and to integrate the state of contemplation into all elements of one's life, to stabilise the view and so gain total realisation. Those able to naturally enter the state of contemplation, abiding continuously in pure awareness, do not need a method of meditation. Practices of 'letting be' help turn the mind from habitual egocentric tendencies. What is then necessary is total, free, all-encompassing 'immersion in the bare immediacy of one's own deepest levels of awareness' (Germano, 1994, p. 254), transcending dualistic divisions between meditation and non-meditation, path and goal, stillness and movement, silence and noise, quiescence and activity (Studstill, 2005, p. 167).

However, it is not as easy as one might think to practice 'letting be' or 'doing nothing'. Hence one might begin with more structured meditations aimed at first stabilising and calming the mind. Such 'preliminary practices' serve to 'refine and pacify consciousness to the point that "letting be" functions as a means of settling even deeper into the here and now, rather than as a sanction for ordinary, egocentric mentation' (Studstill, 2005, pp. 162–163).

## Calm abiding

The purpose of calm abiding practices (*samatha/zhi gnas*) is to find a calm state unperturbed by the movement of the mind. The practice of calm abiding involves maintaining continuous presence, undistracted, beyond judgement and concept, free of thoughts of the past or anticipations of the future. One lightly focuses on an object, which could be one's breathing, emotions, thoughts, sensations or body. Or one might chose an image, prayer word, chant or combinations of these. For example, in the unifying practice, one focuses on one's breathing, chants a mantra and focuses on a visualisation of a deity. When distracted, one gently brings one's attention back to the object. As thoughts arise, they are recognised and they relax back into their own condition. One also recognises that movements, such as the flow of thoughts and emotions and physical sensations, are all also natural aspects of clarity and calm, like birds flying through a vast expanse of space. Gradually one notices the space that exists between the disappearance of one thought and the arising of another. Little by little we integrate such pure presence with all we do: sitting, walking, eating, reading, talking and listening. At first it is like bringing presence to bear on a murky pool of water. If the water is not stirred, it gradually settles and becomes clear. An ancient Tibetan saying is 'Water if you don't stir it, will become clear, mind left unaltered, will find its own natural peace'.

### Śamatha without support

Gradually practitioners find themselves effortlessly resting the mind in the present moment, without distraction, and at this stage they can drop the support and naturally enter *śamatha* without support, where one abides in an objectless state of pure awareness. There is still a sense of presence, a centre of awareness. Whatever thoughts, emotions and images appear in the mind, they just come and go.

This 'presence of mind' that is able to be undistracted can be integrated into daily life, whether sitting, walking, running or singing. You are able to bring conscious awareness to all you do with composure and ease.

## The unaltered state

When, in meditation practice, we examine where thoughts arise, abide and dissolve, we find nowhere and this 'not-finding is finding indeed'. What is found is the clarity of pure awareness, spacious and vast, the nature of mind. We gradually attain an unaltered state of mind:

> Do not alter, do not alter,
> Do not alter this mind of ours.
> Do not grasp, do not grasp,
> Do not grasp at this mind of ours.
> Alter and alter, and you will stir up the cloudy depths of the mind.
> And a mind that is altered obscures its own true nature.
> (Longchenpa, in Sogyal Rinpoche, 2002, p. 15)

When we do not alter our mind, we can rediscover the natural great peace and pure awareness there all the time underneath the clouds of turbulent emotions. Such practices have counterparts in Christian contemplation. A Judeo-Christian metaphor is weather patterns on Mount Zion:

> The marvellous world of thoughts, sensation, emotions, and inspiration, the spectacular world of creation around us, are all patterns of stunning weather on the holy mountain of God. But we are not the weather. We are the mountain. Weather is happening – delightful sunshine, dull sky, or destructive storm – this is undeniable. . . . When the mind is brought to stillness we see that we are the mountain and not the changing patterns of weather appearing on the mountain. We are the awareness in which thoughts and feelings (what we take to be ourselves) appear like so much weather on Mount Zion.
>   For a lifetime we have taken this weather – our thoughts and feelings – to be ourselves, taken ourselves to be this video to which the attention is riveted. Stillness reveals that we are the silent, vast awareness in which the video is playing. To glimpse this fundamental truth is to be liberated, to be set free from the fowler's snare (Ps 123:7). 'Whoever trusts in the Lord is like Mount Zion: Unshakeable, it stands forever (Ps 125:1)'.
> (Laird, 2006, pp. 16–17)

What seemed like a solid brick wall of thoughts melts and becomes a window, or what seemed like an impenetrable cover of clouds is blown away by the winds of awareness revealing the pure primordial sky of infinity, which is always there behind the clouds. Our awareness becomes spacious, free, receptive, open, a luminous presence in which all sense of alienation dissolves, all sense of a separate ego disappears into the vastness of space, without centre or border.

## Insight (*Vipaśyanā/lhagt'ong*)

Insight into ultimate reality (*Vipaśyanā/lhagt'ong*) is required as well as calm abiding. A metaphor used to describe the need for both calm abiding and insight is that of looking at a painting by candlelight. To see the painting clearly the candle must be both still (calm abiding) and bright (insight). We need unwavering light of calm abiding and the light of wisdom. *Vipaśyanā* is a form of inner awakening, at the level of integration of the state of presence and movement.

Meditation in Dzogchen means resting in the nature of mind, without concept, hope or fear, yet imbued with a sense of being at ease, of well-being, of quiet confidence. Cloud-like thoughts and emotions dissolve of their own accord into the vast expanse, revealing the sky-like radiance and clarity of one's true being. Wisdom, compassion, profound love and concern for the needs of others spontaneously radiate from your innermost nature and shine forth like the sun. There is nothing to do, nothing to achieve, just being who you always are at heart. The more one abides in the nature of mind, the more one's own inner wisdom, immeasurable compassion, infinite love and capacity to serve others shine forth of their own accord.

## Integrating meditative awareness into everyday life

The principles of meditation described above are not just applicable to a time set aside for formal meditation. The purpose of formal sessions is to cultivate a capacity for awareness, alertness, non-distraction and continuous presence in all areas of daily life. A simple example is noticing a thought that one is hungry. One doesn't try to block the thought but just notes it. When it is appropriate to make, say, a sandwich, one maintains presence and awareness while making the sandwich. Being present does not require a special practice or body position; it is simply remaining aware and undistracted. Such awareness also gives rise to the presence of mind that enables analytic reverie and free-floating attention.

The principle of being able to integrate or mix (*bsre ba*) is an important element of Dzogchen teachings, referring to the capacity to integrate the state of contemplation, instant presence and primordial awareness in all aspects of body, speech and mind. This relates to awareness of non-duality; there is no duality between calm and movement, between inner and outer, self and other.

This is similar to the Hesychast practice of continuous prayer, when the state of contemplation is formless. Formless contemplation involves an alert, vibrant, open-eyed awareness that is not closed off from one's surroundings and is then integrated into all elements of one's life. Having discovered the calm state (*gnas pa*), one integrates this into ordinary life outside meditation sessions.

## Bodhicitta and compassion

What of the role of love, compassion, kindness, benevolence and equanimity in psychotherapy? Ideally our work is inspired by compassion for the suffering of others, a desire to heal their sorrow, grief and mental affliction, to provide conditions conducive to realising their true nature. Such sentiments in Buddhism are gathered up in the word 'bodhicitta', the 'awakening mind' or 'mind of enlightenment'. *Bodhi* means to awaken, *citta* means mind. Bodhicitta involves both the wish and the active intention to do all one can to remove the suffering of all beings, to attain enlightenment for the sake of all beings, to bring them into the state of enlightenment. In the words of Buddha Maitreya in the *Abhisamayālaṃkāra*, 'Arousing bodhicitta is: for the sake of others, longing to attain complete enlightenment'. This is also predicated on the understanding that all beings have Buddha nature, enlightenment being the realisation of this ultimate nature. In psychotherapy, we might say that all beings have the potential to realise their true self, to heal past trauma, to work through their ingrained destructive tendencies, neuroses and complexes, to come into being the person they are meant to be and to live a full and fulfilling life.

There is relative and absolute bodhicitta. Relative bodhicitta refers to compassion, altruism, benevolence, kindness, equanimity and love in general. Absolute bodhicitta is based on the realisation of *śūnyatā*, an awareness of non-duality, interdependence and ultimate experience of selflessness and egolessness, of primordial wisdom, out of which realisation love and compassion spontaneously flow towards all beings, like the rays of the sun.

Bodhicitta is related to what are known as the four immeasurables: equanimity, love, compassion and joy. Equanimity or impartiality towards patients involves being even-minded. Love is the desire that all beings have happiness, compassion is the desire that they are free from suffering and joy the wish that they are never separated from true happiness. Equanimity enables the qualities of love, compassion and joy to be impartially directed to all beings.

Buddhism has a vast treasury of meditation practices aimed at cultivating bodhicitta. A vital practice for enhancing the therapist's capacity for compassion and bearing the patient's pain is known as *gtong len* which literally means giving and taking. In this practice we focus on the breath. As we breathe in we imagine we are taking inside ourselves all the pain, anguish and suffering of others. As we breathe out we are surrounding them with joy, happiness and healing. It can be applied globally for all, or for specific patients.

What of the patient who cannot feel compassion? 'Paul' came to see me due to his lack of empathy which was threatening his marriage. His mother, who had grown up in an orphanage, made great sacrifices working to provide for his physical needs, but was unable to meet his emotional needs. Through experiencing the analyst's care and compassion, Paul gradually felt compassion for himself, followed eventually by compassion for others, including being able to forgive his mother who had begged for his forgiveness. Finally he felt empathy for his wife. He also found simple loving kindness meditations enhanced his growing sense of compassion and love.

In general meditation practices have a three-fold structure. One begins with cultivating bodhicitta, examining one's motivation for doing the practice and if finding it is solely selfish, transforming it into an altruistic intention to do the practice for the benefit of all others (including oneself). At the end of the practice one dedicates the merit of the meditation practice to attaining enlightenment for the sake of all beings. There are many beautiful prayers that are said at the beginning and end of meditation practices. So too, a therapist might say a short silent prayer before the patient arrives, and dedicate the session with a short silent prayer when they leave.

One such prayer is as follows:

> May all beings have happiness and the cause of happiness.
> May they be free of suffering and the cause of suffering.
> May they never be separated from the great happiness which is without suffering.
> May they abide in the boundless equanimity, free from attachment and aversion.

I finish this chapter with the prayer that I silently say to begin a session. It is from Śāntideva's *Bodhicaryāvatāra*:[4]

> May I become a boat, a raft, a bridge
> For all who wish to cross the water
> May I be an isle for those desiring landfall
> And a lamp for those who wish for light
> May I be a bed for those who need to rest
> And a servant for all those who live in need.
> Like the earth and all other great elements
> And like space itself, May I remain forever
> To support the lives of boundless beings
> Providing all that they may need
> As long as space exists
> And beings endure
> So too may I remain, to dispel the suffering of the world.

## Notes

1  The Buddhist term for meditation (*Bhāvanā/sgom*) refers to mind training/cultivation in general.

2  It is important to note that ignorance (*moha*/*gti mug*), which is one of the three poisons, is not the same as fundamental ignorance (*avidyā*/*ma rig pa*, literally, not seeing, misperceiving). Some people distinguish them by using delusion to translate *moha*/*gti mug*.

3  In Buddhist thought two extremes are those of eternalism (Skt. *nitya dṛṣṭi*) and nihilism (*uccheda dṛṣṭi*). Eternalism refers to the belief in oneself being concrete, independent, eternal and singular. Nihilism is the belief that nothing exists; there is no ultimate reality – the denial of the law of cause and effect.

4  This translation can be found at www.lotsawahouse.org/indian-masters/shantideva/bodhicharyavatara-3.

# Chapter 6

# Primordial purity and spontaneous presence

## The Great Perfection of Dzogchen

### A diamond covered in grime

'Penny' sadly observes:

> It doesn't matter how many university degrees I've completed, how well I dress, however much wealth I accrue, underneath I still feel stupid and shabby. When I was a kid we were very poor. My dad was an alcoholic. There was a lot of domestic violence and there was not enough food to go around. We wore hand-me-downs, including hand-made woollen underpants. School kids would lift up my skirt and taunt me, saying 'can't your mother even afford proper undies?'

Penny is acting in a new job as a social activist. She wants to make a difference so that children who are poor do not feel 'shabby' like she did. But she fears her new boss will see her shabbiness underneath her attempts at power-dressing. Just as she was expelled from high school, she will be expelled from this job. Penny tells me a dream she had the night before starting analysis with me:

> I dreamed I was an old homeless bag-lady. I lived in an old abandoned area by a dirty, polluted canal. I made a lean-to shelter from old bits of cardboard and scraps of wood that I gathered. I stacked all these bits and pieces against a huge, black boulder, covered in dirt and moss. For food I ate what I could scavenge out of rubbish bins.
>
> The boulder provided a bit of shelter and a place to lean my back against. I lived out my life just getting by on scraps of food. But one day I noticed something shining through the moss covering the boulder and I dug away at it. The boulder was in fact a huge diamond covered in dirt and moss. It had been there all along, only I had never noticed it before.

I said, 'So all along, while you thought you were so poor, you were learning against a diamond. Underneath you are not shabby but like a diamond covered in grime. We just need to clear away the grime'.

The dream reminded me of a story which appears in many forms in the Tibetan tradition. Another version found in the *Mahāyānottaratantraśāstra* is as follows:

> If an inexhaustible treasure were buried in the ground beneath a poor man's house, the man would not know of it, and the treasure would not speak and tell him, 'I am here!'.
>
> (in Mingyur and Swanson, 2007, p. 52)

This raises important questions for both the spiritual and psychotherapeutic journey. Is it about *creating* a sense of the true self or is it about *discovering* our true nature? Is individuation something we develop, or does psychotherapy help uncover what has been there in potential from the very beginning but concealed by psychological complexes, entrenched ways of viewing ourselves and the world of others? For John of the Cross, God is always present within us, but we do not realise this. The mystical way is not something we achieve by our own efforts, rather it is effected by God's grace and by emptying of all that is false. In the Buddhist context of Dzogchen, our fundamental condition (*dngos po'i gnas lugs*) is not created but uncovered, recognised and realised. The fundamental nature of the mind is the *tathāgatagarbha*, 'or essence of enlightenment in all beings' which is 'present from the beginning' (Guarisco, 2015, p. 36). Applied to psychotherapy the implication is that therapy is about cutting through the dense thickets of complexes, defence systems and distorted views so that one's true nature can manifest and shine forth.

Dzogchen relates to the direct revelation of ultimate reality, the discovery of the primordial ground of all beings, that, underneath all that conceals and constricts it, is like the adamantine purity of a diamond. Such a ground is ever present, like the sun behind the clouds. The path to realisation is based on pure awareness unconditioned by thought, emotionality or conceptualisation. From the perspective of Dzogchen:

> Everything is naturally perfect just as it is, completely pure and undefiled. . . . With no effort or practice whatsoever, enlightenment and Buddhahood are already fully developed and perfected.
>
> (Trungpa and Shikpo, 1968/2003, p. 462)

## Why Dzogchen?

There has been much written about mindfulness and psychotherapy. Zen Buddhism has been explored in regard to psychotherapy. Dzogchen is less well known in psychoanalytic literature. Dzogchen is, however, a tradition that is becoming increasingly well known in the West. As a living tradition of direct experiential practice with authentic accomplished masters teaching Dzogchen, it has much to offer in the area of psychotherapy and spirituality. The Dzogchen approach may be highly applicable to psychotherapy in a secular modern world, a world where so many patients are seeking a spiritual dimension that is not sectarian, dogmatic, or bound up in cultural mores. It allows for a very ordinary, simple way of life not hide-bound or caught up in complicated rules, regulations and outward show. It may even appeal to those who are drawn to the apophatic but who are agnostic. This is not to proselytise, since psychotherapists take care to not advocate a particular approach but rather encourage the patient's own discovery of what, if any, spiritual tradition they are drawn to. Similarly Dzogchen emphasises personal freedom, individual responsibility and self-observation.

Just as there is a distinction in Christianity between *theologia mystica* and *theologia speculativa*, Dzogchen favours direct experience over intellectual knowledge. The goal of Dzogchen is the direct discovery of one's true nature. In the following I will privilege the authority of Dzogchen masters over academic scholarship. However, I have also tried to reconcile the two approaches.

## Definitions

Dzogchen, or Total Perfection, in itself refers to our primordial nature. Dzogchen teachings derive from an ancient spiritual tradition. Although associated with Tibetan Buddhism, according to teachers such as Chögyal Namkhai Norbu, Dzogchen is, in essence and origin, timeless and beyond school, sect or institutionalised religion. 'The Dzogchen teachings are neither a philosophy, nor a religious doctrine, nor a cultural tradition. Understanding the message of the teachings means discovering one's own true condition, stripped of all the self-deceptions and falsifications which the mind creates' (Namkai Norbu, 1996, p. 23).

The word *Dzogchen* is an abbreviation of *Dzogpachenpo* (*rdzogs pa chen po*, in Sanskrit *Mahāsaṅdhi* or *Atiyoga*) often translated as the 'Great' or 'Total' 'Perfection', or 'Great Completeness'. Dzogchen is called the 'Great Perfection' because:

> it is complete and perfect (*rdzogs-pa*) in itself, with nothing lacking, and because there exists nothing higher or greater (*chen-po*) than it.
> (Reynolds, 1996, p. 21)

Dzogchen teachings are regarded as 'the ultimate expression' in so far as is possible 'of the true nature of Reality, the individual, and the state of awakening' (Studstill, 2005, pp. 127–128). It is 'high' in so far as it is direct, unmediated, uncontrived and non-conceptual. It is also described as essentialising all paths towards realisation. It is seen as all-inclusive, a means of inspiring 'awareness (*rig pa*) of the true nature of reality in its ultimate purity and perfection' (Samuel, 1993, pp. 541, 550). Studstill brings together various definitions of Dzogchen as follows:

> 'Dzogchen' may be used as a term for ultimate Reality (identical with the true nature of the individual) and the ultimate experiential state that realizes Reality. As a term for the Real, Dzogchen 'connotes a natural and effortless

unity underlying and pervading all things,' often described as an empty, yet luminous Ground (*gzhi*) out of which all phenomenal appearances arise. . . . As a label for the realization of the Real, Dzogchen indicates 'a higher-order level of thought, . . . the peak of a person's endeavour to fathom the depth of his being (and) gain an unobstructed view'.

(2005, pp. 128–129)

Dzogchen teachings are transmitted to a student from a fully realised master. Esotericism is 'self-secret', that is, unless one already has received direct transmission as well as cultivating the capacity for participation, diligence, awareness, dedication and spiritual wisdom (*prajñā*), these teachings will naturally remain secret. The following account is merely a theoretical one based on material publicly available in order to preserve the esoteric ethic.[1]

## The origins of Dzogchen

Just as mystery surrounds Dionysius, so too mystery surrounds the founder of Dzogchen in this era, a quasi-mythical figure known as Garab Dorje. Tradition has it that he was born approximately 360 years after the *parinirvāṇa* of Buddha, but scholars speculate that he probably lived in the sixth century CE. He is described as having been born in a kingdom called Oḍḍiyāna, which some scholars identify with the Swat Valley in Pakistan. Garab Dorje is said to have transmitted Dzogchen teachings to his students through an unbroken lineage: to Mañjuśrīmitra, Śrī Siṃha, Jñānasūtra; Vimilamitra, Vairocana and Padmasambhava, then continuing in a similar way to the present. The teachings were passed down from master to disciple through a three-fold method of transmission: direct transmission, symbolic transmission and oral transmission. According to traditional accounts, Mañjuśrīmitra, a scholar at Nālandā, went to Oḍḍiyāna in order to refute Garab Dorje's teachings, because they were reported to transcend the principle of cause and effect. On meeting Garab Dorje and receiving his teachings, Mañjuśrīmitra was filled with remorse at his mistaken views and became a disciple. Garab Dorje transmitted the entire teachings of Dzogchen and summarised the essence for him:

> The nature of mind is the original Buddha,
> Without birth and cessation, like the sky!
> Then you understand that all phenomena are equality beyond birth and cessation,
> Meditating means letting this condition be as it is, without seeking!
> (in Namkhai Norbu and Clemente, 1999, p. 33)

## Three statements of Garab Dorje

Dzogchen teachings are based on what is known as the 'Three Statements of Garab Dorje' or 'Hitting the Essence in Three Words' (*tshig gsum gnad brdegs*). Dzogchen histories relate how when Garab Dorje was leaving this world, 'his body dissolved into space in the midst of a great cloud of rainbow light'. His disciple Mañjuśrīmitra cried in distress:

> Alas, alas! O vast expanse! If the light that is our teacher is extinguished, who will there be to dispel the darkness of the world!
>
> (in the Dalai Lama, 2000, p. 42)

Whereupon Garab Dorje's right arm 'appeared holding a golden casket, the size of a thumbnail, which circled around Mañjuśrīmitra three times, and descended into the palm of his hand' (Dalai Lama, 2000, p. 42). Mañjuśrīmitra immediately attained the same wisdom mind as Garab Dorje. This casket contained the Three Statements.

The Three Statements of Garab Dorje are aimed at bringing one beyond the conceptual and dualistic mind to the nature of mind, to realise and abide within one's primordial state. The Three Statements can be translated as:

1 Direct introduction (*ngo rang thog tu sprad*)
2 Decide directly upon the one thing (*thag gcig thog tu bcad*)
3 Confidence directly in the liberation of rising thoughts (*gdeng grol thog tu bca'*)

The first of the Three Statements of Garab Dorje is also translated as 'directly discover your own state' (Namkhai Norbu and Clemente, 1999, p. 57). It relates to how the student is directly introduced to the nature of mind through mind-to-mind transmission. The teacher, who has fully realised the primordial state of perfect enlightenment reveals the original, uncompounded and unborn condition of all beings. This condition is one of total completeness, plenitude, purity, non-duality, clarity, lucidity and perfection beyond all concepts.

The second statement means to decide directly upon the one thing. Namkhai Norbu translates it as 'not remaining in doubt' in the sense that when we have direct experience of the state of contemplation, rather than purely intellectual knowledge, we are no longer in any doubt regarding the underlying nature of ultimate reality revealed in direct introduction. An example he gives is that of the experience of sweetness. If one has never eaten anything sweet no amount of intellectual explanation makes up for the actual experience. Once one has tasted a piece of chocolate, one knows for certain what sweetness is. Entering the state of contemplation, the student no longer remains in any doubt regarding the underlying nature of reality unveiled in direct introduction. One has decisiveness based on direct, first-hand personal experience (Reynolds, 1996, p. 90). We have discovered it for ourselves.

The third statement, also translated as 'achieve confidence in self-liberation' (Namkhai Norbu and Clemente, 1999, p. 57) relates to how the disciple, who has been introduced to *rig pa*, and who has removed all doubts through the practice of meditation, is able to continue with confidence, integrating the state of contemplation into all elements and situations of life, such that ultimately one has total realisation of one's primordial condition and abides in this condition (Namkhai Norbu, 1986, p. 21). The word 'confidence' (*gdengs*) refers to confidence in the self-liberation of discursive thoughts as they arise. Free of subject-object duality, in the state of contemplation 'thoughts are no longer grasped at nor apprehended' as they naturally liberate 'into their own original condition, which is the state of emptiness' (Reynolds, 1996, pp. 106–107).

Direct introduction can be transmitted in three ways: direct, symbolic and oral. The three modes of introduction in turn relate to the Three Series of Dzogchen teachings: the Mind-Series (*sems sde*), the Series of Space (*klong sde*) and the Essential Series (*man ngag sde* or *upadeśa*). These are all direct paths, where the master first transmits direct introduction. The Three Series are three ways of presenting direct introduction with three associated methods of practice, the aim of which is to bring the practitioner into the state of contemplation, to remain in this state and then integrate it.

The Three Series also relate to the Three Statements of Garab Dorje. The Mind-Series relates to the first statement, direct introduction; the Series of Space to the second statement related to not remaining in doubt; and the Essential Series to the third statement involving continuing in the state of contemplation. The Mind-Series, working more with oral instruction and analysis, aims to bring the practitioner into the state of contemplation. The Series of Space, working with bodily positions and breathing, is designed to provide immediate, direct and spacious approaches to contemplation (Reynolds, 1996, p. 32). The Essential Series takes as a starting point the view that the original condition is one of both primordial purity and spontaneous self-perfected presence (*ka dag* and *lhun grub*). Primordial purity points to the emptiness of the ground while spontaneous presence points to the dynamism and capacity to manifest. Two practices relate to these two qualities: *khregs chod* is based on primordial purity of *ka dag* and *thod rgal* on spontaneous presence of *lhun grub* (Dalai Lama, 2000, p. 32). *Khregs chod* is likened to a woodman cutting loose a bundle of sticks, the bundle being 'all one's emotional and intellectual tensions and rigidities that keep one imprisoned in a self-created cage and prevent one from realizing one's intrinsic freedom' (Reynolds, 1996, p. 33).

Direct introduction from the master to the student is effected in many ways, not just through elaborate rituals. Tilopa slapped Naropa across the face with a shoe. Following a three-year retreat Nyoshul Lungtok was with his master Patrul Rinpoche. Each night Patrul Rinpoche would do a meditation session concerning *Namkha Sumtruk* (three-fold space) stretched on his back. One night Patrul Rinpoche called out to him: 'Lungche! Did you say that you do not know the true nature of the mind?' Lungtok said that was true, he did not. Patrul said, 'Oh, there is nothing not to know. Come here. . . . Lie down, as I am lying, and look at the sky'. They both gazed at the sky. Patrul Rinpoche asked Nyoshul Lungtok:

'Do you see the stars in the sky?'
'Yes'.

'Do you hear the dogs barking in Dzogchen Monastery?'
'Yes'.
'Well, that is the meditation'.

(Tulku Thondup, 1996, pp. 223–224)

Nyoshul Lungtok recalls:

> At that moment I arrived at a certainty (of realisation) from within. I had been liberated from the fetters of 'it is' and 'it is not'. I had realized the primordial wisdom, the naked (union of) emptiness and intrinsic awareness'.
>
> (Tulku Thondup, 1989b, p. 128)

Such introduction to the nature of mind may be instantaneous, and if one has sufficient capacity to discover this real condition and remain unaltered and relaxed in that state, nothing more is needed. However various secondary meditation and purification practices may prepare the ground. As well as discovering our ultimate nature, we also need to understand our relative condition, our psychological and physical limitations and difficulties. Then we can work with our given circumstances with awareness and skilful means. In a similar manner, psychological work is a process of incremental change, as the barnacles of defensiveness are slowly chipped away. Often a patient feels as if nothing is happening. Then, when realisation dawns, it might seem like a major break-through, but the patience, humility and toleration of frustration that preceded it are part of the process of loosening the grip of fixed and distorted modes of being and perceiving.

## Primordial ground

Bion talks of ultimate truth, absolute reality, O. Apophatic Christian mystics talk of inherent godliness, Vedānta of the non-duality of *Ātman* and *Brahman*. Dzogchen describes the primordial condition of each individual as being pure and empty, with infinite potential. 'Self-arising wisdom' in its original condition is 'intrinsically pure', free of dualistic thought, ineffable, inconceivable and the 'base of all primordial purity'. This is the 'natural condition of primordial enlightenment' (Studstill, 2005, p. 130).

A major principle of Dzogchen is the recognition that our pure nature is the fundamental reality underlying all appearance, underneath all the pervasive ignorance that obscures this. 'Self-arising wisdom, the essence of all the Buddhas, exists prior to the division of *saṃsāra* and *nirvāṇa*' and 'this original condition is the uncreated nature of existence'. It is the 'ultimate nature of all phenomena', and 'is utterly free of all the defects of dualistic thought'. 'It is given the name ineffable and inconceivable "base of primordial purity"' and 'pervades all beings without distinction, from glorious Samantabhadra down to the tiniest insect on a blade of grass' (Namkhai Norbu and Clemente, 1999, p. 20).

There is nothing to achieve, nothing to strive for, nothing that needs to be done, for one is 'intrinsically endowed with all'. One is 'always in being', 'never lacking anything' and so 'nothing more is needed' (Karmay, 2007, p. 49). One abides effortlessly and spontaneously in the state of 'such-ness' (Karmay, 2007, p. 54).

> Those who search for an enlightenment outside their actual condition are moving further and further away from it. Reality is the emptiness, the primordial purity, that is the basis from which all phenomena arise, and these phenomena have no essence. . . . Luminous awareness of one's self, beyond subject and object, expands without the need for an intentional meditation . . . one finds that all things are perfect.
>
> (Guarisco et al., 2013, p. 24)

## Rig pa

When one understands the indivisibility of essence, nature and potentiality of energy, such recognition is known as *rig pa* (Sanskrit, *vidyā*). Padmasambhava describes *rig pa* as follows:

> The nature of everything is
> open, empty and naked like the sky.
> Luminous emptiness,
> Without centre or circumference:
> The pure, naked *Rig pa* dawns.
> > (in Sogyal Rinpoche,
> > 2002, p. 263)

Other translations of *rig pa* include intrinsic awareness, knowledge, intellect, pristine cognition, pure presence, intelligence and 'ecstatic intensity' (Guenther, 1992). What is the difference between ordinary mind and the 'open and all-encompassing awareness' of *rig pa*? According to Jigmed Lingpa, mind (Tibetan *sems*, Sanskrit *citta*) 'is not some kind of container within which thoughts take place but a continuing screen of concepts that obscures the true nature of reality'. '*Sems* is like the wind, *rig pa* like the sky through which it blows. *Sems* is a response to the passing images of perceived objects, while *rig pa* is an all-embracing background against which anything can appear' (Samuel, 1993, p. 534).

## Clinical vignette

'Gary' was present at a retreat when direct introduction was given by a realised Dzogchen master. He fears that what he experienced in the conditions of a retreat will quickly fade once he is back at work. The night before coming to see me, he dreams that he is back at the retreat.

> I dream that I am in a Dzogchen retreat. My teacher gazes directly into my eyes, and I feel I am seen utterly to my core. There is no symbol, no

intermediary, just his looking directly into my mind and I look into his and his wisdom is what is transmitted. It is so personal, yet a wisdom that pervades all, beyond all concept, yet it is full of love and unbounded compassion. All last traces of old destructive tendencies and impure vision seem to fall away. I feel I could melt into rainbow light right now and I have no fear of dying, my entire body is filled with peace beyond understanding, the hairs standing on end, I completely melt into light. At the same time I feel at one with the world and full of compassion for all the needless suffering based on ignorance of our true nature that leads to aggression, possessiveness, concepts of me and mine, hope and fear, conflict, war, all the troubles of the world. I find myself crying uncontrollably and I want to do all I can to help others awaken to this realm of pure being.

Afterwards I walk outside and the grass is vibrating with light of the early sun shimmering on the dew fall. Each blade of grass is refracting dancing rainbows of light. The world has never been so radiant, so alive, so real before, as if I had lived all my life with cataracts and only now can I see clearly. I was half asleep, and only now awakened to true reality.

I hope that nothing can take away this realisation, but how will I keep this inner vision clear and untarnished, how will I abide by and in it without grasping it or turning away? That is the question I bring to you.

## From mind to the nature of mind

> If thoughts arise, remain present in that state;
> if no thoughts arise, remain present in that state;
> there is no difference in the presence in either state.
>                                                 (Garab Dorje)

One of the major elements of Dzogchen is how to pass from mind to the nature of mind. The expression 'nature of mind' (Tibetan *sems nyid*) refers to 'the true condition of the mind, which is beyond the limits of intellect and of time'. Other terms for the nature of mind (Tibetan *sems nyid*) include the 'primordial base' (*ye gzhi*), the 'base of all' (*kun gzhi*) and primordial bodhicitta (*ye gzhi snying po byang chub kyi sems*) (Namkhai Norbu, 1996, p. 52). The fundamental nature of the mind is the *tathāgatagarbha*, 'or essence of enlightenment in all beings' that is 'present from the beginning' (Guarisco, 2015, p. 36). Because the nature of mind is primordially pure, with radiant spontaneous presence, nothing can ultimately pollute its fundamental purity. Thoughts and emotional defilements are merely adventitious stains[2] that can be removed.

> From the point of Dzogchen, the understanding is that the adventitious level of mind, which is caught up with concepts and thoughts, is by its very nature permeated by pure awareness. In an experiential manner, the student can be directly introduced by an authentic master to the very nature of his or her own

mind as pure awareness. If the master is able to effect this direct introduction, the student then experiences all these adventitious layers of conceptual thought as permeated by the pure awareness which is their nature, so that these layers of ordinary thoughts and concepts need not continue. Rather, the student experiences the nature that permeates them as the fundamental innate mind of clear light, expressing itself in all its nakedness. That is the principle by which practice proceeds on the path of Dzogchen.

(Dalai Lama, 2000, p. 33)

Direct introduction is a way to reach behind and beyond conceptual thinking, to discover the state of pure contemplation and to abide in it continuously. The state of contemplation is much more all-encompassing, profound and mystical than analytic reverie. Bion would suggest that a state of reverie that has also freed itself of memory, desire or understanding is the state of mind in which O, which cannot be known, may be approached. The state of contemplation is also not properly a 'state' in the sense of being static but is dynamic and ever-flowing. One opens oneself out to the entire 'universe with absolute simplicity and nakedness of mind, ridding oneself of all "protecting" barriers' (Trungpa and Shikpo, 1968/2003, p. 462). This has implications for the ways in which psychological defence systems operate to alienate us from the world of others, where we construct what feels from within a wall of protection from potential hurt, but is experienced from the outside as a wall of hostile fortification fending off others. Dissolving defences opens us to others and affirms a common humanity and continuity of being, the basis of compassion. This is why mystics observe that union with God or the absolute automatically opens the heart.

## Dzogchen and the apophatic

The ground is described as indescribable, unnameable and ineffable. In the Commentary to the *Tun-huang* Manuscript IOL 647, it is said that language is a 'deviation from the principle' and nothing can be predicated of pure being. 'The Absolute (*dharmatā*) has, from the very beginning, never been pronounced' (in Karmay, 1988, pp. 54–55). Although absolute reality cannot be described in words, there is a state of contemplation in which it can be realised, a formless and non-conceptual system of contemplation, a 'direct experience of the true nature of reality, which is immediately present' (Van Schaik, 2004, pp. 4–5) and which goes beyond any form of prayer, spiritual practice or transformational method of meditation. One abides in 'ever-present, nondual and conceptual awareness and spontaneous presence (*lhun gyis grub pa*), indicating immediate and unfabricated presence' (Tiso, 2016, p. 210).

## Self-liberation

A patient may hope to find ways to overcome habitual destructive impulses and afflictive emotions such as rage, anger, depression, anxiety, fear and addiction.

How might Buddhist teachings help such a patient? The Hīnayāna path of renunciation would use methods based on calming the mind, the Mahāyāna path of bodhicitta would apply methods based on compassion, the Vajrayāna is a path of transformation, and Dzogchen a path of self-liberation (*rang grol*).

If one was afflicted by one of the 'five poisons' (desire, anger, delusion, pride and jealousy) in the Hīnayāna path one would seek to overcome destructive emotions through practices based on renunciation. For example if the emotion besetting a person was excessive sexual desire, one might meditate on the desired object as a corpse, or take a vow of celibacy. In the Mahāyāna methods are based on compassion and bodhicitta. If one feels strong antipathy towards someone, one might apply an equalising meditation in which one visualises in front of one the disliked person, a person one likes and a person to whom one feels neutral. One meditates on how all three are equal in desiring happiness and wanting to be free of suffering, and gradually one extends the same feelings of loving kindness felt towards the person who is liked to the disliked person so cultivating the virtue of equanimity. Another practice known as *gtong len*, or giving and receiving, involves imagining one takes in all the suffering of the person in question and sends loving kindness to them.

In the Vajrayāna path of transformation, through symbolically rich deity meditations involving combinations of visualisations, mudras and mantra, one engages directly with disturbing emotions transforming them into their enlightened beneficent counterparts. The strong energy of emotions is linked to our primordial nature and rather than see them as something to be renounced, one transforms them into their creative wisdom aspect. The five 'destructive' emotions become the five enlightened wisdoms: Delusion becomes the wisdom of *dharmadhātu*, anger becomes mirror-like wisdom, pride the wisdom of equality, desire the wisdom of discernment and jealousy all-accomplishing wisdom. Yet from the Dzogchen view, this still involves dualistic thinking, regarding one form of the emotion as negative and needing to be transformed and one as good.

In the Dzogchen approach, being in the state of instant presence, whatever emerges is simply liberated like writing on water. For example, in the very moment of becoming angry, one neither represses nor transforms the anger, but simply observes it without judgement. If there is no aversion or grasping, just pure awareness, the 'anger will dissolve by itself, as if it had been left in its natural condition, allowing it to liberate of itself' (Namkhai Norbu, 1996, p. 59). An analogy is that of a tangled snake naturally uncoiling. Without manipulation or applying an antidote, there is an intrinsic release into freedom. The practice of letting be and simply resting in the nature of mind means that if one allows whatever thought or emotion to arise and disperse of its own accord, neither accepting nor rejecting, all such mental constructions are 'self-liberated': 'All thoughts vanish into emptiness like the imprint of a bird in the sky, or like writing on water' (Trungpa, 2004, xxiv).

The implications for how one lives ordinary life, how one might approach the practice of psychotherapy, is one in which, at the level of pure being, one realises that whatever arises in one's mind is the 'play (*rol pa*) of the ultimate nature' (Tulku Thondup, 1989a, p. 86).

A patient tells me that he has to keep himself frantically busy because if he stops, he feels assailed by a hurricane of disordered thoughts. He sees such thoughts as enemies persecuting him. In the Dzogchen practice of 'liberation through bare attention', having gained confidence in the state of contemplation, even when a thousand thoughts arise, we do not 'become entangled in a net of memories created by the mind'. Instead we 'allow thoughts to dissolve in the sky of the mind without leaving a trace behind':

> When thoughts arise, we turn our attention to them, recognize them for what they are, and without following them, allow them to remain in their own native condition . . . and dissolve of their own accord.
>
> (Reynolds, 1996, p. 111)

Such practices may be helpful for psychotherapy in regard to contemplation, reverie and Freud's free-floating attention in the analytic setting. Practices of 'letting be' enable the mind to find a natural presence and clarity, just as water that is not stirred naturally becomes clear. In the state of analytic reverie, one observes all one's thoughts and emotions like fish in a pool of water, potential sources of communication about what is occurring in the here and now dynamics of the analytic encounter. One is not caught up in them, neither does one reject or grasp after them, but without memory, desire, or understanding, one merely considers how they emerge and how they dissolve again. Longchenpa advises that 'remaining with that state of contemplation, the thoughts release themselves right away like a drawing on water' (in Lipman and Peterson, 1987, p. 37).

## Ground, path and fruit

### Ground (gzhi)

Ultimate reality in Dzogchen is described as the ground (*gzhi*) which is natural, self-originating, unchanging, indestructible, perfect, incorruptible, unborn, non-dual, all-pervasive, spontaneous, luminous, naked and unimpeded. The Tibetan *gzhi* has also been translated as base, foundation, primordial basis and being. In its most general sense, *gzhi* refers to an 'eternal, pure, and luminous reality that is the source of all phenomenal appearance' (Studstill, 2005, p. 148). As described in the *Necklace of Pearls*:

> Its essence is Primordial Purity, and its nature is Natural Perfection.
>
> It is beyond any locality, directionality and partiality. It is neither being nor nothingness, and does not manifest as anything. It is beyond any words or measurements.
>
> (in Nagasawa, 2016, p. 123)

The path involves returning to this fundamental ground of our true nature. The base, ground or *gzhi* denotes

> the fundamental ground of existence, both at the universal level, and at the level of the individual, the two being essentially the same; to realize the one is to realize the other. If you realize yourself you realize the nature of the universe.
>
> (Namkhai Norbu, 1986, p. 56)

## Essence, nature, energy

The primordial state of the ground is described as open and empty in essence, luminous in nature, and its energy is all pervading. These three inseparable aspects are known as the 'three primordial wisdoms' of essence, nature and energy. The essence (*ka dag*) is both empty and 'pure from the beginning' like space. An example of emptiness is thought. When one examines a thought and tries to find where it came from, one finds nothing. If one looks for where it goes, there is nothing; if one looks at where it remains, there is nothing. All phenomena, whether mental or otherwise, however solid they seem, are empty, impermanent, ever-changing and interdependent.

The nature of the ground is clarity or lucidity (*gsal ba*). Although the ground is empty and pure, it manifests spontaneously. Just like in a mirror, it has infinite potentiality to manifest reflections. A clean mirror has the potential to clearly reflect whatever is placed in front of it, good, bad, big, small, beautiful or ugly. Just so, whatever thought arises, thought is not the nature of mind, and the nature of mind is not conditioned by thought. So too, Bion suggests, analysts make themselves available as a mirror that, 'preferably without too much distortion', they can reflect back the meaning of the patient's free associations (Bion, 1976/1994, p. 265).

Energy, or *thugs rje*, has also been translated as 'compassion' or 'resonance' (Studstill, 2005, p. 151). The characteristic of energy is to manifest without interruption. The word 'tantra' in this sense refers to continuity without interruption, the 'condition of infinite potentiality and of uninterrupted manifestation of the energy of our primordial state' (Namkhai Norbu and Clemente, 1999, p. 13). Here it is important to note that bodhicitta in Dzogchen has a specific meaning. The Tibetan is *byang chub kyi sems* where *byang* means primordially pure from the beginning (*ka dag*), *chub* means 'spontaneously self-perfected (*lhun grub*) and *sems* means nature of mind (*sems-nyid*)' (Reynolds, 1996, p. 85).

When direct introduction of the nature of mind is given, one understands how the essence, nature and energy are mutually interdependent, just like a mirror which has three aspects: clarity, reflective capacity and reflection (Namkhai Norbu, 1986, p. 65). Namkhai Norbu shows how this corresponds to three aspects of mind: calm state, movement and presence. The calm state can be found in the gap between the disappearance of one thought and the arising of another thought.

Movement can be found in the continuity of thought without interruption. It is like the movement of fish in the lake. Presence is the pure recognition without judgement, of either the calm state or the movement (Namkhai Norbu, 1996, p. 56). The 'ultimate nature of all phenomena' has the 'condition of original purity (*ka dag*), or emptiness' yet the 'natural energy of emptiness' is 'endowed with movement' and 'manifests as clarity (*gsal ba*), vision (*snang ba*), and pure instantaneous presence (*rig pa*) (Namkhai Norbu and Clemente, 1999, p. 15).

*Path*

From the Dzogchen perspective, we are already self-perfected, the ground of all is inherent purity and we are already being, so to realise enlightenment is 'nothing other than being naturally and spontaneously present in a state of immediate awareness' (Studstill, 2005, p. 160). Dzogchen practice involves letting be, relaxing into the natural state of what is and 'doing nothing' (*bya bral*). One's true nature is already perfect, so 'there is nothing to correct, or alter, or modify' (Namkhai Norbu, 1989, p. x). Structured contemplative practices are replaced with the immediacy of awareness 'beyond all mental constructs and fixation'. Yet such seemingly simple practices of just being are not so easy for the complicated neurotic mind!

> The practice of 'doing nothing' as a resting in the immediacy of the moment is diametrically opposed to the mind's habitual tendencies of grasping and distraction. It requires constant, non-wavering mindfulness, and therefore involves a very *active* and *effortful* 'holding' to the immediacy of present awareness. 'Doing nothing' turns out to be an extremely difficult psychological feat.
>
> (Studstill, 2005, p. 162)

Consequently there are also a wealth of preliminary practices that, while not the state of contemplation itself, prepare one to enter the state of contemplation. The distinction is that in meditation there is something to be done, while in the state of contemplation, there is not (Namkhai Norbu, 1986, p. 77).

### One ground, two paths

Dzogchen speaks of 'one ground, two paths'. Although the ground of our being is primordially pure from the beginning, if we have not recognised our true nature and our mind is distorted by pervasive ignorance and contaminated by erroneous views, this leads to the path of *saṃsāra*. When we recognise our true nature, it leads to the path of liberation. The difference between *saṃsāra* and *nirvāṇa* is simply one of recognition.

> The pure State of Enlightenment is our own mind . . . not some sort of dazzling light coming from outside. If we recognize our primordial State of pure

presence, pure from the beginning, albeit temporarily obscured, and we stay present in this recognition without getting distracted, then all impurities dissolve: this is the essence of the path. Now, the nature of the primordial State as total purity actually manifests, and recognizing it for what it is, we take hold of it forever. It is this decisive knowing, this pure presence of the true original condition, that is called *nirvāṇa*.

(Namkhai Norbu, 2005, p. 22)

Once one has had direct experience of the primordial state, and all doubt dissolves, one abides in the state of contemplation, bringing it into all situations. Another aspect of the path is known as *spyod pa* or attitude or conduct. This is the principle of integrating the state of contemplation into all aspects of daily life. It also involves observing oneself well, working with one's circumstances, being respectful of those around you, and being aware of how to apply the teachings in a given situation so that the teachings are living sources of wisdom inspiring all you are and do.

*Fruition*

In Dzogchen realisation is not something to be constructed or achieved. Realisation and self-liberation merely deepen until one simply remains continuously in the primordial state. There is no need to renounce the world, since 'whatever arises has arisen as the play (*rol pa*) of the ultimate nature' so one can 'simply enjoy all phenomena' (Tulku Thondup, 1989a, p. 86). There is no need to change any outward forms, clothes or habits. Maintaining a vibrant awareness and presence, all that arises spontaneously liberates, without effort. All 'one's habitual vision, the limited cage, the trap of ego' simply collapses, opening 'out into the spacious vision of what is. The bird is free, and can finally fly without hindrance. One can enter and enjoy the dance and play of energies, without limit' (Namkhai Norbu, 1986, p. 118).

As in the Six Vajra Verses:

Seeing that everything is self-perfected from the very beginning
the disease of striving for any achievement is surrendered
and just remaining in the natural state of as it is,
the presence of non-dual contemplation continuously spontaneously arises.

(in Namkhai Norbu, 1986, p. 119)

# Primordial purity

Apophatic and Dzogchen mysticism describe an ultimate, absolute reality that is the ground of being. This ultimate reality is seen as ineffable and beyond the constructions of the conceptual mind. In both traditions the most fundamental problems of existence derive from the alienation arising from an erroneous view of individual selfhood and the experience of separation consequent upon dualistic divisions of self and other, self and Godhead or ultimate reality. Both traditions observe that 'letting be' (Dzogchen) and abandonment (Christian apophaticism) is predicated on the knowledge that the goal is realisation of our primordial nature, awakening to what we already are. Eckhart asks, 'Why do you not stay in yourself and hold on to your own good? After all, you are carrying all truth in you in an essential manner' (1981, p. 184).

The meaning of life is to be found as a return to the primordial ground of being. In Dzogchen we are that reality. For the Christian apophatic mystics we ultimately become one with the Godhead, which is also our true nature. In both traditions intellectual knowledge falls short of this aim in favour of a direct, unmediated, mystical experience of reality. This also entails transcending the strictures of egotism and awakening into a more all- encompassing, expansive state of being spontaneously manifesting universal love and compassion for others. Both traditions teach contemplative methods for achieving their goals, formless supra-conceptual practices which transcend intellect, imagination and sensory perception. Yet ultimately one leaves behind any techniques or methods. The goal of life may be to realise absolute truth, but ultimately goals are also abandoned. One abides in the bare immediacy of pure awareness, an aliveness and vibrancy without clinging to past or future, and without attempts to reify or conceptualise being. One simply is as one is.

## Notes

1  I have taken care not to cite material from restricted teachings for which there is not the permission to cite publicly.
2  Adventitious stains (*glo bur gyi dri ma*) refer to obscuration that intrinsically part of our primordially pure Buddha nature but is layered upon its inherent luminosity. It is possible to remove them, like stains on a mirror. There are four categories of obscuration: karmic, emotional, cognitive and habitual obscuration.

# Chapter 7

# 'I do not exist'

## Śūnyatā and the terror of non-being

## A creation myth

I was sitting in a state of reverie during a session with 'Adam'[1]; who was silent. A statement made by a patient of Winnicott floated into awareness. 'I feel that you are introducing a big problem. I never became human. I have missed it' (Winnicott, 1986, p. 96). It was an uneasy reminder. I thought,

> I just so hope that for Adam this isn't the case. I hope that Adam hasn't missed the boat of life. I hope that through the process of therapy, as well as a gentle practice of meditation guided by loving kindness towards himself, life itself may stitch threads of presence across the void of absence. I can only have faith that these threads of continuity may one day hold him together and support him, rather than his perpetual disappearance through the gaping holes of trauma into the abyss of non-existence.

And in the sometimes empty, sometimes pregnant, sometimes hostile silences something began to float into consciousness. Gradually, in my reverie, a series of misty images began to cohere into a 'myth of origins' that seemed to describe what might be happening for Adam.

> In the beginning there was nothing, an eternal void of no-thing-ness. But there was movement in the huge, vast space, and the movement created droplets of moisture. Out of nothingness a huge cosmic ocean began to emerge: dark, mysterious, primeval, murky, so deep there was no bottom for there was no earth to hold it. But the ocean churned and churned so gradually and imperceptibly one could not see it occurring. Incrementally water became mud and the mud cohered into earth and eventually there was earth beneath the seas which held the ocean. And the ocean churned and churned and slowly, so slowly, the churning stirred and created more mud. Over aeons of time the mud began to cohere into a slimy, viscous form: the first man. And his name was Adam.

## 'Adam'

When Adam arrives for his first session, I hear the gate open, close, then silence. I go to open the door in welcome but intuitively hold back. After a long pause, there is a tentative knock so quiet that I would not have heard it if I wasn't waiting by the door. I open it. Eyes downcast, he says very diffidently, 'Well . . . here I am'. Once inside the room, he sits for a moment on the edge of the couch. Then like a marionette with no puppet master to hold him up, he crumples into the cushions. His face has a haunted, hollowed-out look, covering profound anguish.

Over the course of our analytic journey, his opening phrase 'Well . . . here I am' becomes something of a mantra, transmitting as yet unrealised potential. Like an 'initial dream' encapsulating the patient's psychological predicament, this simple phrase says it all. When he first came to see me, Adam was not 'well'. He had not been psychologically 'born'. He felt that he was no more than an amoeba-like semblance of pre-life with no form, no substance, no past, no future, no sense of on-going being. He was skinless and porous – the emotional states of others passed through him like the tides of an ocean. He was not 'here'. There was no 'I am', no 'I and thou', no 'we', let alone any sense of being real, meaning, or *joi de vivre*.

Adam was a university student studying Philosophy and Religious Studies, where he was particularly drawn to nihilism and deconstructionism in philosophy and teachings on *śūnyatā* in Buddhism. On vacation he found his way to a Tibetan Buddhist retreat and felt that he had finally found the answers to his experience of non-being. Yet, due to excessive application of ascetic and meditative practices, Adam decompensated and was hospitalised. He was advised to seek on-going psychological treatment. He sought a Jungian because, he said, 'Jung, unlike Freud, didn't belittle spirituality'.

Adam feared that he did not exist. Inside was but an empty core, there was no self. He also doubted the existence of the outer world. He suffered both depersonalisation and derealisation,[2] what Bion (1967) calls nameless dread, Winnicott (1974) describes as primitive agony, Clark and others a black hole in the psyche, (Clark, 1983; Tustin, 1988; Grotstein, 1990). Stemming from developmental deficits and relational traumas, such 'pathologies of self' may lead to psychological forms of solipsism, terrors of non-existence and fears of otherness or alterity. Not only suffering abject terror that 'I do not exist', there is a fear that 'others do not exist (for me)'. Others, in their otherness, are experienced as threatening if not annihilating. One defence against such threat is a monadic isolationism, a denial of any need for love or human connection. Another is to render others figments of one's imagination.

Adam sought solace in philosophies, spiritualties and psychologies that seemed to make sense of the experience of derealisation, constructing his own syncretic reading of Western existential, post-modern and neo-Nietzschean noble affirmation in the face of utter nihilism. This was combined with a misreading of Buddhist teachings on *nirvāṇa*, *anātman*, non-self, *śūnyatā*, emptiness or for Adam, 'the void'.[3]

Adam's existential predicament exemplifies a more general area of concern found in situations involving Western practitioners of Buddhism, whether in traditional settings in Asia, or Western settings ostensibly adapted to the Western mind.

Are there problems of translation in regard to Buddhist philosophies of *nirvāṇa, anātman, śūnyatā*, non-attachment, etc.? A misreading of Buddhist teachings may be used for psychologically defensive reasons to make sense of, yet thereby exacerbate, certain forms of psychopathology. In such situations psychotherapy may help a practitioner resolve, dissolve and heal old wounds obscuring the path of realisation.

## Analysis: a relational affair?

Jung saw a person's life-task as involving the gradual bringing together of pre-integrated elements of the psyche into an integrated unity of wholeness, which he called 'individuation'.

> Individuation means becoming a single, homogeneous being, and, in so far as 'individuality' embraces our innermost, last, and incomparable uniqueness, it also implies becoming one's own self. We could therefore translate individuation as 'coming to selfhood' or 'self-realisation'.
>
> (1966, p. 173)

Yet Jung also saw individuation as inherently relational and intersubjective. He said, 'For two personalities to meet is like two different chemical substances: if there is any combination at all, both are transformed' (Jung, *CWXVI*, para 163). Embedded in Jung's observation are implications concerning intersubjectivity, interdependence and the centrality of relationship in the human condition.

Within the psychoanalytic tradition, contemporary relational psychoanalytic approaches also emphasise the centrality of internalised and interpersonal relationships in human development. The Object Relations School signalled a major move away from classical Freudian drive theory towards a relational view of self. Ronald Fairbairn said that 'close relationships [are] the ground of the self'. The task of therapy was to liberate a patient from a closed intrapsychic system into an open, interpersonal one (Fairbairn, 1952, p. 109). Winnicott, Bowlby and Bion also underscore the primacy of relationship in the development of self.

The Relational School of Psychoanalysis, which integrates British Object Relations theory with American interpersonal psychoanalysis, also draws on social constructionism and intersubjectivity theory in philosophy as well as intersubjective infant research. Analytic Field and Link Theory, deriving from parallel traditions in Latin America, North American and France, focuses on the dynamic interplay between intrapsychic, intersubjective, intercultural and intergenerational processes in the constantly evolving and interdependent co-creation of the subject.

In regard to the confluence between Western concepts of self and Buddhist teachings on *anātman*, the significance of the relational turn in psychoanalysis is that it signals a move away from earlier models which tended to construct the self as an isolated independent subject, master in his or her own house, conscious, knowable, whose essence is stable and consistent if not fundamentally unchanging. Emerging relational approaches may bring Western constructions of self closer to those of Buddhist *anātman*. Even the recognition of the unconscious as process not reified entity leads to a decentring of the subject.

Despite the relational turn in psychoanalysis, does psychoanalysis reach beyond the goal of individuation and self-realisation for one's own sake? An essential component of self-realisation is other-realisation, that is, a capacity to respect and enjoy alterity. Responsiveness to the primordial call of others as other and a concomitant out-flowing of care and compassion enable liberation from the confines of a narrow and rigid self-centrism.

Adam is plagued by a waking nightmare.

> I do not exist. All you see is a shell with no being inside, a mask covering nothingness. I am no one and no thing. I am the unborn, the non-existent. Otherwise there is just this enormous sense of space, an infinity that is evil.

Adam defended against such existential dread by attempting to make of it a philosophy and eschewing the need for human connectivity and interdependence. Adam's spirituality emphasised physical and environmental purity and extreme asceticism. Any hint of attachment to body, possessions or people was to be rigorously renounced. His was, one might say, a schizoid split of both mind-body and self-other, fuelled with his particular conglomeration of intellectual and spiritual defences.

The theme of the self and its relations to others permeates the history of psychoanalysis, just as it has permeated Western philosophy. The Jungian goal of individuation derives in part from a post-Scholastic and Neoplatonic Western tradition of self-salvation, reinforced by post-Kantian Idealism, Weimar classical aesthetics, the emphasis on individual salvation in Northern European Protestantism and German Romantic subjectivism. Writers such as Goethe and Novalis emphasised self-cultivation, the primacy of the self and search for wholeness. Schelling's theory of the emergence of consciousness out of the unconsciousness became a basic model for nineteenth-century German psychology and psychiatry. This emergence was seen as cultural, personal and universal, but not interpersonal. Individuation was conceived as ultimately a quest for personal self-realisation, wherein alterity is incorporated within the overarching sphere of the self.

The legacy of such a first-person standpoint, characteristic of much post-scholastic Western thought, can lead to feeling constricted within a psychologically monadic state of alienation. The idea of human autonomy and individualism, stemming from over-emphasis on 'I am' and 'I think', leads to the primacy of the intrapsychic and hence to a position of solipsistic isolation.[4]

Such philosophical issues are not abstract but can be highly disturbing psychological and interpersonal experiences. Psychogenic forms of autism; schizoid states; dissociative, narcissistic and borderline disorders; and other pathologies of self may be compounded by recourse to such philosophically self-centric views.

The question is whether philosophical problems exacerbate psychological, spiritual and interpersonal ones: that is, whether they can universalise or normalise psychological experiences of isolation, existential anxiety and terrors of alterity.

Adam despairs of ever knowing love, or even friendship. He describes feeling like he exists in an empty echo chamber; all he hears is his own voice coming back at himself. For the most part that is the only voice he wants to hear, but it echoes hollowly. He fears that the world does not exist and no one is there to confirm that he exists, yet he finds contact with the world of others overwhelming. Adam's existential loneliness is poignantly described by the Jungian analyst Robert Hobson:

> 'I have no being' carries with it the implication 'No-one is there'. I have no sense of contact with another person who can confirm that 'I am me', capable of having an identity separate from the world of people and things 'out there'. Even my body is alien. There is a threat of *non-being* – a loss of the capacity to speak the word 'I'. . . . In non-being there is some mysterious uncanny sense of the unknown, of an annihilation in which 'I' cease to be.
>
> (1974, p. 76)

A year after Adam began therapy he hands me a note. He is too frightened to say it aloud in my presence. It reads:

> I have come to the realisation that fear of saying 'here I am' touches the core of why I am here. Trusting that I might rise to the occasion of being who I am, and that you will rise to the occasion of meeting me as I am. Here. Now. But I despair. I still don't feel real. I'm so alone. I get sick of sitting at home with only my philosophy books for company, but other people terrify me.

## Being born, being seen, feeling real: the psychological perspective

According to object relations, intersubjective, relational psychoanalysis and attachment theory, we are born into the world as relational beings needing to be welcomed into an atmosphere of care and concern. We feel we exist because we are consistently and lovingly held in the mind of another.

Adam didn't feel real. Adam didn't feel he had even been born. Adam's parents had planned to have a natural birth in a birthing centre. Their first child would be born, 'trailing clouds of glory' (Wordsworth, 1961, p. 628), into a Leboyer pool, in a dimly lit, quiet atmosphere. However, this did not occur. He was born prematurely at 32 weeks. The moment Adam was extracted from the womb, the nurse handed Adam to his father to hold, but he fainted at the sight of the pools of blood on the floor and dropped him. Adam had a recurring nightmare of falling from a great height into a sea of blood. From as long as he could remember, his parents had relayed the story of his traumatic entry into life. In fact, unbeknown to us all, this was a trauma song reverberating through the corridors of intergenerational time.

## A sense of self

> The first and fundamental wonder is existence itself. That I should be alive, conscious, a person, a part of the whole, that I should have emerged out of nothingness, that the Void should have given birth not merely to things, but to me.
>
> (Macneile Dixson, 1958, pp. 72–73)

A sense of self depends on the provision of key intersubjective responsiveness between baby and parent in the early psychological atmosphere. Holding, containment, attunement, synchrony, resonance, mirroring, recognition, being interacted with and loved – all give rise to a feeling of being real, of having a self. Even if this sense of self is no longer master in its own house, unconscious as well as conscious, multiple if not split, ever changing, interdependent, impermanent and decentred, there is nevertheless a sense of self which does a good-enough job of keeping us from falling through the cracks of non-existence.

Psychoanalysts, like philosophers, differ as to whether there is a primary or potential self from the very beginning of life, or whether self is something that develops over time and only under certain conditions. They also define self in very different ways. Self for Jung is 'an extremely composite thing, a "conglomerate soul", to use the Indian expression' (*CWIXi*, para. 634). Jung's view of self is manifold. According to Samuels, one simple definition is that self represents the 'potential for integration of the total personality', including 'all psychological and mental processes, physiology and biology, all positive and negative, realized or unrealized potential, and the spiritual dimension' (2003, p. 72).

The Jungian analyst Michael Fordham puts forward the view of a self that is primary as well as relational, dynamic and developmental, involving processes of deintegration and integration as it meets with the peopled world (1957, p. 127).

For Winnicott 'the central self could be said to be the inherited potential which is experiencing a continuity of being, and acquiring in its own way and at its own speed a personal psychic reality and a personal body-scheme' (1965, p. 46).

## Being seen, feeling real, feeling real, seeing the world

The baby's sense of being real emerges out of feeling seen. 'Not to be seen by the mother, at least at the moment of the spontaneous gesture, is not to exist' (Phillips, 1988, p. 130). However, there is more to this than meets the eye. When a baby looks at mother's face, the baby sees its own reflection in the mother's imitative expression. As Winnicott described it, 'The mother is looking at the baby and *what she looks like reflects what she sees there*' (1971, p. 131, emphasis in the original).

Adapting Berkeley's *esse est percipi*[5] to a psychological context concerning the development of a human being, Winnicott writes:

> When I look I am seen, so I exist.
> I can now afford to look and see.
> I now look creatively and what I apperceive I also perceive.
> In fact I take care not to see what is not there to be seen (unless I am tired).
>
> (1971, p. 134)

The baby begins to see through 'being seen' to being able to 'see' the other as another and not simply a figment of its imagination. This is a relational process that can break down at any stage leading to narcissistic defences, borderline, psychotic or psychogenic autistic-like states, or, as Winnicott (1988) suggested, it leads to philosophy (or at least to post-Kantian idealism). 'Philosophers', Winnicott muses, 'have always been concerned with the meaning of the word "real"' and contemplated the question as to whether 'this stone and this tree continue to be' when 'there's no one about' to observe them. Winnicott sees such philosophical concerns as arising out of 'the initial relationship to external reality' occurring at the 'theoretical first feed' (1988, p. 114). If the mother's 'initial active adaptation to the infant's need was good enough' the infant has the fortunate illusion of 'finding what was created (hallucinated)' (ibid). Winnicott goes on to explain how once the

> capacity for relationships has been established, such babies can take the next step towards recognition of the essential aloneness of the human being. Eventually such a baby grows up to say, 'I know that there is no direct contact between external reality and myself, only an illusion of contact, a midway phenomenon that works very well for me when I am not tired. I couldn't care less that there is a philosophical problem involved'.

However:

> Babies with slightly less fortunate experiences are really bothered by the idea of there being no direct contact with external reality. A sense of threat of loss of capacity for relationships hangs over them all the time. For them the philosophical problem becomes and remains a vital one, a matter of life and death, of feeding or starvation, of love or isolation.
>
> (Winnicott, 1988, pp. 114–115)

## Maternal reverie, containment of unthinkable anxieties

As explained more fully in Chapter 4, according to Bion, the mother, in her reverie, takes in unthinkable anxieties, thereby containing, bearing and thinking what had been uncontainable, unbearable and unthinkable. The infant now reassured is able to sleep, feel safe and secure, and is also able to dream. The infant then can 'reintroject' dreadful anxieties rendered thinkable and endurable.

Bion gives the example of a baby, who is so wracked by anxiety that it 'messes itself and cries. The mother picks it up, feeds it and comforts it'. Through her containment the mother has metabolised the baby's fears of impeding death, transmuting nameless dread 'into vitality and confidence' (Bion, 1963, p. 31). However Adam's mother was not capable of experiencing Adam's terror of dying and so he was left re-introjecting the threat of non-being made infinitely worse.

> I was around three. I was playing on a headland near our house and I slipped and fell down the cliff. I only fell half way and was rescued by a passer-by who took me home. I ran to my mother for comfort but she was not there. I didn't know it at the time but she had been hospitalized again for post-natal depression. I was overwhelmed with the terror that she had died. I couldn't stop crying but my father just hit me and told me 'boys don't cry!'

Such a traumatic event exacerbated Adam's original fall off the operating table into the world with no one to hold him together. He felt himself to be falling forever in an alien universe without limits.

## Continuity and going on being

Feeling real involves a sense of continuity, that we are integrated, coherent and continuous, even if we are also de-integrated, incoherent and discontinuous.

Winnicott's 'going on being' (1956, p. 303) depicts how in the earliest stages the mother's physical and emotional holding gradually gives rise to a sense of being real, creatively alive and deeply connected. 'Going on being' is also relational: the sense that another continuously holds us in mind as well as in her arms gives rise to a sense of continuity of being. As Ogden observes, 'Holding, for Winnicott, is an ontological concept' which relates to the 'experience of being alive . . . as well as the changing intrapsychic-interpersonal means by which the sense of continuity of being is sustained over time' (2004, p. 1349).

In Vajrayāna Buddhism, the word 'tantra' also means 'continuity'. Etymologically tantra means a loom, and figuratively 'a weaving of one's life' (Guenther, 1996, p. ix).[6] 'In Tibetan tantra is called *rgyud*, which is like the thread that runs through beads' (Trungpa, 1975, p. 8).

> This is a continuity of being which divides into two grounds: we have to start somewhere, and then go a certain way (and perhaps arrive at a goal). This is the way tantra was presented. It refers to an immediate human situation which arises out of the question of how we are going to *be*. Tantra also sees the question of how we are going to be in terms of relationship, realizing that [one] is always related to something or someone.
>
> (Guenther, 1975, p. 2)

## Discontinuity, disruption, deintegration, disintegration

New experiences may initially feel disruptive to our sense of going on being. But as we integrate such experiences, the flow of life continues, ideally enriched by such experience. Some experiences, however, may be so overwhelming that integration is not immediately possible, resulting in trauma. What is the consequence for being creatively alive if we have suffered too long a separation at too early a time for this to be repaired? According to Winnicott a baby might be able to face mother's absence for $x$ minutes, possibly recover from $x + y$ minutes, but that $x + y + z$ minutes leads to a fissuring in the psyche.

> If a breaking point is reached, the sense of continuity is lost. This rupture of continuity is associated with such primitive agonies as a return to an unintegrated state, falling forever, loss of psychosomatic unity, and loss of the sense of reality and the capacity to relate to objects . . . the subject tries to find some way of organizing himself in the face of an unthinkable agony, in which the personality is threatened by a fate worse than nothingness.
>
> (Eigen, 1993, p. 120)

We are all marked by areas of sensitivity, wounds and traumatic complexes. But, as Eigen observes, we may also suffer a sense of pervasive deadness, that at the deepest level bears witness to a 'fissuring, dissolving, breaking' lapse in the continuity of existence, that once was unendurable and endless, an 'evil eternity' (1993, p. 121). Eigen writes:

> The blanking out pointed to here is more primitive than denial. An elemental response to agony, it threatens to continue endlessly. To various degrees, the infant tones down, shuts off, and dies out. The infant does not yet know about physical death. What is lost is his implicit sense of on going being, his psychophysical aliveness, his dawning awareness of being there, his primordial self-feeling. Over and over he goes through the experience of dying out and coming back, the most ghastly horror and the saving bliss.
>
> (1993, pp. 121)

Adam's own experience of an 'evil eternity' derived from an emotionally dead mother, a sense not of a pregnant absence, but an annihilating absence thus engendering a primordial break in life's continuity, a psychic black hole. Nothingness for Adam was non-existence, annihilation, not the state of no-thing-ness that is ecstatic for the apophatic mystics.

## Nameless dread

I open the door to a white, frozen mask. I know immediately that Adam has disappeared again into what he calls 'the void'. He sits down like an automaton, stares in stony silence at the wall as if staring into space. I do not exist for him; he is totally isolated in his own realm of non-existence. The sense of deadly despair pervades the room. I feel myself fading into nothingness, a realm of absence, unmitigated bleakness and blankness.

We sit in silence, sometimes for session after session. I wonder what on earth do I have to offer him?

I long to reassure him that things will get better, that I am with him, silently present rather than silently absent like his mother. An abyss opens up between us. On his side he is sucked into the evil eternity of a psychic black hole, evil because the isolation is, for him, totally absolute, negative O. On my side, I want to find a way to cross the abyss of agonised alienation, to offer some gesture of hope. All I can do is silently but emotionally connect to this unbearable zone, hoping he senses and has some faith I am with him in his hell-realm of nothingness.

## Transitional space, the me and the not-me, play leading to capacity to be alone

The subject comes into being in the potential space between mother and infant. In this space, self and other are neither one nor two but somehow make up an inter-penetrating interpersonal field. Transitional space is a protected realm of trust, in which imagination, creativity and culture are generated. One can withdraw attention from the outer environment because one is being 'minded'. Paradoxically, being held *in* mind gives rise to a capacity to be alone in the presence of another. Such a sense of presence enables one to bear absence. A baby also develops the capacity to be alone, to enjoy solitude as well as fulfilling relationships. We need to be minded in all senses of the word. Unfortunately, Adam was not minded in any sense of the word.

Feeling terribly apprehensive about going on another Buddhist retreat, Adam asked, 'Will you hold me in mind?' I answered, 'Of course I will'. In fact, I thought, I always hold you in mind. I have minded him since our first session. One of the things that psychotherapy offers, rare in this world of fleeting contractual arrange-ments, is that we hold the patient in our hearts and mind, perhaps not always at the forefront of our awareness, but at a subliminal level, session to session, week to week, year by year. We commit to be there with the patient on their life journey for as long as we are needed, like a companion on the way. This 'companion-ship', the feeling another is with you, cares for you, tries to understand you in all your complexity and alterity, brings presence into the absences, understanding into misunderstanding, yet cognizant of what is ever elusive and unknowable. That it continues over time, gives rise to threads of continuity that are woven into the on-going, interdependent, ever changing and evolving tapestry of a life. Gradually, imperceptibly, Adam began to feel alive. He began to trust that he was held in mind, trust in the sense of continuity of being. Being minded he could mind him-self and come to be able to mind others. He began to work with clay, building out of the mud human figures, sculpting being out of the amorphous mud of non-being.

## Notes

1 'Adam' is inspired by work with many patients suffering derealisation and depersonalisation but 'Adam' himself is fictional.

2 I am using the diagnostic terms 'depersonalisation' and 'derealisation' in a *style métaphorique*, to describe the subjective experience of feeling one does not truly exist and has no self (depersonalisation) and the fear that the world does not exist (derealisation). As a diagnostic term, 'depersonalisation' was first used by Dugas in 1898, to refer to 'a state in which there is the feeling or sensation that thoughts and acts elude the self and become strange; there is an alienation of personality; in other words, a depersonalisation' (Dugas and Moutier, 1911, p. 13, in Sierra, 2009, p. 9). Dugas in fact derived the term 'depersonalisation' from the diary of the Swiss philosopher Amiel (1821–1881) who had written, 'All is strange to me; I am, as it were, outside my own body and individuality; I am *depersonalised*, detached, cut adrift' (1933, p. 275, in Sierra, 2009, p. 9).

3 As explained in Chapter 5, *anātman* is conventionally translated as no-self, not-self or non-self, and refers to the negation of a construct of a permanent, changeless, independent self. *Śūnyatā*, usually rendered as 'emptiness' or 'voidness', refers to the negation of all possible conceptualisations of 'reality', and a transcendence of both eternalism and nihilism. Likewise, *anātman*, or the emptiness of self, is a negation of a construct of a permanent, solid, unchanging, eternal and independent self.

4 The term 'monad' originally comes from the Greek meaning unity. As developed by the philosopher Leibniz, monads are infinite, eternal, mind-like, self-reflecting substances. Applied psychologically the monadic stance refers to treating oneself as a self-sufficient system, depending on nothing or no one else outside to be what one is.

5 Berkeley meant by this that I exist because I am seen by God. Winnicott's version is that I exist because I am held in the mind of Mother.

6 Tantra etymologically derives from *tana* meaning warp and *bantar* as weft. It is related to *prabhandha* and *santāna* which also means continuity.

# Chapter 8

# Bearing the unbearable

## Intergenerational transmission of trauma

### Rachael

I was thrown in the deep end with 'Rachael', submerged in subterranean realms beyond anything I had ever previously encountered. I was challenged to bear what seemed utterly unbearable, my capacity for compassionate witness stretched to breaking point, analytic reverie plunging into ghastly nightmarish realms beyond imagination. We both had to bear being with something sensed as sinister, uncanny, but the terrible nature of which we had no conscious knowledge.

In her first session she said, 'It's been a watery year for me, full of tears. I'm really depressed, like I'm stuck in some kind of drain'. She spoke of 'treading water' unable to fully enter the 'swim of things'. Sometimes she felt submerged in a watery grave, which she called her 'deathy mode'.

She brought many dreams of swimming pools representing both terror and fascination with plumbing her depths. There was a sense that we were feeling our way together into such zones: sometimes tentatively dipping our toes in the water; sometimes colluding in an unspoken reluctance to dive into the unknown; sometimes drawing breath ready to take the plunge. A sense of immersion in dark gloomy waters permeated our imaginal and affective space, a necessary induction into her world. A recurring dream of a waterless concrete swimming pool signalled a malignant 'heart of darkness', whose significance only gradually emerged.

Throughout six years of analysis, watery motifs and images of pools and drains welled up recurrently in Rachael's dreams, evoking recovered memories and generating the metaphoric vocabulary between us. Why did Rachael and I unconsciously use so many metaphors concerning water, pools and drowning to describe her internal landscape?

### Dreams and moving metaphors as conduits for intergenerational transmission

Analytic reverie is a form of compassionate witness, bearing the unbearable load of trauma, bringing light into areas of darkness and hope where hope has been lost. Dreaming and reverie in the analytic field may generate 'moving metaphors'

(Hobson, 1985) which take on a life of their own, amplifying the language of experience that develops between patient and analyst. Hobson argues that a vital therapeutic task is to 'share in creating moving metaphors which forward personal growth and open up new possibilities'. The 'colourful, vigorous, ambiguous language of metaphor generates a sense of immediacy and life which lures us on to explore what is dimly sensed' (Hobson, 1985, p. 56). Hobson observes how in clinical work we use metaphors but more accurately we are used by them. Rachael and I found ourselves being used by such a metaphoric process. Harrowing and torturous experience revealed, darkly as through a glass, an unknown but dimly sensed ancestral story.

## Transgenerational transmission

Descendants of ancestors who have suffered unimaginable trauma may inherit the psychic task of processing difficult matters their forebears did not have the conditions to face. They may be driven to seek therapy by an unconscious need to uncover past secrets, to piece together an ancestral and cultural history, before the stories and the keys to comprehending what they carry die with their forebears. As Jung wrote:

> The patient who comes to us has a story that is not told, and which as a rule no one knows of. . . . It is the patient's secret, the rock against which he is shattered.
>
> (1963, p. 117)

Yet the children of survivors of trauma may be carriers for that which was unendurable for their ancestors. They may not consciously realise their psychic inheritance. When the handing down of family and cultural stories is dissociated due to pain, fear or shame, it impoverishes the next generation. In place of ever-vitalising myths of origin is a humming hollowness.

When, in the attempt to move on, the past is rendered a closed book, it enters the stream of unconscious transmission. Dreams and their metaphoric representations may function as conduits for walled-off psychic chambers of horror which were previously unthinkable and hence unspeakable. Such ancestral matters will haunt the analytic space until they are uncovered, emotionally faced and gradually transformed by the analytic couple.

The primary vehicle for transformation is the analytic relationship, nested within the healing ambience of the analytic field. Such emotional containment may enable the unthinkable to be thought, the unbearable to be borne. Once borne, an effective metaphoric language emerges out of shared symbolising. It is the analyst's role to not only bear the unbearable with and for the patient, but create a healing sanctuary in which the patient begins to feel that such unbearable pain can be borne.

Bion proposed that the capacity to dream requires relational containment: there is an intersubjective matrix in which dreaming, thinking and symbolising occurs. The analyst, through a state of reverie, models how it is possible to sit with inchoate, fragmented psychic material (Bion, 1967, p. 105). Psychological patience, the ability to tolerate confusing and painful emotional matters, creates the necessary conditions for such raw psychic material to be transformed into food for thought, that is, to become thinkable. The analytic space becomes an empty vessel for the incarnation of dreams and dreaming. Dreams are re-membered and re-presented: their emotional tonality, multivalent meanings, symbolic imagery and narrative structure are related in the analytic field. This inter-relational 'storytelling' becomes part of the discovery of the symbolic depth of the dream. That is, we often only truly 'realise' a dream in the interpersonal activity of its telling, a potentiality which continues to unfold over time. The form of language used to convey the symbolic potential of dreaming is metaphoric and symbolic associative rather than linear and factual.

The moving metaphor is moving in two significant ways: it is continually transforming, and it is emotionally moving. This points to the emergent and relational aspects of the moving metaphor. It is both generated by and generative of a symbolic attitude. The moving metaphor is a 'kind of living symbol' opening up 'depths of experiencing "where silence reigns"' (Hobson, 1985, p. 61). Once the deepest truths transmitted by the moving metaphor are fully understood by the analytic couple, they also become profoundly moving realisations.

## Metaphor and symbol

Moving metaphors are vehicles of communication conveying as yet unknown symbolic truths emerging in the analytic space. As Jung put it, the meaning of a symbol resides 'in the fact that it is an attempt to elucidate, by a more or less apt analogy, something that is still entirely unknown or still in the process of formation' (Jung, 1967, p. 492). The dream imagery that Rachael brought contained symbolic analogies for buried psychic matters. In turn these images generated a language rich with metaphoric association which further served the process of unveiling vital truths. The moving metaphors expressed multiple layers of symbolic meanings, never to be pinned down as representing a single concrete 'fact' or literal event. A capacity for uncertainty and negative capability was essential, a form of analytic apophatic reverie.

Moving metaphors are dynamic communications emerging out of the co-created realisation of mutual participation in symbolic processes within the therapeutic field. In turn dreaming, which gives rise to living symbols, depends upon relational containment. There is a continuous movement between relational containment as a necessary precondition for the patient to dream, for the emergence of waking dream thoughts in the analytic field through analytic reverie, the internalisation of a capacity for reverie leading to mutually generated waking dream thoughts giving rise to further symbolic images. In turn moving metaphors convey incipient symbolic truths that are initially revealed (but not necessarily fully understood) in dreams, which in turn depend on relational containment . . . a kind of benign circle.

## Rachael: early memories

Rachael, a single mother of two girls, did not remember much about her early life. She felt haunted by fragmented and fragmenting pieces of information she gleaned as a child: a baby brother who died; her father's Ukrainian heritage and his alcohol-fueled violent rages, and a grandfather who, like her father, served in the war. Her mother was oblivious to this history and point-blank refused to discuss it. Prior to coming to see me, there had been no one to help Rachael weave together the threads of palpable emotional experience into a coherent whole.

One day she recovered an early memory. She related how she had been in the bath the night before and heard herself singing a childish song:

> I was in the bath and I was singing 'don't step into the water or you'll drown.' I said, 'hold on a minute, what am I saying?' I suddenly remembered, that was what I did when I was three. My father had just left my mother and I wanted to die.

A powerful memory flooded back. As a 3-year-old Rachael stepped into the backyard swimming pool wanting to die. The overwhelming shock of water filling her lungs evoked an unexpected will to live. Her father re-appeared, gathering her limp body in his strong arms. However, having saved her from drowning, he did not fulfil her desperate longing that he would stay. He left again, abandoning her to her silent mother, a bullying older brother and a shroud of mystery concerning a baby brother who had died just before he left.

## Maternal matters: transference and countertransference

She remembered the maternal environment after her father left as deathly quiet and joyless. She described her mother as unresponsive, deadly and depressed. Rachael herself felt dissociated, autistic and deaf, as if incorporating her mother's emotional deafness into her own sense of self.

Often in analysis Rachael behaved like a young child, hoping that an enlivening, appreciative mother-analyst would delight in her stories. Bright shining eyes peeped out almost mischievously under a mane of cropped short black hair, animated facial gestures willing me to respond. Our analytic conversations sounded like we were singing together, akin to what Bateson (1979) described as the protoconversation. I noticed a vital need for vocal attunement and facial mirroring. These involved making emotionally concordant responses to subtle nuances of facial expressions, matching the tone, pitch and melodic contour of her voice, the rhythm of her speech. When immersed in an atmosphere of such finely attuned responsiveness, she would communicate in a sing-song voice. I found myself intuitively cooing in response, indicating my understanding of her world through musical imitation. Rachael tells me how:

> I left here last time thinking I had babbled my head off, I was a bit embarrassed. I was thinking 'Oh God, I don't have to tell Judith I scratched my nose yesterday!' It was like you were my mum!

She burst into tears, saying her mother never listened and how much this hurt. Reminded of her mother's emotional absence of mind, she subsided into a flat monotone, a vocal indicator that she had been triggered into a monotonous dissociated zone, a traumatic memory system (Meares, 2000).

## Hierarchy of memory and unconscious traumatic memory systems

Meares defines the 'unconscious traumatic memory system' as 'a collection of memories concerning similar traumatic events, which is stored in a memory system beyond the reach of reflective awareness'. This system is 'triggered by contextual cues which resemble, in some way, the original trauma' (2000, p. 53). Traumatic memory systems involve a layered hierarchy of different memory systems, 'earlier and less accessible traumata underpinning those which are nearer to consciousness' (Meares, 2005, p. 102). Trauma causes the individual's consciousness (and memory) to fall down the developmental ladder of memory. When traumatic memories are evoked by sensory, verbal or other means of 'priming' (Tulving and Schacter, 1990) they become 'implicit' (Graf and Schacter, 1985), lacking episodic or reflective function.[1] A person catapulted into a traumatic memory system may be flooded with associated emotional and physiological responses to the original trauma without necessarily realising such memories are being stirred up. When Rachael was thus triggered, the relational space between us seemed permeated with ghostly presences, a gloomy and emotionally charged atmosphere, a sense of confusion and despair that nothing would ever change or get better, her 'deathly mode'.

Any inkling of hope that I might provide longed-for maternal attunement elicited anxiety in Rachael, triggering unconscious traumatic memories. Ephemeral threads of attachment between us evoked grief for what had not been, overlaid by fear, not only of losing, but what was transpiring between us. Hence Rachael's growing capacity for reflective function, mentalisation and a symbolic attitude was not a straightforward development through her analysis. It oscillated wildly in the transference-countertransference dynamics. As well as significant linguistic markers, there were aural indicators which alerted me to whether Rachael felt inter-subjectively immersed with me in 'moments of meeting' (Stern, 2004) and engaged in symbolic play, or catapulted back into the concrete literalism and arrested time zone of a traumatic memory system. When relating narratives of self, Rachael's tonality was sing-song, featuring the musical tone-set *la so mi*, identified by ethnomusicologists as the first tone set used in children's songs the world over. When triggered back into a traumatic memory zone Rachael reverted to a featureless monotone. For example, the musical notation for her song in the bath was as follows:

She went from singing a childish melody to a sudden harsh monotone on the word 'drown'. Modell notes that if

> our analysand is in a state of nonrelatedness, his or her speech becomes boring and monotonous and therefore without meaning. To respond to the other empathically, speech must contain an element of prosody, of musicality, consisting of variations in pitch, tone, and rhythm. Language becomes alive and meaningful only in the presence of feeling.
>
> (2008, pp. 161–162)

Rachael put great store on my ability to remember all the bits and pieces of her life that she relayed but was unable to hold in her own conscious episodic memory. Functioning as the gatherer of the disparate fragments of her life, analytically holding her in mind was part of the relational containment that enabled her to remember the past and develop her own capacity for dream-work alpha function.

Yet there was a continual fluctuation between Rachael's growth of a capacity for metaphor, reflection and symbolic attitude, and a rebound to a concrete zone dominated by literal thinking, an inability to distinguish between symbol and what is being symbolised and acting out rather than sitting with her painfully confusing experience.

## Paternal transferences

Despite his repeated abandonment of her, Rachael clung tightly to an idealised image of her father. Her descriptions of visits to his theatre restaurant were like a fairy tale: 'I was treated as his little princess. I would come home full and glowing, only to return to being pale, gaunt and skinny – the match girl'. She blamed her demonised 'witch-mother' for her father's abandonment.

> He came here at the age of 20 with nothing. He built his way up, working his guts out. But, when I was about 4, Mum got him committed to a psych ward. I don't know the details. This is the silent mum who never told me anything.

Parents who hide the past due to fear of the terror they experienced or exposure of their own terrible deeds transmit 'no-go zones', sending unspoken signals 'that's not something we talk about'. Dan Bar-On (1989) describes this as the 'double wall of silence', where parents refuse to speak about their past and where children dare not ask. A similar dynamic played itself out in our analytic work: Rachael communicated fragmented shards of information about her father, which left me with a sense of foreboding. Yet I felt great reluctance to push her to reveal more lest I seemed intrusive if not interrogatory.

Rachael enjoyed bathing in the aura of my analytic attention but if she perceived the slightest hint of disapproval it could shock her as if I was holding a gun to her head.

> I feel like a naughty girl. You must be representing something authoritarian now. You've just put on a uniform with a starched collar. Now gun me down!

Rachael anticipated a punitive reaction to the confession that followed. 'I have to tell you something really terrible. I was really bad'. She described how she witnessed her 5-year-old daughter Mila bully her little sister Vera.

> I screamed at Mila, 'you little Hitler' and threw her across the room. Now I realise it was a throw-back to my childhood when my father bashed my older brother. I felt so guilty not coming to his rescue. I hate myself so much!

Children who witnessed trauma but were unable to intervene may later engage in repeated enactments of the original scene in an attempt to overcome pervasive feelings of guilt. Yet, as Rachael found to her dismay, they often unwittingly take the part of the aggressor. Freyberg (1989) describes how survivors' identification with their aggressors may spill out towards their own children, such as calling them 'swine' or 'little Hitler'. Furthermore, a child's intuited sense of horrific events preceding their birth leads to a tendency to repeat the suffering that perpetuates the persecutor/persecuted scenario. The dissociation of parents may be transmitted to children like a bizarre object. Such was Rachael's suicidal ideation, her outbursts of rage towards her father and then the identification of her own son as a 'little Hitler'.

The paternal arena within Rachael was compounded by the unresolved issues of her forefathers. The 'law of the fathers' was difficult to negotiate, shifting from protector, boundary-setter and moral watch-dog to tyrannical Gestapo-like interrogator. This rendered her current relationships highly problematic. She related a dream she had the previous weekend about her boyfriend Pete.

> I dreamed last night that there were harp strings attached between my heart and Pete's. Fucking harp strings, playing my heart-strings. I just want to break them!

So, too, heart strings of attachment between us sounded a mournful tune, evoking a desperate longing for connection, triggering pre-emptive impulses to avert the pain of disconnection by snapping the ties she also feared would bind.

The dream image of the harp strings also depicts the process that develops between image, symbol and metaphor, and how this continually generates the metaphoric language of experience in the analytic relationship. The symbol of the harp resonated on multiple levels. Through being able to play creatively with me, Rachael found her Orphic voice and a more cohesive sense of self, evidenced by joyful sing-song modes of communication. However her Orphic complex also signalled the compulsive allure of looking back to Hades (Pickering, 2008). The harp also represented Rachael's romanticised ancestry of Ukrainian folk-music. She tried repeatedly to reach her father through playing such music, only to have him disparage it as 'Jewish'.

Dim intimations of her father's dark past began to float into awareness:

> I was reading the childhood of Adolf Hitler and it brought all this stuff up for me. It made me think of my father. Hitler's father was brought up to feel shame without any memory. That was how I was brought up with my family, no history, no understanding of that Ukrainian side, and there's a lot of horror around that.

We both entered deathly toxic waters. My own body seemed to act as a container, leading to a sense of being contaminated with poisonous material I could not metabolise, somatically manifesting in a painful attack of colitis. The next day Rachael brought the following dream:

> I woke up in the middle of the night from a dream thinking 'Judith, we need to work on this'. Something about making a cut in a baby's anus.

Rachael told me she had been hospitalised as a baby for colitis. Feeling my way into and containing her primitive experience through embodied counter-transference was precursory to her capacity to dream it into conscious aware-ness. As Eli Humbert observed, 'Here in the body, where the early traumatic incidents were imprinted' is where 'their reactivation takes place' (1988, p. 10). Similarly Kestenberg (1982) describes a patient whose bodily symptoms functioned as metaphoric manifestations of her immersion in her ancestor's traumatic experience. She imaged her intestines as being a tunnel where her grandmother could hide, protecting her grandmother from the concentration camp in which she died.

It was as if the sorrows and horrors inflicted by the ancestors rose like bruises upon our bodies. Rachael and I slowly began to emerge from what Rachael called our 'carnival of horrors'. She brought me some Kabuki tea, suggesting I might need 'detoxing', as if subliminally aware that I had been somatically bearing her familial devastations.

Gradually her dream images of a swimming pool transmuted into something seemingly less sinister:

> I dreamed about a house being renovated. When I was asked to enter the bathroom I was scared, you know what swimming pools mean to me. But it was only a bath, and it had no water in it. It was the bottom that I remember so clearly, just concrete.
>     And I thought when I woke up: there's a shift there, because it used to be a huge Olympic pool, now it's domesticated.

Six months later she related a dream in which she was sitting by rock pools, dangling her toes in the water, enjoying the ambiguous beauty of the scene. She felt her life was now like the rock pools.

> Despite my daily struggle to keep my head above water, I'm much more confident mothering my two kids, I've begun a uni prep course and you won't believe it, I've finally met Mr Right. He's a lawyer specialising in international law and wants to marry me!

Things were going so 'swimmingly', as she put it, that she felt ready to move out of 'our pond' into the 'river of life'. It was as if we had been able to co-create a therapeutic pool side-by-side with the swimming pool of trauma, and that being implicitly present to the reality of both zones allowed for generative movement in the analytic field.

## Unto the fourth generation: the emergence of transgenerational matters

A year after Rachael finished analysis, I moved to a different city. For the sake of my patients I set up a year's transitional period of commuting between the two cities. Out of the blue Rachael rang saying she felt 'deathy' again and needed to sit with the one person she felt really knew her. Her fiancé didn't understand her moody, dark temperament. Marrying Mr Right suddenly felt like chopping off her left hand.

In our first analytic reunion, Rachael launched into a dream within a dream of a square swimming pool, filled with a huge and deep body of clear but stark, lifeless water.

> There was nothing beautiful about the pool, it's just a box. I had a flash of memory of hitting the bottom, pushing up with my legs. I shot right out of the water and soared into the sky. This was more frightening than being in a huge body of water. There I was, no parachute, just suspended in the air looking down and knowing if I fall that'll be it.

I realised that I had been naively idealistic when I accepted her decision to finish analysis, a therapeutic version of 'and they lived happily ever after'. In fact, in my absence she felt polarised between feeling manically suspended in mid-air with no emotional backing or smashed against the concrete of a swimming pool.

Rachael experienced a constant battle between the courage to be against the desire not to be:

> I almost need to get to a point where I say, 'Look Rachael, let's do life!' not, 'I can't do that because of what happened in my past'.

Yet her fatally absent mother had provided no containing environment in which 'doing life' seemed a viable proposition. It was more like being catapulted into an abyss of disintegration. Her 'deathy mode' was familiar territory and so felt safe although in fact it was a form of anti-life.

In the aching absence of both analyst and fiancé in the present, she felt mired in a claustrophobic situation as a single mother. Her propulsive reaction was wanderlust: she bought a caravan to take her children around Australia. This lust to 'wander lost' represented both a romantic idealisation of a rootless Romany world and intimations of racial persecution.

Her father stepped in again, announcing that he wasn't going to let his grandchildren go waltzing about the countryside like gypsies. Her life might be a write-off but his grandchildren should have a proper schooling.

> He asked me to send the children's birth certificates, no I mean their school reports, sorry, I get so hazy around all this!
>
> He said, 'Well they've got to come and live with me, I'm going to pay for their schooling and you won't be allowed to visit them' – as if my influence is contaminating. He was an absolute bastard, if only I could have filmed it to show you: 'Judith, this is my father!'

I wondered what 'unthought known' (Bollas, 1987) was expressed in her slip about the birth certificates. As we later realised, it revealed Rachael's introjection of her father's disavowed 'known'. That she was 'hazy' was a sign of dissociation. Rachael was suffering the fate that Lieberman observed, where the child becomes the 'carrier of the parent's unconscious fears, impulses and other repressed or disowned parts of themselves' such 'negative attributions' becoming an 'integral part of the child's sense of self' (1999, p. 737). In a bizarre twist, her father identified her as being 'contaminated' while he was the bastion of middle-class virtue. Lifton (1986) observes how perpetrators often maintain a paradoxical sense of morality by doubling thus creating an inner wall between their unspeakable acts of violence and their later highly moralistic personal lives.

Rachael finally came to exorcise such contamination by returning it to its sender.

> Why does it have to be me? I look at my Mum, and she's not carrying anything into the next generation. I'll do anything not to let it contaminate my children's lives. It's like I'm in this court of law, I have to have the answers, I have to go to the source.

When her father next came to visit, although terminally ill with cancer, he brought a new girlfriend no older than Rachael in tow.

> She waltzed in, dripping gold, rubbishing everything I was. I was reduced to a heap. I couldn't help it, you do take that stuff on. I kept making an effort to reach my Dad. I played a CD of harp music from the tiny village where he came from. She said, 'Oh this is Jewish music!' She and my father are really racist. Then she said, 'Oh she's probably got a Jewish boyfriend' and at that point, I turned around and I looked her in the eye. Time stood still, no one breathed. I turned to her and said:
>
> 'Are you just a puppet?'
>
> I can't explain, like all my anger on behalf of all the people who suffered under such racist attitudes was encapsulated in that moment. I repeated it:
>
> 'Are you a puppet?'
>
> He had never seen me stand up like this. I'm the good one who meekly sits there. She just laughed nervously. I just looked at her and said it again:
>
> 'Are you a puppet?'
>
> Each time I asked it the atmosphere got more intense. In my mind she had to say 'yes', or that fixed moment wasn't going to end, nothing was going to break the spell.
>
> Eventually she looked at me, and she said 'yes' and she sunk back into herself and was silent.

Rachael was unknowingly alluding to Hitler's puppets, and of her father being a puppet of a puppet state, as well as his girlfriend being her father's puppet mouthpiece in the present.

## The blindness of the seeing eye

After this session I felt enclosed in some opaque veil through which I peered as through a glass darkly, as if suffering a 'blindness of the seeing eye in which one knows and does not know a thing at the same time' (Freud, 1925, p. 235).

How could I expect Rachael to face what I had not been able to face? I knew I had to enter the arena represented by the empty swimming pool and not back away. After the session I sat alone and in a waking dream reverie, entered her dreamscape. I found myself behind a membrane which held back a build-up of a flood of amniotic-like fluid. It perforated. I burst through into a huge, white concrete enclosure. At the end of the enclosure was a door. I opened it and went through. I was flooded with horrendous imagery concerning drains loaded with the skeletons of dead babies, chambers piled with discarded bodies. I intuited that this shocking imagery in some way related to Rachael's paternal ancestry but not how. I felt myself vicariously immersed in a place of razor-blade cruelties and cold-blooded torture. Such images invaded my dreams and waking analytic reverie in the days following.

My waking dream reverie was an attempt to re-avow what had been denied, to break through the defences I too had adopted, such as making a neat wrap-up if not cover-up of the case. Was the membrane I broke through a metaphoric depiction of the double wall of silence Rachael had experienced in her family, replicated in the transference-countertransference dynamics of analysis? Was it symbolic of the membrane Rachael burst through, not into life, but a time tunnel into the world of the dead, a transposition 'into the world of the past, similar . . . to the spiritualist's journey into the world of the dead' (Kestenberg, 1982, p. 794).

Fonagy (1999) describes how actual imagery of unmetabolised horror may be transposed into the child's imagination. In turn such imagery was transposed into my analytic imagination. The concrete zone I entered in my reverie represented a non-metaphoric psychopathic dimension incapable of moving or being moved, leading to a sense of deadliness. It also represented an introjection of a patrilineal concrete, ruthless mind. As Grubrich-Simitis observes, 'A timeless concretism' operates in 'psychic functioning which manifests itself in the second generation' involving an inability to metaphorise (1984, p. 303).

Although it was unlikely we would ever fully know the full history there were strong indications that Rachael's father was a link in a chain of ancestral participation in atrocity. He transmitted into his daughter a split-off representation of this. Aspects of such introjections were then transmitted into me and were played out between us. The starkness of such states led me to adopt defensive manoeuvres such as making a neat wrap-up of the case.

Once I had unblinkingly faced this terrible truth, without my saying a word, Rachael herself realised it. Like watching the scattered shards of glass in a kaleidoscope suddenly cohere, all the many vital clues to her ancestry suddenly came together. It was Rachael who spoke, 'You know I've been thinking a lot about that swimming pool image. And I've been digging into the past. I found out something utterly appalling. My father was a member of the Schutzmannschaften in Reichskommissariat Ukraine. Do you know what that implies?' We sat in silence, breathing in the implications of this truth. I knew that Rachael knew, and I knew that Rachael knew that I knew, of the real possibility of his involvement in atrocity.

Realisation of the horrendous implications of her ancestry did not break Rachael apart, it brought her together, as if she were the shards of glass, each reflecting an element of the story, but only making sense when seen within the context of the whole. This was the true beginning of her individuation. She no longer had to bear alone that which her ancestors had not borne for themselves.

Once the ghostly projective identification with the hidden executioner had been shockingly revealed to both of us Rachael was able to shake off its haunting. The desire to heal the past and redeem her father's humanity continued unabated, begging another vital question:

> When does it end? Now my dad's really dying I still want to be able to throw away all the history and say let bygones be bygones, before it's too late.

Can a child of a perpetrator, themselves shockingly neglected, ever truly integrate and heal the sins of the father?

## Theoretical discussion: intergenerational transmission of the executioner's guilt

The intergenerational transmission of trauma has been discussed by many theorists, who have noted that where a traumatic past is disavowed it leads to confusion in the next generation. Such confusion is repeated in the therapy of the offspring 'when that which is not known cannot be dealt with until the secret has been exposed' (Pines, 1993, p. 205).

But what about intergenerational transmission of the executioner's disavowed guilt? Rachael's family did not discuss the past: it was a closed book. She shared a similar fate to children of post-war German society as described by Mitscherlich and Mitscherlich (1975), leading to pathologies of remembrance, inability to mourn, defences against facing intuited horrific events and psychic numbing. The silence and denial concerning her father's participation in atrocity and the gaps in family history exacerbated her own sense of unreality and 'borrowed unconscious sense of guilt' (Eickhoff, 1989).

McGrath observes a 'transgenerational transposition of trauma which is tantamount to the patient's immersion in another reality' not their own. Where the core of self is dissociated due to absence, this creates an openness to 'colonization' by the 'mental states' of the parental figure (2000, p. 127).

If a patient can be colonised by untransformed mental states of an ancestor which are thus 'unknowable' for the patient, might such states in turn be transmitted into the analyst? Had I been colonised by material originating in Rachael's father's disavowed guilt? Rachael was pervaded by a sense of intuiting more than she was conscious of. Her dreams and our moving metaphors gave ample clues, but it was as if she was awaiting my capacity to host the unthought known so the burden she was bearing could be shared. Being open to receive the full implications of the underground sub-texts in our work allowed the unthinkable to be thought and thereby known.

My countertransference disease was bystander and survivor guilt: for escaping her claustrum (Meltzer, 1992) filled with psychopathic toxicity and images of unredeemable violence. In addition to unconsciously enacting her father's rescuing her from drowning and then leaving her, had I repeated his flight from an intolerable place of ancestral history? Had I too incorporated a transposition of borrowed unconscious guilt, which, as long as it was not fully understood, was liable to being re-enacted?

Confronted with what I saw and bore, I felt profoundly ashamed. I also inherit my society's offloading of guilt. I was brought up in an educated, middle-class circumstance of peace and security. I am moved to do what I can to atone for cultural acts of historical ignorance.

## Conclusion

Rachael brought an initial dream of a swimming pool. Neither of us knew its full import, but allowed ourselves to be submerged in unknowing. The dream images became a moving metaphor which took on a life of its own, generating a language of experience that developed between us. Images emerging in her dreams became processes of symbolisation as they were poetically expressed in a shared language, transmuting from unconscious symbolisation (being used by symbols without quite knowing what was being symbolised) through to using symbols reflectively via metaphoric language that organically emerged. Her ensuing dream series, symbolic imagery and metaphors featuring pools of water and waterless pools were multivalent. There was the depiction and communication of a traumatic event in her own childhood: a suicidal near-drowning associated with her father's abandonment. The dream encapsulated a traumatic memory system repeatedly played out in her current relational and analytic life. There was symbolic imagery associated with the primal pool of amniotic fluid, the womb of life. The womb could as easily turn into a watery coffin, a deadly non-alive zone of experience. There were gestures towards the pool of life she was too terrified to enter. The moving metaphor was also a conduit for transmitting a terrible ancestral burden of guilt, the untold stories which formed the rock against which Rachael was shattered again and again.

The moving metaphor led to a re-evaluation of all that had transpired between us. The dream image of an empty concrete swimming pool represented the transposition of her father's ruthless concrete mind. He transposed into his daughter a psychic representation of his participation in torture as well as a legacy of disavowal and dissociation. Facing this dark history enabled the first signs of true aliveness to emerge, heralded in dream images of rock pools by the sea, the moving metaphors of a flowing yet safely contained, creative and related self.

Being with Rachael in our analytic crucible taught me how vital it is to be aware of the ways in which the offspring of both victims and perpetrators of trauma may inherit that which was too unimaginable for the previous generations to face. Where psychological birth implies bursting out of an amniotic sac into a torture chamber, how is life possible? Our being beside one another in such a crucible, emotionally laying ourselves on the line, opening the heart of true compassion, is a terrible yet necessarily moving aspect of analytic work. When one human being, as closely as is humanly possible, is able to take inside their heart the full weight of another person's unbearable burdens of ancestral trauma, without even knowing the full extent and import of this burden, and so enters the dark pools of another's past, this loving *participation mystique* begins to transmute terror and horror into hope. Just as the mother takes in a baby's fear of dying and anni-hilation, the analyst takes in an unknown intimation of unimaginable horror that a patient such as Rachael had no means to bear. From her first session Rachael and I both entered a shared subterranean realm of unknowing, where that which was dimly sensed was slowly revealed through nightmares, dreams and dreaming in the analytic space, through syntonic congruent forms of embodied countertransference.

Entering the imaginal world of the patient through unknowing, the story of Rachael is the story of how we both entered unknown territory. Neither of us knew where she came from or where we were going. She did not know her ances-tral history and neither did I, yet the unmetabolised nature of this history threat-ened her sanity with its undercurrents of unspeakable torture.

The apophatic dimension of psychotherapy is not abstract theory; it is the sear-ing, stark, dark, agonising experience of being with another human being through and in unknowing. We may feel expected to be experts who can formulate inter-pretations and diagnostics in order to effect a cure and so defend against the *massa confussa* with psychoanalytic theory but such false knowledge impedes rather than aids healing.

In these two cases concerning Adam and Rachael we see the apophatic at work in therapy. Adam didn't feel he was real and suffered the abject annihilating terror of non-existence the shadow side of the apophatic, negative O. Rachael and I were in a psychological cloud of unknowing, a dark night of the senses, deprived of any guiding principle of knowledge. One form of suffering concerned questions of being, the other questions of unknowing.

This is the meaning of apophatic reverie and contemplation; this is true com-passionate participation and witness. This is being with another in an actively engaged state of contemplation with faith, hope, *agapē*, intuition and compassion, forming the only sources of illumination. The commitment a therapist makes is to be there with the patient on a long path of discovery, through labyrinthine pas-sages of darkness, confusion and despair, to plumb the deep caverns where angels fear to tread, and, we hope, to emerge into new spaces of possibility and life.

## Note

1 Meares, personal communication, May 2012.

# Part Two

# A ray of divine darkness

## Psychotherapy and the apophatic way

# Chapter 9

# The trace of the infinite in the face of the other

## Lévinas' ethics of alterity

### Bobby the dog

During WW2 Emmanuel Lévinas was imprisoned just outside Hanover by the Nazis in Camp 1492. Lévinas saw himself reflected in the eyes of his captors, eyes that 'stripped us of our human skin' rendering them 'subhuman'. All that was left was a 'small inner murmur, the strength and wretchedness of persecuted people' that 'reminded us of our essence as thinking creatures, but we were no longer part of the world' (*DF*, 153).

A stray dog wandered into the camp, momentarily relieving the 'numbing inhumanity' of the camp.

> For a few short weeks, before the sentinels chased him away, a wandering dog entered our lives. One day he came to meet this rabble as we returned under guard from work. He survived in some wild patch. . . . We called him Bobby . . . as one does with a cherished dog.
>
> (*DF*, 153)

Lévinas asks:

> Are we not men? In his own way, Bobby answers: 'yes! and again, yes!' He would appear at morning assembly and was waiting for us as we returned, jumping up and down and barking in delight. For him, there was no doubt that we were men.
>
> (*DF*, 153)

Through his tail-wagging friendly greeting, Bobby, a dog, restored Lévinas' humanity.

### Psychotherapy: a relational affair?

Psychotherapy may aim towards 'self-realisation' (Jung, 1966, para 266). Yet, being inter-relational and interdependent, the path of self-realisation requires other-realisation. It also requires transcending any such dualities. It requires a capacity for alterity. Alterity is the interpersonal dimension of the apophatic. It concerns a sense of humble veneration for the sanctity of another being who comes before me face to face, who is utterly enigmatic, unknowable, vulnerable, and worthy of my care.

## Alterity undefined

Alterity[1] as a term derives etymologically from the Latin 'alter', meaning 'other', which we also find in the term 'altruism', coined by August Compt (1798–1857). Yet alterity is more than a synonym for otherness or difference. Although including awareness of otherness, respect for difference and heteropathic forms of empathy, an ethics of alterity embraces the discipline of not-knowing, or what Lévinas refers to as the philosophy of the enigma.

*Alterité* also signals the attempt to resolve the problem of casting the not-I as Other, making 'I' the central, privileged term. Since Descartes, the 'not-I' has been a philosophical concern in terms of epistemology. Adopting the term alterity aims to shift the focus from the epistemic other to the ethical relation. That is, an actual being (human, animal or divine) who is located in a particular political, cultural or religious context. There is a sense of immediacy in the other who comes before me which breaks through the various ways we seek to mediate if not control relationships through ideologies, prejudice and judgement: all of which occlude the face of the actual other, creating alienation and dualistic divisions.

There is absolute ineffability and absolute alterity, the absolutely Other (*l'absolument Autre*) to be found within oneself and without, the otherness of the self, the otherness of the other. How does one respond to others, not as 'another me', or covered with projections of our own uncanny strangeness, but as subjects in their own right, with vastly different ways of being and seeing the world?

In the context of psychotherapy, there is a need to avoid the dangers of imposing a totalising psychoanalytic model upon the patient, delivered through interpretations that assume superior knowledge. The alterity, irreplaceable uniqueness and actuality of a given patient transcends all formulations, theoretical constructs and diagnostic criteria. We need to be open, receptive to all the patient wishes to express, all that is seeking expression behind their expression and all that cannot be expressed. This expression, for Lévinas, overflows any idea or concept, yet it is also a welcoming (*accueillance*) in which 'the very epiphany of the face is produced' (*TI*, 51).

Alterity for Lévinas is more redolent of mystery, enigma, transcendence and incomprehensibility. Here we can see Lévinas as an apophatic philosopher.

## The ethical (*l'éthique*)

'The ethical' (*l'éthique*) in the context of an ethics of alterity has a specific meaning. It does not imply an ethical system, a set of moral standards, or a 'code of ethics'. It is more about recognition of the enigmatic sanctity and holiness of another human being and the responsibility such recognition invites:

You know, they often speak of ethics to describe what I do, but what interests me when all is said and done is not ethics . . . it's the holy, the holiness of the holy.

(Lévinas, in conversation with Derrida, 1999, p. 4)

## Selving and othering in philosophy and depth psychology

> Your wisdom and knowledge mislead you when you say to yourself, 'I am, and there is none besides me'.
>
> (Isaiah 47:10)

A fundamental problem that has occupied both Western philosophy and psychology is the relation of self to others. The origin of the philosophical problem derives from the conceptual primacy of a private, sovereign subject or perceiving ego. How does that self then relate to other selves? Are others similar or different? How can I know another? Or, at least, to what extent is it subjective apperception and projective, and how much is it 'objective'?

If our starting premise is a concept of an independent, autonomous, unchanging self then it inevitably makes relations with others problematic. Quoting the Russian philosopher Vladimir Solovyov, 'Egoism consists in this: absolute opposition, an impassable gulf is fixed between one's own self and other beings. I am everything to myself ... but others are nothing in themselves and become something only as a means for me...I am the centre and the world only a circumference' (1918/2010, p. 72).

Charles Taylor argues that a root cause of relational pathology is a self-centred orientation towards the world, 'relating everything to ourselves, dominating and possessing things which surround us'. It leads to a form of psychological 'slavery, a condition in which we are in turn dominated, captured by our obsessions' (1989, pp. 138–139).

The existential philosopher Gabriel Marcel (1888–1973) warns that so long as the 'ego remains shut up within itself', it has not 'awakened to reality', a reality which is relational. It is a 'prisoner of its own feelings, of its covetous desires'. A 'dull anxiety' permeates is existence (Marcel, 1945, pp. 28–29, in Moyn, 2005, p. 223). Rosenzweig (1921/2005) depicts this form of alienation chillingly:

> The same sound resounded and yet was everywhere heard only in one's own interior; no one felt the human element as the human element in others, each one only immediately in his own self. The self remained without a view beyond its walls; all that was world remained without. If it possessed the world within itself, it did so as personal property, not as world. . . . The ethical norms of the world thus lost all their own meaning in this field of vision of the self-willed self; they became the mere content of his self-inspection.
>
> (Rosenzweig, 1921/2005, p. 91)

## Philosophical solutions to the problem of solipsism and individualism

Lévinas is an inheritor of the legacy of philosophical attempts to address the problem of the isolated mind. The absolute of subjective idealism of absolute idealism, Hegel's historicism, Schopenhauer's inference of the partial knowing of the unknowable reality of the thing-in-itself (extrapolated from subjectively embodied experience of the Will) and Nietzsche's will-to-power were all motivated by a need to transcend the idea of the solitary and disembodied self. Yet attempts to resolve the problem of solipsism from within the confines of subjective idealism lead to being trapped within a hall of mirrors.

Phenomenology prior to Heidegger also floundered over inherently solipsistic assumptions. Heidegger's solution to solipsism and the problem of the isolated mind was to postulate that we are primordially *with others* already and that care and *Mitsein* (being-with) is more primordial than *Dasein* (being-in-the-world). Yet Heidegger wedded his concept of co-being and 'heedful being-with-one-another' with National Socialism, recasting ethics as a post-metaphysical form of 'dwelling' in the homeland. This reinforced a communal politics of *Kampf, Volk* and *Heimat* (struggle, folk and homeland) (Bambach, 2007, p. 210). Consequently the other as foreigner was out-ed from his realm of the 'originary'. Furthermore, for Heidegger, the other person is but part of the crowd that surrounds me and limits my freedom. Lévinas observed that Heidegger's increasing over-emphasis on ontological formulations had a direct bearing on his chilling perversion of his own important insights.

Continental philosophy after Heidegger, particularly that of Merleau-Ponty, Buber and Lévinas, sought to overturn the tyranny of the isolated subject, by recourse to love, the mutuality of self and other (I-thou relations) and by completely turning the question of the relationship of self and others around and starting with otherness itself.

'In the beginning is relation' (Buber, 1923, p. 32), pre-empting relational currents in psychoanalysis. Buber's solution was to begin with relationship, the interhuman spaces between people and the 'I-thou' subject-to-subject encounter, rather than 'I-It' where the other is treated as a thing or object. 'I require a You to become; becoming I, I say You. All actual life is encounter' (Buber, 1970, p. 62).

## Lévinas: subjectivity is founded in the idea of infinity

Rather than starting with the self, Lévinas starts with the other. The other is not a threat, except to my unmitigated power, autonomous freedom and narcissism. An ethics of alterity puts into question the 'liberty, spontaneity and cognitive emprise of the ego . . . that seeks to reduce all otherness to itself' (Critchley, 2002, p. 15). 'The focus is a relationship of respect and responsibility for the other person' rather than presumption of reciprocity. Here Lévinas departs from Buber, for whom the

I-thou infers a 'symmetrical co-presence'. Lévinas said, 'I must always demand more of myself than of the other; and this is why I disagree with Buber's description of the I-thou ethical relation as a symmetrical copresence'. He saw such 'essential asymmetry' as the 'very basis of ethics' (Lévinas and Kearney, 1986, p. 31).

Lévinas presents 'a defence of subjectivity' but one that is not based on ego-centrism but as 'founded in the idea of infinity' (*TI*, 26). The human being, in having 'an idea of infinity', is by definition, a 'thought which contains more than can be thought' (Lévinas, 1987a, p. 54). This phrase is an allusion to the third of Descartes' Meditations (1664)[2] concerning the relation between the *res cogitans* and the infinity of God. Here we have parallels between Bion's O, which cannot be known, and the apophatic mystical tradition. In recognising the unknowable incomprehensibility of the other, yet also recognising the ethical relation to the other, there is a relation of inequality, non-reciprocity and asymmetry. The other always exceeds and escapes any concept.

For Lévinas, alterity intimates encounter with infinity itself. Although such encounter is 'utterly resistant to the solipsism of the transcendental Ego' it does not endanger or annihilate the subject, but on the contrary enables its constitution' (Davis, 1996, p. 39). If I orient myself towards traces of the infinite in the other it points toward the infinite itself. This outward flowing orientation into the world of others and beyond them to the infinite itself, frees me from the horrifying isolation of solipsism.

For Heidegger the other becomes absorbed into the self via *Mitsein*. For Sartre the other is a threat, creating a 'little particular crack in my universe' stealing the world from me (Wright, 1991, p. 31). For Lévinas the relationship with the other implies peace and non-violence:

> The face in which the other – the absolutely other – presents himself does not negate. . . . It remains commensurate with him who welcomes; it remains terrestrial. This presentation is pre-eminently non-violence, for instead of offending my freedom it calls it to responsibility and founds it. As non-violence it nonetheless maintains the plurality of the same and the other. It is peace.
>
> (*TI*, 203)

## Lévinas: ethics precedes ontology

> *la philosophie: sagesse de l'amour au service de l'amour* (AE, 207) Philosophy is the wisdom of love at the service of love.
>
> (Lévinas, *OB*, 162)

Central to the philosophy of Lévinas is the idea that ethics precedes ontology. Ethical responsibility towards beings precedes how we conceptualise being, that is, the 'hungering, thirsting, suffering' human being in all his or her corporality (Waldenfels, 2002, p. 65). Bobby the dog did not need a degree in ontology to lick the hand of Lévinas and so restore his humanity. Lévinas did not need to *know* Bobby, only to *respond* as one being to another being welcoming him with loving kindness and friendliness.

From this perspective, concern for beings and how we ethically relate to beings is prior to concerns about being and how we conceptualise it. This is not that being does not matter since being and beings are on a continuum. Lévinas felt that such ethical priority had been ignored by Western philosophy, from Plato to Hegel and Husserl and on to Heidegger, through over-preoccupation with ontology, a prioritising of 'the Same' (*le Même*) over the alterity of the Other (*l'Autre*), as well as attempts to reduce 'the Other to the Same' through a relationship of knowledge (*TI*, 43). Such 'ontological' and epistemological 'imperialism' has the purpose of 'offsetting the shock of alterity' leading to a form of egology (Davis, 1996, p. 40).

In a psychological sense the ethics of how we respond to the call of the other who comes before us, face to face, has an ontological dimension as a mover of psychological becoming. We confirm the other in their being by how we respond to their implicit statement 'Here I am'. If we disregard or misapprehend them, they may feel unreal. If we narcissistically expect them to accommodate themselves to our reality they may feel a coercion to comply, fearing rejection and expulsion.

Lévinas suggests that self comes into being through recognition of the other and that we become substantial through being subject to the ethical call of the other for our solicitude and care. Here he is playing on the words subject, subjectivity and substantial. Subjectivity is not based on egocentrism but as 'founded in the idea of infinity' (*TI*, 26).

Metaphysical, theological and philosophical concepts 'remain empty and formal frameworks' 'without the signification they draw from ethics. . . . It is from moral relationships that every metaphysical affirmation takes on a "spiritual" meaning' (*TI*, 79).

## Totalisation and fundamentalism

Lévinas was deeply concerned with the ways in which Western civilisation has been dominated by a striving for totalisation and reduction of all phenomena to a spurious unity or sameness.

Attempts at totalisation may use different methods to achieve its aim – assimilation, incorporation, conversion or homogenisation – and when this fails, expulsion, if not obliteration. Lévinas believed there is a direct correlation between totalitarian violence, fundamentalism and over-emphasis on totalising forms of ontology and ideology when such totalisation leads to a failure to apprehend others as beings in their own right. In extreme they may be treated as non-entities, to be ignored, exploited or annihilated. He warns that we damage our own subjectivity and humanity by doing so.

## The apophatic in Lévinas

> When in the presence of the Other, I say 'Here I am!' This 'Here I am!' is the place through which the Infinite enters into language, but without giving itself to be seen.
>
> (*EI*, 106)

Lévinas engages in apophatic languages of unsaying in such pronouncements as '*The other qua other is the Other*' ('*L'Autre en tant qu'autre est Autrui*') (*TI*, 71). Here alterity resonates with apophatic epistemology. Lévinas suggests any theology is too positive. 'God reveals himself as absence rather than presence' (1986, p. 32). Lévinas, when referring to God, 'frequently writes *à-Dieu* (to-God) rather than *Dieu* in order to avoid the implication that the noun refers to a substance with separate existence. Instead God is to be *approached* but never reached' (Davis, 1996, p. 98).

Words such as transcendence, exteriority, infinity, the other, alterity and ethics are used with deceptive simplicity, poetically, almost like koans, to shift their associations from philosophical investigation towards a realisation beyond the reaches of philosophical enquiry.

## Face to face (*le face à face*)

> The welcoming of the face is peaceable from the first, for it answers to the unquenching Desire for Infinity.
>
> (*TI*, 150)

Lévinas held that ethics begins in apprehending the face of the other. The face-to-face encounter is iconic of a relational context in which ethical responsiveness towards another's inviolable yet unknowable mystery is primordial. The face-to-face relation (*le face à face*) is an epiphany of holiness, inviolability and vulnerability. It is a revelation of the invisible in the visible, the manifestation of infinity in the finitude of the being of beings.

The immediacy of the face paradoxically reveals hiddenness – defying categorisation, representation or comprehension: 'the encounter with a face which at once gives and conceals the other' (*TO*, 78–79). The face of the actual other transcends the mere idea I have of the other: 'The way in which the Other presents himself, exceeding *the idea of the Other in* me, we here name face' (*TI*, 50).

The face of the other does not threaten to negate our self; it 'gives a proper foundation to freedom. The transcendental Ego would like to be the sole source of its own knowledge, actions and meanings; the encounter with the Other shows such freedom to be' narcissistic and erroneous (Davis, 1996, p. 49).

Such bestowal of freedom grants the possibility of creative expansion beyond the narrow horizons of insular systems of belief, liberation from the strictures of egocentrism, a brush with eternity: 'The Infinite comes in the signifyingness of the face. The face *signifies* the infinite' (*EI*, 105). Paradoxically, encounter with the irreducible otherness of the other frees us from solipsism because it shows the other is separate, independent, different and not a figment of my idealistic fantasy. This is implicit in Winnicott's tracing of the observation that it is through the mother's capacity to survive the baby's destructiveness that the baby makes the transition from treating mother as an extension of itself to an externally perceived, separate person, an other.

Lévinas also observed that it is very difficult to kill someone you truly look at face to face.

> The first word of the face is . . . 'Thou shalt not kill'. . . . [*tu ne tueras point*]. There is a commandment in the appearance of the face, as if a master spoke to me. However, at the same time, the face of the Other is destitute; it is the poor for whom I can do all and to whom I owe all. And me, whoever I may be, but as a 'first person', I am he who finds the resources to respond to the call.
>
> (*EI*, 89)

## The saying (*le Dire*) and the said (*le Dit*)

The face of the other transcends knowledge, yet it belongs to someone with whom I am engaged in conversation. Lévinas makes a distinction between 'the saying' (*le Dire*) and 'the said' (*le Dit*). Before the face of the other 'I do not remain simply contemplating it, I respond to it. The saying is a way of greeting the Other. . . . It is difficult to be silent in someone's presence' for their vulnerability invites response (*EI*, 88). The ethical choice is to welcome the other, to share their world by speaking to them, using a form of language where there is a readiness to listen without prejudice, an openness, where 'I am never sure just what he will say, and there is always room for reinterpretation and spontaneity on both sides' (Wild, 1969, p. 14).

In essence this points to the ways in which language, whose purpose is to communicate, also falls short of the mark when it comes to alterity. Just as the word 'apophatic' means 'away from saying', a key phrase for Lévinas is 'a saying that must also be unsaid'. Lévinas was acutely aware of the apophatic problem of attempts to describe the indescribable. He deliberately uses enigmatic, at times fragmented and repetitive language where any saying 'is in the necessity of unsaying itself' (*EI*, 107). First, the very words that attempt to convey meaning are the same words that endanger the meaning behind the expression being conveyed. Second, saying is always intersubjective and part of the present moment: once uttered it is part of the past, the 'said'. Lévinas uses terms such as 'expression', 'invocation' and 'prayer'.

He cites Socrates in Plato's *Phaedrus* who preferred conversational speech to the written word because spoken speech is intersubjective and dialogically relational. Saying is something happening here and now between you and me. Further the written word 'being unable to defend . . . itself', can all too easily be misinterpreted (in Davis, 1996, p. 37).

Lévinas and Bion both employ language which is congruent with what they are pointing towards, truths that may be conveyed but cannot be contained in words. Saying is always inter-subjectively responsive and dialogic. The said is like a monologue that leaves no room for the other to speak, interrupt or disrupt.

## The trace of infinity

When I respond to the primordial call of the alterity of the other with a concomitant out-flowing of welcome, this leads to true self-liberation, that is, liberation from the strictures of egocentrism. We realise our own subjectivity through recognition of both the humanity and the alterity of the other, which in turn is a trace of the infinity of God. Such ethical responsiveness bestows true subjectivity, true freedom and true enjoyment: we can cry out, as did Abraham, 'Here I am!' (*heneni*).

> When in the presence of the Other, I say 'Here I am!', this 'Here I am!' is the place through which the Infinite enters into language, but without giving itself to be seen.
>
> (*EI*, 106)

Such 'exigency of holiness' is an opening beyond limitation, a manifestation of the infinite. Although such manifestation of the infinite is not something that can be 'thematised', represented or comprehended, 'the subject who says "Here I am"' in response to the 'illeity' of the Infinite, '*testifies* to the Infinite. It is through this testimony whose truth is not the truth of representation or perception, that the revelation of the Infinite occurs' (*EI*, 106).

A trace of the infinite also implies something beyond, transcendent, utterly Other, the Otherness of God. Here is Lévinas' third. The gesture of homage to the sanctity of the other passes beyond the other to the infinite itself, yet without losing the interpersonal dimension. Through the trace of infinity in you, I intuit the infinite without losing sight of you. Nor, in considering my ethical relation to you, do I lose sight of other others, for whom I am an other (*OB*, 158). Lévinas is also aware of a world of other others outside my relationship with my neighbour, thus extending consideration of ethical responsibility and bringing in the notion of the third. Lévinas increasingly uses the term 'neighbour' (*prochain*) instead of the more abstract 'The Other' (*Autrui*) to emphasise the proximity of a real person rather than abstract principle (Davis, 1996, p. 82).

## The third (*le tiers*)

Lévinas considers the ethical relation with the alterity of another human being who comes before me face to face. But this person is also an other to others. This other to the other is the third (*le tiers*). My neighbour is a neighbour to the third party.

> The third party is other than the neighbour, but also another neighbour, and also a neighbour of the Other, and not simply his fellow. What then are the

other and the third party for one another? The other stands in a relationship with the third party, for whom I cannot entirely answer, even if I alone answer, before any question, for my neighbour.

(*OB*, 157)

Lévinas cites Isaiah, 'Peace, peace to the neighbour and the other one far-off' (Isaiah 57:19), as showing how the third also brings in the question of justice and its relationship to conscience, consciousness and co-existence (*OB*, 157).

Just as Lévinas describes the primal responsibility I have towards the other, so too in therapy my first concern is my ethical relationship towards the patient. This ethical relationship takes place within an intersubjective field-as-third. According to Ogden, the relationship gives rise to a third subject, which 'stands in dialectical tension with the separate, individual subjectivities of analyst and analysand in such a way that the individual subjectivities and the third create, negate, and preserve one another' (1994, p. 5). In an analytic relationship, the notion of individual subjectivity and the idea of a co-created third subject are devoid of meaning except in relation to one another.

Alterity itself could be considered as a third. If alterity is the trace of the infinite in the other, then alterity has as its source, infinity itself. I often think of the analytic third as like a 'still quiet voice' that arrives, unbidden, hidden and inspiring yet requiring a stillness, a receptivity, to be intuited.

## The asymmetry of the ethical relationship

For Lévinas, my subjectivity arises out of the obligation to assume responsibility for the other. This 'essential asymmetry' is the 'very basis of ethics' (*DEL* 31) producing 'a curvature of intersubjective space' (*TI*, 291). Lévinas does not impose his ethic on anyone but himself. The I who is responsible and 'from whom the Other might require substitution and sacrifice' is only me and no one else (*OB*, 126).

Lévinas' focus on the responsibility that 'I have towards the Other' without expectation of reciprocity has sometimes been interpreted as a one-sided exhortation to self-effacement. On the contrary:

The Other precisely reveals himself in his alterity not in a shock negating the I, but as the primordial phenomenon of gentleness.

(*TI*, 150)

Altruistic response to alterity restores my true face through freeing me from the isolation of solipsism. Self comes into being through recognition of the trace of infinity, the trace of God, the mystery of being that is refracted through *L'Autri*. When we encounter the other and respond welcomingly to their alterity we enhance our own humanity, our participation in the world, our intimation of infinity beyond us.

The therapeutic relationship is also asymmetric: the focus of care and responsibility is towards the patient. We take care to not impose our own needs upon the patient, nor expect acknowledgement or gratitude. No patient fits neatly into preconceived formulae, models or diagnostic straight jackets. Each patient and every analysis is as unique as the patient is. This was recognised by Jung, who wrote, 'Psychotherapy and analysis are as varied as are human individuals. I treat every patient as individually as possible, because the solution to the problem is always an individual one' (1963, p. 130). He said, 'I am unsystematic very much by intention' since 'in dealing with individuals, only individual understanding will do' (1963, p. 131). He also commented that the analyst must 'guard against falling into any specific routine approach' and also 'guard against theoretical assumptions' (1963, p. 131).

Perhaps we have cast the issue of the relations between self and others from the wrong starting point. For example, in response to claims that psychoanalysis is dying, Jonathan Lear suggests that the question is not whether psychoanalysis is obsolete 'but whether the individual is. The commitment to the individual is a tradition in the West, and psychoanalysis is itself a manifestation of that commitment'. The debate about individualism is a false debate because it assumes we are individuals. 'Are we?' Lear asks (1990, pp. 18–19).

## The development of a capacity for alterity

How does a child come to appreciate alterity, uncertainty and unpredictability? How does a child intuitively imagine the emotional states of others, their inner worlds and experience 'the problem of other minds'? A capacity for alterity develops from having care-givers who were receptive to a child's ever-changing alterity. Such parents are able to enjoy the child's unique 'spontaneous gestures' of the true self, rather than expecting the child to conform to their expectations and world view. In other words, for a child to develop a capacity for alterity, the child's parents had to have had a capacity for alterity.

When a child fears disapproval, distain or anger in place of being valued, the child retreats. In the case of reverse mirroring the child receives the unconscious demand to mirror the parent, the unspoken message, 'Don't be yourself: be my unknown and unfulfilled needs. You are here to become my existence, my identity; you must not exist for yourself' (Clark, 1983, p. 75).

'Adam' was never able to be angry, be a naughty 2-year-old, stamp his foot, say, 'No!' lest a withering look of utter disapprobation left Adam cowering, shivering and withered if not obliterated.

Any signs of being a rambunctious child with his own personhood, desires and proclivities were not even disapproved of, they were ignored. He felt a continual tug-of-war between his desire to be himself and a need for recognition. He loved painting and expressed his emotions through the medium of colour. 'I cannot believe', he told me, 'that no one in the family ever once even commented on my huge murals. Eventually I simply gave up'.

According to Winnicott, mother's capacity to attune and attend to her baby is, at first, so close that the baby almost believes that mother is an extension of its own mind, that is, a subjectively conceived object. Gradually, over time, mother misses the mark just a little, and this creates slight cracks in the seamlessness of the baby's subjective universe. The baby becomes more able to tolerate the paradox of being neither one entity nor entirely separate.

A baby has aggressive fantasies involving destruction of mother. Her survival leads to the realisation that mother is not simply a figment of the baby's imagination, that she has an existence beyond the baby's mind:

> The subject says, 'Hello object. I destroyed you. I love you. You have value for me because of your survival of my destruction of you. While I am loving you I am all the time destroying you in unconscious fantasy'.
>
> (Winnicott, 1971, p. 105)

The baby asserts its own agency and separate identity, and does so through temper tantrums, foot stamping and the famous 'no' word. Eventually the baby develops a desire for reparation and 'ruth' (Winnicott reclaimed the original meaning of 'ruth' meaning care). Prior to this, relations are based on ruthless love; there is little consideration for pain inflicted on the other as another being. Yet this stage is vital, for without it the baby may develop an overly compliant false self. If a child's authentic spontaneous gestures are validated and encouraged, a child grows in confidence. The child is paradoxically more able to empathise with the parent's joys and sorrows, their separate experience and alterity, without feeling threatened. The child comes to recognise the other as a whole person, overcomes the problem of other minds, distinguishes otherness within from otherness without and enjoys, rather than fears, the unpredictable, ever-changing and inter-relational dynamics of being alive.

## Qualifications

There are vital distinctions to be made when discussing Lévinas' ethics of alterity. An encounter with the other represents a primordial ethical moment, but this does not necessarily imply that we *will* respond ethically. However hard we try to deny or obliterate the alterity of another, alterity itself cannot be destroyed. Even when citing the Judeo-Christian commandment 'Thou shalt not kill', Lévinas suggests that the commandment is paradoxical. The other can be killed but not their alterity. 'Lévinas does not tell us that we *should not* kill the Other; he tells us rather that the Other [in their inviolable alterilty] *cannot* be killed' (Davis, 1996, p. 50).

So too, Behrouzin Boochani's *No Friend but the Mountain: Writing from Manus Prison* is a testament to the triumph of the freedom of the human spirit over physical imprisonment. As an asylum seeker detained without charge, conviction or sentence on Manus Island, he proclaims that Australia may have imprisoned his body, but his spirit remains free.

## Conclusion

Lévinas directs our gaze towards the holiness of the other in their unknowable, ineffable mystery. This is ordinary as well as extraordinary. It is in the actuality of our everyday, messy, unpredictable and confusing relationships with others that we come face to face with each other and ourselves, with our ever-changing elusive being, our alterity. The humanity of another may challenge my egocentrism, but this liberates me from the alienation of solipsism. The ethics of alterity inspires altruistic love. Lévinas describes how in authentic love relations neither self nor other are abolished, both are confirmed because the other is desired as other, not an other reduced to the same.

## Notes

1  In regard to problems of translation, Lévinas differentiates two terms for 'other' in French. *l'Autre* refers to the 'other' as non-personalised other, usually translated with lower case 'other', and the personalised *l'Autrui*, the Other, distinguished in English with upper case. Lévinas uses various terms all translated in English as 'other' (*Autre, autre, Autrui*) and is not always consistent. Lévinas scholars have tended to capitalise Other when referring to the human other and lower case other when referring to otherness in general. The term *autrui* usually means the 'personal other' and *autre* otherness or alterity. But sometimes *Autre* refers to God. Alterity is deliberately used to differentiate the sense of enigma from difference as in Derrida's *Différance* (a deliberately homophonic misspelling of difference).

2  Lévinas isolates the movement of Descartes' thought as follows: first the 'subject confirms its own existence as beyond doubt' in the Cogito. Second the 'subject proves to itself the existence of God and thus finds itself to be created by something which transcends it' (Davis, 1996, p. 39).

# Chapter 10

# The origins of the apophatic way

## Introduction

'Eve' lies on the couch, her eyes half-closed. She has bought her diary but does not open it. From time to time she alludes to its contents, but she does not trust anyone enough to confide her deepest longings. She continues to find people disappointing. All significant people in her life have failed to make the appointment with her reality. Her parents were caught up in the quotidian concerns of middle-class life. Her art teacher was more concerned with kudos than the deeper spiritual meaning of art. She suspects that I too am only interested in treating her mental health issues, her capacity to work and to have fulfilling relationships, not questions of meaning and spirituality. She stirs and begins to speak:

> All this is well and good, this slow progress I've been making in therapy. Psychologically I am so much more stable than when I first came to see you, I'm building up my life as an artist. I have more friends. But underneath there is still something fundamentally wrong. A sense of uneasiness is eating away at me that I am not being true to the inner essence of why I am here on this earth. There must be more to therapy than holding down a job and getting on better with people?
>
> When I was 16 and depressed I left school and volunteered on an aid project in Uganda. I went through terrible times. It was harrowing, not just the extreme poverty, but psychologically I was a mess. But at least I felt that I was more in tune with some inner sense of purpose. I just want to go to some wild remote place away from it all, until I have clarity about what truly all this is about.

I respond:

> You feel drawn to finding a way to follow your true destiny, to go for the bull's eye. You are not sure how. Being an artist is part of the process but is not the goal itself. You sense there is more to it all.

What is the goal of therapy? Is it to enable patients to heal all that has wounded them, to help loosen the psychological binds preventing them from achieving their highest potentialities? Is it to identify and cut through the tangled thickets of illusions and delusions and so uncover their true nature? Is it to enable human flourishing, self-knowledge, and well-being? What is the role of religious or philosophical questions concerning the meaning of life and ultimate truth? Is meaning given, intrinsic or made?

For Freud, the goal of therapy is the capacity to love and to work. For Jung it is the realisation of self through the process of individuation: 'The self is our life's goal' (*CWVII*, para. 404). For many psychoanalysts it is to 'know thyself'. For Bion, the ultimate aim of analysis is the search for truth and being that which is real (Bion, 1965, p. 148).

The apophatic tradition is radical in seeking the meaning of life through unknowing, un-finding and relinquishing false certitudes. An essential element of the apophatic way is not self-knowledge but *agnōsia* is a form of true gnosis. In order to be united with the unknowable One loses oneself, stands outside oneself and suffers apophasis of the self.

I am deliberately using the word 'way' in conjunction with the term 'apophatic'. This 'way' towards at-one-ment with ultimate reality is through unsaying, where language is used to defeat language, opening the mind to a reality beyond our conceptual mind.

The goal of life for the apophatic mystics is realisation of a natural and inherent divinity effected through continuous love of the unknown 'God and of things divine' (*EH* 1 376A). Love of God 'moves us towards the divine', and the

> sacred enactment of the divine command brings about in unspeakable fashion our divine existence. And divinisation is to have a divine birth. No one could understand, let alone put into practice, the truths received from God if he did not have a divine beginning.
>
> (*EH* 2 392B)

The spiritual path is a return to the One, however one might undefine that One. Related to the theme of divinisation through union with God, is union with one another. It is not possible to attain union with the One whilst divided among each another (*EH* 3.8 437A). An apophatic might then expand Freud's goals of work and love as the work towards union with the unknowable absolute and love of all unknowable beings.

The next four chapters trace the history of the apophatic way in the Western tradition, relating the apophatic to the practice of psychoanalysis. I will show the extent to which Bion was inspired by the apophatic tradition through the authors he quotes, such as the anonymous author of *The Cloud of Unknowing*, John of the Cross and Meister Eckhart. This chapter forms an introduction and early history, Chapter 11 focuses on Dionysius, Chapter 12 the later apophatic mystics and Chapter 13 the practice of contemplation in apophatic Christian mysticism.

## Relevance for psychotherapy and the search for the meaning of life

The search for a deeper meaning has inspired countless mystics and philosophers throughout history who observed that material and hedonistic pursuits do not bring lasting satisfaction. For example Hilary of Poitiers (310–368) writes:

> I began the search for the meaning of life. At first I was attracted by riches and leisure. . . . But most people discover that human nature wants something better to do than just gormandize and kill time. They have been given life in order to achieve something worth while, to make use of their talents. It could not have been given them without some benefit in eternity. . . .
>
> Then I sought to know God better . . . I discovered that God bears witness to himself in these terms: 'I AM who I am,' . . . I was filled with wonder at this perfect definition which translates into intelligible words the incomprehensible knowledge of God.
>
> (Hilary of Poitiers in Clément, 1993, pp. 18–19)

So too, many people feel a sense of dissatisfaction until they uncover a core sense of truth and purpose. In Buddhist teaching beings are tossed around in *saṃsāra* until they discover the profound natural great peace and clarity when their mind is brought home to its real nature. In a Christian formulation they are 'restless until they rest in God'. Dionysius continually returns to the theme that all beings

> must desire, must yearn for, must love, the Beautiful and the Good . . . each bestirs itself and all are stirred to do and to will whatever it is they do and will because of the yearning for the Beautiful and the Good.

According to the apophatic mystics, the inability to comprehend absolute reality is due to the very incomprehensibility of the absolute. This alterity is linked to the incomprehensible alterity of oneself. In the analytic context, the implication is that the alterity of the patient is linked to their godliness, and their ineffable godliness is linked to the ineffable alterity of God, the Divine, the absolute, the thing-in-itself, O. Yet patients such as Eve ask us: How might they discover and incarnate this truth in their own way for themselves?

## The apophatic way: definitions and etymology

The apophatic way is so called due to an intimation that at-one-ment with ultimate reality is found through negation of mental ideas based on the conceptual mind. Apophatic, meaning unsaying or negation, comes from the Greek *apophasis*, literally 'saying no' or 'saying negatively'. *Phasis* comes from *phemi* which means to speak or assert. *Apo* means 'from' or 'away' and so it could be translated as 'away from saying' or non-assertion. Such unsaying is in the service of mystical union with unknowable, unspeakable and transcendent divinity. By negating names and constructs we clear space for the mystery to dawn within us, for true revelation (*apophaino*) or enlightenment, for union with the divine.

In the fourth century BC *apophasis* was used as a legal term meaning 'special investigation', a 'showing forth', a 'declaration' referring to the procedure of investigation, report or prosecution in relation to threats to Athenian democracy, whereby a report or special investigation (*apophasis*) would be presented to the *ekklesia*, giving its recommendations for prosecution and so forth (Cartledge et al., 2002, p. 217). Aristotle applied the term to logic, as one of the two logical categories: affirmation (*kataphasis*) and denial (*apophasis*).

> An *affirmation* (*kataphasis*) is a statement (*apophansis*) affirming something of something, a *negation* (*apophasis*) is a statement (*apophansis*) denying something of something.
>
> (Aristotle, *Int.* vi 17a 25–26, in Lameer, 1994, p. 76)

The kataphatic denotes affirmative strands of mysticism: *kataphatikos* meaning 'saying' or 'affirming'. The apophatic mystics continually juxtapose the *kataphatikē* as being towards speech and *apophatikē* as away from speech, pairing assertions with denials, affirmations with negations, procession with return, knowing with unknowing and words with silence. All such pairings are put to the service of being able to reach beyond such pairs to a non-duality that transcends them. For Dionysius, kataphatic theologies descend from affirmations about the being of God, through the incarnation, to the concepts we use of God and the images that scripture applies to him. The further we descend with kataphatic theology, following the way of procession, the more verbose our explanations become. When we trace the way of return, the way of apophatic theology, speech fails.

## Common themes found on the apophatic way

### Apophatic epistemology

A central principle of much Greek and Neoplatonic thought is 'that to be is to be intelligible'. Being, or 'that which is' (*tò ón*), 'can be apprehended by intellection' (*nóēsis*) (Perl, 2007, p. 5). However, for the apophatic philosophers, the source of reality, the One (*hen*), is beyond being and cannot be comprehended by intellection. Plato wrote that 'the One has no name, nor is there any description (*logos*) or knowledge (*epistēmē*) or perception (*aisthēsis*) or opinion (*doxa*) of it. . . . And it is neither named nor described nor thought nor known, nor does any existing thing perceive it' (142A, in McGinn, 1991, p. 33). For Plato the One as absolute is beyond being (*ousia*) but does reveal itself 'to the *nous* in the philosopher's soul in a form of direct intuition' as *nóēsis*. Such intuition is not cognition, but realisation 'of a potential identity between the Absolute' and the absolute within the human being (Dodds, 1928, p. 141).

The Christian apophatic mystics suggest that God is shrouded in the darkness of unknowing and that ineffable, dark unknowing is the way towards divinising union with the source of all, and that the person is also fundamentally shrouded in mystery. How might this relate to the psychoanalytic aim of attaining self-knowledge and making the unconscious conscious?

Unknowing in the apophatic tradition is a form of apophatic epistemology. Recognition of unknowing is an aspect of true knowing, which is always an active verb, experiential and not a static piece of stale knowledge. Apophatic contemplation is an active spiritual discipline in which the inconceivable presence of God breaks through all affirmations and negations, leading to divinisation with God beyond being through unknowing. This is sometimes described as a 'knowing beyond knowing' (*excessus mentis*).

Meister Eckhart advised us to 'be in a state of forgetting and not knowing and it will be revealed' (in Vermote, 2011, p. 355). A refrain was 'willing nothing, knowing nothing, and having nothing' (Meister Eckhart in Sells, 1994, p. 181).

Where Christian apophatic theology concerns itself with the One, the God beyond being and the spiritual search for union with the unknowable Godhead, Bion uses the word O as a symbol unsaturated with preconceptions, to denote absolute truth. Going back to these sources shows that apophatic mysticism permeates Bion's writings about O and being without memory, desire and understanding. Bion draws on apophatic mystics such as Meister Eckhart, John Ruysbroeck and St John of the Cross, all of whom were influenced by Dionysius in their mystical theology. He frequently refers to Freud's quotation 'a beam of intense darkness' which in fact derives from *The Mystical Theology* of Dionysius. This takes analysis right into the heart of apophatic practice. The analyst sits with the patient in a state of contemplation, empty of memory, desire, understanding and comprehension, undistracted, tranquil, emanating compassion, radiating pure presence, generosity of spirit and loving kindness. The analyst may be agnostic as to whether patients should seek to discover such a state of contemplation for themselves, but nevertheless the analyst's state of mind remains a vital element of healing. This relates to the theme of whether psychotherapy could be considered a form of spiritual practice for the therapist, regardless of the patient's spiritual leanings. On the other hand, the analyst who can dwell in a state of contemplation will be more able to rise to the challenge of meeting spiritual questions poised explicitly or implicitly by patients.

## Apophatic anthropology: union of the unknown self with the unknown Godhead

How we view self and the search for our true self is a very different trajectory in contemporary times than it was in the times of Dionysius. The early Greek and pre-medieval notion of self is 'collective and extensive, sharing a common consciousness with other selves . . . and embracing as well the forms of the things of the external world known to it' (Trinkaus, 2000, pp. xix–xx).

Apophatic theology is a form of apophatic mystical anthropology, the *via negativa* a form of spiritual practice enabling one to realise the non-duality of divine and human subjectivity. Purged of all that the mind can perceive, imagine, conceive, the mystic who enters the divine gloom in a state of nakedness and emptiness, becomes a receptive receptacle for the inflow of divine alterity. Just as the ultimate is beyond all affirmation and all negation, the self is beyond all definitions and all negations. Apophatic mystical practice involves freeing the self as well as God from constructs that obscure divinity, shedding oneself of all knowing in the service of being 'uplifted to the ray of the divine shadow'. Further 'this ascent to the luminous, divine darkness also requires that we stand outside ourselves, that we suffer ecstasy' (Stang, 2009, p. 42). Unknowing the self clears space not only for God but the indwelling of the other (Stang, 2012, p. 204).

For Dionysius, union with the 'God beyond Being' takes place through a continual process of 'unknowing' (*agnōsia*) (Stang, 2012, p. 2).

> Dionysius' entire mystical theology narrates the self's efforts to unite with the 'God beyond being' as a perpetual process of affirming (*kataphasis*) and negating (*apophasis*) the divine names, on the conviction that only by contemplating and then 'clearing away' (*aphaeresis*) all of our concepts and categories can we clear a space for the divine to descend free of idolatrous accretions.

Through ascending to the unknowable Godhead, the self is 'cleared away of its own names, unsaid, rendered unknown to itself – in other words, *no longer I*'. Stang argues this amounts to a form of apophatic anthropology in which the apophatic way becomes 'an exercise of freeing the self as much as God from the concepts and categories that prevent its deification' (Stang, 2012, p. 3). To be united with the unknowable God, one must become less than unknown. Union involves self-naughting, self-emptying, *kenosis*.

## The nameless

> But Moses said to God, 'If I come to the Israelites and say to them, "The God of your ancestors has sent me to you", and they ask me, "What is his name?" what shall I say to them?' God said to Moses, 'I am who I am.' He said further, 'Thus you shall say to the Israelites, "I am has sent me to you"'.
>
> (Exodus 3: 13–14)

A central dilemma for all apophatic theology is how to name the nameless. For the Hebrews God's ineffability and inscrutability means that God's name is inutterable. Dionysius also wrote that the Godhead is nameless (*DN* 1.6 596A). Dionysius poses the question: how can one 'investigate the meaning of the Divine

Names, when the superessential Deity is shewn to be without Name, and above Name?' (*DN* 1.4 593A, in Stang, 2012, p. 120). The Divine Names can only be written about 'in a manner surpassing speech and knowledge' since 'the unknowing of what is beyond being (*hyperousiotetos agnousia*) is something above and beyond speech, mind, or being itself' (*DN* 1.1 588A).

The One is invisible, inscrutable and untraceable, and no one can penetrate its hidden infinitude (*DN* 1.2 588C). The 'Light beyond all divinity' is identical with 'the Nameless Itself' (*anonymon autēn*). It is beyond imagination, discourse, conception and conjecture, 'being, rest, dwelling, unity, limit, infinity, the totality of existence' (*DN* 1.5 593C–593D).

For Meister Eckhart too, the self is nameless, the finest names are 'telling lies' for the self is 'free of all names', 'bare of all forms, wholly empty and free, as God . . . is empty and free' (*Sermon 2, Intravit Jesus* in Turner, 1995, p. 141).

Apophatic mystics use the way of unsaying and paradox to point to the relationship between the self and God:

> He gives birth not only to me, his Son, but he gives birth to me as himself and himself as me and to me as his being and nature. In the innermost source, there I spring out in the Holy Spirit, where there is one life and one being and one work.
>
> (Meister Eckhart, in Harmless, 2008, p. 120)

### Limits of language

> What is to be said of it remains unsayable; what is to be understood of it remains unknowable.
>
> (Dionysius, *Ep.3* 1069B)

There is a paradox regarding the attempt to find language to describe the indescribable. If ultimate reality is inexpressible, language has no direct access to it. Yet language is deliberately used to unsay itself. The Advaita Vedānta, Prajñāpāramitā, Dzogchen, Dionysius, other apophatic Christian mystics, Bion and Lévinas all concur that ultimate reality is beyond description, yet nevertheless language is used to convey this impossibility. The language of the *via negativa* is used to undo itself in the service of transmitting glimpses of that reality beyond language. Enigmatic symbols, negations (*aphaireseis*) and denials are used to point to what lies beyond speech. What is extraordinary about the apophatic language of those like Dionysius is that the very paradoxes and negations have the potential to shock us out of the ordinary conceptual mind into the ineffable realisation of the absolute. Language points beyond itself, and the paradox removes mental constructs that obstruct direct vision of the absolute. Transcendence contains an *aporia*, an unresolvable dilemma. Plotinus wrote: 'We find ourselves in an *aporia*, in agony over how to speak. We speak of the unsayable (*au rhētou*); wishing to signify it as best we can, we name it' (in Sells, 1994, p. 16). Proclus wrote, 'Language when conversant with that which is ineffable, being subverted about itself has no cessation and opposes itself' (*Platonic Theology* 2.10, in Stang, 2012, p. 130). Sells writes that 'apophasis is a discourse in which any single proposition is acknowledged as falsifying, as reifying. It is a discourse of double propositions, in which meaning is generated through the tension between saying and unsaying' (1994, p. 12). He sees this as part of a 'guiding semantic force' that is characteristic of apophatic mysticism, that searches for an absolute reality which 'slips continually back beyond each effort to name it or even to deny its unnameability' (1994, p. 2). As Webb and Sells explain:

> Apophatic language uses double propositions – no single proposition on its own can be true or false, can be a meaningful utterance. In the tension between two propositions, meaning can occur. The meaning is fleeting. The language-conditioned mind tends to fix (or fixate) upon the second proposition as if it were meaningful in itself. Ever-new critical propositions are needed to keep meaning from reifying into a fixed image.
>
> (1995, p. 199)

Sells also differentiates between apophatic *theory* which 'affirms the ultimate ineffability of the transcendent' and apophatic *discourse* in which 'unnameability is not only asserted but performed' (1994, p. 3). Sells delineates three features of apophatic writing in the Classical Western tradition:

> (1) the metaphor of overflowing or 'emanation' which is often in creative tension with the language of intentional, demiurgic creation; (2) dis-ontological discursive effort to avoid reifying the transcendent as an 'entity' or 'being' or 'thing'; (3) a distinctive dialectic of transcendence and immanence in which the utterly transcendent is revealed as the utterly immanent.
>
> (1994, p. 6)

Ultimate reality transcends language, name and form, yet Dionysius does not avoid attempting to find language to describe the indescribable. Tomasic describes his methodology as using 'collision statements', which dialectically combine contrary predicates, negations of negations and even affirmation and negation of contradictory predicates (Tomasic in McGinn, 1991, p. 176). Dionysius advocates a ceaseless negation of negation: 'It is beyond assertion and denial . . . it is free of every limitation, beyond every limitation; it is also beyond every denial' (*MT* 5 1048B). God is not just ineffable but beyond ineffability, not just unknowable but beyond unknowing, not just incomprehensible but beyond incomprehensibility. Negative theology ultimately leads to 'the absolute silence of the mind' (Perl, 2007, p. 14).

So too, the Buddhist school of philosophy known as Prāsaṅgika Mādhyamika used what are called non-affirming negations. A non-affirming negation is a negation which does not leave something in the place of what has been negated. For Dionysius language collapses under the weight of internal contradictions and so passes over into the silence of eternity. The higher one proceeds to the transcendent, the more language fails, until it becomes silently one with the indescribable One (*MT* 3 1033C). Meister Eckhart also 'twists the discourse, breaks it up, recomposes it . . . he will use speech, necessarily broken, contradictory, absurd, paradoxical, conceptually hyperbolic speech, to bring to insight the ineffability of God' (Turner, 1995, p. 151).

Likewise Bion seeks to purge psychoanalytic language of the 'trammels imposed by the penumbra' of sensuous associations that accrue to psychoanalytic terminology (1965, p. 138), instead coining linguistic symbols such as O and alpha function which are 'intentionally devoid of meaning' (Bion, 1962, p. 3). For Bion, language is inadequate when it comes to representing 'that aspect of the human personality' and of the One, the Alpha and the Omega, 'that is concerned with the unknown and ultimately unknowable – with O' (Bion, 1970, p. 88).

### Nothingness and union with the One

Union with God beyond being is not just a state of unknowing but an encounter with no-thing-ness: knowing nothing, having nothing, desiring nothing. In the darkness of unknowing there is direct encounter with that One beyond all being. For Eckhart, union with the Godhead in the soul occurs in a state of nothingness, when the person gives up reliance on image, imagination and mentation, and the deity is divested of properties and attributes (Sells, 1994, p. 12).

Nothingness can denote both emptiness and meaninglessness. Yet it can also point to a transcendent experience of ineffability. Psychologically, for patients such as Adam (who we met in Chapter 7), nothingness is experienced as persecutory annihilation, a horrifying state of non-being, a psychic black hole. How we experience nothingness relates to how our early care-givers mediated, metabolised and transformed existential terrors, rendering bearable what we could not initially bear. In turn this leads to the gradual development of a sense of on-going being, a capacity to tolerate the frustration of uncertainty that enhances a capacity for creativity, and perhaps for some, an apophatic sensibility.

In mysticism nothingness requires *kenosis* and renunciation of ego, as well as a capacity to bear absence, emptiness and boundlessness. This requires courage, grace, faith and love. Psychologically the mystic also needs to have found sufficient containment of nameless dread. Rigid fundamentalist ideologies may be used defensively to ward off the anguish of uncertainty. We can see that the no-thing-ness of mysticism requires psychological maturity, such that it is an experience of 'primal emptiness' awaiting realisation, rather than primal meaninglessness. No-thing-ness is either experienced as an opening to pristine plenitude of infinity possibility or a 'black hole' filled with 'tormenting nothingness paradoxically mixed with nameless dread, the decathected chards or residues of abandoned meaning' (Grotstein, 1990, p. 267).

For Bion there is a distinction between nothingness related to meaninglessness and no-thing-ness related to the meaningful ineffable. No-thing-ness is 'the matrix or "ether" of primary meaninglessness and is the emptiness which must be experienced in order for meaningful experience to be realized' (Grotstein, 1990, p. 268). Nothingness in a negative sense refers to 'negation of being' and 'negation of meaning' when there is a failure to tolerate absence, separation and gaps, leading to a 'default into the disintegrative nothingness of the "black-hole"' (Grotstein, 1990, p. 270). Paradoxically, as Stevens points out, a capacity to contemplate absence and emptiness leads 'to the ability to give meaning to experience' (2005, p. 622). So too, embracing the emptiness of self in both Buddhist and Christian apophatic approaches is an experience of awakening and realisation, a manifestation of one's deepest being and a liberation from the constricting cage of ego.

## Early history of the apophatic

The history of the *via negativa* or apophatic way is generally traced through Plato (428/427–348/347 BCE) to Plotinus (204/5–270 CE). Apophasis is also found in the synthesis of Platonic and Hebraic traditions in the work of the Jewish philosopher Philo of Alexandria (15/10 BCE–45/50 CE). Philo's themes of transcendence and immanence were taken up by the early church fathers and mothers, inspiring the negative theology of Gregory of Nyssa, as well as Plotinus. Plotinus held that the unlimited is beyond being (*epekeina ontos*).

### Proclus

Proclus of Athens (410 or 412–85 CE) was also influenced by Plotinus. Platonists such as Plotinus and Proclus discovered an apophatic strand in the Platonic dialogues. Proclus distinguishes two ways that the One can be revealed as being through analogy and negation. The first is 'through analogy (*di' analogias*) and through likeness to what is posterior'. In the second way 'through negation (*dia ton apophaseon*)' the transcendence of the One' over everything can be shown (Proclus, in Louth, 2012, p. 139). Proclus also distinguished between the *via affirmativa* and the *via negativa* in the epistemological approach to God (Mondello, 2010, p. 31).

We are reminded that negations are not simple contradictions of kataphatic affirmations; apophatic and kataphatic theology complement each other. Proclus warns against the dangers of misinterpreting the negations (*apophaseis*) as privations (*stereseis*), 'or the analogies as identities', as this will impede the 'journey which raises us to the first principle'.

According to Proclus, 'every effect remains (*monē*) in its cause, proceeds (*proodos*) from it, and returns (*epistrophē*) to it' (Proclus, 1963, p. 38). Apophatic and kataphatic are related to procession and return, 'procession corresponding to apophatic theology and return corresponding to cataphatic theology' (Louth, 2012, p. 140).

### Clement of Alexandra (150–215 CE)

Clement of Alexandria wove a rich tapestry of Hellenistic, Jewish and Christian thought that also influenced the Cappadocians, particularly Basil of Caesarea (329–379), his brother Gregory of Nyssa (335–394) and Gregory of Nazianzus (330–389). All such strands were later taken up and further synthesised by Dionysius in Syria in the early sixth century.

For Clement divine love is the core of Christianity. His non-duality is based on the Platonic relation between simple and complex unity, of there being one in the other and the other in the one, such as the Father in the Son and the Son in the Father. Clement also follows the apophatic in suggesting that nothing can be predicated of God who has no limit, no form and no name. Clement uses the term *mystikos* to describe the 'secret modes of manifestation of the hidden divine reality in scripture, rite, and prayer' (McGinn, 1991, p. 171).

### John Chrysostom (347–407 CE)

John Chrysostom wrote a series of sermons called *On the Incomprehensibility of God* which describe God as shrouded in incomprehensibility. He also describes the 'fearful wonder' and sense of vertigo attendant upon realising this incomprehensibility.

> His judgements are inscrutable, his ways are unsearchable, his peace surpasses all understanding, his gift is indescribable, what God has prepared for those who love him has not entered into the heart of man, his greatness has no bound, his understanding is infinite.
>
> (Chrysostom, 1982, pp. 57–58)

### Gregory of Nyssa (about 335–395 CE)

At the heart of the negative theology of Gregory of Nyssa is the relationship between the radical alterity and the unknowable Godhead and the profound intimacy of our relationship with this transcendent, uncreated and unbegotten God. For Gregory the purpose of apophasis is to progressively lay aside inappropriate depictions of the trinity who share an essence that is ineffable (Stang, 2013, p. 168).

Just as Dionysius and Gallus were to do later, Gregory of Nyssa takes Moses' ascent of Mount Sinai as an allegory of mystical theology or apophatic epistemology in which all sensory perception, intellection and other attempts to know God are to be abandoned. Moses, having ascended Mount Sinai, declares 'that he had seen God in the darkness' 'beyond all knowledge and comprehension, for the text says, *Moses approached the dark cloud where God was*' (Exod., 20,21). So the mystic leaves 'behind everything that is observed, not only what sense comprehends but also what the intelligence thinks it sees' and 'keeps on penetrating deeper until' it:

gains access to the invisible and the incomprehensible, and there it sees God. This is the true knowledge of what is sought; this is the seeing which consists in not seeing, because that which is sought transcends all knowledge, being separated on all sides by incomprehensibility as by a kind of darkness.

(Gregory of Nyssa, 1978, pp. 94–95)

As we shall see, Bion's negative epistemology has its antecedents in such apophatic epistemology as expressed by apophatic mystics. Bion's application of Keats' 'negative capability' and being able to dwell 'in uncertainties, mysteries, doubts' (Keats, 1817, in Bion, 1970, p. 125), is related to apophatic epistemology: the ability to seek union with ultimate reality through unknowing. In approaching the absolute reality of O, we actively lay aside all preconception, intellectual mentation, ideas and desires to approach that which is beyond knowing.

# Chapter 11

# The apophatic mysticism
# of Dionysius

## Who was Dionysius?

The identity, location and date of Dionysius, also called pseudo-Dionysius or pseudo-Dionysius the Areopagite, are shrouded in mystery. It is probable that he was a Syrian monk writing in the late fifth and early sixth century who took on the pseudonym of a disciple of Paul. As recorded in Acts 17:23, this disciple, in his speech to the court of the Areopagus, invoked the 'unknown God' (*agnōstos theos*): 'That which you therefore worship through unknowing, this I proclaim to you' (in Stang, 2012, p. 118). This pseudonym sets the scene for a mystical theology based on worshipping the unknowable God through unknowing. According to Stang, the pseudonym itself is intimately related to apophatic anthropology. Pseudonymity for Dionysius is:

> an ecstatic devotional practice in the service of the apophasis of the self, and thereby of soliciting deifying union with the unknown God. . . . Pseudonymous writing is for our author a practice that stretches the self to the point that it splits, renders the self unsaid, that is, unseated from its knowing centre, unknown to itself and so better placed, because displaced, to suffer union with 'Him, Who has placed darkness as His hiding-place'.
>
> (2012, p. 204)

The earliest known reference to the works of Dionysius was in 532 in a record of a conference between followers of the decrees of the Council of Chalcedon (451) and followers of Severus of Antioch (465–538). The extant[1] *Corpus Dionysiacum*[2] consists of four treatises and ten letters: *The Divine Names* (*DN*), *The Mystical Theology* (*MT*), *The Celestial Hierarchy* (*CH*), The *Ecclesiastical Hierarchy* (*EH*) and the *Letters*. In the following I will be drawing out themes that are relevant to an apophatic spirituality of psychotherapy. Quotations from the *Corpus Dionysiacum* are included in order to make key selections from Dionysius' oeuvre available to the reader not familiar with Dionysius. His writings, even in translation, have an almost poetic mystical power to evoke intimations of the states being described. I will outline key principles and terms such as the three-fold mystical path consisting of purification, illumination and union; unknowing and the *via negativa*; denial, kataphasis and apophasis, and their relationship to the Neoplatonic triad of procession, return and remaining; the metaphors of hiddenness, darkness, illumination, light and shadow; uplifting; transcendence; the role of scripture and liturgy; hierarchy; *erōs*; ecstasy; union; divinisation; and the clinical relevance of Dionysius.

## The Mystical Theology

Dionysius opens *The Mystical Theology* (Greek: *Peri mustikes theologias*, Latin: *De mystica theologia*) with a prayer that God will 'lead us up beyond unknowing (*hyperagnouston*)' (*MT* 1.1 997A) and a plea to 'strive upward as much as you can toward union (*henōsin*) with him who is beyond all being and knowledge (*agnoustous*)' (*MT* 1.1 997B). Invoking the trinity as beyond being, it begins with the theme of divine darkness:

> O Trinity
> beyond being
> beyond divinity,
> beyond goodness, and
> guide of Christians in divine wisdom,
> direct us to the mystical summits
> more than unknown and beyond light,
> There the simple, absolved, and
> unchanged mysteries of theology
> lie hidden in the darkness beyond light
> of the hidden mystical silence,
> there, in the greatest darkness,
> that beyond all that is most evident
> exceedingly illuminates the sightless intellects.
> There, in the wholly imperceptible and invisible,
> that beyond all that is most evident
> fills to overflowing the sightless intellects
> With the glories beyond all beauty.
> (*MT* 1.1 997A-B in Jones, 2011, p. 211)

Dionysius prays that his addressee, a certain 'Timothy', should abandon all sense perceptions, all conceptual knowledge, all understanding, 'all that is not and all that is', and strive for union with the divine darkness of God, beyond all being and beyond all knowledge, so as to 'be uplifted to the ray of the divine shadow'.

> This is my prayer.
> And you, dear Timothy,
> in the earnest exercise of mystical contemplation, abandon

all sensation and all intellectual activities,
all that is sensed and intelligible,
and all non-beings and all beings.
Thus you will be unknowingly be elevated,
as far as possible,
to the unity with that beyond all being and knowledge.
By the irrepressible and absolving ecstasis
of yourself and of all,
absolved from all, and
going away from all,
you will be purely raised up
to the rays of the divine darkness
beyond being.
       (*MT* 1.1 997B-1000A in Jones, 2011, pp. 211–212)

Embedded in this prayer is the essence of Dionysius' apophatic mystical teaching. This teaching is one involving the practice of self-abandonment to God, eschewing ordinary ways of knowing such as knowledge gained through the senses, intellect and rationality, transcending both being and non-being, the ecstasy of renouncing self and all that is not God, all inadequate and false ways of knowing and being, plunging into the rays of divine darkness beyond being.

## Purification, illumination, union

Dionysius depicts Moses' ascent of Mount Sinai as the archetype in describing the mystic assent to the Godhead. He outlines three stages in this process: purification (*katharsis*), illumination or contemplation (*theōria*) and union (*henōsis*). This three-fold division had its antecedents in Gregory of Nyssa and was taken up by later Christian mystics as the three-fold way of mysticism: the purgative, illuminative and unitive. The way of purification was ascetical, the illuminative that of intellectual contemplation and the unitive that of infused contemplation leading to union with God. For Dionysius all three are successive apophatic stages relating to the passage from sensory perception to intellect and finally towards deifying union in total darkness beyond all perception, intellection and knowledge.

Moses submits to every form of purification and separates himself, representing the first stage of *katharsis*. He then enters the second stage, *theōria*, and 'hears the many-voiced trumpets' and 'beholds many lights'. Moving past the crowds, sounds of trumpets and lights, he 'arrives at the summit of the divine ascents'. Yet 'he still meets not with God, for he sees not Him – since he is not to be seen – but the place where He stands'. This is 'the highest and most divine of the things which are seen and grasped by intuitive knowing . . . through which His Presence is indicated which is above any conception' (*MT* 1.3 1000C-1A, in Golitzin, 2013, p. 38). Moses then ascends further, entering the third stage, *henōsis*, where through darkness, cloud and silence, he 'plunges into the truly mystical darkness of unknowing' (*MT* 1.3 1001A). He is 'supremely united by a completely unknowing inactivity of all knowledge' (*MT* 1.3 1001A). Entering the 'gloom of unknowing', a 'gloom of the *Agnosia*', Moses realises that he is 'wholly of Him Who is beyond all' (*MT* 1.3 1001A, in Stang, 2012, p. 137).[3]

> And then, abandoning both what is seen and those who see them, he enters the truly secret darkness of unknowing . . . and enters into Him Who is altogether untouchable and invisible and beyond all things. Beyond all things, and belonging to nothing else, whether to himself or to any other, he is, in accordance with what is greater and by a complete cessation of all his own activity of knowing, united to Him Who is wholly unknowable, and by knowing nothing, knows in a manner beyond intellect.
>
> (*MT* 1.3 1000C-1A, in Golitzin, 2013, pp. 38–39)

According to Dionysius the mystical path involves surrendering the conceptual mind in successive stages in order to reach union with ultimate reality. In such a union, inspired by divine love (*erōs*), borne of mystical ecstasy (*ekstasis*), we are 'taken wholly out of ourselves' (*DN* 7.1 867–868A). Through plunging 'into the truly mysterious darkness of unknowing' (*MT* 1.3. 1001A in Stang, 2012, p. 204), we become one with the Unknown One. Not 'seeing and not knowing' is 'veritably to see and to know and to celebrate superessentially the Superessential, through the abstraction of all existing things' (*MT* 1.3 1001A, in Stang, 2012, p. 138).

Apophatic purification involves renouncing 'all perceptions open to knowledge' so as to come to have one's being in God who 'is altogether untouchable and invisible and beyond all things'. Belonging to no one, neither oneself or another, one comes to be united to a greater faculty of contemplation 'by the cessation of all knowledge'. 'Through knowing not at all' one 'knows in a manner beyond mind' (*MT* 1.3 1000D-10001A in Golitzin, 2013, p. 228).

## *Unknowing* (agnōsia, agnousia, agnoustos, agnoustous, hyperagnoustos)

Unknowing for Dionysius is not simply lack of knowledge but the realisation that God is beyond being and therefore is beyond the limits of human comprehension, and that it is through unknowing that we attain union with the unknowable One. The One is 'the unknown (*agnouston*) . . . beyond all unknowing (*hyperagnoustou*) and . . . unknowable (*agnoustoi*)' (*DN* 1.5 593B). 'For if all knowledges are of beings and have their limit in beings, that which is beyond all being also transcends all knowledge' (*DN* 1.4 593A, in Perl, 2007, p. 13).

Such unknowing is central to contemplation, in which sensory perception, desire, imagination and reason are surrendered as the soul draws ever closer to God in a state of darkness. In *The Divine Names* Dionysius describes unknowing as an understanding beyond being:

> Since the unknowing of what is beyond being is something above and beyond speech, mind, or being itself, one should ascribe to it an understanding

beyond being. . . . Just as the senses can neither grasp nor perceive the things of the mind, just as representation and shape cannot take in the simple and the shapeless, just as corporal form cannot lay hold of the intangible and incorporeal, by the same standard of truth beings are surpassed by the infinity beyond being, intelligences by that oneness which is beyond intelligence. . . . Mind beyond mind, word beyond speech, it is gathered up by no discourse, by no intuition, by no name. It is and it is as no other being is. Cause of all existence, and therefore itself transcending existence, it alone could give an authoritative account of what it really is.

(*DN* 1.1 588AC)

All false modes of knowing that obstruct realisation of the God beyond being and beyond knowing must be cleared away:

[The Cause of all is] manifested without veil and in truth, to those alone who pass through both all things consecrated and pure, and ascend above every ascent of all holy summits, and leave behind all divine lights and sounds, and heavenly words, and enter into the gloom, where really is, as the Oracles say, He Who is beyond all.

(*MT* 1.3 1000C in Stang, 2012, p. 160)

The 'superessential Deity' is 'without Name, and above Name' and is 'superior to every expression and every knowledge, and is altogether placed above mind and essence'. While embracing, uniting, comprehending and anticipating all things, it is 'altogether incomprehensible to all'. There is 'neither perception nor imagination, nor surmise, nor name, nor expression, nor contact, nor science' (*DN* 1.4 593A, in Stang, 2012, p. 120).

Likewise Bion advises us to have 'faith that there is an ultimate reality and truth – the unknown, unknowable, "formless infinite"' (1970, p. 31). Faith needs to be 'unstained by any element of memory or desire' (Bion, 1970, p. 32). At-one-ment is a return to our original at-one-ment, in a state of unknowing beyond memory, desire or understanding, eschewing all that is derived from the world of perceptions and conceptions. Bion continually reminds us of the unknowable ultimate reality, the 'thing-in-itself' (*Ding an sich*) lies beyond knowledge and perception. 'The dominant feature of a session is the unknown personality and not what the analysand or analyst thinks he knows' (1970, p. 87). But further than this, O, which cannot be known, is something one aspires to be at-one with.

## Via negativa

If the One is beyond all comprehension, all names and all attributes, then negation is one of the ways to clear away all that delimits and constricts true realisation of the One. Whereas in affirmative theology analogies are used to describe God from what is perceived, in negative theology,

as we plunge into that darkness which is beyond intellect, we shall find ourselves not simply running short of words but actually speechless and unknowing . . . the more [my argument] climbs the more language falters, and when
it has passed up and beyond the ascent, it will turn silent completely, since it
will finally be at one with him who is indescribable.

(MT 3 1033BC)

Yet even negation must be negated. In Chapter Five of The Mystical Theology
Dionysius observes that the Cause is beyond both affirmative and negative theology, beyond assertion and denial. It is non-dual:

We therefore say that the universal Cause, which is situated beyond the whole
universe, is neither matter . . . nor body; that has neither figure or form, nor
quality nor mass; that it is not in any place, that it defies all apprehension
by the senses. . . . Rising higher, we now say that this Cause is neither soul
nor intelligence . . . that it can be neither expressed nor conceived, that it
has neither number nor order, nor greatness, nor littleness, nor equality, nor
inequality, nor likeness, nor unlikeness . . . that it is neither essence nor per-
petuity, . . . it eludes all reasoning, all nomenclature, all knowing . . . nothing
can be asserted of it and absolutely nothing denied . . . all affirmation remains
on this side of the transcendence of him who is divested of everything and
stands beyond everything.

(MT 5 1048A-1048B in Clément, 1993, pp. 30–31)

By not seeing and by unknowing (ablepsias kai agnosias) one attains that which
is above seeing and above knowledge (MT 2 1025B). God is above both intellect and being, and so is only known beyond intellect by total unknowing (Ep.1
1065AB).

## Denial (aphaeresis)

Another term Dionysius uses is aphaeresis or denial. It is found in such paradoxical statements as 'Denial (aphaeresis) of all beings' praises 'the Light
beyond all deity' (DN 1.5 593C). Like the reductio ad absurdum of the Buddhist philosophical school Prāsaṅgika Mādhyamika, such practice of denial
shocks one out of the conceptual mind, giving rise to a glimpse of that which
is beyond mind. Here the term aphaeresis is used in the service of clearing
aside all predicates of God, a form of negative abstraction towards illuminative
revelation and union with God so that through denying all that is not God, 'we
may unhiddenly know that unknowing which itself is hidden from all those
possessed of knowing amid all beings' (MT 2 1025B).

Through stripping away all predicates, aphaeresis leads to direct revelation
through unknowing (agnōsia), 'And this quite positively complete unknowing is
knowledge of him who is above everything that is known' (Ep. 11065AB).

It is beyond assertion (*thesis*) and denial (*aphaeresis*). We make assertions (*theseis*) and denials (*aphaeresis*) of what is next to it, but never of it, for it is both beyond every assertion, being the perfect and unique cause of all things, and by virtue of its preeminently simple and absolute nature, free of every limitation beyond every limitation; it is also beyond every denial (*aphairesin*).

(*MT* 5 1048B)

The purpose of denial is to point towards transcendence by negating all that is not the One: 'Every affirmation regarding Jesus' love for humanity has the force of a negation (*apophaseous*) pointing towards transcendence' (*Ep*.4 1072B). Such 'unknowing' is a transcendent knowing indeed.

## *Kataphasis* and *apophasis*, procession, return and remaining

Dionysius takes the Neoplatonic pairing of procession-return but switches them so that the kataphatic represents procession and the apophatic the return to the source. There is a triad consisting of *kataphasis, apophasis* and *ekstasis* relating to the Neoplatonic triad of *monē, proodos* and *epistrophē* (remaining, proceeding and returning). *Erōs* is the energy inspiring all three. Yearning for the One as a cyclical process of procession and return, which

> starts out from the Good, reaches down to the lowliest creation, returns then in due order through all the stages back to the Good, and thus turns from itself and through itself and upon itself and toward itself in an everlasting circle.
>
> (*DN* 3.17 713D)

God also 'remains' (*monē*) while overflowing into creation. Kataphatic and apophatic are interdependent and qualify each other:

> God is known both through knowing and through unknowing. . . . He is nothing of what is, and therefore cannot be known through anything that is; and yet he is all in all. He is nothing in anything; and yet he is known by all in all, at the same time as he is not known by anything in anything . . . the way of knowing God that is most worthy of him is to know him through unknowing, in a union that rises above all intellect.
>
> (*DN* 7.2 872AB in Clément, 1993, p. 231)

Negations (*apophaseis*) are not 'simply the opposites of the affirmations', nor are they to be regarded as in any way superior. The Cause of all is beyond privation, beyond both denial (*aphairesein*) and assertion (*MT* 1.2 1000B). The means for indwelling union with the divine is through a process of affirming then negating the Divine Names, negating the negation and transcending any such dichotomy.

The interdependence of the kataphatic and apophatic, the affirmative and nega-tive, and the immanent and transcendent gives rise to a third way that transcends all such paired opposites. In later thought these three ways were known as the *via affirmationis*, *via negationis* and *via eminentiae*.

The goal of all affirmations and negations is that 'without veil, we may know that *agnōsia* which is enshrouded under all the known, in all things that be' (*MT* 2 1025B, in Stang, 2012, p. 138). This is relevant to Bion's search for what he describes as unsaturated ways to denote absolute truth, free of accretions and saturated ways of knowing, and of his thesis that we cannot know O but we can become it through a process of 'at-one-ment' with the Godhead, through 'incarnation of a part of an independent Person, wholly outside the personality' (1965, p. 139).

## Hiddenness, darkness, illumination, light, shadow

Just as the kataphatic and apophatic condition each other in a circle of interdepen-dence, negative metaphors such as darkness, hiddenness, shadow and blindness are juxtaposed with positive metaphors such as light, illumination and sight. The apophatic way leads one to the darkness of unknowing in which one is blinded by divine light. The

> Divine gloom is the unapproachable light in which God is said to dwell. And in this gloom, invisible indeed, on account of its surpassing brightness, and unapproachable on account of the excess of the super-essential stream of light, enters every one deemed worth to know and to see God, by the very fact of neither seeing nor knowing, really entering in Him, Who is above vision and knowledge.
>
> (*Ep. 5* 1073A, in Stang, 2012, pp. 122–123)

Darkness does not mean an absence of light in the sense of deprivation but in the sense that the 'darkness' of God is beyond light.

> I pray we could come to this darkness so far above light! If only we lacked sight and knowledge so as to see, so as to know, unseeing and unknowing, that which lies beyond all vision and knowledge. For this would be really to see and to know: to praise the Transcendent One in a transcending way, namely through the denial of all beings.
>
> (*MT* 2 1025B)

Mystical experience is often described by mystics in terms of the symbolism of light and illumination, conjoined with that of darkness, such as 'luminous darkness', 'beam of intense darkness'. God communicates through a 'transcen-dent outpouring of light', a light which is 'invisible because of its superabundant clarity, and unapproachable because of its transcendent outpouring of light'

(*Ep.* 5 1073A in Golitzin, 2013, p. 42). Maximus the Confessor (580–662) took up the theme of light as a dazzling darkness, a darkness beyond radiance (*hyperphotos gnophos*). The Byzantine mystics such as Symeon the New Theologian (949–1022) and the Hesychasts of Mount Athos such as Gregory Palamas (1296–1359) likewise drew on Dionysius' theme of uncreated light. Bion observes that 'many mystics express their experience of direct access to the deity in terms of light' (1970, p. 81).

## Uplifting (*anagou, anagoge*) and symbolic theology

Dionysius uses the terms *anagou* and *anagoge*, translated as 'uplifting', to describe the anagogical element in the interpretation of symbols, whereby one is first uplifted from the realm of sensory perception to conceptual perception, then beyond all conception to the realm of the inconceivable (Rorem, 1993, p. 186). Dionysius describes a three-fold process of ascent from symbolic theology to kataphatic theology to apophatic theology. In the first perceptible symbols are used so as to be raised through analogy towards the kataphatic conceptions symbolised. After turning to the kataphatic theology concerning the names of God such as wisdom, being, life, truth and so forth, we then go by the way of apophatic theology, in which we 'leave behind us all our own notions of the divine' and 'call a halt to the activities of our minds and . . . approach the ray which transcends being' (*DN* 1.4 592D). Symbols are used by Dionysius to refer to the sensible representations of God in scripture and liturgy.

> We make use of elements and symbols and words and writings and reasonings for the sake of the senses, but when our soul is moved by its intellective powers towards intelligible things, the senses together with sensible things become superfluous as do, indeed the intellective powers themselves, once the soul, having arrived at the likeness of God, is impelled by an unknown union to the rays of the light unapproachable by means of sightless impulsions.
>
> (*DN* 4.2 708D, in Golitzin, 2013, p. 131)

We ascend from symbols based on sensory perception and images to intellect and then to unknowing. Being both similar and dissimilar, symbols both reveal and conceal that which they symbolise. To reveal God is to conceal God. Ultimately symbols have to be transcended, as no form of cognition, even symbolic, can reveal God. 'We take away all things . . . so that we may unhiddenly . . . know that unknowing which is hidden . . . by all that is known in all beings, and may see the darkness beyond being which is concealed by all light in beings' (*MT* 2, 1025B in Perl, 2007, p. 105).[4]

Symbols, metaphors, images and analogies are a vital aspect of both kataphatic theology and psychoanalysis. The potential space of therapy and the analyst's capacity for reverie, for unknowing and negative capability help the patient to move beyond concrete literalism to symbolisation. Symbolic thinking enables the patient to enter a realm of uncertainty and openness to ambiguity, multiplicity and new possibilities rather than be mired in fixed, static literalism and rigid beliefs about themselves and their world. Yet the symbol is not to be reified or grasped at. Like a finger pointing to the moon one looks to where the finger points and does not grasp the finger.

## Transcendence (*exaireou, epekeina*)

Transcendence can take two forms: epistemological and ontological. One transcends the knowing mind but the One also transcends being. The One transcends both being and knowledge, since 'whatever transcends (*epekeina*) being must also transcend (*exeremene*) knowledge' (*DN* 1.4 593A). Two Greek terms are used by Dionysius to depict the transcendence of the One, *exaireou* and *epekeina*. The One transcends, 'surpasses by far (*exairemene*) every sacred thing' (*CH* 3.1 165C). The 'Godhead transcends (*exeretai*) and surpasses every real and every conceivable power' (*DN* 8.1 889C). Another word that is often translated as transcendent or beyond is *epekeina*, found in such phrases as: 'It's supremely individual identity beyond (*epekeina*) all that is, its oneness beyond (*epekeina*) the source of oneness' (*DN* 2.3 641A), or 'When talking of that peace which transcends (*epekeina*) all things, let it be spoken of as ineffable and unknowable' (*DN* 11.1 949B). Yet God is also immanent, descending 'by means of an ecstatic and super-essential power while remaining within itself' (*DN* 4.13 712B in Golitzin, 2013, p. 63) and by so doing, enabling us to become at one with the One.

## Saying the unsayable: scripture as revelation

For Dionysius, both scripture and liturgy serve as vehicles transmitting revelation and disclosing the 'hidden, transcendent God' (*DN* 1.1 588C). 'In the scriptures the Deity has benevolently taught us that understanding and direct contemplation of itself is inaccessible to beings, since it actually surpasses being' (*DN* 1.1 588C). Dionysius quotes Romans 11:33 that the divinity is 'unsearchable and inscrutable'. Yet the Good is not 'absolutely incommunicable', for it reveals a 'transcendent beam' drawing mystics to contemplation and to be 'unswervingly' raised upward towards the 'ray which enlightens them' (*DN* 1.2 588D-589A).

## Hierarchy (*hierarchia*)

In *The Ecclesiastical Hierarchy* Dionysius created the abstract noun *hierarchy* from *hierarch* to refer to a system for channelling (sourcing) the sacred. The purpose of hierarchy is 'to enable beings to be as like as possible to God at to be at one with him' (*CH* 3.2 165A in McGinn, 1991, p. 165). It is deification and 'the assimilation and union, as far as attainable, with God' (*CH* 3.2 165A in Stang, 2012, p. 102). This in turn makes us 'co-workers with God', allowing the work of God to move through us into creation. The word 'hierarch', meaning 'source (*arche*) of the sacred (*hieros*)', was used prior to Dionysius in non-Christian contexts to refer to the leader of sacred ritual (Rorem, 1993, p. 21). Hierarchy for Dionysius encompasses order, understanding and activity: 'In my opinion, a hierarchy is a sacred order (*taxis hiera*), an understanding (*epistēmē*), and an activity (*energeia*) being approximated as closely as possible to the divine' (*CH* 3.1 164D in Stang, 2012, p. 2).

## Erōs: love of God, love of all beings

*Erōs* is the energy of interconnection between God and beings leading to a cycle of procession and return consisting of God's procession into creation and our return to God who is our true self. God's presence is 'in all things' and God's going out is his going in. God is the self of all things (Perl, 2007, p. 47). Through love one becomes ecstatic, going out of oneself into the beloved. 'The divine love is ecstatic, not allowing lovers to belong to themselves, but to those beloved' (*DN* 4.13, 712A in Perl, 2007, p. 47).

Recognition of interdependence and our place in the whole enables the work of God (*theurgy*) to flow through creation. So too, out of love God moves through all creation.

> The very cause of all things, by the beautiful and good love of all things, through excess of erotic goodness, becomes out of himself . . . in his providences towards all beings, and is as it were enticed by goodness and affection . . . and love and is led down, from above all things and beyond all things, to in all things . . . according to an ecstatic power beyond being, without going out from himself.
>
> (*DN* 4.13 712B, in Perl, 2007, p. 46)

Each person must make an active choice to become co-workers with God. Such cooperation is a process of divinisation wherein we attain union with the Source of all. It involves stripping ourselves bare, shedding our identity. We are carried away by divine love (*theios erōs*) to stand outside ourselves, responding to the call of God to return to our source. As Stang puts it, '*Erōs* is the engine of apophasis, a yearning that stretches language to the point that it breaks, stretches the love to the point that he splits' (2012, pp. 169–170).

## Ecstasy (*ekstasis* or *ekstatikos*)

*Erōs* towards God leads one to stand outside oneself in ecstasy, rendering one open to non-duality, an ecstasy that divinises the human being, just as God is humanised in Christ. 'Standing outside . . . of our whole selves' we become 'wholly of God. For it is better to be of God, and not of ourselves' (*DN* 7.1 865D–868A, in Stang, 2012, pp. 171–172). God too, in his yearning for the well-being of all is also led outside of his transcendent dwelling place. 'On account of an overflowing of loving goodness', God is 'carried outside of himself in the loving care he has for everything' (*DN* 4.13 712B, in Perl, 2007, p. 46).

The ecstatic mystical experience is a return to the One in 'whom we live and move and have our being' (Acts 17:28). This process is reciprocal. The activity of divine *exstasis* is the energy of divine love at work in the heart of the neophyte. God pours out divine love to enable beings to transcend themselves in and through God in a divine cycle:

> The circle imagery is indeed apt, suggesting both the process of divine activity proceeding outwards to bring all back to itself, and the principle of the double exstasis having its beginning and end in God.
>
> (Golitzin, 1994, p. 47)

Dionysius makes a play on the words 'understanding' (*epistēmē*) and 'ecstasy' (*ekstatikos*). 'Understanding' means 'I stand upon' and 'ecstasy' that 'I stand outside' (myself). Understanding leads to an 'ecstatic *epistēmē*, that is, an understanding predicated precisely on standing-outside ourselves' (Stang, 2012, p. 9). The ecstasy of standing outside oneself in a state of unknowing delivers true understanding.

So too, the ecstatic process of self-abandonment to God is a process of true self-realisation. At the ultimate level God is the being of all, and the heart of the meaning of life is the erotic self-transcending union between God and all creation. We are not separate, independent and autonomous beings but partake of the divine energy. 'Herein the divine love eminently shows its endlessness and beginninglessness, as an eternal circle, whirling around through the Good, from the Good, and in the Good and to the Good in unerring coiling up, always proceeding and remaining and returning in the same and by the same' (*DN* 4.14, 712D–713A, in Perl, 2007, p. 48).

## Union (*henousis*)

The purpose of life for Dionysius is 'union of divinised minds with the Light beyond all deity' which occurs only through 'the cessation of all intelligent activity' (*DN* 1.5 593C). One belongs no longer to oneself but to the Divine Beloved (*DN* 3.13 712A). The paradox is that self-realisation implies renunciation of self to become 'neither oneself nor someone else' (*MT* 1. 3 1001A).

Union is brought about through the ecstasy of divine love which leads one out of oneself in a return to the One. Dionysius quotes Paul (Gal 2:20) who was so taken up by divine love and yearning for God that he suffered ecstasy, standing outside himself and declaring that 'it is no longer I but Christ lives in me'.

> Wherefore the great Paul, having come to be in possession of divine love, and participating in its ecstatic power, says with inspired mouth, 'I live, and yet

not I, but Christ lives in me,' as a true lover and, as he says, ecstatic to God, and living not his own life but the life of the beloved, as greatly cherished.

(*DN* 4.13 712A, in Perl, 2007, p. 47)

## Divinisation (*theosis*)

*Theosis* means divinisation, 'being as much as possible like and in union with God' (*EH* 373D). Divinisation is the means by which separations between self and other, beings and ultimate reality dissolve and melt away. Divinisation, *theosis* or at-one-ment with the unknown God is a relational activity, including not just the relationship with the divine, but love of others and recognition of our interdependence.

The hierarchy is a means of divinisation, 'lifting us upward hierarchically until we are brought as far as we can be into the unity of divinisation (*theousin*)' (*EH* 373A). Here the soteriological importance of sacred liturgy comes in, for it is in the Eucharist that 'our fragmented lives' are drawn 'together into a one-like divinization'. It forges a divine unity out of the divisions among us. It grants us communion and union with the One (*koinōnian kai henōsin pros ton Hena*) (*EH* 3.1.1 424CD in McGinn, 1991, pp. 177–178). Through the Eucharist, a 'perfecting divinisation (*theousesin*)' may occur, so arriving 'at the highest possible measure of divinisation (*theousei*) and will be both the temple and the companion of the Spirit of the Deity' (*EH* 433C).

## Clinical relevance of Dionysius

Bion follows the tradition of Dionysius when he observes that although we ordinarily do not have direct access to O, mystics attest to direct experience of O, with whom they aim to be at one. Similarly Dionysius continually reminds the reader that 'one can neither discuss nor understand the One, the Supra-unknowable, the Transcendent, Goodness itself' (*DN* 1.5 593B). It is not a matter of whether we can know the absolute; it is a matter of becoming the absolute.

Apophatic contemplative practice affirms then negates the Divine Names in order to break through the paradox of God's presence and absence, immanence and transcendence, and attain union of the unknown self with the unknown God. Although the One transcends all thought, the meaning of life is union with that which is beyond, unknowable, inscrutable and ineffable, yet immanent. Here Dionysius also focuses on the saving activity of incarnation. Just as Christ becomes human, we become divinised. 'Out of love for humanity Christ emerged from the hiddenness of his divinity to take on human shape, to be utterly incarnate among us while yet remaining unmixed' (*EH* 3.13 444C). Through Christ's procession downwards to humanity, the human race may return to God. To

enter participation with himself and to have a share in his own goodness, if we would make ourselves one with his divine life and imitate it as much as we can, so that we may achieve perfection and truly enter into communion with God and with the divine things.

(*EH* 3 444CD)

The activity of soteriological compassion takes place through procession and return from the Ultimate to the level of beings, in order to enable them to return to their inherent godliness or primordial purity. It is divine compassion that inspires the descent from the One to the Many to bring them back 'that they may be one even as we are one' (John 17:21). So too, for Jung the goal of therapy was to enable un-dividedness, which he called 'individuation', for the patient to realise his or her own true self, which is also utterly transcendent, fathomless:

That is to say even the enlightened person remains what he is, and is never more than his own limited ego before the One who dwells within him, whose form has no knowable boundaries, who encompasses him on all sides, fathomless as the abysms of the earth and as vast as the sky.

(*CWXI*, para. 758)

Dionysius was not advocating abstract theology but direct mystical experience aiming for total transformation, involving recognition that we are as unknown to ourselves as God is to the human intellect, leading to indwelling of the unknown God as Christ. Here in terms of apophatic psychotherapy, the way to realise true selfhood is through an apophasis of the self, through negation of the self, clearing away fabrications and constructs, splitting it open to indwelling in a greater dimension of absolute reality, in O. Leaving ourselves empty we await true insight to dawn. The apophatic way is a training in openness and *kenosis*. It is an ascetical practice involving a radical epistemological renunciation, stripping away all constructs about reality, all sensory perceptions, imagination, reason, intellectual ideas but knowing nothing, being nothing, one is lead through darkness towards a state of ecstasy where one is neither oneself nor other, a ecstasy that opens the way for 'Him Who is beyond all' to effect union with the Unknown beyond knowing. The utterly unknown Godhead also suffers ecstatic yearning that all creation return to its source and so the unmanifest manifests in creation so that all beings might return to their source, a source beyond being and knowing.

Likewise the movement between the kataphatic and apophatic is a form of deconstruction, when imagery and emotional reactions burn themselves out and we enter the state of contemplation beyond knowing. Dionysius continually displays a vision that transcends ordinary human knowing yet is not remote or impersonal. Through becoming the divinity in which we share, there is loving movement from the Source to embrace all humanity, in which we realise our own 'godlike oneness'. 'We, in the diversity of what we are, are drawn together by it and are led into a godlike oneness, into a unity reflecting God' (*DN* 1.4 589D).

For both Dionysius and Bion the apophatic way is an active spiritual discipline. Although the emphasis for Dionysius is spiritual and for Bion it is psychoanalytic, at-one-ment with ultimate reality is a shared aim. Bion continually advises us to actively shed memory, desire, understanding and sense impressions to ready us for the state of mind in which O can transform in us. There is a meditative practice of self-emptying and breaking through the gaps between thoughts to a reality beyond. 'It is important that the analyst should avoid mental activity, memory and desire' which are 'harmful' (Bion, 1970, p. 42) to the mind's capacity to gaze nakedly upon the ultimate beyond all sense impressions, imagination, concepts, theory and reason.

In the darkness of unknowing there is direct encounter with that One beyond all being, all attributes, all conceptions. All polarities such as between self and other are transcended. Ultimately one is one with the One, as we are all at-one.

## Notes

1 Dionysius refers to two other treatises which have either been lost or he never completed: *Theological Representations* and *Symbolic Theology*.
2 A note on translation: unless otherwise indicated the translation I am using is that of Luibheid and Rorem (1987). I follow the convention of giving the name of the work in initials followed by the line number. Where another translation is used, I include the name of the translator, date and page number for that version. I am indebted to Henderson (2014) for his ground-breaking work on Dionysius and Psychoanalysis who has added Greek transliterations to many of these excerpts.
3 Stang follows the 1897–9 Parker translation as being closer to the Greek. He has made some slight changes. All citations from Stang are therefore those of Parker as edited by Stang.
4 Perl contends that the Parker translation is imperfect and the Luibheid translation 'so far from the Greek as to be almost a paraphrase rather than a translation, and disregards Dionysius' use of traditional philosophical terms' (Perl, 2007, p. ix). Hence any citation I have used from Perl is his own translation.

# Chapter 12

# The apophatic way after Dionysius

## The influence of Dionysius

Dionysius' *Corpus Dionysiacum* influenced a long line of apophatic mystics and theologians after him, including Thomas Aquinas, Meister Eckhart, John Tauler, Henry Suso, John Ruysbroeck, Julian of Norwich, Jean Gerson, Nicholas of Cusa, Denis the Carthusian, Marsilio Ficino, Theresa of Ávila and John of the Cross. He was a major inspiration for Orthodox traditions including twentieth-century mystics such as Vladimir Solovyov, Vladimir Lossky and Christos Yannaras. He indirectly influenced Freud, directly influenced Jung and was a major source for the apophatic mystics inspiring Bion's apophatic epistemology and ontology of O.

Dionysius' influence spread after his works were translated into Latin, the first translation being Abbot Hilduin at the abbey of Saint Denys in the ninth century. The anonymous author of *The Cloud of Unknowing* wrote a translation of *The Mystical Theology* called *Deonise Hid Divinite*. By the sixteenth century 'except for the Bible and perhaps the works of Boethius, no writing of the early Christian era received' as much attention as the *Corpus Dionysiacum* in terms of 'translations, excerpts, commentaries . . . that combined these elements into veritable encyclopaedias of Dionysian scholarship' (Froehlich, 1987, p. 33). The Florentine Academy, who advocated Neoplatonic philosophy not as abstract speculation but as a way of life, championed Dionysius for his combination of Platonic philosophy and Christian mysticism. Giovanni Pico della Mirandola hailed Dionysius as 'the master of the true Christian *cabbala*' and for Ficino the three 'pillars of his religious synthesis were Plato, Paul and Dionysius' (Froehlich, 1987, p. 36).

Dionysius influenced medieval mysticism on one hand and Scholastic theology on the other. In the thirteenth century, there was a balance between experiential and scholastic intellectual approaches, known respectively as *theologia mystica* and *theologia speculativa*. Similarly philosophy in the premodern time was more allied to spiritual philosophy with its emphasis on *theoria, gnosis, speculatio, contemplation* and *visio* (Waaijman, 2005, p. 24). *Theoria* is philosophical and epistemological, whereas contemplation belongs to spiritual theology. The experiential strain of Dionysianism has been referred to as *Affective Dionysianism* and is associated with the theologians at the Abbey of Saint-Denis and the Abbey of St Victor in Paris. Ecstatic union with God is affected through love rather than intellect. The *theologia mystica* as defined by Jean Gerson (1363–1429) is 'the extension of the soul in God through the desire of love', 'an experimental cognition of God through the union of the spiritual *affectus* with him' which 'takes place through ecstatic love'. This is a 'rising movement in God, through fervent and pure love', a 'cognition experienced of God through the embrace of unitive love'. Furthermore 'mystical theology is irrational and beyond mind and foolish wisdom, exceeding all praise' (Gerson, in Tyler, 2010, p. 63).

I briefly mention some of the apophatic writers influenced by Dionysius. Moses Maimonides is cited as an exemplar of the apophatic in Jewish thought who greatly influenced Meister Eckhart. I then focus on Meister Eckhart and John of the Cross due to their critical influence on Bion's writings.

## John the Scot Eriugena (810–877)

John the Scot Eriugena was commissioned by Charles the Bald to make a better translation of the *Corpus Dionysius*. This inspired him to compose his own work *Periphyseon (On the Divine Nature)*. God is seen as beyond being, yet at the same time 'the being of all things', that which 'overflows all things', that which 'makes all things and is made in all things' and that which 'limits all things yet is their boundless infinitude' (*Periphyseon*, in Sells, 1994, p. 37). Apophatic theology and apophatic anthropology are linked: 'Negative theology and negative anthropology are grounded in the conviction that divine and human subjectivity are one and the same in essence' (Stang, 2012, p. 156).

Eriugena follows the Neoplatonic and Dionysian procession and return where all returns ultimately into a primal unity. Eriugena uses the term 'theophany' (*theophania*) to denote the appearance or manifestation of the deity, from the words *theos*, God and *phaino* meaning 'bring to light, make appear'.

> For everything that is understood and sensed is nothing other than the apparition of the non-apparent, the manifestation of the hidden, the affirmation of the negated, the comprehension of the incomprehensible, the utterance of the unutterable, the access to the inaccessible, the intellection of the unintelligible, the body of the bodiless, the essence of the beyond-essence, the form of the formless, the measure of the immeasurable, the number of the unnumberable, the weight of the weightless, the materialization of the spiritual, the visibility of the invisible, the place of the placeless, the time of the timeless, the definition of the infinite, the circumscription of the uncircumscribed, and the other things which are both conceived and perceived by the intellect alone and cannot be retained within the recesses of memory and which escape even the blade of the mind.
>
> (Eriugena, in Sells, 1994, p. 44)

## Moses Maimonides (1137–1204)

Followers of the apophatic way are also to be found in Judaism and Islam, Maimonides being a major exponent of Jewish apophaticism. Maimonides was born in Cordoba, Spain, at the time of the Almohad dynasty. His family moved to Alexandria in 1166, settling in Old Cairo (Fustat) where he became a spiritual leader to the Jewish community. He was also a physician, judge and lawyer. It was here that he composed, in Judeo-Arabic, his *Guide of the Perplexed* (*Dalālat al-ḥā'irīn*). Its aim was to reconcile faith and reason. One method was to view biblical parables not only symbolically, but apophatically, through contradictions that enable truth to be glimpsed then concealed again. The essence of Maimonides' negative theology is that one cannot posit any attributes of God. Ultimately the highest form of praise for God is silence, which arises through the understanding of the negation of divine attributes. Maimonides held that God is indescribable and incomprehensible, and can only be expressed by negation.

> Between our knowledge and His knowledge there is nothing in common, as there is nothing in common between our essence and His essence. With regard to this point, only the equivocality of the term 'knowledge' occasions the error; for there is a community only in the terms, whereas in the true reality of the things there is a difference. It is from this that incongruities follow necessarily, as we imagine that things that obligatorily pertain to our knowledge pertain also to His knowledge.
>
> (1963, p. 482)

Owing to God's absolute transcendence, any attempt to describe God leads to the dangers of idolatrous anthropomorphism.

> It has also become clear in metaphysics that by our intellects we are unable to attain perfect comprehension of His existence, may He be exalted. This is due to the perfection of His existence and the deficiency of our intellects. His existence has no causes by which He could be known. . . . It therefore follows that we do not know His knowledge either, nor do we comprehend it in any way, since He is His knowledge and His knowledge is He.
>
> (Maimonides, 1975, p. 95)

## Thomas Gallus of Vercelli (1200–1246)

Gallus' translation and commentary on Dionysius emphasised the affective implications of the expressions 'ray of darkness' and 'cloud of unknowing' that gave rise to the understanding of *theologica mystica* as union with God through love. The mystical ascent requires embracing the darkness of unknowing where *intellectus* is replaced with *affectus*.

> Why is this summit of the divine secrets said to be 'unknown above all unknowns', 'brilliant beyond all brilliance' and 'the highest'?
>
> It is said to be 'unknown beyond all unknowns', because rational enquiry falls short of it; it is said to be 'brilliant beyond all brilliance' because

understanding fails of it, being overwhelmed by the overflowing outpourings of light; it is said to be 'the highest' because intelligence cannot reach up to it because of its *transcending union of love.*

> (Gallus, *Glossa* on *The Mystical Theology*, PL. 122, 271A,
> in Turner, 1995, p. 191, emphasis in the original)

Taking Dionysius' account of Moses' ascent wherein Moses 'plunges into the truly mysterious darkness of unknowing' Gallus describes Moses, who, when he

> enters into the cloud of unknowing [*ad caliginem ignorantiae*], that is, he is made one with the incomprehensibility of the Godhead, which intelligence cannot reach into: this [cloud] shuts out all else and encloses within it and hides in the deepest secrecy all those knowings and understandings as in the first cause of all. And by means of this [cloud] all who are united with God, who is above all things, are confirmed in an eminence which no reason is able to explore nor intellect contemplate; and being set apart from all things and in a manner of speaking from itself, it is united with God, who is unknown to intellect, *through a union of love* . . . which is effective of true knowing, far superior to the knowing of intellect; and in so far as it leaves the knowing of intellect behind, it knows God beyond all knowing and mind.
>
> (Gallus, in Turner, 1995, pp. 192–193)

## Nicholas of Cusa (1401–1464)

Nicholas of Cusa (Cusanus) was born in Kues, Germany. He was sent Dionysius' *The Mystical Theology* by Paolo del Pozzo Toscanelli in 1443. On his journey back from Constantinople in 1437, Cusanus had a revelation showing the way to express the inexpressible:

> I was led to this, that I embrace incomprehensibles incomprehensibly in instructed ignorance by the transcending of incorruptible truths which are humanly knowable.
>
> (Nicholas of Cusa, *De docta ignorantia*, in Cranz, 2000, p. 103)

*De docta ignorantia* (1440) was his most famous work, embracing the themes of learnt ignorance, the coincidences of opposites, 'the contraction of the universal to the particular, and the unfolding of the infinite in the finite and the enfolding of the finite in the infinite' (Nicholas of Cusa, 1997, p. 19). In *De docta ignorantia* he suggests that the human mind should raise itself 'to that simplicity where contradictories coincide' (Nicholas of Cusa, in Bond, 1997, p. 103). The goal of the intellect is 'neither that which it understands nor that which it completely fails to understand but that which it understands by not understanding (*id quod non intelligendo intelligit*) (*De vision Dei*, xvi, in Cranz, 2000, p. 90). The 'instructed ignorance' that embraces 'incomprehensibles incomprehensibly' 'involves an active use of the mind in relation to God', it 'proceeds with energy toward the ineffable' (in Cranz, 2000, p. 34). The 'mind moves beyond reason and intellect to grasp God through the coincidence of opposites or contradictories' (Cranz, 2000, p. 34).

### Coincidentia oppositorum

Cusanus put forward a non-dualist perspective in which the distinction between the finite and infinite and the temporal and eternal is transcended in creation (Cranz, 2000, p. 91). We approach the Godhead through the capacity to hold unknowing as the way to true gnosis and *coincidentia oppositorum*. The term *coincidentia oppositorum*, which was coined by Cusanus in *De Docta Ignorantia* (1440), was taken up by Jung, Mircea Eliade, Henry Corbin, Gershom Scholem and Abraham Joshua Heschel.

The *coincidentia oppositorum* is related to the cloud of unknowing: one leaps into and through the cloud of unknowing where invisible light is seen. In *On the Vision of God*, 9:36 he writes:

> I experience how necessary it is for me to enter into the cloud and to admit the coincidence of opposites, above all capacity of reason, and to seek there the truth where impossibility confronts me. And above reason, above even every highest intellectual ascent when I will have attained to that which is unknown to every intellect and which every intellect judges to be the most removed from truth, there are you, my God, who are absolute necessity. And the more that cloud of impossibility is recognised as obscure and impossible, the more truly the necessity shines forth and the less veiled it appears and draws near.
>
> (Nicholas of Cusa, 1997, p. 251)

Cusanus also describes the alterity of God: 'Therefore in the otherness (*alteritate*) of the intellect, we participate in infinity above all reason' (Cusanus, *De coniecturis*, II, 6#104, h III, 101, in Cranz, 2000, p. 36). Union with the Beyond involves entering divine darkness, a union transcending all earlier theology, utterly beyond intellect and conception:

> If you could indeed conceive it, then it would not be the principle of all, which signifies all in all. Every human concept is the concept of a one something. But the *non aliud* (Not Other) is before concept . . . Therefore let the *non aliud* be called the absolute concept (*conceptus absolutus*) which is seen by the mind but which cannot itself be conceived.
>
> (Cusanus, *Directio speculantis seu de non aliud*, in Cranz, 2000, p. 146)

## Meister Eckhart (1260–1327/1328)

Meister Eckhart was born around 1260 in Hochheim, Thuringia. He became a Dominican at Erfurt where he received an education in liberal arts and Latin. He then went to the Dominican monastery at Cologne for higher education. He moved between Paris and Germany. It was in 1302 in Paris that he was given the title *magister*, or in German *Meister*.

### Influence of Maimonides

Meister Eckhart draws on Maimonides' radical way of negation and also takes up his discourse on the Tetragrammaton: 'A name that is so unpronounceable and thereby, through its silence, protects the one so named from linguistic reification'. The 'I am that I am' (*ehyeh asher ehyeh*) is a 'negation of negation' (Sells, 1994, p. 151). 'God is not a concept or a term, but Reality, that in its own "is-ness" (*isticheit*) is nameless' (Studstill, 2005, p. 193). Eckhart also drew on Maimonides' approach to biblical exegesis in regard to the hidden or 'mystical' meaning, 'figure' and 'parabolical manner' (*parabolice*) (Colledge and McGinn, 1981, pp. 28–29).

### The unmanifest unity of the Godhead and soul

Eckhart refers to the unmanifest unity in a variety of ways: as the desert; nothingness (*nihtheit*); the godhead (*gotheit*); the ground (*grunt*) of the soul which is also the ground of the deity; the spark (*vünkelîn*) of the soul; naked (*blos*) being; the castle (*castellum*) into which Jesus was received (Sells, 1994, pp. 147–148); the refuge of the spirit; and silence. The spark of the soul is identical with the godhead. This can only take place through self-emptying: the soul becomes 'equal to nothing', empties itself and goes out of itself (Sells, 1994, p. 163).

God's 'is-ness' is the same as the soul's 'is-ness': 'if my life is God's being, then God's existence (*sîn*) must be my existence, and God's is-ness (*isticheit*) is my is-ness, neither less nor more' (Eckhart, in Studstill, 2005, p. 204). There is a power in the spirit that is utterly free, but also 'free of all names', 'bare of all forms, wholly empty and free, as God in himself is empty and free. It is so utterly one and simple, as God is one and simple, that man cannot in way look into it' (Eckhart, in Studstill, 2005, p. 204).

### Procession and return

Eckhart's version of the Neoplatonic theme of procession and return is expressed in such statements as 'God's outgoing is his ingoing' (*Gotes ûzgang ist sîn îngang*) (*Predigt* 53; DW 2:530, in Sells, 1994, p. 175). There is a dynamic process of evolution from God involving a 'flowing out (*exitus, effluxus, ûzvliezen*) of all things' and 'a flowing back or return to this ineffable source (*reditus, reflexus, durchbrechen, îngânc*)' (Colledge and McGinn, 1981, p. 30).

In terms of the process of emanation and return there is 'the inner emanation of the Trinitarian Persons' which Eckhart calls *bullitio* (bubbling up) and the 'flowing out of all things from the divine ground' in the act of creation (Colledge and McGinn, 1981, p. 31). Eckhart describes the bubbling up of the trinity within itself that takes the form of 'procession of the son' from the Father. 'The birth of the divine son (which is also the self-birth of the divine) takes place "in eternity" (*in aeternis*)'. This is a process continually occurring beyond time and this continually occurring birth takes place in the soul: 'The birth of the son in the soul is the very same eternal birth that always has occurred and always is occurring within the trinity' (Sells, 1994, p. 148). Eckhart writes:

> The father gives birth to his son in eternity, equal to himself. 'The word was with God, and God was the word' (John 12:1). It was the same in the same nature. Yet I say more: he has given him birth in my soul. Not only is the soul with him and he equal to it, but he is in it, and the father gives his son birth in eternity. . . . The father gives birth to his son without cease; and I say more: he gives me birth, his same son. I say more: he gives me birth not only as his son, but he gives birth to me as himself and himself as me and to me as his being and nature. In the innermost source, there I spring out in the holy spirit, where there is one life and one being and one work. Everything God works is one; therefore he gives me, his son, birth without any distinction.
>
> (*Predigt* 1: 109–110, in Sells, 1994, p. 172)

Just as God is beyond names, the self is beyond name. In a passage reminiscent of Buddhist doctrines of *anātman*, non-self, or Advaita Vedānta '*neti, neti'(not this, not this)*, the self is 'neither this nor that . . . it is bare of all forms, wholly empty and free, as God in himself is empty and free. It is so utterly one and simple, as God is one and simple, that man cannot in any way look into it' (Sermon 2, in Turner, 1995, p. 141). And:

> God, who has no name – who is beyond names – is inexpressible and the soul in its ground is also inexpressible, as he is inexpressible.
>
> (in Turner, 1995, p. 141)

The 'ground of the soul is identical with the ground of the deity, with the godhead' (Sells, 1994, p. 163). This involves giving up attachment, images and will, and becoming nothing: then the soul becomes virgin. One 'must "break through" into the very ground of God' (Turner, 1995, p. 141). Further,

> when all images have departed from the soul and it sees single unity, then the pure being of the soul, passive and resting within itself, encounters the pure formless being of the Divine Unity, which is being beyond all being.
>
> (in Turner, 1995, p. 141)

## Path

For Eckhart there is an uncreated element in the soul that pre-exists one's birth. The goal for the mystic is a return to this original uncreated ground, the birth of the Son or Word in the soul. Yet 'seeking a goal' even union with God, 'sets up a dualistic frame of reference that negates realizing the goal' (Studstill, 2005, p. 216). Hence the path involves 'seeking nothing' and abandoning all desire for the goal. Those who attain to the Godhead do so by pulling 'off the coat from God' and apprehending him 'bare, as he is stripped of goodness and of being and of all names' (Eckhart, *Predigt* 9 in Baudinette, 2012, p. 29). For this to take place 'God actually has to become me and I have to become God' (Eckhart in Studstill, 2005, p. 206).

The mystic must, therefore, realise a pure, empty, uncontrived and non-discriminating mode of experience. She must become unconditioned unity herself in order to experience the unconditioned unity that is God (Studstill, 2005, p. 206). The path is one in which one cultivates unconditioned unity through detachment (*abegescheidenheit*) and self-effacement, involving letting go of self-desire and the sense of distinct selfhood and the dualism inherent in attachment which is predicated upon distinguishing between what is desirable and what is to be rejected. Likewise 'detachment is a mystical practice, involving the "radical deconstruction of the created self"' (Studstill, 2005, p. 207).

## Contemplation

Contemplative practice for Eckhart is a form of inner silence. Contemplation has its stages, the first of which is self-emptying. This involves 'denuding the soul of all images, concepts and attachments' and leads to a second stage that Eckhart calls the 'desert' in which 'the mystic has finally become empty and is able to rest in a state of quiet, unmoving stillness' (Studstill, 2005, p. 219). The third stage, the 'birth of the Word or Son in the soul', is marked by an awakening of 'uncreated light' which 'comprehends God without medium' (McGinn, 2001, p. 45). Through this birth the mystic is 'taken up into the immanent activity of the Trinity' (Studstill, 2005, p. 219). 'The birth in eternity already is a ceaseless birth in the soul' (Studstill, 2005, p. 220). But there is more:

> The noble and humble man is not satisfied to be born as the only-begotten Son whom the Father has eternally born, but he wants to be also the Father and to enter into the same equality of eternal paternity and to bear him, from whom I am eternally born.
>
> (Eckhart, in Studstill, 2005, p. 220)

In this ground 'I am neither God nor creature, but I am what I was and what I shall remain, now and eternally'. Like a drop of water poured into a cask of wine, union entails there being no difference, 'we become the same being and substance and nature as [God] is himself' (Eckhart, in Studstill, 2005, p. 221).

As with Dionysius, union with God is effected through divine love. It is a 'contact, meeting and union' in which 'both sides kiss each other and embrace in a natural and essential love that is inward and very delightful' (*Parables of Genesis*, in Turner, 1995, p. 142).

## Self-emptying

Eckhart's term for *kenosis* or self-emptying is *Abgeschiedenheit* or solitude. The 'birth of the son in the soul' occurs through 'letting go or self-abandon through which the soul gives up its attachments, desires, works, and becomes "equal to nothing"' (Sells, 1994, p. 173). The son can only be born in the soul when the soul is empty of self-will, of images, and 'sinks back into nothingness' breaking 'through to the divine ground where the soul's ground and God's ground are one' (Sells, 1994, p. 174).

> The mystic empties herself *because* of God's fullness of being, which no concept, image, or name can ever approximate. Emptying and negation are both premised on affirmation and function as a means of realizing the highest mode of affirmation, God Himself.
>
> (Studstill, 2005, p. 193)

## Love of God, love of neighbour

A common theme is that to love God is to love all beings. So too for Eckhart, whoever loves God:

> must love his neighbour as himself, rejoicing in his joys as his own and desiring his honour as much as his own and loving a stranger as one of his own. This way a person is always joyful, honoured, and advantages, just as if he were in heaven.
>
> (in Sells, 1994, p. 176)

## Influence on Bion

Bion considers Meister Eckhart's distinction between the Godhead and God, quoting Tractate XI, 'God in the Godhead is spiritual substance, so elemental that we can say nothing about it' (in Bion, 1965, p. 139). According to Bion, God is regarded by Meister Eckhart as 'a Person independent of the human mind'. Furthermore, 'the phenomenon does not "remind" the individual' of God, but 'enables the person to achieve union with an incarnation of the Godhead, or the thing-in-itself (or Person-in-Himself)' (Bion, 1965, p. 139). The main question for Meister Eckhart concerns our identity with the deity and how 'we are transformed and changed into God' (Bion, 1970, p. 116). Bion notes that there 'is a suggestion that there is an ultimate reality with which it is possible to have direct contact' (1965, p. 139).

## St Teresa of Ávila (1515–1582)

The mysticism of Teresa of Ávila bursts to breaking point with kaleidoscopic arrays of images, visions, metaphors and ecstatic experiences. Kataphatic elements are then shaken up to be balanced with apophatic, active discursive meditations by passive prayer of quietude which transcend all natural faculties of sense, intellect and imagination.

Her writings remind us that the apophatic and kataphatic are not mutually exclusive but stand in paradoxical tension as a language of unsaying, where the purpose is not simply to describe spiritual experience but to evoke the experience in the reader. Teresa also counsels that different personalities need different approaches, that the apophatic way may leave some as 'dry as sticks' (Teresa of Ávila, 1976, p. 200).

Teresa was of *converso* origins, her grandfather forcibly converting from Judaism to Christianity after being accused of apostasy in Toledo in 1485. She entered a Carmelite convent at Ávila when she was 21. She practiced what was known as recollection (*recogimiento*) that she learnt from the book *El tercer abecedario espiritual* (1537) by the Franciscan mystic Francisco de Osuna. This is a form of meditation in which one withdraws into oneself, shutting out all external stimuli, so that the soul may be open to divine presence. The outer senses are stilled so inner senses can intuit God's illumination. The soul becomes increasingly attuned to the inner radiance of God. This involves *kenosis*, emptying the self so as to be transformed into the Godhead, our true original state, fleeing 'from the all to the All' as she wrote to her brother Lorenzo in 1576 (in Hamilton, 1960, p. 30).

Teresa had mystic experiences of union from early on, but then felt that she had lost her way for many years until she saw a statue of Christ in agony and experienced a second conversion. Through meditating on the scene of Christ in the Garden of Gethsemane, she realised a reciprocal mutuality, the equality of friends, between God and the soul. God needs us as we need him. Prayer is that of intimate sharing between friends. Her emphasis on the equality of friendship between God and human extended into her reforms: communities of contemplatives were communities of equality not hierarchy.

Teresa's *Interior Castle* uses the symbol of the soul as being like a castle made of diamond or crystal. The soul ascends through the seven concentric dwelling places (*moradas*) moving from the outer to the innermost centre of the soul where Christ the King dwells within and like the sun radiates outwards. The outer dwellings are based on meditation and active effort, the inspiration of sermons, books, trials, works of charity and virtue, as well as the call of God. But the further one ascends, the more that contemplation replaces prayer, and passive recollection and the prayer of quiet replaces active efforts. In the fifth dwelling place contemplation deepens into the prayer of union in which one 'neither sees, nor hears, nor understands' (Teresa of Ávila, 1944/2002, p. 251). She uses the metaphor of a silkworm dying in its cocoon to be reborn as a butterfly. In the inmost dwelling the soul attains spiritual marriage with God and becomes ever more renewed in its original image, that of God. In this 'spiritual marriage the union is like what we have when rain falls from the sky into a river or fount; all is water, for the rain that fell from heaven cannot be divided or separated from the water of the river. Or it is like what we have when a little stream enters the sea: there is no means of separating the two' (Teresa of Ávila, 1980, p. 434). This too is a form of procession and return, as one processes and returns to the centre of one's being, and returns to the world, the waters of union flowing outward such that union flows out into creation, inspiring contemplative action in the world.

# Chapter 13

# Transcending all knowledge

## St John of the Cross

> I entered into unknowing
> and there I remained unknowing
> transcending all knowledge
> (John of the Cross in
> Girón-Negrón, 2009, p. 173)

### The wound of love

According to John of the Cross, a sense of incompleteness alerts us to a deeper dimension, calling us back to our source. We may experience 'immense torment and yearning to see God'. The 'spiritual wounds of love' in our soul and the hiddenness of God are essential aspects of the mystical path. It is through the wound that God enters, inspiring the soul to renounce all that is false, to 'go out of herself and enter into God' (*CB*, 1, 19, 2017, p. 485). The soul must renounce all that the intellect knows, all that understanding comprehends, all sense, feeling, imagination of its own. The memory must be stripped, the will conformed to the will of God and through such purification of the senses and spirit, one enters a divine darkness in which spiritual marriage takes place with the source of all, the divine Bridegroom.

Bion's work cannot be fully appreciated without understanding the apophatic mysticism of John of the Cross. This chapter focuses on the writings of John of the Cross, particularly the necessity for the annihilation of the potencies of the understanding, the memory and the will. This is the original source for Bion's advice to abandon memory, desire and understanding. The chapter also outlines what is meant by contemplation for John of the Cross.

### Some brief biographical details

Juan de Yepes y Álvarez was born in 1542 in Fontiveros on the Castillian plain. His father belonged to a family of silk merchants from Toledo with *converso* origins. There is some evidence that his mother, a poor weaver, might have been of *moriscos* or Muslim ancestry. His father died when John was 8, and his childhood was spent in poverty. He found work at the Plague Hospital where his mentor encouraged him to enrol at the Jesuit College in Medina where, between 1559 and 1563, he studied metaphysics, grammar, Greek, Latin, and Spanish literature. In 1563, when he was 21, he joined the Carmelite *Convento* of Santa Ana in Medina, taking his vows in 1564 and the name Juan de Santo Matía. He entered the Carmelite college of San Andrés at Salamanca in 1565. In 1567 he was ordained a priest and shortly after met the founder of the Discalced Carmelites, St Teresa of Ávila, who persuaded him to help reform the Carmelites from within. John set up the first reformed Carmelite house for men taking on the new Primitive Rule of Our Lady of Mount Carmel and his new name, San Juan de la Cruz.

The reforms were an attempt to focus on the original eremitical, cenobitic and mendicant elements of the Carmelite rule. A major aspect was to create more space for the practice of contemplation. Due to major tensions concerning the reforms, a group of those who were opposed to such reforms took John prisoner in 1577 in the Carmelite monastery in Toledo where he was imprisoned in a tiny cell for nine months. Here he wrote his *Spiritual Canticle*. Despite such privation and torture, he felt spiritually transformed. John eventually managed to escape on 15 August 1578 and eventually was able to recuperate in Sierra de Cazorla where he was able to expand and write commentaries on the works written in prison such as *The Dark Night of the Soul*, *The Ascent of Mount Carmel*, *The Living Flame of Love* and *The Spiritual Canticle*. He became prior of the Carmel of Los Mártires in the Alhambra, Granada. In 1580 approval was finally given for the independence of the Discalced Carmelites, only a year before Teresa's death. In 1588 he moved to Segovia and spent his last years in Sierra Morena. On becoming seriously ill in 1591 he was moved to Ubeda in Andalusia where he died on 13 December 1591. His relics were returned to Segovia.

## *Teología Mística* and dark contemplation in John of the Cross

John of the Cross is an inheritor of the Dionysian apophatic tradition of dark knowledge (*sapientia oscura*), linking dark contemplation (*contemplación tenebrosa*), mystical theology (*theologia mystica*) and Dionysius' 'ray of darkness' (*rayo de tiniebla*). He is also a follower of *Affective Dionysianism* with its emphasis on the experiential and mystical rather than intellectual approach to contemplation.

John also equates mystical theology with infused contemplation (*contemplación infusa*) and relates them to the dark night of the soul.

> This dark night is an inflow of God into the soul, which purges it of its habitual ignorances and imperfections, natural and spiritual, and which the contemplatives call infused contemplation or mystical theology.
>
> (*DN* II. 5.1, 2017, p. 401)

In the *Spiritual Canticle* 39:12 he describes the links between the dark night, contemplation, unknowing and mystical theology as the hidden knowledge of God:

> This night is the contemplation in which the soul desires to behold these things. Because of its obscurity, she calls contemplation night. On this account contemplation is also termed mystical theology, meaning the secret or hidden knowledge of God. In contemplation God teaches the soul very quietly and secretly, without its knowing how, without the sound of words, and without the help of any bodily or spiritual faculty, in silence and quietude, in darkness to all sensory and natural things. Some spiritual persons call this contemplation knowing by unknowing.
>
> (*CB* Commentary on Stanza 39.12, 2017, p. 626)

The 'divine light of contemplation' creates 'spiritual darkness' in the soul because it surpasses all understanding. It also deprives the soul of the act of understanding and so 'darkens it'. This is why infused contemplation is called a 'ray of darkness'. 'As a result, when God communicates this bright ray of his secret wisdom to the soul not yet transformed, he causes thick darkness in its intellect' (*DN* II. 5.3, 2017, p. 402).

Diego de Jésus (1570–1621), who edited the first complete edition of the works of John of the Cross in 1618, points out that *Teología Mística* 'treats of things very high, sacred and secret and touches on experience more than speculation – on taste (*gusto*) and divine savour (*sabor divino*) rather than knowledge (*saber*), and this in a high state of supernatural and loving union with God' (in Tyler, 2010 p. 69).

### *Rayo de tiniebla*: a ray of darkness

Union with God 'demands that we be united with the darkness (*unirse con la tinie bla*)' and takes place through the darkness of unknowing, 'fathomless and obscure' (*A* II. 94, 2017, p. 178). Darkness is both means and end: the soul must travel in darkness, deliberately blinding itself to all the mind can know, and God is shrouded in darkness. The path is one of *noche*, night, *nada*, nothingness, and darkness (*tiniebla*). Gathering the terms used for the purifications undergone on the dark night we find words such as deprivation, privation, mortification, detachment, negation, denial, annihilation, nothingness, night, darkness, quietude, purgation, void, ridding and suspension.

In *The Ascent of Mount Carmel* John writes:

> Neither the understanding with its intelligence will be able to understand aught that is like Him, nor can the will taste pleasure and sweetness that bears any resemblance to that which is God, neither can the memory set in the imagination ideas and images that represent Him. It is clear, then, that none of these kinds of knowledge can lead the understanding direct to God; and that,

in order to reach Him, a soul must rather proceed by not understanding than by desiring to understand; and by blinding itself and setting itself in darkness rather than by opening its eyes, in order the more nearly to approach the ray Divine.

And thus it is that contemplation, whereby the understanding has the loftiest knowledge of God, is called mystical theology, which signifies secret wisdom of God; for it is secret even to the understanding that receives it. For that reason Saint Dionysius calls it a ray of darkness (*rayo de tiniebla*). . . . It is clear, then, that the understanding must be blind to all paths that are open to it in order that it may be united with God.

(A II, 8.5–6, 1953, pp. 91–92)

When the soul is struck by 'the divine light of contemplation', it 'causes spiritual darkness' because it deprives the soul of understanding (*A* II, 5.3). The soul is pierced with a shaft of love and wounded and cries out to her Beloved 'where have you hidden?' (*CB* I, 2017, p. 471).

## Meditation and contemplation in John of the Cross

John advises that meditation, discursive prayer, reflection and 'interior acts of love' are for beginners. But the 'road to God consists not in a multiplicity of meditations nor in ways or methods of such, nor in consolations' (*A* II. 7.8, 1953, p. 86). Through 'withdrawing the soul from the life of the senses and placing it in that of the spirit' God brings the soul from meditation to contemplation which is 'beyond the range of the imagination and discursive reflection' (*DN* I.10.1, 2017, p. 381). The soul must then abandon the ordinary way of meditation and be

> perfectly detached, calm, peaceful, and serene, as God is; it must be like the atmosphere, which the sun illumines and warms in proportion to its calmness and purity. Thus the soul must be attached to nothing, not even to meditation . . . for every act of the soul . . . will hinder and disturb it, and break that profound silence of sense and spirit necessary for hearing the deep and soft voice of God, Who speaks to the heart in solitude; it is in profound peace and tranquillity that the soul is to listen to God.

(LF III. 38, 2007b, p. 81)

## *En una noche oscura:* one dark night

The *summum bonum* for John is mystical union with the hidden God in love through the apophatic path of unknowing. In order to ascend towards such union, John teaches us, 'A soul must ordinarily pass through two principle kinds of night – which spiritual persons call purgations or purifications of the soul'. Both are called nights because the 'soul journeys in darkness as though by night' (*A* I.1.1, 2017, p. 118). John delineates two broad stages of the dark night of contemplation, the dark nights of the senses and the spirit, corresponding to the two parts of the soul, the sensory and spiritual.

> Hence one night of purgation is sensory, by which the senses are purged and accommodated to the spirit; and the other night or purgation is spiritual, by which the spirit is purged and denuded as well as accommodated and pre-pared for union with God through love.
>
> (*DN* I.8.1, 2017, p. 375)

Within these two basic divisions are active and passive nights. Thus there are four nights: the active night of the senses, the passive night of the senses, the active night of the spirit and passive night of the spirit. The dark night can also be considered as tripartite, the dark night of the senses (with active and passive phases), the dark night of the spirit (with active and passive phases) and the dark night of union with God. These three relate also to the three-fold way of purga-tion (*vía purgativa*), illumination (*vía iluminativa*) and union (*vía unitiva*). Yet in *The Ascent of Mount Carmel* (I.2.5), John writes that there is only one night with three phases. The night of the senses resembles the twilight of early evening, the night of the spirit like midnight since it consists of faith and faith is totally dark to the understanding. The third part, representing God, is like the time before early dawn. Yet we are also reminded that 'to enter upon the road is to leave the road' and 'to enter upon that which has no way, which is God. For the soul that attains to this state has no longer any ways or methods … I mean ways of understanding, or of perception, or of feeling' (*A* II. 4.5, 1953, p. 72).

The poem 'Dark Night' contains John's teachings on the stages towards union with God. Hence I will quote the poem in full:

1. One dark night,
   fired with love's urgent longings
   – ah, the sheer grace! –
   I went out unseen,
   my house being now all stilled.
2. In darkness, and secure,
   by the secret ladder, disguised,
   – ah, the sheer grace! –
   in darkness and concealment,
   my house being now all stilled.
3. On that glad night,
   in secret, for no one saw me,
   nor did I look at anything,
   with no other light or guide
   than the one that burned in my heart.
4. This guided me
   more surely than the light of noon

to where he was awaiting me
– him I knew so well –
there in a place where no one appeared.

5. O guiding night!
O night more lovely than the dawn!
O night that has united
the Lover with his beloved,
transforming the beloved in her Lover.

6. Upon my flowering breast
which I kept for him alone,
there he lay sleeping,
and I caressing him
there in a breeze from the fanning cedars.

7. When the breeze blew from the turret,
as I parted his hair,
it wounded my neck
with its gentle hand
suspending all my senses.

8. I abandoned and forgot myself,
laying my face on my Beloved;
All things ceased: I went out from myself,
leaving my cares
forgotten among the lilies.

(*A*, 2017, pp. 113–114)

## The psychology of John of the Cross

The nights of the senses and spirit relate to two of the three dimensions of the person. The dark night of the senses relates to the purification of the lower, sensitive soul and the dark night of the spirit to the higher rational and more interior spiritual soul. John, propounding his own version of scholastic psychology, views the person as a psychosomatic unity of body and soul (*un solo supuesto*), within which there is a further tripartite division consisting of body, lower sensitive soul (*la parte inferior*) and higher spiritual soul (*la parte superior*). The sensitive soul includes the exterior sense (*los sentidos corporales exteriors*) and interior senses (*los sentidos corporales interiors*) as well as imagination (*imaginación*), fantasy (*fantasía*), the sensible memory and the sensitive appetite from which the passions arise. The higher spiritual soul (*el espíritu*) is the seat of three potencies (*potencias*, many translators translate *potencias* as 'faculty', 'function' or 'power'): understanding (*entendimiento*), memory (*la memoria*) and will (*la voluntad*). In short the function of understanding is to know, of memory to both recall and anticipate, and of will to choose. These three potencies are what Bion refers to (in a different order) when he says the analyst should abandon memory, desire and understanding. The Spanish word for understanding that John uses is *entendimiento*, often translated as intellect, meaning the power of understanding and of comprehension. It is *entendimiento* that Bion translates as 'understanding'. Knowledge (*sciencia*) that arises from the understanding is of two kinds, natural and supernatural. Natural apprehensions (*aprehensiones naturales*) include understanding, judgement and discursive reasoning. Supernatural apprehensions (*las sobrenaturales*) involve divine intervention, such as 'visions, revelations, locutions and spiritual feelings' (*visiones, revelaciones, locutions y sentimentos espirituales*) (*A* II. 23.1, 1953, p. 173).

Memory (*la memoria*) forms 'like an archive and receptacle' for the understanding 'in which all intelligible forms and images are received' (*A* II. 16.2, 2017, p. 200). Memory includes not just memories of the past but also anticipations of the future. So too, Bion sees memory as 'the past tense of "desire", "anticipation" being its future tense' (1967/2014, *CWVI*, p. 208).

The will (*la voluntad*) is the agent of volition and linked to desire. All the 'faculties, passions and desires' are 'governed by the will'. Will or volition ordinarily governs the potencies, appetites, affections and the four passions, namely joy, hope, grief and fear. Affections are the passions once accepted into the higher soul where they become affections of the will (*afeciones de la voluntad*) (Luévano, 1990, p. 57). The will is the agent that, through desire, appropriates an object to consciousness, hence John counsels one to 'desire nothing'. It is not the actual objects of consciousness that cause problems, but the will and possessive desire that we attach to them. The noetic apprehension augmented by desire leads to the soul being cluttered with preoccupations, leaving no room for the inflow of grace, of intimations of eternity, a brush with divine presence.

## The dark night of the senses

Upon a dark night the soul 'went forth while its house was still at rest', enkindled with love of God and led by God through darkness. The dark night of the senses that it has entered is dark because of 'the privation and purgation of all its sensual desires, with respect to all outward things of the world' and 'likewise with respect to the desires of its will'. The house, referring to the sensual part of the soul, is at rest and asleep (A. I. 4, 1953, p. 18). The senses need to be emptied of 'every imaginative form and apprehension', all images and even their residues. 'Night' here refers to 'a deprival of gratification of the soul's appetites in all things' which is 'like living in darkness and in a void' (*A* I. 3.1, 2017, pp. 121–122).

The aim of the purification effected by the active night of the senses is to actively engage in asceticism in order to release one from subtle forms of spiritual pride, spiritual avarice, anger, envy and sloth, attachment to sensory experience and self-cherishing. This alone is not enough and so the soul enters the passive night of the senses, indicated by such signs as the inability to meditate, a sense of spiritual torpor. The dark night of the senses is necessary because God cannot be cognised through the senses:

Inasmuch as this union and transformation are not cognizable by sense or any human power, the soul must be completely and voluntarily empty of all that can enter into it, of every affection and inclination so far as it concerns itself. Who shall hinder God from doing His own will in a soul that is resigned, detached, and self-annihilated? . . . not trusting to anything it understands, tastes, feels, or imagines – for all this is darkness, which will lead it astray, or keep it back; and faith is above all understanding, taste and sense.

(*A* II. 4.2, 1906/2007a, p. 72)

The purification of desires is necessary for the soul in which such desires dwell is 'wearied, tormented, darkened, defiles and weakened' (*A*. I.6.1, 1953, p. 33). A person must be liberated from all desires because 'in the state of divine union a person's will is so completely transformed into God's will that it excludes everything contrary to God's will, and in all and through all is motivated by the will of God' (*A* I. 11.2, 2017, p. 142). John gives lengthy instructions for this night of the senses concluding with a poem summing up the need for complete renunciation of all desires, particularly the negation of being and knowing: 'To arrive at being all' one must 'desire to be nothing', to 'come to the knowledge that you have not, you must go by a way in which you know not' and 'to come to be what you are not, you must go by a way in which you are not' (*A* I. 13.11, 2017, pp. 150–151).

## The dark night of the spirit

The soul, enkindled with 'love's urgent longings' for union with the divine Bridegroom, then enters the illuminative way of infused contemplation, the active followed by passive nights of the spirit. In the passive night of the spirit faith is the only guide. The individual having actively engaged in self-emptying and renunciation of attachments to fixed beliefs and rigid ways of seeing, thinking, frozen memories and expectations, enters a realm of utter darkness, a radical negation of self and all things. An analogy John uses to compare the night of the senses and night of the spirit is the difference between cutting off a branch and pulling up a plant by the roots. The night of the senses is like cutting off the branches, whereas the night of the spirit uproots the most deep-seated habitual tendencies, removing the oldest and most subtle stains on the soul (*DN* II. 2).

## Purification of understanding, memory and the will through faith, hope and love

The mystical ascent involves a continual process of self-emptying and excavation of 'the caverns of the heart' in order to be filled with God's Holy Spirit. The 'three faculties of the soul —understanding, memory and will— are brought into this spiritual night, which is the means to Divine union' by means of the 'three theological virtues—faith, hope and charity' (*fe, esperanza y caridad*), all of which serve to 'produce the same emptiness and darkness, each one in its own faculty' or potency (*A* II. 6.1, 1953, pp. 79–80). Understanding is perfected by being emptied and darkened by faith, memory is freed 'in the emptiness of hope' and will is 'buried by withdrawing and detaching' all desire by charity. The three virtues 'cause emptiness in the faculties: faith, in the understanding, causes an emptiness and darkness with respect to understanding; hope, in the memory, causes emptiness of all possessions; and charity causes emptiness in the will and detachment from all affection and from rejoicing in all that is not God' (*A* II. 6.2, 1953, p. 80).

> The first cavern is the understanding; its emptiness is the thirst for God.
>
> The second cavern is the will, and the emptiness thereof is a great hunger for God.
>
> The third cavern is the memory, and the emptiness thereof is the soul's melting away and languishing for the possession of God.
>
> (*LF* III. 22, 1934/1974, p. 125)

It is the understanding, will and memory that create suffering in the soul on the path towards union with God.

> In the understanding it languishes because it does not see God, Who is its salvation. . . . In the will it suffers, because it possesses not God, Who is its comfort and delight. . . . In the memory it dies, because it remembers its privation of all the blessings of the understanding, which are the vision of God, and of the delights of the will, which are the fruition of Him, and that it is very possible also that it may lose Him for ever. . . . In the memory, therefore, the soul labours under a sensation like that of death.
>
> (*CB* II. 7, 1934/1974, pp. 150–151)

The dark night involves the pain of darkness in the understanding, emptiness in the memory, spiritual aridity in the will. Impure understanding is likened to murky air, memory to muddy water and the will to a mirror that is cloudy (all metaphors also found in Dzogchen). Air, water and a mirror are not murky, muddy or cloudy in themselves but inherently pure. They are obscured and contaminated by desire and so prevent God's likeness being purely reflected in the soul.

Understanding 'should be withdrawn from all particular knowledge, whether temporal or spiritual' lest the soul be preoccupied (*A* II. 14.12, 1953, p. 118). Faith is the means of entering this night, a night so dark as to be comparable to midnight. The divinity of God is concealed in the obscurity of faith.

> In order for the understanding to be prepared for this Divine Union, it must be pure and void of all that pertains to sense, and detached and freed from

all that can clearly be perceived by the understanding, profoundly hushed and put to silence, and leaning upon faith, which alone is the proximate and proportionate means whereby the soul is united with God. . . . For, as God is infinite, so faith sets Him before us as infinite . . . and as God is darkness to our understanding, even so does faith likewise blind and dazzle our understanding.

(*A* II. 91, 1953, p. 93)

The darkness of faith is intimately connected to the apophatic way, the *via negationis*.

In order to be united with God through hope, memory must be stripped of all forms and impression such that it is 'in total oblivion and suspension' and is 'bare and clear, as though nothing passed through it'. For 'there is no way to union with God without annihilating the memory as to all forms . . . since God has no form or image comprehensible to the memory' (*A* III. 2.4, 2017, p. 269). Acts of remembrance and anticipation can function as possessions, over which one is possessive, and this impedes the path to union. 'By removing these "possessions", the empty and liberated memory is filled solely with the hope for God' (Luévano, 1990, p. 56).

Through the virtue of love human will is transformed into God's will and human desire becomes divine love. The will is thereby stripped of all its old desires and redirected towards God. Desiring nothing, possessing nothing, 'in the state of divine union a person's will is so completely transformed into God's will that it . . . in all and through all is motivated by the will of God' (*A* I. 2, 2017, p. 142).

Now when these faculties, passions and desires are directed by the will toward God, and turned away from all that is not God, then the strength of the soul is kept for God, and thus the soul is able to love God with all its strength.

(*A* III. 16.2, 1953, p. 243)

For John, as for Bion, there is the ascetic discipline of eschewing the tendency to fill our minds with sensory, intellectual and spiritual gratification. John advocates absence of desire and understanding because desire takes up space in the container of the human soul, leaving no room to be filled with the pure presence of God.

Bion also describes how memories saturate the analytic container, leaving no space for transformations in O. For Bion the analytic state of mind is one of emptiness, allowing the analyst to listen to the patient, free of memory, desire and understanding in order to 'deprive itself for all the worldly things', to become in O 'which is as dark as night to the understanding' (John of the Cross in Bion, 1965, p. 159).

The dark night of the spirit is full of darkness and trials beyond imagination. The soul undergoes 'dryness . . . insipidity and bitterness' (*sequedad, sinsabor y amargura*) (*DN* I. 8.3), an unbearable sense of desolation in which the soul cannot 'cling with the intellect, rejoice with the will, nor discourse with the memory' (*arrimo en el entendimiento, ni jugo en la voluntad, ni discourse en la memoria*) (*DN* I. 9.7). The soul is pierced by 'a divine ray of contemplation' (*divino rayo de contemplación*) which 'darkens, voids and annihilates the soul of its passion concerning its particularised apprehensions and affections' (*divina luz. . . . la oscurece, vada y aniquila de la pasión acerca de sus aprehensiones y afecciones particulares*) (*DN* II. 2.2). The person entering such a cloud may feel that they cannot even understand themselves, let alone find anyone else who understands the experience they are going through. Here the psychotherapist or spiritual director has to take care not to interfere but just be with them in this darkness.

> God does all this by means of dark contemplation. And the soul not only suffers the void and suspension of these natural supports and apprehensions, which is a terrible anguish (like hanging in midair, unable to breathe), but it is also purged by this contemplation. As fire consumes the tarnish and rust of metal, this contemplation annihilates, empties, and consumes all the affections and imperfect habits the soul contracted throughout its life.
>
> (*A* II. 5.5, 2017, p. 405)

## The purpose of life is union with the Divine Bridegroom

The goal of life is for the soul to realise its own inherent divinity through ecstatic union of the lover with the Divine Bridegroom. This is the third Dark night, that of the light just before dawn. The soul becomes one with God, like a spark of fire melting into the fire:

> So too the soul . . . when transformed, and glowing interiorly in the fire of love, is not only united with the divine fire, but becomes a living flame, and itself conscious of it.
>
> (*LF* Prologue 4. 2007b. p. 3)

Union with God is based on the transformational power of the union of unknowing and divine love. John uses erotic poetic imagery of union with the Bridegroom. Union with God is a spiritual marriage, a total transformation into the Divine Beloved, in 'the Beloved lives in the love and the lover in the Beloved. Love produces such likeness in this transformation of lovers that one can say each is the other and both are one'. John, like Dionysius, draws on St Paul's statement 'I live, now not I, but Christ lives in me' for 'his life and Christ's were one life through union of love' (*CB* Commentary on Stanza 12. 7–8, 2017, p. 518). Union takes place in caverns of mystery:

> The high caverns of this rock are the sublime, exalted, and deep mysteries of God's wisdom in Christ, in the hypostatic union of the human nature with the

divine Word, and in the corresponding union of human beings with God, and the mystery of the harmony between God's justice and mercy with respect to the manifestations of his judgements in the salvation of the human race.

(*CB* 37.3, 2017, p. 615)

The soul that is totally purified and emptied of 'all forms and images that can be apprehended' and is 'transformed' 'into a state of perfection'. Once all the veils that obscure God are removed, the soul is perfectly detached and is transformed into the 'Wisdom, which is the Son of God' and is 'imbued with that which is divine' (*A* II. 15.4).

## The role of the spiritual director, the role of the analyst

John warns of the dangers of wrong direction, such as encouraging a person to continue with meditation when they have attained infused contemplation. How might we think of the parallels with the role of the analyst? In the following passage John warns the director to remember that it is the Holy Ghost who is the director. So too in analysis it is the analytic third, the 'still quiet voice' that enables the analytic journey to unfold organically. In the *Living Flame of Love* John writes:

> Let spiritual directors . . . remember that the Holy Ghost is the principle agent here, and the real guide of souls; that He never ceases to take care of them and never neglects any means by which they may profit and draw near unto God as quickly as possible, and in the best way. Let them remember that they are not the agents, but instruments only to guide souls by the rule of the faith and the law of God, according to the spirit which God gives to everyone.
>
> (*LF* III. 47, 1912/2007b, p. 87)

John also warns that 'some spiritual fathers are likely to be a hinderance and harm rather than a help to these souls that journey on this road' since they 'have neither understanding or experience of these ways'. The person who is being guided by God 'along a sublime path of dark contemplation and aridity, in which they feel lost and filled with darkness, trials, conflicts, and temptations' might be told this is 'due to melancholia, depression, or temperament or to some hidden wickedness' (*A* Prologue 4, 2017, p. 116). St John suggests that directors at this stage need to know not to interfere with God's work of purgation. It is instead a time to 'give comfort and encouragement' (ibid., p. 117). The difficulty of discernment for the therapist or director is also to know when a patient is suffering a spiritual crisis pertaining to the dark night of the soul rather than melancholia or depression. The authentic experience of a dark night will eventually transform into the dawning of wisdom, love and light in the mystical betrothal with the divine Bridegroom.

## Silent music

> The tranquil night
> at the time of the rising dawn,
> Silent music,
> Sounding solitude,
> the supper that refreshes, and deepens love.
>                     (*CB* 15, 2017, p. 473)

After the anguish, emptiness and desolation of the dark night, there is the possibility of the dawning of light, illumination, joy, beatitude and wisdom. 'At the time of rising dawn' the soul who is asleep 'in the bosom of the Beloved', is illuminated by divine love and wisdom. 'She receives in God' a 'fathomless and obscure divine knowledge', a 'tranquillity and quietude in divine light, in the new knowledge of God' and rightly 'calls this divine light "the rising dawn"' which 'dispels the darkness of night and unveils the light of day'. The soul is 'elevated from the darkness of natural knowledge to the morning light of the supernatural knowledge of God' (*CB* 14–15, 22–24, 2017, pp. 534–535).

> There he gave me his breast;
> there he taught me a sweet and living knowledge:
> and I gave myself to him,
> keeping nothing back:
> there I promised to be his bride.
>                     (*CB* 27, 2017, p. 475)

# Chapter 14

# Apophatic contemplation in Christianity

Bede Griffiths, an English Benedictine monk devoted to Hindu-Christian dialogue, describes how, when he was a child at boarding school, he went for a walk one evening. He heard the birds singing, but it was a hearing like nothing before. 'It seemed to me that I had never heard the birds singing before and I wondered whether they sang like this all the year round and I had never noticed it'. Bede walked on and 'came upon some hawthorn trees in full bloom'. Again, it was as if he

> had never seen such a sight or experienced such sweetness before. If I had been brought suddenly among the trees of the Garden of Paradise and heard a choir of angels singing I could not have been more surprised. I came then to where the sun was setting over the playing fields. A lark rose suddenly from the ground beside the tree where I was standing and poured out its song above my head, and then sank still singing to rest. Everything then grew still as the sunset faded and the veil of dusk began to cover the earth. I remember now the feeling of awe which came over me. I felt inclined to kneel on the ground, as though I had been standing in the presence of an angel; and I hardly dared to look on the face of the sky, because it seemed as though it was but a veil before the face of God.
>
> (Griffiths, 1954, p. 9)

Bede Griffiths had the sense he was in 'the presence of an unfathomable mystery', an experience of awe, as if a veil has been lifted 'and we see for the first time behind the façade which the world has built around us' (1954, p. 10).

> These are the moments when we really come face to face with reality. . . . We see our life for a moment in its true perspective in relation to eternity. We are freed from the flux of time and see something of the eternal order which underlies it. We are no longer isolated individuals in conflict with our surroundings; we are parts of a whole, elements in a universal harmony.
>
> (Griffiths, 1954, p. 11)

Contemplation in the apophatic mystical tradition is not the same as mindfulness, analytical meditation, discursive prayer, ritual or liturgical worship. Although the exact definitions vary, meditation in the Christian context is seen to be dependent on methods, images and concepts, whereas contemplation is not something to be achieved, it is a grace which, like 'a flash of brilliant darkness', enters the soul at prayer. Prayer, meditation, study, liturgy and leading a virtuous life are all like tilling the soil and planting seeds. Whether the seed takes root or not depends upon something intangible that transcends human 'will' or 'effort'. The contemplative mystics would say it depends on grace. Contemplation can refer to the state of being with, or abiding in the Godhead or absolute.

## Etymology

The Western word 'contemplation' derives from the Latin *contemplātiō* or *contemplātiōnis*. *Contemplātiō* in turn derives from *contemplō*. The word *templum* refers to the space within the temple, not the structure itself. The prefix *con* can mean 'with', 'thoroughly', 'connectivity', and the suffix *-tion* a state. The *templum* was the heavenly place where the gods dwelt, as well as the earthly temple where one communed with the gods. Within the sacred space, the Roman priest as augur, in a state of contemplation, paid attention, observed and interpreted the messages of the gods. It also relates to the Greek *temenos*, a sacred space. The temple is within oneself, as well as without. The apophatic way is a process of clearing away all that clutters the temple of the soul so that it becomes a suitable dwelling for the inflow of divine wisdom. We 'live, we move and have our being' in God (Acts 17:28), and God dwells in our hearts (John 17:23).

In antiquity contemplation referred to a deliberate turning away from the distractions of 'corporeal' vision and the cultivation of inner sight leading to a 'rational reflection on incorporeal things'. For the Platonic philosopher, contemplation was the only means to ascend to the One, and hence contemplation 'was the ultimate goal of the enlightened individual's earthly life' (Watson, 2011, p. 11).

Plato wrote about contemplation as the search for truth as a form of love of wisdom. Aristotle also describes the contemplative life and contemplative moments when one becomes almost like God. Plotinus and the Neoplatonists taught that contemplation was the 'supreme expression of human existence', which was also available to all who sought it. 'Plotinus followed the contemplative path set out in Plato's *Symposium*' and experienced contemplative union with the One: 'That God who has neither shape nor any conceptual form but is seated above intellect and everything intelligible' (*Vita Plotini* in Kenney, 2013b, p. 32). He held that apophatic contemplation involves dissolution of the boundaries of consciousness into communion with the One, through turning away from seeing the external world and rising up to be 'alone with the alone' via a sense of 'presence beyond knowledge' (Kenney, 2013b, p. 32).

In the following, I shall focus on contemplation from the apophatic perspective. I argue that such contemplation has much to offer the psychotherapist seeking to enter a state of analytic reverie. In turn, analytic reverie is a way to attune to the O of a given session.

## What is contemplation?

Contemplation (*contemplatio*) was a word used before *mystica*, and was the Latin translation of the Greek *theoria* which means 'gazing at' or 'being aware of'. The word for contemplation, *theōria*, is related to the word for God, *theos*, which is derived from *theasthai*, to behold. Contemplation was used in favour of mysticism by Augustine, Gregory and Bernard. In the tradition of Christian contemplative prayer, contemplation was commonly understood as gazing on God with the inner eye of love.

St Gregory the Great, at the end of the sixth century CE, describes contemplation as the knowledge of God impregnated with love. He also saw contemplation as the fruit of reflection on the word of God and calls it 'resting in God'. Thomas Aquinas defines contemplation as 'a simple gaze on God and divine things proceeding from love and tending thereto' (Aquinas in Johnston, 1978, p. 24). Francis de Sales defines contemplation as 'a loving, simple, and permanent attentiveness of the mind to divine things' (in Johnston, 1978, p. 24).

There is often an overlap between the terms contemplation, mysticism, mystical theology and spirituality. John of the Cross writes of how 'because of its obscurity, she calls contemplation night. On this account contemplation is also termed mystical theology' (John of the Cross, 1964, p. 626).

Many writers from Origen in the third century onwards drew on the gospel passage where Jesus visited two sisters, Mary and Martha (Luke, 10: 38–42) to differentiate the contemplative and active ways (*vita contemplativa* and *vita activa*). Martha busied herself offering physical hospitality while Mary sat, rapt in contemplation gazing on Jesus and taking in his every word. Martha resented Mary for not helping her and asked Jesus to get Mary to help. Jesus replied that Martha was anxious and troubled by many things, but that only one thing was necessary and that Mary had chosen the better part. This distinction between Mary and Martha became an archetypal story illustrating two different callings, one the active life and the other the life of contemplation. Origen saw in this story a depiction of the dichotomy articulated by Aristotle between the practical and theoretical life. Yet for others such as Thomas Aquinas, mystical contemplation had a necessary overflow in sharing the fruits of contemplation in order to help others. Mary and Martha represent two necessary dimensions of the religious life.

From the twelfth century there were distinctions made between *lecto divina*, meditation, prayer and contemplation, with further distinctions between acquired and infused contemplation. Acquired contemplation, like meditation, was achieved by one's own effort aided by grace. Efforts might include the repetition of the prayer word as in the prayer of the heart. Infused contemplation is sometimes called mystical contemplation, which followed a calling to a deeper level of prayer, signalled by such signs as a longing for solitude, an inability to engage in discursive prayer, a profound sense of inner silence and awareness of the presence of God. There comes a stage where the prayer word dissolves into a luminous sense of vastness and infinity in which 'contemplative practice is mainly a silent and uncluttered gazing into luminous vastness that streams out as our own awareness, a riverbed of awareness in which all things appear and disappear' (Laird, 2006, p. 69).

Thomas Merton wrote that 'the Christian contemplative is called mainly to penetrate the wordless darkness and apophatic light of an experience beyond concepts, and here he gradually becomes familiar with a God who is "absent" and as it were "non-existent" to all human experience' (1973, p. 186).

## Contemplative prayer

Contemplative prayer was practiced among the desert fathers and mothers in Egypt, Palestine and Syria, and propounded by Evagrius, Augustine, St Gregory the Great, Dionysius and the Hesychasts. In the medieval period it is associated with mystics such as Bernard of Clarivaux, Hildegard of Bingen, William of St Thierry, Guigo the Carthusian, Francis and Clare of Assisi, Mechtilde of Magdeburg, Meister Eckhart and other Rhineland mystics, Ruysbroek, Tauler, the author of *The Cloud of Unknowing*, Richard Rolle, Walter Hilton, and Julian of Norwich. Later there was also Teresa of Ávila, John of the Cross and Francis de Sales, among many others.

## Hesychasm

The Egyptian desert fathers originally used the term hesychast (from the Greek *hesychasmos* meaning stillness, rest, silence) to refer to a person leading a life of solitude and contemplation. This understanding broadened to include the method of apophatic prayer, known as 'prayer of the heart', based on the passage in the Sermon on the Mount in Matthew's gospel: 'When you pray, go into your room and shut the door and pray to your Father who is in secret; and your Father, who sees in secret, will reward you' (Matthew 6:6).

Evagrius Ponticus (345–399) described a three-fold path 'involving purification from passion (*praxis*), contemplation of nature as the work of God (*physike theoria*) and the vision of God (*theologia*)' (Strezova, 2014, p. 11). Evagrius also advised the contemplative to pass beyond images:

> When you pray, do not try to represent the divine in yourself, do not let any specific form be imprinted on your mind. Instead approach the Immaterial immaterially, and then you will understand.
>
> (*De oration 66* in Harmless, 2004, p. 351)

God is beyond image, beyond materiality, thus for Evagrius to pray before an image even a mental one, is tantamount to idolatry. Evagrius continues:

Blessed the mind which in time of prayer has attained perfect formlessness.

Blessed the mind which in undistracted prayer receives an ever-growing desire for God.

Blessed the mind which in time of prayer becomes immaterial and stripped of everything.

Blessed the mind which in time of prayer possesses perfect insensibility.

(*De oration 57*, in Harmless, 2004, p. 351)

## Philokalia, the Orthodox tradition and the Jesus Prayer

We have seen etymological links between spirit, spirituality and the breath. Many early texts on Christian contemplation and hesychasm advocate synchronising breathing with the prayer word. This is very similar to teachings in Buddhism combining mantra meditation with breathing. Hesychios says, 'With your breathing combine watchfulness and the name of Jesus' (Hesychios, 1983, p. 196). Incorporating awareness of breathing is a way to overcome distracting thoughts, eliciting stillness, calm, concentration and wisdom.

> You know, brother, how we breathe: we breathe the air in and out. On this is based the life of the body and on this depends its warmth. So, sitting down in your cell, collect your mind, lead it into the path of the breath along which the air enters in, constrain it to enter the heart altogether with the inhaled air, and keep it there. Keep it there, but do not leave it silent and idle; instead give it the following prayer: 'Lord, Jesus Christ, Son of God, have mercy on me'.
>
> (in Johnston, 1997, p. 80)

The classic prayer of the heart is the Jesus Prayer, first mentioned by Diadochos of Photiki (c. 450). In shortened form it is 'Lord Jesus Christ, have mercy on me'. An extended version is 'Lord Jesus Christ, Son of God, have mercy on me, a sinner'. Following St Paul's direction to 'pray without ceasing', it was taught as a way to practice continuous prayer, through the discipline of frequent repetition and the quest for inner silence and quietude (*hēsuchia*). The prayer word acts as an anchor for non-discursive, imageless prayer, similar to Buddhist calm-abiding meditations. Some writers, such as the Cloud author, advised that the word itself was not important, and the shorter the better. Other writers held that the name of Jesus carried a sacramental power. The aim of continuous prayer was to preserve awareness of divine presence through the remembrance of God (*mnēmē Theou*) in all one was doing, whether eating, resting, working or sleeping as well as in dedicated times of prayer and contemplation a principle also espoused in Dzogchen.

Hesychios advised one to combine breathing with watchfulness and the name of Jesus. 'If you really wish . . . to be still and calm, and to watch over your heart without hindrance, let the Jesus Prayer cleave to your breath, and in a few days you will find that this is possible' (1983, p. 196). St Gregory Palamas advised one to silently pray 'Lord Jesus Christ, Son of God,' as one inhales, pause a moment, then as one exhales pray 'have mercy on me, a sinner.'

The repetition of a phrase has the benefit of focusing the mind, enabling it to transcend discursive prayer into the state of pure contemplation. It enables one to overcome what Cassian called the 'monkey mind' which is disquieted, 'boiling over with a multitude of different distractions . . . unable to control my wandering thoughts' or curb 'imagining foolish phantasies' (1997, p. 381). So too, Buddhists use the analogy of the monkey mind, jumping from one thing to another, never at rest.

The Monk of Mount Athos gives the following instructions for repetition of the prayer word or phrase.

> The words of prayer should be spoken very slowly, one by one, each engross-ing the whole being. The entire person focuses into a single point. The breath-ing changes and becomes . . . secret . . . the mind, the heart, the body to its very bones, are all drawn into this one point. Unseeing, the mind contem-plates the world; unseeing the heart lives the sufferings of the world, and in the heart itself suffering reaches its utmost limit. The heart – or rather, the whole being – is submerged in tears.
>
> (Sophrony, 1973, p. 33)

He also observes that contemplative prayer leads naturally to true compassion for the world. This is a vital theme, for the contemplative's search for union with God also entails a natural out-flowing of love and compassion for all beings, as an 'ontological community of being' since the Son of Man takes into himself all beings. 'When you pray, keep your mind quite free from any imagining, any irrelevant thought. . . . Enclose your mind in the words of your prayer' (Sophrony, 1973, p. 25).

## Contemplation in Augustine of Hippo (354–430)

Augustine, in his *Confessions*, describes contemplation as revealing the 'amaz-ing depth' of the soul, and the potential for divine communion with God. For Augustine, the source and inspiration for contemplation is the indwelling of the Holy Spirit:

> The contemplative soul is inhabited by the spirit and knows 'the things of God' only through the Spirit (XIII. xxxi [46]). The activity of the spirit is the agent of divine self-contemplation. It is this divine contemplative motion, out into creation and back through the 'things of God,' that establishes the great rhythm of creation. It is this majestic spiritual movement that is discovered in contemplation.
>
> Contemplation is the sight of God directed towards creation and then back upon himself through contemplation. God's contemplative presence is the

active force holding reality in existence, and the Christian soul can connect
up with that divine intellection.

(Kenney, 2013b, p. 200)

## Contemplation in Dionysius

For Dionysius contemplation passes from the outward symbols in scripture and
liturgy to their inner meanings, to higher contemplations, to those of 'hidden mystical contemplations' (*ta mystika theamata*), to not seeing that is seeing indeed
(*MT* 1.1 997B) in 'the brilliant darkness of hidden silence' (*MT* 1.1 997B). When
all that can be seen falls away and one enters the gloom of the *Agnosia*, words,
language and symbols fail and one enters a mystic silence, becoming 'wholly
speechless' in order 'to be united with the unutterable' (*MT* 1033C in Golitzin,
2013, p. 61).

> Do thou, then, in the intent practice of mystic contemplation, leave behind
> the senses and the operations of the intellect, and all things that the senses
> or the intellect can perceive, all things which are not and things which are,
> and strain upwards in unknowing, as far as may be, towards the union with
> Him Who is above all things and knowledge. For by unceasing and absolute
> withdrawal from thyself and all things in purity, abandoning all and set free
> from all, thou shalt be borne up to the ray of divine darkness that surpasseth
> all being.
>
> (Dionysius, *MT* I. 1 in Johnston, 1967, p. 33)

For Dionysius contemplation has a trajectory, from passing from the outward
symbols in scripture and liturgy to their inner meanings, to higher, hidden and
mystical contemplations (*ta mystika theamata*), beyond symbolisation towards
union in 'the brilliant darkness of hidden silence' (*MT* 1.1 997B). Unknowing
(*agnōsia*) begins with contemplation (*theōria*) of the Godhead beyond contemplation, thus freeing the contemplative from the seer and the seen, plunging into
'the truly mysterious darkness of unknowing' (*ton gnophon tēs agnosias ton ontōs
mystikon*) (in Sells, 1994, p. 35). Dionysius outlines three stages in the process of
union with our own inherent divinity: purification (*katharsis*), followed by contemplation (*theōria*), and finally union (*henōsis*). The word for contemplation,
*theōria*, is related to the word for God, *theos*, which is derived from *theasthai*, to
behold.

## Contemplation in *The Cloud of Unknowing*

It is thought that the anonymous author of *The Cloud of Unknowing* was writing
in the late fourteenth century in the northeast midlands of England. The author
also translated Dionysius' *The Mystical Theology* under the title *Deonise Hid
Diuinite*. The title derives from the phrase in *The Mystical Theology, tōn gnophon*

*tēs agnōsias* or 'the darkness of unknowing' (*MT* 1.3.1001A). Its commentary interpreted *The Mystical Theology* as a guide to the darkness of unknowing, in which the soul is united with God in ecstatic love. Love, not thought, is the way to penetrate the cloud of unknowing: 'Of God himself can no man think. . . . Whence he may well be loved, but not thought. By love may be he gotten and holden; but by thought never' (*Cloud of Unknowing*, in Underhill, 1922, 6. p. 89).

   *The Cloud of Unknowing* takes the form of a long letter to a disciple addressed as 'My spiritual friend in God'. In this sense it is an experiential guide to the path of apophatic contemplation. This path is seen to be a work of grace and divine love. God asks for nothing except to 'fix your love' on God, and 'let this be the sole concern of your mind and heart' forgetting all else. The spiritual friend is warned that at first there will be 'nothing but a kind of darkness about your mind, or as it were, *a cloud of unknowing*. You will seem to know nothing and to feel nothing except a naked intent toward God in the depth of your being (in Johnston, 1973, p. 40).

> This darkness and this cloud is always between you and your God, no matter what you do, and it prevents you from seeing him clearly by the light of understanding in your reason, and from feeling him in the sweetness of love in your affection.
>
>                                             (in Walsh, 1981, pp. 120–121)

*The Cloud* author also advises that just as there is a '*cloud of unknowing*' that 'lies above you between you and your God, so you must fashion a *cloud of forgetting* beneath you' (in Johnston, 1973, p. 45, emphasis in the original). The *cloude of forgetyng* involves a deliberate forgetting that eschews memory of creatures, and even all spiritual activity borne of imagination, reason and sense.

> Wholly intent upon God, this simple love beats unceasingly upon the dark *cloud of unknowing*, leaving all discursive thought beneath the *cloud of forgetting* . . . the very heart of this work is nothing else but a naked intent toward God for his own sake.
>
>                                       (in Johnston, 1973, pp. 70–71)

The importance of the double cloud is that such 'double darkness intervenes "between" (*betwixt*) creation and the mystic, as well as "between" the mystic and God'. Such 'betweenness' or 'liminality' serves to deconstruct 'categories of spatiality and temporality. God is outside time and space: he cannot be found "here" or "there"' (McGinn, 2012, p. 404), yet God is our being.

   Love is the central theme for the contemplative life:

> Try to understand this point. Rational creatures . . . possess two principle faculties, a knowing power and a loving power. No one can fully comprehend the uncreated God with his knowledge; but each one, in a different way, can

grasp him fully through love. Truly this is the unending miracle of love: that one loving person, through his love, can embrace God, whose being fills and transcends the entire creation. And this marvellous work of love goes on forever, for he whom we love is eternal.

(*Cloud of Unknowing*, 4, Johnston, 1973, p. 42)

On a practical level *The Cloud* suggests that the contemplative begin by engaging in monologistic prayer, selecting a simple one-syllable word such as 'God' or 'love'. One should

> fasten this word to your heart, so that whatever happens it will never go away. . . . With this word you are to beat on this darkness above you. With this word you shall smite down every kind of thought under the cloud of forgetting.
>
> (in McGinn, 2012, pp. 407–408)

You should 'choose a short word rather than a long one', a 'one-syllable word such as "God" or "love" is best'. Then simply 'fix' the word 'in your mind so that it will remain there come what may'. It is your 'defence in conflict and in peace. Use it to beat upon the cloud of darkness above you' and consign all distractions to the cloud of forgetting below you. If a niggling thought distracts you,

> demanding to know what you are doing, answer with this one word alone. If your mind begins to intellectualise over the meaning and connotations of this little word, remind yourself that its value lies in its simplicity. Do this and I assure you these thoughts will vanish. Why? Because you have refused to develop them with arguing.
>
> (in Johnston, 1973, pp. 7–8)

As is the case in Dzogchen and John of the Cross, the author of *The Cloud of Unknowing* differentiates between meditation and contemplation. Meditation is more akin to discursive, active prayer. Contemplation involves darkness, silence and mystical unknowing. Yet the apophatic is always grounded in the kataphatic foundation. The beginner starts with conceptual kataphatic spiritual exercises as well as participating in sacramental, scriptural, devotional and liturgical life. Meditation, devotion, reason, intelligence, scripture, conscience and reliance on a spiritual director are supports for apophatic contemplation. But then the contemplative begins to feel a blind desire leading to a deeper sense of presence in which one's awareness shifts to 'the weight of love'. There may be an intrusion of blind love preventing one's usual prayers and ever deeper desire for contemplation, both signs indicating that one is being called to contemplation, the 'singular' way in which one learns to 'live now at the deep solitary core of' one's 'being' (in Egan, 1978, p. 406).

Ultimately God may send illuminating light revealing divine secrets and setting the heart aflame: a supra-cognitive enlightenment that is incommunicable, a 'knowing by unknowing' that 'includes faith, love and wisdom. It is founded on faith, directed by love, and at its summit may be granted a "dark wisdom" known only to the one who receives it' (McGinn, 2012, p. 411).

> Then perhaps it will be his will to send out a ray of spiritual light, piercing this cloud of unknowing between you and him, and he will show you some of his secrets, of which many may not or cannot speak (2 Cor. 12:4). Then you shall feel your affection all aflame with the fire of his love, far more than I know how to tell you, or may, or wish to at this time.
>
> (in Walsh, 1981, pp. 174–175)

In *The Book of Privy Counseling* the methodology is ever more apophatic: to reject all thoughts about what one is, what God is and focus nakedly only on 'that I am' and 'that God is'.

> This awareness, stripped of ideas and . . . anchored in faith, shall leave your thought and affection in emptiness, except for a naked thought and blind feeling of your own being . . . let that quiet darkness be your whole mind and a mirror to you.
>
> (in Johnston, 1973, p. 138)

The final step is to reject all thought of one's own being, enter a state of total self-forgetfulness and concentrate only on the Being beyond being of God, abandoning all thoughts 'be they good or bad':

> Leave your thought quite naked, your affection uninvolved, and your self simply as you are, so that grace may touch and nourish you with the experiential knowledge of God as he really is. See that nothing remains in your conscious mind save a naked intent stretching out toward God. Leave it stripped of every particular idea *about* God . . . and keep only the simple awareness *that he is as he is*.
>
> (in Johnston, 1973, p. 139, emphasis in the original)

The goal for the contemplative is deifying union with God. This requires embracing a process of self-naughting: 'Leave this everywhere and this something in exchange for this nowhere and this nothing' (in McGinn, 2012, p. 417). Similar to Dionysius' 'beam of intense darkness', one experiences a blindness due to an *'habundaunce of goostly light*, so that while the outer person calls it "Nothing", the inner person calls it "All"' (in McGinn, 2012, p. 417). Leaving behind egocentric clinging to the false self, one passes into the beatitude of nothingness, into the limitless infinity of God's truth.

The *Book of Privy Counseling* continues the themes of self-negation and blind stirring of love towards God essentialised in the prayer:

> That which I am I offer to you, O Lord,
> Without looking to any quality of your
> Being but only to the fact that you
> are as you are; this, and nothing more.
>                       (in Johnston, 1973, p. 138)

He continues: 'Go no further, but rest in this naked, stark, elemental awareness that you are as you are' (in Johnston, 1973, p. 139).

Just as the *Cloud* featured the double cloud of forgetting and unknowing, the *Book of Privy Counseling* features a double negation, the naked being of the soul and the naked being of God. This

> aims at a radical stripping away, not only of all the created qualities of the soul but also of all the particular attributes of God. Having nothing to do with our ordinary levels of experience, the work involves no imaginative or intellectual activities. Because it negates even the awareness of our own naked being when it attains direct perception of God, the work can be described as perfect union. The surpassing love and wisdom found at this highest stage, always brief, cannot be understood, let alone communicated to others.
>                       (McGinn, 2012, pp. 420–421)

The *Cloud* author is also advocating non-dualism in which distinctions between inner and outer are transcended. Here the need is to

> become detached from, that is liberated from, the very dualism itself between interiority and exteriority in theory and in practice, so that we do not any longer have to see ourselves as caught between their opposed polarities.
>                       (Turner, 1995, p. 209)

Difficulties arise if we become attached to a way, even the apophatic way. All spiritual methods and techniques, grasping after results, clinging to mystical experience must be abandoned. We are also warned to remain anchored in sacramental, liturgical and scriptural life as well as rooted in one's community.

## Conclusion

The call to contemplation requires surrender, darkness, nothingness, penetrating the abyss with awe, wonder and reverence. Contemplation is not something achieved but a grace, which like a flash of brilliant darkness, enters the soul at prayer. Prayer, meditation, study and leading a virtuous life are all like tilling the soil and planting seeds. Whether the seed takes root or not is, according to the mystics, dependent upon something intangible and transcends 'will' or 'effort'. It depends on grace. Ultimately too, prayer, ascetical practices and mediation all fall away in the cloud of unknowing. What is required is abandoning all memory, desire, understanding, conceptualisation and the ratio-centric machinations of the ordinary mind, opening into awe, wonder, gratitude, awareness, a sense of the sacred, of holiness itself, of divinity beyond understanding.

> It is nothing that can be grasped by thoughts, feelings, words. Language wilts. The prayer word opens. It reveals not another object of awareness, but the groundless ground that is the core of all being . . . and indescribable vastness, streaming from all sides, streaming from no sides, an ocean full and overflowing with a luminous nothing . . . where no word has ever gone, but out of which the Word emerges. And so this silence washes onto the shores of perception, making it stretch in metaphors of light, union, calm, spaciousness.
>
> (Laird, 2006, p. 66)

# Chapter 15

# Apophatic epistemology in Bion

## The search for knowledge

'Know thyself', Socrates instructs us. There is an intrinsic desire to know ourselves, to know each other. We seek to know the truth, the nature of reality, the meaning of our existence. If we are religious, we seek to know God. Aristotle observed that:

> All men by nature desire to know. An indication of this is the delight we take in our senses; for even apart from their usefulness they are loved for themselves; and above all others the sense of sight. . . . The reason is that this, most of all the senses, makes us know and brings to light many differences between things.
> (*Metaphysics* I.I, 980a21–7, in Lear, 1988, p. 1)

According to Freud (1905) there is a drive to know, an 'instinct for knowledge' (*Wissenstrieb*) or epistemophilic instinct. For Freud, this was largely infantile sexual curiosity. Klein developed the concept of the epistemophilic instinct further, describing the 'child's urge to knowledge' of mother's body and mind (1923, p. 435). Self-knowledge may be a crucial aim of psychoanalysis (Bion, 1963, p. 91), but can we truly know ourselves? As Nietzsche observed:

> How can a human being know himself? He is a dark and shrouded thing; and if a hare has seven skins, a human being could strip off seven times seventy and would still be unable to say, 'now this is really you, this is no longer a rind'.
> (in Kaufmann, 1966, pp. 7–8)

What if the very thing we wanted to know was beyond knowledge; what if it cannot be apprehended through the senses or even the rational mind? For the apophatic mystics as well as for Bion, ultimate reality is not accessible through ordinary ways of knowing. In such 'apophatic epistemology' knowledge is replaced by a recognition of unknowing, sight by deliberate blinding, since

> in order to see clearly one really needs to be pretty well blind – metaphorically and literally. It is really a sort of positive lack of anything in one's mind . . . that the darker the spot that you wish to illuminate, the darker you have

to be – you have to shut out all light in order to be able to see it. Only in that way is it possible to get the conditions in which a real object – but one which is formless and not in any way appreciable to what we ordinarily regard as the senses – emerges, evolves, and becomes possible for us to be aware of.

(Bion, 1965/2014, *CWVI*, p. 13)

Within psychoanalysis the discovery of the unconscious is the discovery of those aspects of the self that are unknown. There is a correlation between inner and outer alterity, between our alter ego, what Freud called the uncanny, what Jung referred to as the shadow, and the alterity of another. The epistemological paradox expressed by Bion is that the *search* to know is different from the *assumption* that we know. Similarly a *piece* of knowledge gets in the way of the search to know, which is a dynamic inter-relational link predicated on uncertainty.

For Bion, psychoanalysis is not properly a theory or body of knowledge but 'an expedition' into the unknown. Bion writes that it is a mistake to view 'psychoanalysis as a body of knowledge or a therapeutic procedure rather than as a research into the domain of mind itself, an expedition' (1968/2014, *CWXV*, p. 62).

Bion follows in the footsteps of the apophatic mystics who realised that ineffable, dark unknowing is the way to realise ultimate reality. The soul meets God by plunging 'into the truly mysterious darkness of unknowing' (Dionysius, *MT* 1.3. 1001A). The 'darkness of unknowing' (*caligo ignorantiae*) is a deliberate discipline. Dionysius writes that the 'most divine knowledge of God . . . comes through unknowing', achieving a 'union far beyond mind, when mind turns away from all things, even from itself, and when it is made one with the dazzling rays, being then and there enlightened by the inscrutable depth of Wisdom' (*DN* 7.3 872B).

Bion, in *Attention and Interpretation* (1970, p. 27), describes self-vigilance and discipline of not knowing, enabling 'epistemological purity, naivety, and freedom from ready-made previous theories, in order to be directly in contact with the ultimate reality of what is actually taking place in each session of psychoanalysis, and thus be an effective psychoanalyst' (Torres, 2013, p. 32).

This is a different form of epistemophilic instinct, apophatic epistemology: the yearning to understand absolute reality requires the knowing that consists in unknowing, the seeing that consists in not seeing, the wisdom beyond all conceptual mentation. It is such apophatic epistemology that Bion embraces in his descriptions of O.

The analyst must focus his attention on O, the unknown and unknowable.

(Bion, 1970, p. 27)

If such a *via negativa* is to be applied to analysis, it creates an interesting epistemological problem for psychoanalysis, which seeks to develop insight, self-knowledge, to make the unconscious conscious. Even the term 'analysis' suggests detailed examination and investigation in order to know. Yet, for Bion, 'the dominant feature of a session is the unknown personality and not what the analysand or analyst thinks he knows' (1970, p. 87). It is 'as difficult to see the centre of one's personality as it is to view the centre of the galaxy' (Bion, 1991, p. 254).

## Negative epistemology and the unconscious

Psychotherapy is concerned with the unconscious which by definition is as yet unknown. Negative epistemology is an intrinsic aspect of psychoanalytic methodology. There is a need to sit with uncertainty, mystery and doubt. Jung spoke of scintillae, the sparks of consciousness which come from the 'Ruach Elohim', the 'Spirit of God' which illuminates the darkness, the 'lumen naturae' which 'is the light of the darkness' (*CWVIII*, para. 388). The therapist, like the alchemist, seeks to discover how in 'the very darkness of nature a light is hidden, a little spark without which the darkness would not be darkness . . . the lumen naturae is the light of the darkness itself, which illuminates its own darkness, and this light the darkness comprehends' (Jung, *CWXIV*, para. 197).

Bion reminds us that we do not have direct access to psychic phenomena. We can see a chair, a couch, a person's body, but not the contents of their mind. We cannot see, touch, hear, smell or touch anxiety: 'The phenomena of mental life . . . are shapeless, untouchable, invisible, odourless, tasteless'. Yet 'these psychically real . . . elements are what the analyst has to work with' (Bion, 1970, p. 70).

In regard to the application of negative epistemology to psychotherapy, issues of relevance could be summarised as follows:

- There is a natural desire to know, what Freud and Klein called the epistemophilic instinct, originating in the infantile desire to know the mother's body/ mind.
- Self-knowledge is a major aim for psychoanalysis. The patient comes seeking greater self-awareness. The analyst also seeks to understand the patient. Very often the patient derives not only a sense of reassurance through feeling understood, but a sense of feeling real through being known deeply with a concomitant sense of being cared for.
- Yet the mystery and alterity as well as the dynamic ever-changing nature of reality means one cannot ever be fully known. There are tensions between the desire to know and be known and the incomprehensibility of a person.
- Ultimate truth, absolute reality, the divine, the Godhead are not to be known through ordinary ways of knowing. The absolute cannot be apprehended through sensory perception, imagination, intellect, rational knowledge, doctrine and affirmative kataphatic theology.

- How does one pass from knowing to being or from knowing about reality to realising it? In psychoanalysis, there is the issue of how to turn intellectual insight into structural change, to move from diagnosis to cure. A simple clinical example might be that through analysis one recognises that one is beset by a particular complex, addiction, or repetition compulsion, but how does one actively succeed in loosening its pernicious hold on our life? How might one go from *knowing* one should be more compassionate to *being* more compassionate, from intention to action?
- Apperception, presupposition, presumption, prejudice and judgment can create psychic dust storms obscuring intimations of ultimate reality. It is not that such mental activity is 'bad' or 'wrong' but that it tends to form a curtain or cloudy film obscuring what lies beyond. How does one create a space to see beyond thought, to apprehend a deeper dimension beyond appearance?
- 'Knowledge' can obstruct 'knowing'. A static piece of knowledge can serve as a blockage to the activity of trying to know. Conceptualisation, interpretations, bodies of knowledge, ideology, dogma and doctrine all have their place but also have limitations: they can get in the way of the actively engaged activity of trying to understand what one does not know, and being receptive to what one does not, even perhaps, cannot fully understand.
- In Dzogchen there is the central issue of how one passes from ordinary 'mind' to the 'nature of mind', clearing away egocentric and dualistic constructions of reality to pass through to the primordially pure, free and luminous base of all.
- For John of the Cross the emptying and purification of understanding, memory and will clears the soul for the infilling of the dark wisdom of God.

## Bion's apophatic epistemology

Bion's apophatic analytic epistemology includes his writings on the K link, the psychoanalytic application of Keats' concept of negative capability, Henri Poincaré's selected fact, the Language of Achievement and, following John of the Cross's *Ascent of Mount Carmel*, Bion's suggestion that analysts should renounce memory, desire understanding and sense impressions.

The crucial point is that the activity of seeking to know is not the same as a piece of knowledge or the assumption that one knows, such assumptions getting in the way of the search to know. For Bion the activity of seeking to know as an emotionally engaged activity is denoted by what he calls the K link.

### The K link

Bion recognised that emotional experience is always embedded in relationship: 'An emotional experience cannot be conceived of in isolation from a relationship' (1962, p. 42). He notates three emotional intersubjective links between human beings as Love (L), Hate (H) and Knowledge (K) (1962, p. 43). Their negatives are −L, −H and −K.

The K link is an emotional link between two people seeking to know and be known while realising that they cannot ever fully know another. The emotionally engaged, compassionate activity of searching to know while tolerating the difficult frustration of not knowing forms two paradoxical components, both of which are needed in creating a worthy container for hosting the possibility of new insight. This is reminiscent of the Spanish word *recordar*, that John of the Cross used in regard to mystical union, to denote not so much recollection, but coming to know, to awaken and to discover.

Awareness of unknowing is painful and may be defended against by attempts at modification or evasion of pain, depending on the capacity of the individual to 'tolerate frustration' (Bion, 1962, p. 48). One can defend against the pain of not knowing via positing a *piece* of knowledge which one grasps like a possession, in place of the emotional activity of seeking to know. Evasion may take the form of positing a quick answer to a question that circumvents the spirit of enquiry and forecloses on further questioning. Any given answer tends to evoke more questions and any interpretation is only provisional, a hypothesis, a wondering. There is a need to be cognizant of complexity, multi-factorial analyses, the intersecting and interdependence of myriad dynamic factors involved in any given situation. Both modification and evasion preclude the establishment of a K link and learning through emotional experience.

False knowledge can become a tyranny, a way of categorising and thus controlling the other. What Bion calls minus K (−K) is a tyrannous imposition of a false 'knowledge' fuelled by envy for the other being outside the sphere of one's epistemological control. Minus K is an evasion of the pain of not being able to know, predict and control the other. The emotional aspects of −K are envy and greed, a spoiling, destructive impulse where meaning is denuded of vitality, thus occluding against discovery. According to Bion, this belongs to the psychotic part of the personality. Meltzer describes such a process thus:

> Generosity becomes *quid pro quo*, receptiveness becomes inveiglement, reciprocity becomes collusion, understanding becomes penetration of secrets, knowledge becomes information, symbol formation becomes metonymy, art becomes fashion.
>
> (Meltzer, 1992, pp. 72–73)

We all have a right to remain hidden. There is a tension between the desire to be understood and the desire to retain a private inner core, to choose when and how much to confide. A patient 'Ben', took six months before feeling he could trust me enough to confide his darkest secrets that he had never divulged to anyone before. His mother was not only very intrusive, but she assumed she knew what he was thinking and feeling. He so hated anyone knowing anything about him that he closeted himself away in his bedroom. Yet he felt terribly isolated and lonely.

Another part of him longed to feel understood. When he finally did reveal his ter-rible secret, he felt enormous relief, followed by fear and suspicion it might be used against him, or that I might not have really got it right. I had to take great care to respect his need to be in control of when, how and if this matter was brought up again.

Realising one cannot ever penetrate inside another's inner world, respecting privacy coupled with genuine interest is a feature of the capacity to enjoy alterity. It gives rise to a sense of richness, nuanced by 'generosity, receptiveness, aes-thetic reciprocity' and is 'the locus of symbol formation, and thus of art, poetry, imagination' (Meltzer, 1992, p. 72).

We need to be open to meet a natural fear of the unknown and the unpre-dictable. For analysts this requires the openness and vulnerability of meeting the patient for each session as if for the first time. We often seek to overcome this fear of uncertainty with being 'all-knowing' and by arming ourselves with formulaic interpretations and spurious truisms.

Presuming we *can* know another fully, or, even more erroneously presuming that we *do* know, inhibits the K activity of *getting* to know. But this is not to sub-stitute the desire to know with apathy and disinterest: if we can't know we might as well not bother trying. This merely leads to a vacuous and dismissive form of epistemological laziness. Lévinas articulates something close to what Bion means by the K link: the desire to comprehend while recognising the other is not a con-cept and transcends comprehension:

> Our relation with the other (*autrui*) certainly consists in wanting to com-prehend him, but this relation overflows comprehension. Not only because knowledge of the other (*autrui*) requires, outside of all curiosity, also sym-pathy or love, ways of being distinct from impassable contemplation, but because in our relation with the other, he does not affect us in terms of a concept. He is a being (*étant*) and counts as such.
>
> (*TI*, 6)

## Thoughts and thinking

Although the apophatic seeks to transcend the conceptual mind, thinking is also a natural activity of the mind. The state of contemplation or meditation is not a blanked out, absent-minded or trance-like state. For Bion, thoughts are not them-selves negative and he is in fact advocating ways to enhance a capacity for think-ing and hosting thoughts. It is more that one does not seek to grasp thoughts but entertains them, just as a host welcomes guests into the container of one's home but does not take them hostage:

> The patient's activity most in evidence in an analysis is thinking. The analyst can see the use he makes of the analytic situation. He may appeal for help, exploit the possibilities of cruelty to the analyst, seek an outlet for love and

generosity and so on. This he does by thinking silently, talking to the analyst, thinking aloud and occasionally by action.

(Bion, 1963, p. 91)

## The truth drive

Although acknowledging unknowing as an analytic discipline, the search for truth inspires our quest. Truth is vital for psychic health. Conversely deprivation of truth leads to psychic starvation (Bion, 1962, p. 56). For Bion, the search for truth supersedes the pleasure principle and desire to evade the pain of unknowing. Bion cites Kipling's 'six honest serving men': 'What and Why and When and How and Where and Who' (Bion, 1977). All the 'six honest serving men' can be seen to be servants of the seventh: the drive for truth, the instinct to know, *Wissentrieb*, the K link.

The philosopher Yovel talks of *the conatus intelligendi*, meaning the inherent endeavour to understand, to 'interpret our existence, to make sense of it, to endow it with *meaning*', that 'human beings *strive to exist in an interpreted, meaning endowed way*'. This means we are 'existentially, both a question – which breaks down our compact being in the present – and a rudimentary answer, which does not repair it' (Yovel, 1999, pp. 54–55).

Schelling also wrote about 'intellectual intuition', a concept derived from Spinoza who wrote about 'intuitive knowledge', or 'knowledge of the third kind'. Both can be related to Poincaré's selected fact, the insight that serves to harmonise and make sense of a mass of seemingly scattered elements. Before we can elaborate on Bion's application of the selected fact to analysis, we need to understand his use of Keats' term 'negative capability'.

## Negative capability

The K link, the ability to sit with unknowing while seeking to know, is linked to what Keats called 'negative capability', meaning the capacity to be 'in uncertainties, mysteries, doubts, without any irritable reaching after fact and reason' (Keats, 1817, in Bion, 1970, p. 125).

In a letter to Richard Woodhouse dated 27 October 1818, Keats elaborates on the qualities of a 'poetical Character' as distinguished from 'an egotistical Sublime'. To be a poet requires a capacity for ecstasy, the ability to stand outside oneself and become one with the moon, sun and sea, to inhabit the identity of others. It involves having 'no self' and the absence of ego as well as an ability to embrace the dark as well as bright side of life.

> As to the poetical Character itself . . . it is not itself – it has no self – It is everything and nothing – It has no character – it enjoys light and shade; it lives in gusto, be it foul or fair, high or low, rich or poor, mean or elevated – It has as much delight in conceiving an Iago as an Imogen. . . .

> A poet is the most unpoetical of anything in existence, because he has no Identity – he is continually in for and filling some other body. The Sun – the Moon – the Sea, and men and women, who are creatures of impulse, are poetical, and have about them an unchangeable attribute; the poet has none, no identity.
>
> (Keats, 2002, p. 194)

Keats says that the poet should have to have 'no identity', 'no self', and 'make up one's mind about nothing' (2002, p. 380). For Bion, a capacity for uncertainty is central to analysis:

> The 'analytic situation' must be one in which two people can have a relationship in which neither is compelled to search 'irritably' for certainty as a method of stifling doubts, uncertainties, mysteries, half-truths and neither is compelled to assert anything as a means by which doubt and uncertainties are evaded.
>
> (1968/2014, *CWXV*, p. 70)

Just as Descartes applied doubt to his philosophical procedure, therapists need to dwell in doubt, mystery and uncertainty with an attitude of open-mindedness that can host a new dawning of insight. Opening with Keats' letter to Dilke, Bion's final chapter of 'Attention and Interpretation' suggests that 'any session should be judged by comparison with the Keats formulation' (Bion, 1970, p. 125).

## Language of Achievement, transmission and transformations

Bion also takes up Keats' term 'the Man of Achievement' and applies it to the form of language that expresses negative capability. To elucidate truth the analyst needs to employ the Language of Achievement, that is, 'employ methods which have the counterpart of durability or extension in a domain where there is no time or space as those terms are used in the world of sense' (1970, p. 2).

Bion was concerned to find a way to communicate psychoanalytic experience. This issue is highly pertinent to apophatic mysticism and transmission of revelation. How does an analyst communicate vital observations about analysis or depict the analytic process? How does an artist convey a transitory moment in time when the flowers are blooming and fluttering in the wind?

There is a link between evolution and Bion's theory of transformations. An example he gives is that of a field of poppies that is painted on a canvas. An artist, through the transformation of an actual field of poppies moving in the breeze into an artistic representation of the field of poppies, is able to convey something consistent with the actual experience. There is an 'invariant' element that allows one to see a consonance between the painting and the landscape it represents. Yet a painting is static, a field of poppies a mutable moment in time and in flux.

Suppose a painter sees a path through a field sown with poppies and paints it: at one end of the chain of events is the field of poppies, at the other a canvas with pigment disposed on its surface. We can recognize that the latter represents the former, so I shall suppose that despite the differences between a field of poppies and a piece of canvas, despite the transformation that the artist has effected in what he saw to make it take the form of a picture, *something* has remained unaltered and on this *something* recognition depends. The elements that go to make up the unaltered aspect of the transformation I shall call invariants.

(Bion, 1965, p. 1)

The criteria for the psychoanalyst's writing is that it

should stimulate in the reader the emotional experience that the writer intends, that its power to stimulate should be durable, and that the emotional experience thus stimulated should be an accurate representation of the psychoanalytic experience ($Oa$) that stimulated the writer in the first place.

(Bion, 1965, p. 32)

If one intuits 'truth O' from this, then the Language of Achievement has achieved durability, it has transmitted transient evolutions of truth beyond that which is apprehended by the senses.

The *Corpus Dionysiacum*, the poetry of John of the Cross and the sacred texts of religion all seek to convey a truth beyond words. Despite the impossibility of expressing in language ultimate reality, 'poetic and religious experience have made possible a degree of "public-ation" in that formulations exist which have achieved durability and extensibility' (Bion, 1970, p. 1). Likewise, to elucidate truth the analyst needs to 'employ the Language of Achievement'. This means employing methods that point to a 'domain where there is no time or space as those terms are used in the world of sense' (Bion, 1970, p. 2).

## The selected fact

Negative capability is the mental state required for the dawning of a new realisation or for intuition of the selected fact.

By Selected Fact I mean that by which coherence and meaning is given to facts already known but whose relatedness has not hitherto been seen.

(Bion, 1963, p. 19)

The 'selected fact' is a term coined by the French mathematician Poincaré. Bion applies this to the analytic situation to refer to one of those moments where, out of the chaos of a mass of disparate, disunited elements, there is a dawning of insight that makes sense of it all. This crystallises all the mass of material the patient was manifesting into an understanding, such that one feels that what was previously a seeming mass of confusing and fragmented elements suddenly makes sense. This is like a detective, who, out of all the trails of evidence, clues and false-leads, suddenly 'gets it', or a mathematician suddenly resolves a previously unresolved problem, a scientist makes a break-through discovery, or a koan is realised, or a meditation experiences the nature of mind. In analysis it refers to a particular thought or insight which suddenly occurs to the analyst, an 'emotional experience of a sense of discovery of coherence' (Bion, 1983, p. 73). Poincaré describes it thus:

> If a new result is to have any value, it must unite elements long since known, but till then scattered and seemingly foreign to each other, and suddenly introduce order where the appearance of disorder reigned. Then it enables us to see at a glance each of these elements in the place it occupies in the whole. Not only is the new fact valuable on its own account, but it alone gives a value to the old facts it unites.
>
> (1952, p. 30)

The selected fact emerges when an

> inchoate mass of incoherent, or apparently incoherent, elements can, by selection of the appropriate fact, be made to appear to the observer to come together as a whole in which the elements are now seen to be related to each other as parts of the whole.
>
> (Bion, 1992, p. 193)

It occurs in the process of synthesis.

> I have used the term 'selected fact' to describe that which the psycho-analyst must experience in the process of synthesis. The name of one element is used to particularize the selected fact, that is to say the name of that element in the realization that appears to link together elements not hitherto seen to be connected.
>
> (Bion, 1962, p. 72)

It takes a considerable degree of negative capability and courage on the part of the therapist to withstand being in a 'cloud of unknowing', when immersed in a sea of psychic confusion. The disunited, inchoate elements presented by the patient are like a kaleidoscope being shaken and its contents spilled into the room. If one can sit long enough with the *massa confusa*, the fragmented bits may begin to cohere into a pattern. Patients often expect the analyst to know what is going on, to have the answer to their problems. The analyst needs to resist the patient's pressure to know, without seeming to withhold, helping the patient develop patience and curiosity, in fact, negative capability. Such a state of mind, unsaturated with premature judgements, is required if a central truth is to be discerned out of the seeming chaos and confusion. The analyst's ability to sit patiently and calmly with complexity and confusion, seeking to know but not jumping to hasty conclusions, may enable a selected fact to occur in the mind of the patient.

Bion describes how in analysis we are listening to 'the totality of a person' and the 'amount of information we get is infinite: it has no boundaries whatever. So out of this mass of material we have to do some selecting' (1976/2014, *CWXV*, p. 34). Yet Bion warns this can mean selecting out what not to hear. Bion also cites Freud who advised that 'it is important to be able to pay attention to the patient; to watch, listen and hear what is going on until a pattern emerges' (1990, p. 117). In the intersubjective analytic field consciousness emerges out of unconscious processes, clarity out of patiently allowing confusion to settle.

Bion links the selected fact with his non-pathological reformulation of the transitions between the paranoid-schizoid position and the depressive position. For Klein, the paranoid-schizoid position involves a primitive form of splitting of self and others into good and bad, in which one cannot tolerate the ambivalence of hate and love and there is no ability to integrate. In Bion's new formulation, in the paranoid-schizoid position one must tolerate the tensions between disunited elements until transformation occurs, whereby they are become integrated via a third thing that brings coherence. Being the 'element that gives coherence to the objects of the paranoid-schizoid position' the selected fact 'initiates the depressive position' (1962, p. 87). The paranoid-schizoid position refers to differentiation, the depressive to transcending of opposites. The formula Ps$\longleftrightarrow$becomes differentiation$\longleftrightarrow$integration (Grotstein, 2007, p. 95). Ps$\longleftrightarrow$D thus dialectically mediate each other, each having different mental functions.

Bion (1970) discusses how the analyst must patiently suffer the sense of disunity and deintegration concomitant with contending with a mass of incompatible disparate psychic material until such time as a pattern emerges. 'Analogous to the paranoid-schizoid position', Bion renames this state of mind as 'patience' (retaining 'its association with suffering and tolerance of frustration') in order to differentiate it from the pathological implications of Klein's formulation. Bion links patience with negative capability when he suggests that:

> 'Patience' should be retained without 'irritable reaching after fact and reason' until a pattern 'evolves'.
>
> (1970, p. 124)

The sense of coherence when the selected fact emerges is linked to the achievement of the depressive position, renamed 'security' (associated with 'safety and diminished anxiety'). Yet a 'sense of achievement of a correct interpretation will be commonly found to be followed almost immediately by a sense of depression'. Thus the 'experience of oscillation between "patience" and "security" [is an] indication that valuable work is being achieved' (Bion, 1970, p. 124).

## Without memory, desire and understanding

> The 'act of faith' (*F*) depends on disciplined denial of memory and desire. A bad memory is not enough: what is ordinarily called forgetting is as bad as remembering. It is necessary to inhibit dwelling on memories and desires.
>
> (Bion, 1970, p 41)

Bion advises therapists to cultivate a state of mind that renounces 'memory, desire and understanding'. The next chapter will focus on the apophatic and mystical dimensions of the state in which there is no memory, desire and understanding, and its antecedents in John of the Cross. But before this can be explained, we need to understand more generally how these terms function as major elements in Bion's negative epistemology.

Bion's original presentation on the need for the analyst to relinquish memory and desire was given without notes to the British Psychoanalytical Society in 1965. He then wrote it up as a two-page article in 1967. In *Attention and Interpretation* (1970) he adds 'understanding' as a third element to be eschewed along with 'sense perception'.

Memories and desires, he tells us, are 'already formulated', they 'derive from experience gained through the senses' and are 'evocations of feelings of pleasure and pain' (Bion, 1970, p. 31). Because psychic realities cannot be apprehended by the senses, the 'suspension of memory, desire, understanding, and sense impressions' is necessary for they all impede contact with psychic reality, 'namely, the evolved characteristics of O' (Bion, 1970, p. 43). The analyst is asked to 'impose upon himself a positive discipline of eschewing memory and desire. I don't mean that "forgetting" is enough: what is required is a positive act of refraining from memory and desire' (Bion, 1970, p. 31). Bion is advocating a form of contemplative discipline in which one practices suppressing the functions of memory, desire, understanding and sense perception one by one or all together (Bion, 1970, p. 44).

Just as John of the Cross warned us, memories litter the mind and need to be cleared away. Not only assumptions predicated on memories of previous sessions, every insight however true and revelatory in its inception becomes part of the new resistance to freshly realising. Bion suggests that patience and negative capability are needed, because in the moment of realisation, the 'revelation' begins to degenerate into but a memory of an insight. Negative capability teaches us a form of faith that depends on patience and uncertainty: not-knowing is a prerequisite for the activity of seeking to know, which is never a static piece of knowledge about something or someone, but an epistemophilic movement towards the one that one wants to know. Even the most profound realisation requires being rendered unknown and rediscovered afresh.

Desire may be simple, such as wishing the session to end, looking forward to the evening when one can relax with a delicious dinner and a glass of wine. It can be a seemingly noble desire to cure the patient or to understand them properly. All such desires obstruct naked awareness of what is going on in the session. Bion warns that

> it is wrong for the analyst to allow himself either memories or desires, the one being the future tense of the other, because memories and desires are opaque. They hide what is going on. This, I believe, is equally true of understanding. While you are *trying* to understand what the patient says he goes on talking and you do not hear what he says.
>
> (Bion, 1990, p. 88)

John of the Cross also warned that the soul needs to avoid leaning 'on its own understanding, sense, imagination, judgement' in the search for illumination of divine realities which are not apprehensible by these mental and sensual faculties (1934/1974, p. 15).

The discipline of eschewing understanding is necessary because fear of uncertainty and ignorance tend to lead to quick formulations that 'deny ignorance – the dark night of the senses' (Bion, 1965, p. 159). The attempt to deny unknowing leads to an obstruction of intuition which requires 'faith' and the 'dark night' that John of the Cross articulates (Bion, 1965, p. 159). Bion is drawing on the Ascent of Mount Carmel (II:6) regarding the role of faith in purifying the caverns of the soul of all understanding. The faculty of understanding is emptied by the darkness of faith, for that which is sought, O, ultimate reality, God, cannot be comprehended by understanding, so needs to be disarmed, silenced, put to rest. In its place the darkness of faith can approach the unapproachable light, but through darkness and obscurity. Here John quotes St Paul's *Fides est sperandarum substantia rerum, argumentum non apparentium*.

### Memory, desire and understanding: qualifications

It is vital we too don't misconstrue Bion's guidance. Memory as a saturated element is different from the act of remembering together which is an active re-creation in the present, a shared remembering (Bion, 1970, p. 107).

Bion distinguishes memory from evolution, which is where an image, idea or dream floats into mind 'unbidden and as a whole' (1967/1992, p. 383). Related to the selected fact, an 'evolution' is 'the coming together, by a sudden precipitating intuition, of a mass of apparently unrelated incoherent phenomena which are thereby given coherence and meaning not previously possessed' (Bion, 1967, p. 127).

Eschewing memory does not mean we do not remember what patients reveal. Remembering is vital for a sense of continuity to develop in a patient whose sense of on-going being has been ruptured. Yet we are in a continual and dynamic process of becoming. The patient today is not the same as the patient last week. To think that either a patient or analyst is the same today as yesterday is 'suspect', a 'sign of a collusive relationship intended to prevent emergence of an unknown, incoherent, formless void and an associated sense of persecution by the elements of an evolving O' (Bion, 1970, p. 52). We are continually in a creative dynamic of movement, flux and mutual shaping of each other's reality and newly experiencing one another in the here and now: a present that 'creates us' – and then is gone. In the empty space created by deliberate forgetfulness and unknowing, we await new beginnings.

Just as suppressing desire does not imply apathy or indifference, being without understanding does not imply disinterestedness, but involves using every fibre of our being to try to be open to understanding, respectfully and non-intrusively, while simultaneously remembering that others are beyond understanding. Patients often come into therapy because they feel no one has truly understood them. Bion notes that reverie and alpha function is the psychological source for love and understanding, vital for well-being. Feeling understood connects to feeling real, held in mind. But assuming we understand obstructs trying to understand.

Bion concludes his discussion of memory, desire and understanding, by saying that the 'practising analyst' ought to be able 'to be aware of the aspects of the material that, however familiar they may seem to be, relate to what is unknown both to him and to the analysand'. All attempts 'to cling to what' is known should be 'resisted' so as to achieve a state of mind which Bion calls 'patience', retaining 'its association with suffering and toleration of frustration'. Such 'patience' should be 'retained without "irritable reaching after fact and reason" until a pattern "evolves"' (1970, p. 124).

## Faith

Bion poses the question: 'It may be wondered what state of mind is welcome if desires and memories are not'. It is one of faith, 'faith that there is an ultimate reality and truth – the unknown, unknowable, "formless infinite"' (1970, p. 31). Eschewing memory, desire and understanding allows for something unbidden to emerge and have its being. 'The transformation in K must be replaced by transformation in O and K must be replaced by F' (Bion, 1970, p. 46). John of the Cross writes of how when the understanding is completely emptied of 'all that pertains to sense, and detached and freed from all that can clearly be perceived by the understanding', it is replaced by faith, for 'as God is darkness to our understanding, even so does faith likewise blind and dazzle our understanding' (A II. 91, 1946/2008, p. 98).

## A beam of intense darkness

In attempting to describe the role of faith (F), Bion quotes a letter Freud wrote to Lou Andreas Salomé in 1916 in which Freud describes 'blinding himself artificially' in order to 'focus all light on one spot'. One achieves faith by 'rendering oneself "artificially blind" through the exclusion of memory and desire'. The 'piercing shaft of darkness can be directed on the dark features of the analytic situation' and it is through faith that 'one can "see", "hear", and "feel" that which cannot be apprehended through the senses or faculty of understanding' (Bion, 1970, p. 57).

Bion says: 'I would like to borrow from Freud and divert his statement to suit my problem' (1990, p. 20). In fact, the original 'borrowing' is from Dionysius' *The Mystical Theology* 1:1 where he describes being borne up to the 'ray of divine darkness that surpasseth all being'. Bion continually returns to the theme of darkness and deliberate blinding, a 'penetrating beam of darkness' (1990, p. 20) or a 'piercing shaft of darkness' (1970, p. 57), all being expressions relating to the themes of how, according to Dionysius, the sight of God is so overwhelming that it blinds, ultimate reality is unsearchable, inscrutable, unutterable, and passes all understanding.

Milton also described the need for deliberate blinding to see what is 'invisible to mortal sight'. As Bion quotes: 'Be shelled eyes with double dark . . . and find the uncreated light' (Milton, in Bion, 1991, p. 271).

So too, O is a ' "dark spot" that must be illuminated by "blindness" ' (Bion, 1970, p. 69). 'The analyst must cast a beam of intense darkness into the interior of the patient's associations so that some object that has hitherto been obscured in the light can now glow in that darkness' (Bion, personal communication to Grotstein, 2007, p. 1). Being artificially blinded 'through the exclusion of memory and desire' enables the 'piercing shaft of darkness' of faith to be directed into the darkness of an analytic session (Bion, 1970, pp. 57–58). Bion says:

> We could try to bring a brilliant illumination to bear on this obscure thing in order to show up the dark space so clearly that even something dark and difficult to see would become visible. Freud gave a clue to another approach when he said, 'I often try artificially to blind myself in order to examine these obscure places'.
>
> (1990, p. 20)

Applying this principle 'to suit his problem' he continues:

> Instead of trying to bring a brilliant, intelligent, knowledgeable light to bear on obscure problems, I suggest we bring to bear a diminution of the 'light' – a penetrating beam of darkness: a reciprocal of the searchlight. The peculiarity of this penetrating ray is that it could be directed towards the object of our curiosity, and this object would absorb whatever light already existed, leaving the area of examination exhausted of any light that it possessed. The darkness would be so absolute that it would achieve a luminous, absolute vacuum. So that, if any object existed, however faint, it would show up very clearly. Thus, a very faint light would become visible in maximum conditions of darkness.
>
> (1990, p. 20)

Instead of trying to know, one deliberately practices unknowing, emptying the mind of all 'knowns'. *Kenosis* is also epistemological, emptying one's mind so that the caverns of the soul are purified of all conceptual traces, memories and anticipations, thereby becoming a suitable vessel for newly emerging realities to be intuited. When considering the next day's session with a patient, it is better to 'blind ourselves artificially so that the dark should be so pervasive that any very faint subject will show up' and so that 'our intuition, however feeble, can have a chance of seeing something, however faint and however obscure, in what the patient is saying to us' (Bion, 1990, p. 105).

Faith and at-one-ment represent mystical apophatic epistemology and apophatic ontology respectively. How we come to bear another's reality is to incarnate it in ourselves, to dream it, to feel and suffer it in the pith and marrow of our bones. We enter a process of becoming what we do not yet know, will never know, yet can become.

Faith (F) in ultimate reality (O) as unknowable enhances precision in acknowledging opacity: it enables one to be more attuned and perceptive of subtle nuances of experience concomitant with the appreciation of what remains forever out of reach. Faith in O 'approaches an attitude of pure receptiveness. It is an alert readiness, an alive waiting' (Eigen, 1998, pp. 219–220). It is about being fully present in the moment, neither getting caught up in memories of the past, nor anticipating the future, laying aside all concepts and opening out to intimations of infinity.

> The analyst has to *become infinite* by the suspension of memory, desire, understanding.
>
> (Bion, 1970, p. 46)

# Chapter 16

# Without memory, desire and understanding

## A commentary

### The Ascent of Mount Carmel

Bion concludes *Attention and Interpretation* (1970) with a ground-breaking state-ment. He counsels analysts to cultivate a state of mind which renounces 'memory, desire and understanding' in order that god, that which is 'formless, infinite, inef-fable, non-existent', may be discovered, restored and evolve.

> What is to be sought is an activity that is both the restoration of god (the Mother) and the evolution of god (the formless, infinite, ineffable, non-existent), which can be found only in the state in which there is no memory, desire, understanding.
>
> (1970, p. 129)

This statement is dense with a profundity of apophatic implications which Bion does not spell out, leaving the reader to discover their own realisations. The fol-lowing is an attempt to elaborate on my own reflections about Bion's writings on memory, desire and understanding. In contemplating the enormity of this task, I feel a little like I am venturing forth up Mount Carmel, with nothing to guide me. There is no guarantee I will do more than slip on the rocky scree of ignorance and misunderstanding. I do not suggest that such reflections will be 'on the mark'. I am acutely aware of the paradox that to truly 'understand' is to stand under, in awe and emptiness, placing a 'cloud of forgetting' beneath and a 'cloud of unknowing' above and deliberately leave behind understanding based on the conceptual mind.

## A personal commentary on Bion's passage

I am going to break down the elements of this passage and consider each in turn. However, a linear mode will not suffice and the passage also has to be considered as a whole.

The elements for consideration are as follows:

- What is to be sought is an activity
- That is both the restoration of god (the Mother)

- And the evolution of god
- The formless, infinite, ineffable, non-existent
- Which can only be found in the state in which there is no memory, desire, understanding.

This statement is pregnant with apophatic mystical inspiration, such as John of the Cross, who describes how for the mystic, understanding is purged of light, desire of its affects and memory of its contents. According to Mawson (*CWVI*, 2014, p. 5–6), one of Bion's personal copies of St John of the Cross has the following passage marked from *The Ascent of Mount Carmel*, III, 2, 2–5:

> All these sensory means and exercises of the faculties must be left behind and in silence so that God Himself may effect the divine union in the soul. As a result one has to follow this method of disencumbering, emptying, and depriving the faculties of their natural rights and operations to make room for the inflow and illumination of the supernatural. If a person does not turn his eyes from his natural capacity, he will not attain so lofty a communication; rather he will hinder it.
>
> Thus, if it is true—as indeed it is—that the soul must journey by knowing God through what He is not, rather than through what He is, it must journey, insofar as possible, by way of the denial and rejecting of natural and supernatural apprehensions. This is our task now with the memory. We must draw it away from its natural props and capacities and raise it above itself (above all distinct knowledge and apprehensible possession) to supreme hope in the incomprehensible God. . . . The annihilation of the memory in regard to all forms (including the five senses) is an absolute requirement. . . . This union cannot be wrought without a complete separation of the memory from all forms.
>
> (John of the Cross, in Kavanaugh and Rodriguez, 1964, pp. 214–215)

As outlined in more detail in Chapter 12, the purpose of purifying the three potencies of understanding, memory and will in the dark night of the spirit is the inflow and illumination of God and union with God. For the soul to attain restoration of its divinity it has to undergo the purgation of all sensory desires, of all memory, will and understanding through the virtues of faith, hope and love.

## What is to be sought is an activity

What is this activity – an 'activity that is both the restoration of god (the Mother) and the evolution of god (the formless, infinite, ineffable, non-existent), which can be found only in the state in which there is no memory, desire, understanding' (Bion, 1970, p. 129)? Activity implies movement – actively being present, actively laying aside the conceptual mind, actively renouncing memory, desire and understanding, an activity of conscious intent. Yet for mystics such as John of the Cross, active engagement in practices of contemplation is superseded by passivity. The active night of the senses, involving our own efforts to detach ourselves from distraction, is supplanted by the passive night of the senses, followed by the active then passive nights of the spirit. In the *Ascent of Mount Carmel*, Book I John writes:

> Ordinarily, the soul enters this night in two ways: one is the active way, the other is the passive. The active way is that by which the soul is able to make, and does make, efforts of its own to enter in, assisted by divine grace. . . . The passive way is that in which the soul does nothing as of itself, neither does it make therein any efforts of its own; but it is God who works in it, giving special aids, and the soul is, as it were, patient, freely consenting thereto.
>
> (John of the Cross, 1934/1974, p. 10)

One may initially do all one can to be ready for this night through *kenosis* but ultimately it is a path of 'active inaction', where the activity spoken of is the activity of the Spirit, of grace. Here passivity is related to being receptive to the dawning of a realisation, such as the selected fact (Bion, 1963, p. 19).

Although most mystics warn that the mystical path is dependent on grace and that mystical experience cannot be manufactured, the seeker of truth still has to actively seek, actively turn towards the source of truth and actively surrender all that gets in the way. There is the activity of re-orientation towards the source of grace through metanoia, repentance, confession and renunciation. There is the activity of purification, emptying and doing what is necessary to become a suitable vessel for grace to enter. This may be as simple as putting aside time for prayer, sitting on one's mediation cushion, going on retreat. It also includes emptying the mind and soul of all that would contaminate divine inspiration.

The author of *The Cloud of Unknowing* writes of how although the loving desire for God is 'certainly God's gift, it is up to you to nurture it'. The author gives the following advice regarding cultivating the activity of contemplation:

> And so, to stand firmly and avoid pitfalls, keep to the path you are on. Let your longing relentlessly beat upon the *cloud of unknowing* that lies beneath you and your God. Pierce that cloud with the keen shaft of your love, spurn the thought of anything less than God, and do not give up this work for anything.
>
> (in Johnston, 1973, p. 55)

We have the advice to 'stand firmly', 'keep to the path', 'relentlessly beat', 'pierce that cloud' 'spurn thought' and 'do not give up this work'. These are all phrases denoting activity. Elsewhere the author advises his charge to 'pursue your course relentlessly' (in Johnston, 1973, p. 39).

John of the Cross, in describing the active night of the spirit in *The Ascent of Mount Carmel*, also advises of the need for an active discipline of renouncing 'all that can enter by the eye, all that the ear receives, all that the fancy may imagine, or the heart conceive' (John of the Cross, 1934/1974, Book 2, p. 15).

Philosophically the word activity is sometimes related to the distinction between activity and passivity, active versus passive emotions, passion and action. Passive emotions are those such as fear or sadness which one suffers. Bion's six emotional links Love (L), Hate (H), Knowledge (K) and their negatives −L, −H, −K are active links (Bion, 1962, p. 47). Thought is an activity of consciousness. In terms of Bion's 'thoughts without a thinker', the thinker has to be capable of hosting a thought or realisation. To be a thinker capable of instantiating a thought is to be an active, yet empty, recipient.

How does a profound realisation inspire us to act? Buddhists talk of three aspects of enlightenment: view, meditation and action. We may experience a moment of revelation, but that moment fades, becomes but a memory of a revelation and needs to be not only renewed but rediscovered as if for the first time. A valuable epiphany loses value when we possessively attempt to preserve it. Revelation needs also to lived, suffusing and inspiring our actions. Buddhists also talk of *trinle*, translated as enlightened activity that is spontaneous, everlasting and all pervasive. So too the Christian mystics, including Dionysius, describe the activity of God (*Energeia*). The essence, power and *energeia* of God are one; the divine and luminous energy of love flows throughout all creation. There is the theurgy or work of God, elaborated on by Dionysius, wherein one becomes a co-worker of God (*sunergos theou*) through the activity of cooperation (*sunergeia*) with the work of God, whereby we become vehicles through which God's activity can manifest in the world.

## The restoration of god (the Mother)

What might be implied by Bion's connection of god to the Mother? And what might he mean by god without a capital G but mother with a capitalised M? Bion here suggests a correspondence between what apophatic mystics mean by 'god' and O as denoting 'ultimate reality, absolute truth, the godhead, the infinite, the thing-in-itself', 'darkness, formlessness' (1970, p. 26), the 'unknown, "the void and formless infinite"' (1965, p. 171). The ultimate goal is at-one-ment with O, becoming one with our godhead. Bion quotes Meister Eckhart who wrote that 'we are changed and transformed into God' (Meister Eckhart, in Bion, 1970, p. 116).

### god (the Mother)

Is Bion alluding to the primal sense of oneness with god (the Mother) as a corollary of the transformation in O, a transcendence from the personal self into the All, 'at-one-ment with O'? For St Julian of Norwich divine wisdom is the 'ground of moderhed' and of a metaphysical Motherhood as the foundation of creation (McGinn, 2012, p. 461). Martin Buber writes of how 'every developing human child rests, like all developing beings, in the womb of the great mother – the undifferentiated, not yet formed primal world' (Buber, 1970, pp. 76–77).

## Restoration

The word 'restoration' implies that something forgotten, lost or tarnished is remembered, re-found and renewed. When we restore a piece of furniture or a work of art we attempt to take it back to its original condition. What is it that needs restoration? Bion says it is restoration of god (the Mother). Does this imply restoration of an original unity with the godhead or the Great Mother? Or does the image of god (the Mother) within us need restoring? This brings up the theme of whether the task is to achieve union with god, or whether it is to regain, re-find and re-discover it. The early church fathers and mothers understood union with God as reunion, a restoration of the *imago dei* that was obscured by original sin. An original state of consonance, harmony and oneness with the divinity was lost through the fall. The consequence of such loss is also a loss of 'the intuitive apprehension of God' and 'our very cognition of the Divinity is held to have been impaired as well. From this perspective, the task of mystical theology' is the restoration of the original consonance with God in which 'apprehension of God' is 'immediate' (Mondello, 2010, p. 21). This restoration involves stripping away from consciousness all that is not God, and the negative epistemology is that of the *via negativa*. As Stein puts it, 'We are utterly indeterminate, infinitely potential, never fully realized, and linked to (even fused with) the Divine' (2008, p. 307). 'The self, as the fundamental psychic ground of all human images and ideas of Deity, is itself grounded in and fused with Divinity' (Stein, 2008, p. 314).

For John of the Cross, restoration is about reunion with God, a union that was lost when Adam and Eve broke away from the original condition of being made in the image of God.

> Beneath the apple tree:
> there I took you for my own,
> there I offered you my hand, and restored you
> where your mother was corrupted.
> (John of the Cross, *CB* Commentary
> on Stanza 23.2, 2017, p. 563)

Christ's crucifixion enables the restoration of the original condition of grace that had been lost. 'For human nature, your mother, was corrupted in your first parents under the tree, and you too under the tree of the cross were restored' (John of the Cross, *CB* Commentary on Stanza 23.2, 2017, p. 564). The Bridegroom redeems and espouses the soul to himself

> through the very means by which human nature was corrupted and ruined, telling her that as human nature was ruined through Adam and so corrupted by means of the forbidden tree in the Garden of Paradise, so on the tree of the cross it was redeemed and restored when he gave it there, through his passion and death, the hand of his favour and mercy, and broke down the barriers between God and humans that were built up through original sin.
> (John of the Cross, *CB* Commentary on Stanza 23.2, 2017, p. 563)

## Original blessing, primordial purity

Traditional cosmogonic myths depict, through symbolic narratives, an 'aboriginal' time in which there was consonance between humanity and divinity, earth and heaven. Humans could ascend and descend at will via an *axis mundi* between heaven and earth, like the angels ascending and descending Jacob's ladder. Through some form of turning away, this connection was severed and the task is to restore this original state of blessing.

Religious myths and rituals express nostalgia for the original state of purity. They also show the means by which restoration can take place.

## Restoration of a posited state of uterine unity

The theme of restoration is linked to speculation about uterine life as a state of oneness and wholeness that is lost, and the consequent yearning to restore this original condition. Freud cites Romain Rolland's 'oceanic feeling' who saw it as the source of religious feeling, 'a sentiment of eternity', a 'feeling as of something limitless, unbounded' (Freud, 1930, p. 64). Freud links 'oceanic feeling' to the state of primary narcissism, where for the infant there is no distinction between oneself, mother and the external world. There is a sense of 'an indissoluble bond, of being one with the external world as a whole' (Freud, 1930, p. 65), a feeling of 'oneness with the universe'.

Martin Buber, in *I and Thou*, writes of prenatal life as

> one of purely natural combination, bodily interaction and flowing from one to the other. Its life's horizon, as it comes into being, seems in a unique way to be, and yet again not to be, traced in that of the life that bears it. For it does not rest only in the womb of the human mother . . . Yet this connation has a cosmic quality that the mythical saying of the Jews, 'in the mother's body man knows the universe, in birth he forgets it,' reads like the imperfect decipherment of an inscription from earliest times.
>
> (1987, p. 40)

A metaphor found in both Christianity and Dzogchen is that of a grimy mirror: when the mirror is cleaned our true nature is revealed. For Catherine of Genoa, (1447–1510) this is to realise the *imago dei*.

> Once stripped of all its imperfections, the soul rests in God, *with no characteristics of its own*, since its purification is the stripping away of the lower self in us. *Our being is then God.*
>
> (in Turner, 1995, p. 143)

We break through the veils of illusion that separate us into an undivided reality of which we a part, with which we are not dual.

When all images have departed from the soul and it sees single unity, then the pure being of the soul, passive and resting within itself, encounters the pure formless being of the Divine Unity, which is being beyond all beings.

(Meister Eckhart, in Davies, 1988, p. 51)

## The evolution of god

What does the word 'evolution' mean when applied to 'god (the formless, infinite, ineffable, non-existent)'? Let us first reconsider Bion's definition of O:

> I shall use the sign O to denote that which is the ultimate reality represented by terms such as ultimate reality, absolute truth, the godhead, the infinite, the thing-in-itself. O does not fall in the domain of knowledge or learning save incidentally; it can be 'become', but it cannot be 'known'. It is darkness and formlessness but it enters the domain when it has evolved to a point where it can be known, through knowledge gained by experience, and formulated in terms derived from sensuous experience; its existence is conjectured phenomenologically.
>
> (Bion, 1970, p. 26)

Bion applies the word 'evolution' to both O ('evolved aspects of O') and to the analytic session. The unknowable ultimate evolves until such time as it is apprehensible through the K link:

> Every object known or knowable by man, including himself, must be an evolution of O. It is O when it has evolved sufficiently to be met by K capacities in the psycho-analyst. He does not know the 'ultimate reality' of a chair or anxiety or time or space, but he knows a chair, anxiety, time, and space. In so far as the analyst becomes O he is able to know the events that are *evolutions* of O . . . the psycho-analyst can know what the patient says, does and appears to be, but cannot know the O of which the patient is an evolution: he can only 'be' it.
>
> (1970, p. 27)

O can 'evolve' by 'becoming manifest', 'by becoming a "reminder"', an "incarnation" or "embodiment" or an "incorporation"' (Bion, 1965, p. 163). O, as ultimate reality, is the heart of psychoanalysis: 'No psychoanalytic discovery is possible without recognition of its existence, at-one-ment with it and evolution' (Bion, 1970, p. 30). The analyst 'must be at one' with O and identify 'with the *evolution* of' O in order to be able to 'formulate it in an interpretation' (Bion, 1970, p. 89).

Bion describes how evolution of O takes place in a given session:

> In any session, evolution takes place. Out of the darkness and formlessness something evolves. That evolution can bear a superficial resemblance to memory, but once it has been experienced it can never be confounded with memory. It shares with dreams the quality of being wholly present or

unaccountably and suddenly absent. This evolution is what the analyst must be ready to interpret.

(1967/1992, p. 381)

Such evolution is related to the practice of deliberate blinding, an essential feature of Bion's apophatic epistemology. Deliberate blinding, along with suspending 'memory, desire, understandings and sense impressions' (Bion, 1970, p. 43) enables 'the piercing shaft of darkness' to be 'directed on the dark features of the analytic situation'. Through the 'freedom from being "blinded" by the qualities . . . that belong to the domain of the senses' the analyst is able to '"see" those evolved aspects of O that are invariant in the analysand' (Bion, 1970, pp. 57–58).

The analyst 'must wait for the analytic session to "evolve"'. He must wait 'for an evolution to take place so that O becomes manifest in K through the emergence of actual events' (Bion, 1970, p. 28). O is at the centre of analysis, and the analyst must be 'at one' with O: and 'with the *evolution* of this he must identify so that he can formulate it in an interpretation' (Bion, 1970, p. 89).

## Transformations and evolution of O

O may be represented in a Zen koan, or a symbol, or a sacrament, all of which are not the thing itself but must have some element that enables access to becoming at one with O.

> In order to express adequately the original essentially unknowable reality O, the transformations must contain these invariants or elements which are unchanged in the process of transformation.
>
> (Symington and Symington, 1996, p. 108)

All that we have access to is an evolution of O, not O itself. At-one-ment with O cannot be attained through knowledge, phenomena or the appearance aspect of reality. It is beyond appearance.

> The psycho-analyst is concerned with O, which is incommunicable save through K activity. O may appear to be attainable by K through phenomena, but in fact that is not so. K depends on the evolution of O → K. At-one-ment with O would seem to be possible through the transformation K → O, but it is not so.
>
> (Bion, 1970, p. 30)

O resides within appearance, within objects and within all phenomena:

> In any object, material or immaterial, resides the unknowable ultimate reality, the 'thing-in-itself'. Objects have emanations or emergent qualities or evolving characteristics that impinge upon the human personality as phenomena.
>
> (Bion, 1970, p. 87)

## Evolution and the Neoplatonic doctrine of remaining, procession and return

In discussing evolution in terms of 'emanation of the deity' and 'incarnation of the deity', Bion is implicitly drawing on the Neoplatonic doctrine of remaining, procession and return (*monē, proodos, epistrophē*) which, as we have seen, Dionysius, John of the Cross, Meister Eckhart and other apophatic mystics describe. 'Using the Proclean procession of *monē*, (remaining), *proodos* (proceeding) and *epistrophē* (reverting), God in God's being as *erōs* is able to proceed out to all creation and remain in the Godhead at the same time' (Tyler, 2010, pp. 66–67). In the *Corpus Dionysiacum* Dionysius replaces the Neoplatonic triad of *monē, proodos* and *epistrophē* with a triad consisting of affirmation (*kataphasis*), negation (*apophasis*) and ecstasy (*ekstasis*). Dionysius talks of procession and return, and that the way towards union with God is through affirmation and negation of the attributes or of God, which follows 'divine procession and return, transcendence and immanence' leading to union with the unknown God, who 'has placed darkness as His hiding-place' (*MT* 1.2 1000A, in Stang, 2012, p. 204). The One transcends all thought and the meaning of life is union with that which is beyond, unknowable, inscrutable and ineffable, yet immanent. Here Dionysius also focuses on the saving activity of incarnation, the purpose of which is that as Christ becomes human, we become divinised, or as Eckhart puts it, we are 'changed and transformed into God' (Bion, quoting Meister Eckhart, 1970, p. 116). For Dionysius, such union is affected through love (*erōs*), God's love for us and our love for God. Dionysius writes of how God, by *agápē* and by *erōs*, is enticed away from his dwelling place 'and is led down, from above all things and beyond all things', to abide and be 'in all things' 'according to an ecstatic power beyond being, without going out from himself' (Dionysius, *DN* 4.13. 712B in Perl, 2007, p. 46). This is close to what Bion means by evolution.

Just as Dionysius draws on the Neoplatonic theme of procession and return, Bion explores how all that can be discussed are the 'evolved characteristics of O (K) whereas F is related to O itself' (1970, p. 45). This is like Dionysius' discussion of the procession from the absolute. Similarly, although we cannot ever know the O of which an emanation or evolution points, we can become O through transformations in O and this is like Dionysius's return (*monē*). Bion cites Meister Eckhart's understanding of the godhead which in itself cannot be the object of knowledge but that which emanates from it can be known.

The godhead, according to Eckhart, 'evolves to a point where it becomes apprehensible by man as the Trinity'. But the godhead in itself 'is formless and infinite'. There is a distinction between the 'evolution characteristic of the godhead' and the 'capacity of the apprehending object to apprehend'. Yet evolution and apprehension are linked: aspects of an ultimate reality, which is formless and infinite, evolve, like the trinity, 'until it intersects the personality of the observer' (Bion, 1970, p. 88).

Bion reconsiders O 'with the help of … Platonic Forms and their "reminders" (phenomena); "godhead", "god" and "his" incarnations; Ultimate Reality or Truth and the phenomena which are all that human beings can know of the 'thing-in-itself' (1965, p. 162). The value of the 'reminder' is not that it reminds the individual of the form but that it 'enables the person to achieve union with an incarnation of the Godhead' (Bion, 1965, p. 139).

Bion cites Eckhart on the distinction between the darkness and formlessness of the Godhead and the trinity that flows out from the Godhead:

> Eckhart considers Godhead to contain all distinctions as yet undeveloped and to be Darkness and Formlessness. It cannot be the object of Knowledge until there flows out from it Trinity and the Trinity *can* be known.
>
> (1965, p. 162)

The Godhead is distinguished from God by both 'Meister Eckhart and the Blessed John Ruysbroeck'. Bion quotes Ruysbroek's 'Tractate XI "God in the Godhead is spiritual substance, so elemental we can say nothing about it"' (Bion, 1965, p. 139).

Bion also discusses Kant's distinction between the thing-in-itself that 'cannot be known' and the 'secondary and primary qualities' that can be (1965, p. 162).

At an ultimate level there is no such thing as restoration or evolution. There is nothing to be restored, for it was ever thus and ever will be. There is nothing to evolve for it is already O, no-thing, the thing-in-itself, absolute truth, the ineffable, infinity, the 'world of darkness, the Void, the formless Infinite' (Bion, 1977/2014, *CWXIII*, p. 55).

## Which can only be found in the state in which there is no memory, desire, understanding

In *Caesura* Bion gives two quotes from *The Ascent of Mount Carmel* referring specifically to the need to renounce memory. The first quotation is simply:

> The memory must also strip itself of all those forms and kinds of knowledge, that it may unite itself with God in hope.
>
> (John of the Cross in Bion, 1977/2014, *CWX*, p. 36)

The second is more detailed:

> The love which the memory always has for other forms and kinds of knowledge which are of supernatural things, such as visions, revelations, locutions and feelings which come in a super-natural way. When these things have passed through the soul, there is wont to remain impressed upon it some image, form, figure or idea, whether in the soul or in the memory of fancy, at times very vividly and effectively. Concerning these images it is also needful to give advice lest the memory becomes encumbered with them and they be a hindrance to its union with God in perfect and pure hope.
>
> (John of the Cross in Bion, 1977/2014, *CWX*, p. 36)

As we saw in Chapter 12, John of the Cross counselled that in order to travel along the dark nocturnal path towards union with God, the soul must be completely emptied of understanding, memory, will, sense, imagination, judgement, affection and inclination. All reliance on sensory perception and mental conceptualisation must be actively renounced. As regards memory, John of the Cross writes in *The Ascent of Mount Carmel* that memory must be stripped and emptied of all natural forms of knowledge formed 'about the objects of the five bodily senses'. 'The memory must labour to destroy all sense of them, so that no impression whatever of them shall be left behind; it must forget them, and withdraw itself from them, and that as completely as if they had never entered into it. Nothing less than the annihilation of the memory as to all these forms will serve, if it is to be united with God' (John of the Cross, 1934/1974, p. 53).

Union with the Godhead, becoming O, realising our true nature, is not achieved through any epistemophilic faculty. Memory, desire and understanding are all forms of obscuration which 'act like a mist that makes it impossible for internal eyes to "see and tell"' (Bion, 1977/2014, *CWXIII*, p. 39).

Applying St John to the analytic situation, Bion articulates what I have condensed as five principles concerning being without memory, desire and understanding.

- Analysis is a meeting in the here and now of patient and analyst in which 'what takes place in the consulting room is an emotional situation which is itself the intersection of an evolving O with another evolving O' (Bion, 1970, p. 118).
- In order for evolution of O to take place the container needs to be purified and emptied of all that contaminates and clutters the space.
- Memory relates to the past, and desire relates to the future. Both memory and desire obscure and obstruct evolutions of O taking place in the present.
- Desire begets desire and must be actively resisted. Desire may relate to either the patient or analyst: desires may be seemingly altruistic such as wanting the patient's cure, or selfish, such as wanting the session to end.
- Memory and desire are derived from sense impressions. Psychic reality, let alone O, cannot be apprehended through the senses. We can see a chair but we cannot see anxiety, pain, fear, love and hate, although we do sense and are affected by the manifestations of their symptoms. We cannot see the unapproachable light of God with human eyes but only through the darkness of faith.

## A suitable vessel to receive the unknown

Both memories and desires may become mental possessions that saturate our mind leaving little room for new information to penetrate. Memory, desire and understanding crowd and contaminate the empty vessel of the container leaving no room to be filled with the unadulterated presence of evolutions of O at a given moment. To use a Buddhist analogy: a container that is upside down, dirty or leaky will not function as a suitable vessel to receive the patient in their ineffable alterity.

'If the psycho-analyst has allowed himself the unfettered play of memory, desire and understanding, his preconceptions will be habitually saturated and his 'habits' will lead him to resort to instantaneous and well-practiced saturation from 'meaning' rather than from O' (Bion, 1970, p. 51).

Nor will such a container be able to receive and host revelations that are beyond understanding. John of the Cross writes:

> This light is ever ready to be communicated to the soul, but does not flow in, because of the forms and veils of the creature which infold and embarrass the soul. Take away these hinderances and coverings, as I shall hereafter explain, and the soul in detachment and poverty of spirit will then, being pure and simple, be transformed in the pure and sincere divine Wisdom who is the Son of God.
>
> (*A* II, 15.2, 1934/1974, p. 37)

But 'when the soul frees itself of all things and attains to emptiness and dispossession concerning them' then, just as light will enter in 'if you open the shutters, so God . . . will enter the soul that is empty and fill it with divine goods' (*LF* III. 46, 2017, p. 691).

### Memory and desire, past and future

Bion explains how memory functions as a container for past experiences whereas desire attempts to contain the future. Desire obviously fails, since the future does not yet exist, but desire generates fantasies based on wishes and expectations for the future. Memories of the past fill the mind and create assumptions that obscure how the patient is today. Desire also fills the mind leaving little space for the present moment to unfold. Desires can be nostalgic or anticipatory, 'reminiscences or anticipations' (Bion, 1970, p. 31). Such desire-laden fantasies clutter our awareness and cloak the face of the patient just as memories do.

Memory is untrustworthy because when recompiling past events a host of unconscious forces sort and distort our reconstructions. 'Memory is always misleading as a record of fact since it is distorted by the influence of unconscious forces' (Bion, 1967/1992, p. 380).

Whether the desire is for the future or past, such desire will interfere with the ability to 'attend to the present moment which is neither the past nor the future' and 'while we are thinking about the past and the future we are blind and deaf to what is going on at the present moment' (Bion, 1990, p. 67). Thus 'every session attended by the psychoanalyst must have no history and no future' (Bion, 1967/1992, p. 381). I am reminded of the Buddhist advice to be fully present in the moment, neither getting caught up in memories of the past, nor anticipating the future. Memory and recall get in the way of free-floating attention, freedom and intuition. Bion suggests that the analyst, in preparation for the next day's session with the patient should spend time 'banishing any memory of the patient whatsoever, and any aim or ambition in regard to his cure' (Bion, 1965/2014, *CWVI*, p. 12).

> To spend time on what has been discovered is to concentrate on an irrelevance. What matters is the unknown and on this the psycho-analyst must focus his attention. Therefore 'memory' is a dwelling on the unimportant to the exclusion of the important. Similarly 'desire' is an intrusion into the analyst's state of mind which covers up, disguises and blinds him to, the point at issue: that aspect of O that is currently presenting the unknown and unknowable though it is manifested to the two people present in its evolved character. This is the 'dark spot' that must be illuminated by 'blindness'. Memory and desire are 'illuminations' that destroy the value of the analyst's capacity for observation as a leakage of light into a camera might destroy the value of the film being exposed.
>
> (Bion, 1970, p. 69)

A patient tells me how 'earth-shattering' the insight was that she had had in the last session. 'It was life-changing, an epiphany! I realized how much I push men away while seeming to seek affirmation'. She then says, 'So I am hoping for another epiphany today'. There was an the expectation that each session should result in a new earth-shattering epiphany. If it didn't occur, I was failing to 'deliver the goods' and she became despondent. 'This is getting nowhere' she crossly exclaimed. 'Yes', I thought wryly to myself, 'no-where is probably where we need to be'.

Even the most profound realisation requires being rendered unknown and rediscovered afresh, again and again. Buber also writes about an I-thou encounter that is unmediated in the present, without intervention of any concept, prior knowledge, imagination or memory, no greed or anticipation:

> The relation to the You is unmediated. Nothing conceptual intervenes between I and You, no prior knowledge and no imagination; and memory itself is changed as it plunges from particularity into wholeness. No purpose intervenes between I and You, no greed and no anticipation; and longing itself is changed as it plunges from the dream into appearance. Every means is an obstacle. Only where all means have disintegrated encounters occur.
>
> (Buber, 1970, pp. 62–63)

## Desire begets desire

Desire begets desire: the more one allows oneself to be preoccupied with memories and desires, the 'more the tendency to harbour them increases'. Evocation of memory and desire is associated with 'impulses of possessiveness and sensuous greed: the impulses generate memory and desire; memory and desire generate sensuous greed' (Bion, 1970, p. 33).

Desire may be for the patient, such as 'desires for the patient's cure, or well-being'. Or desire may be for the analyst's benefit, such as desiring 'the end of a session, or week, or term' (Bion, 1970, p. 56).

> You may, for example, feel that you would like to be at home. If that idea becomes more and more possessive you then think, 'How marvellous it would be to be at home!' If you are spending your time thinking about that, it becomes very difficult to pay attention to what is happening in the present. The perception of the immediate experience becomes opaque.
>
> (Bion, 1990, p. 67)

'Desires distort judgement by selection and suppression of material to be judged' (Bion, 1967/1992, p. 380) and lead to the 'progressive deterioration' of analytic intuition (Bion, 1970, p. 56).

Bion argued that

> the desire to cure the patient should have no place whatsoever in the consulting room . . . because . . . nothing will throw your judgement out more than to be concerned with trying to remember what the patient or you yourself have said, or wanting to cure the patient, or to entertain any other desire.
>
> (1965/2014, *CWVI*, p. 12)

For the analyst who is used 'to remembering what patients say and to desiring their welfare, it will be hard to entertain the harm to analytic intuition that is inseparable from *any* memories and *any* desires' (Bion, 1970, p. 31). The possessiveness of memory and desire is particularly harmful to analytic work. As well as imposing on and stealing from patients, 'memories' can be regarded as 'possessions' and desires can possess the mind of the other.

> A certain class of patient feels 'possessed' by or imprisoned 'in' the mind of the analyst if he considers the analyst desires something relative to him – his presence, or his cure, or his welfare.
>
> (Bion, 1970, p. 42)

## Clinical vignette

The early atmosphere into which Anna was born was filled with a sense of foreboding and lack of emotional containment. Anna was haunted by images of her mother's grief-struck, locked-in face. When describing this, her voice trailed away into little more than a whisper, as if replicating the atmosphere of nameless dread in her description. Listening, I found myself fading into this realm of absence and blankness.

I long to reassure her things would get better, that I am with her, silently present rather than silently absent like her mother. But Anna seems unreachable. A void opens up between us. On her side she plummets into a black hole, evil because the isolation felt absolute. On my side there is a longing to enter her psychological hell realm and offer some gesture of hope, but any attempt only exacerbates her sense of alienation. I realise that I need to ward off the desire to reassure her. All I can do is vicariously enter this unspeakable and unbearable zone, not try to make it better, just be with her.

We sit for what feels like an agonising eternity, listening to the deafening silence of the void. Yet Anna senses my immersion with her in the state of 'dreadfulness incarnate'. Her 'evil eternity' originated in questioning her mother when she was 4: 'What happens when I die? Will you be with me?' Her mother didn't even register the import of the question, let alone offer comfort. Abandoned into carelessness, Anna plummeted into an unendurable state of no-thing-ness and no-one-there-ness. My capacity to bear the unbearable *with her* was part of such 'being with' – feeling her sense of utter alienation in the marrow of my bones was a precursor for any spark of incipient aliveness. Laying aside memory, desire and understanding, I invoke a sense of faith, knowing that I have to bear the unbearable with her in darkness and obscurity.

## O and psychic reality are not apprehended through the senses

Memories and desires are 'two facets of the same thing: both are composed of elements based on sense impressions' (Bion, 1970, p. 41). They are ready-made 'formulations which contain pleasure and pain' (Bion, 1970, p. 31). Memory deals with 'sense impressions of what is supposed to have happened' whereas desire deals with 'what has not yet happened' (Bion, 1967/1992, p. 380). The 'invariants' for both memory and desire 'are an inside and an outside composed of objects which are sensible'. Furthermore, 'Both imply the absence of immediate sensual satisfaction; one supposes a store of sensual objects, the memory being the container, and the other a conjunction of sensually satisfying objects' (Bion, 1970, p. 41).

Psychic reality, as well as mystical realities, cannot be apprehended by the senses. 'The realities with which psycho-analysis deals, for example fear, panic, love, anxiety, passion, have no sensuous background' (Bion, 1970, p. 89). As a consequence, Bion specifically adds sense impressions to the list of what must be renounced: 'The suspension of memory, desire, understanding and sense perception' are all 'to be eschewed' (1970, p. 43).

## Without understanding: the cloud of forgetting and cloud of unknowing

Memory, desire and understanding obstruct becoming in O, union with the Godhead. The apophatic way is beyond understanding, for 'God, being incomprehensible, surpasses infinitely all the powers of human intelligence to understand Him. So the understanding, having neither the knowledge nor the power of comprehending God, advances towards Him by not understanding' (John of the Cross, 1934/1974, pp. 133–134).

# Chapter 17

# Bion's O and the apophatic way

Ultimate truth is ineffable.

(Bion, 1977/2014, *CWXIII*, p. 12)

There is, according to apophatic mystics, an ineffable reality beyond appearance, beyond comprehension and beyond dualistically constricted perspectives of the egocentric mind. This absolute reality of which we are part, is beyond the capacity of the ordinary mind to conceive because concepts are limited and this reality is beyond limitation. It is beyond imagination because imagination is based on images. G. K. Chesterton wrote that 'The imagination is supposed to work towards the infinite; though in that sense the infinite is the opposite of imagination. For the imagination deals with an image. And an image is in its nature a thing that has an outline and therefore a limit' (1938, p. 107). Meister Eckhart suggested that one 'should love God unspiritually, that is, your soul should be unspiritual and stripped of all spirituality, for so long as your soul has a spirit's form, it has images', and images mean that oneness with God is mediated through image. Instead one 'should love him as he is nonGod, a nonspirit, a nonperson, a nonimage, but as he is pure, unmixed, bright "One", separated from all duality; and in that One we should eternally sink down, out of "something" into "nothing"' (1981, p. 208).

The mystic path towards ultimate reality is often described as one of ever-closer union with God. Yet at an ultimate level at-one-ment is not actually becoming one with reality because we were never separate to begin with. We do not attain anything because there is nothing to attain. It is *alétheia*, unconcealment. We break through myriad layers of psychological, intellectual, emotional and spiritual obscuration preventing this realisation.

## Defining the indefinable

Bion saw the quest to become at-one with absolute reality as the essential goal of analysis. Ultimate reality, the 'thing-in-itself' (*Ding an sich*) is a numinous domain of pure being, beyond all understanding.

There is a 'thing-in-itself', which can never be known; by contrast the religious mystic claims direct access to the deity with whom he aspires to be at one.

(Bion, 1970, p. 87)

Bion's O is akin to the Eternal Light in canto xxxiii of Dante's Paradiso:

Eternal Light, that in Thyself alone
Dwelling, alone, dost know Thyself, and smile
On Thy self-love, so knowing and so known!
(in Bion, 1965, p. 13)

O as ultimate reality cannot be known, but it can be realised through 'at-one-ment'.

[O] stands for the absolute truth in and of any object; it is assumed that this cannot be known by any human being; it can be known about, its presence can be recognized and felt, but it cannot be known. It is possible to be at one with it. . . . No psycho-analytic discovery is possible without recognition of its existence, at-one-ment with it and evolution. The religious mystics have probably approximated most closely to expression of experience of it.

(Bion, 1970, p. 30)

O is an ineffable, inscrutable, constantly evolving domain of reality, the 'world of darkness, the Void, the formless Infinite' (Bion, 1991, p. 275). Like the infinite expanse of sky behind the clouds, O is always there, behind the restless turbulence of our emotional confusion and delusion. O remains unaltered, radiant, clear light, infinite space, omnipresent, beyond any conceptualisation, beyond comprehension. Yet even a glimpse of O brings forth profound compassion, loving kindness, equanimity and immeasurable joy as well as the pathos of the tears of things, *lacrimae rerum*.

## The mystical dimensions of O

For many analysts, what Bion meant by O is understood as solely clinical, referring to the core truth of an analytic situation, of a patient, of the analytic relationship.[1] But Bion, who first mentions O in 1963, increasingly explores O as an apophatic dimension of analysis, until, in Chapter Ten of *Transformations* (1965), he begins using language redolent of apophatic mystical writings, a theme he continues in *Attention and Interpretation* (1970) and *Cogitations* (1992).

Many mystics have been able to describe a situation in which it is believed that there really is a power, a force that cannot be measured or weighed or assessed by the mere human being with the mere human mind.

(Bion, 1992, p. 371)

As well as citing apophatic mystics such as Meister Eckhart, John of the Cross, Isaac Luria, John Ruysbroeck and the *Bhagavad Gita*, Bion advises therapists to read John of the Cross and poets such as John Milton. In pointing to O, Bion repeatedly draws on Milton's expression from *Paradise Lost*:

> The rising world of waters dark and deep
> Won from the void and formless infinite.
> (Milton, in Bion, 1965, p. 151)

In the Brazilian lectures Bion points out that '*Paradise Lost* and the end of the Fifth Book of the *Aeneid* are both serious attempts to formulate, and thus communicate, something about religion, about a god representing the ultimate reality' (1973/1990, p. 20).

> In the third book of *Paradise Lost* Milton says, 'Hail, holy Light, offspring of heaven first-born! Or of the Eternal coeternal beam May I express thee unblamed? Since God is light, And never but in unapproached light Dwelt from eternity – dwelt then in thee, Bright effluence of bright essence increate! . . . Won from the void and formless infinite!' There seems to be no doubt, and Milton certainly had no doubt, that he was blind – 'so thick a drop serene hath quenched these orbs which roll in vain'; although they can feel the warmth he can see nothing.
> (Bion, 1974/1990, p. 104)

## Unknowability of O

As we have seen, Bion belongs to those apophatic mystical and philosophical traditions that view ultimate reality as inaccessible through sensual and intellectual experience. In ascribing to the unknowable nature of absolute truth, Bion also places himself in the same Idealist and Transcendentalist tradition as Plato, Berkeley and Kant. This shows 'the extent to which they believe that a curtain of illusion separates us from reality' (Bion, 1965, p. 147). Bion refers to philosophers such as Kant for whom the 'thing-in-itself cannot be known but secondary and primary qualities can be' (1965, p. 162). He refers to how 'the writer of *Job* . . . expressed in unforgettable language the feebleness of human pretensions to knowledge' (Bion, 1991, p. 230). He writes:

> It is not knowledge of reality that is at stake, nor yet the human equipment for knowing. The belief that reality is or could be known is mistaken because reality is not something which lends itself to being known. It is impossible to know reality for the same reason that makes it impossible to sing potatoes; they may be grown, or pulled, or eaten, but not sung. Reality has to be 'been'; there should be a transitive verb 'to be' expressly for use with the term 'reality'.
> (Bion, 1965, p. 148)

All attempts to point towards the unknowable O break down: all attempts to represent O are but transformations of O, not O. 'The most and the least that the individual person can do is to be it' (Bion, 1965, p. 140).

Mystics may have access to O, but cannot express it through 'words, gestures, art or music' since all such 'methods of communication are transformations and transformations deal with phenomena and are dealt with by being known, loved or hated' (Bion, 1965, p. 147). In this sense, the links of loving, hating and knowing (L, H, K) are but 'substitutes for the ultimate relationship with O which is not a relationship or an identification or an atonement or a reunion':

> The qualities attributed to O, the links with O, are all transformations of O and *being* O. . . . The human person *is* himself and by 'is' I mean . . . a positive act of being for which L, H, K are only substitutes and approximations.
>
> (Bion, 1965, p. 140)

It is not that O cannot be represented by a formulation of a transformation. But the links K, L, H are only 'appropriate' to transformations of O, not O itself.

> O, representing the unknowable ultimate reality can be represented by any formulation of a transformation – such as 'unknowable ultimate reality' which I have just formulated. . . . But I wish to make it clear that my reason for saying O is unknowable is not that I consider human capacity unequal to the task, but because K, L, or H are inappropriate to O. They are appropriate to transformations of O but not to O.
>
> (Bion, 1965, p. 140)

## Fear of the unknown

> Confronted with the unknown, 'the void and formless infinite', the personality of whatever age fills the void (saturates the element), provides a form (names and binds a constant conjunction) and gives boundaries to the infinite (number and position). Pascal's phrase '*Le silence éternel de ces espaces in nis m'effraie*' can serve as an expression of intolerance and fear of the 'unknowable' and hence of the unconscious in the sense of the undiscovered or the unevolved.
>
> (Bion, 1965, p. 171)

We fear the 'eternal silence' of 'infinite space' and defend against our fear by filling the void with concepts, names and theories. Just as at-one-ment with O cannot be attained through knowledge, it is also not attained through methods or techniques of prayer. In *A Memoir of the Future* Bion warns that all such methods and all dogmata need to be transcended to move towards the reality beyond. He quotes John of the Cross who said that even 'reading his own works could be a stumbling block if they were revered to the detriment of direct experience.

Teachings, dogma, hymns, congregational worship, are supposed to be preludes to religion proper – not final ends in themselves' (1991, p. 267).

## Transformations from knowing to being

A patient 'Andy' tells me about how, after a late-term miscarriage, his wife wanted them both to participate in a private ritual where they scattered the ashes of the foetus in their backyard garden, to plant a new rose bush to represent the unborn child. He went through the motions of showing support but internally he was feeling impatient and thinking to himself, 'Can't she just get over it? She'll have another. Doesn't she realise how busy I am with my new business?'

As he related this event, something 'clicked' inside and he realised how utterly self-preoccupied he had become with the new business, which on the face of it was to support his wife in her desire to have a family, yet he himself was ambivalent about having a child at this stage in his career. He was mortified realising how alone she must have felt. He also realised how much fear surrounded the thought of having a baby, fear about the helplessness and vulnerability of a little baby, fear about his capacity to support it, fear about being a good father. He resolved to go home and have a heart-to-heart with his wife, to tell her how sorry he was that he had not been supportive, to show her how much he did in fact care.

But when Andy came to see me for the next session, it was as if he had never had this realisation. Instead he filled the session with an account of his excitement that another business had agreed to seed-fund his business proposal. He mentioned in passing that his wife had gone to the doctor and the doctor had prescribed anti-depressants for post-partum depression 'so now it should all be fine again when the pills kick in and do their job'.

A patient might have a profound insight but resist the implications such insight brings: to become rather than know. Intellectual knowledge of one's limitations is very different from realisation leading to change. Bion asks, 'Is it possible through psychoanalytic interpretation to effect a transition from knowing the phenomena of the real self to being the real self?' (1965, p. 148).

> The gap between 'knowing phenomena' and 'being reality' resembles the gap between 'Knowing about psychoanalysis' and 'Being psychoanalysed'.
> (Bion, 1965, p. 149)

This relates to the distinction between insight and structural change in analysis. It is much easier to have insight into our complexes than to do what it takes to liberate ourselves from their grip. Change requires consistent and incremental and sometimes humbling practice. We bump up against our habitual tendencies over and over. Symington and Symington describe how the analytic couple may come to an understanding 'through the K relationship only to find that it then degenerates into having a piece of intellectualized knowledge of it'. Such a 'reversal occurs as a way of evading the painful realisation achieved through the K link. . . . There is a continuing decision to be made as to whether to evade pain or to tolerate and thus modify it' (Symington and Symington, 1996, p. 28).

For Bion, resistance is related to the fear of moving from knowing to becoming:

> The gap between reality and the personality, or, as I prefer to call it, the inaccessibility of O, is an aspect of life with which analysts are familiar under the guise of resistance. Resistance is only manifest when the threat is contact with what is believed to be real. . . . Resistance operates because it is feared that the reality of the object is imminent.
>
> (Bion, 1965, p. 147)

There is a difference between knowing and being. Interpretations are part of the K link. The anxiety lest transformation in K leads to transformations in O is responsible for the form of resistance in which interpretations appear to be accepted but in fact the acceptance is with the intention of 'knowing about' rather than 'becoming' (Bion, 1965, pp. 159–160). Transformations in K may be described loosely as akin to 'knowing about' something whereas transformations in O are related to becoming or being O or to being 'become' by O (Bion, 1965, p. 163).

> [Acceptance] in O means that acceptance of an interpretation enabling the patient to 'know' that part of himself to which attention has been drawn is felt to involve 'being' or 'becoming' that person.
>
> (Bion, 1965, p. 164)

There is often 'intolerance and fear of the "unknowable" and hence of the unconscious in the sense of the undiscovered or the unevolved' (Bion, 1965, p. 171). Patients may seem to agree with an interpretation but their hidden intention is to 'know about' rather than undergo the transformation required by truly accepting an interpretation. Furthermore, the patient attempts by 'agreeing with the interpretation' to inveigle the analyst 'into a collusive relationship to preserve K' rather than become O (Bion, 1965, p. 162).

Bion explores the theme of the difference between 'knowing phenomena' and 'being reality'. It is possible to be reminded of the 'form' through phenomena and it is also 'possible through "incarnation" to be united with a part, the incarnate part, of the Godhead'. But, 'is it possible through psycho-analytic interpretations to effect a transition from knowing the phenomena of the real self to being the real self?' (1965, p. 148). Both patient and analyst need to face the fear of the transformation from knowing about to becoming, that is, being, O.

> The psycho-analyst can know what the patient says, does, and appears to be, but cannot know the O of which the patient is an evolution: he can only 'be'

it. He knows phenomena by virtue of his senses but, since his concern is with O, events must be regarded as possessing either the defects of irrelevancies obstructing, or the merits of pointers initiating, the process of 'becoming' O. Yet interpretations depend on 'becoming' (since he cannot know O).

(Bion, 1970, p. 27)

Bion compares the psychological pain and turbulence involved when there is the 'emergence of transformation in O' (1965, p. 158) with the first dark night of the soul. He quotes John of the Cross who describes how:

The first [night of the soul] has to do with the point from which the soul goes forth, for it has gradually to deprive itself of desire for all the worldly things which it possessed, by denying them to itself; the which denial and depriva-tion are, as it were, night to all the senses of man. The second reason has to do with the mean, or the road along which the soul must travel to this union – that is, faith, which is likewise as dark as night to the understanding. The third has to do with point to which it travels – namely God, Who, equally, is dark night to the soul in this life.

(John of the Cross, *The Ascent of Mount Carmel*,
Book I, chapter II[2], Allison Peers trans, 1935/1953,
pp. 19–20, in Bion, 1965, pp. 158–159)

In the Allison Peers translation of John of the Cross quoted by Bion in *Trans-formations,* the word 'understanding' is used to translate *entendimiento*. In trans-lations by Kavanaugh and Rodriguez (1964)) *entendimiento* has been translated as 'intellect'. The Spanish *entendimiento* means the potency, faculty or power (*potencias*) of understanding, knowing, intellection. The raw data communicated to the senses is 'apprehension', which means the simple perception of something without the attribution of predicates to it, without affirming or denying. The understanding is the window for memory and will. Knowledge that arises from the understanding is of two kinds, natural and supernatural. The way supernatural understanding is imparted to the soul transcends natural capacity.

Bion describes the fear of unknowing, of ignorance due to the fact that such transformation in O requires faith and is 'not amenable to apprehension by the senses' and says this faith is that described by John of the Cross as the 'dark night of the soul'. The third dark night represents the transformation of K to O, which for John of the Cross is union with God:

The third 'dark night' is associated with the transformation in O, that is from K → O. The transformation that involves 'becoming' is felt as inseparable from becoming God, ultimate reality, the First Cause. The 'dark night' pain is fear of megalomania. This fear inhibits acceptance of being responsible, that is mature, because it appears to involve *being* God, being the First Cause, being ultimate reality with a pain that can be, though inadequately expressed by 'megalomania'.

(1965, p. 159)

Yet as John of the Cross also teaches, the aim is to transform the beloved into her Lover, just as 'fire converts all things into fire' (in Tyler, 2010, p. 47).

This latter distinction between becoming O or being become by O is what John of the Cross calls the distinction between the 'active' and 'passive' night. The 'active' night refers to all one's attempts to reach union with God, the 'passive' night to one being become by God.

For Bion, interpretations 'should be such that the transition from *knowing about* reality to *becoming real* is furthered' (1965, p. 153).

> If I am right in suggesting that phenomena are known but reality is 'become' the interpretation must do more than increase knowledge. It can be argued that this is not a matter for the analyst and that he can only increase knowledge; that the further steps required to bridge the gap must come from the analysand; or from a particular part of the analysand, namely his 'godhead', which must consent to incarnation in the person of the analysand.
>
> (Bion, 1965, p. 148)

'James' had read all Thomas Merton's books and was very inspired by them but always stopped short of actually going near a church, let alone a monastery. The church was a symbol of all he hated in his fundamentalist parents. Yet he eventually decided to take seriously the voice that kept coming to him in quiet moments, that he should actually do a retreat at a Trappist monastery rather than just read about it. In the end it was abject despair that propelled him to visit Merton's monastery and there, on retreat, he felt a subtle yet radical shift from 'knowing about' the contemplative path to 'experiencing it', from resisting belief in God to finding a strange sense of peace. On retreat, James 'consented' to letting something indefinably mysterious into his heart. He felt more alive than ever before, as if he had lived in the shadows, merely going through the motions of life. The gnawing emptiness of futility and despair now felt like the emptiness of a cave open to being filled with inspiration, the cave of the heart. Something utterly precious entered his heart. James then feared what would occur when he left the monastery. He feared he would harden his heart and cover over this deep sense of peace and inspiration. He wished the monks could have intuited what he was going through and without further ado, accept him into their enclosure. But he stopped short of asking.

Returning from retreat he discussed his dilemma with me, the fear he would return to the state of knowing about rather than being at one with his contemplative experience. Just as he wished the monks had bolted the gate with him still inside, he wanted my help to 'keep me on track' pleading 'don't let me fall away from this'.

Taking one's life 'watered down' and 'diluted' was the dilemma James described in therapy. How could he keep the flame burning within? How to avoid indefinitely postponing 'the state of "being" O'? (Bion, 1965, p. 149).

Not only the analysand, but also the analyst needs to confront fear of becoming in O.

> [The] psycho-analyst can know what the patient says, does, and appears to be, but cannot know the O of which the patient is an evolution: he can only

'be' it. He knows phenomena by virtue of his senses but, since his concern is with O, events must be regarded as possessing either the defects of irrelevancies obstructing, or the merits of pointers initiating, the process of 'becoming' O. Yet interpretations depend on 'becoming' (since he cannot know O). The interpretation is an actual event in an evolution of O that is common to analyst and analysand.

(Bion, 1970, p. 27)

Here we return to the theme of the spiritual practice of the therapist. Even when sitting with patients who are anti-religious, atheistic or disinterested in spiritual questions a capacity for negative capability, reverie and contemplation remain vital.

## O, Platonic Forms and incarnation

If ultimate reality is ineffable, how do we approach the unapproachable light? The nature of the Godhead in itself, and the Godhead's relationship to the cosmos, is a common Neoplatonic dilemma, discussed by Jewish and Christian Neoplatonists alike. It also relates to the Neoplatonic themes of procession and return and the great chain of being from the Godhead to the cosmos. For Plotinus, the One is above being, followed in turn by Being, World Soul and Nature. For Proclus, the One is above being followed by *henads*, Limit and Unlimited, One-being, Life, Intellect, Soul and Nature.

Bion draws on both 'Plato's theories of Forms' (Bion, 1965, p. 138) and the Christian doctrine of the Incarnation, the latter yielding for the analyst 'the rewarding model' (Bion, 1970, p. 88). The unknowable O may be made manifest through various forms, including emanation, incarnation, evolution and transformation. Bion links manifestations of O to both Plato's Forms and the Christian doctrine of the incarnation as implying an 'absolute essence', O, with which the analyst 'must be at one'. The analyst must also identify with the evolution of O in order to formulate it in an interpretation (Bion, 1970, p. 89).

Bion makes a subtle but important distinction between Plato's Forms and the Christian doctrine of the Incarnation. To begin with, Bion outlines his understanding of Plato's theories of Forms.

As I understand the term, various phenomena, such as the appearance of a beautiful object, are significant not because they are beautiful or good but because they serve to 'remind' the beholder of the beauty or the good which was once, but no longer is, known. This object, of which the phenomenon serves as a reminder, is a Form. I claim Plato as a supporter for the pre-conception, the Kleinian internal object, the inborn anticipation. . . . Phenomena, the term being used as Kant might use it, are transformed into representations . . . the significance of O derives from and inheres in the Platonic Form.

(1965, p. 138)

Bion goes on to describe how in Christian Platonism the 'balance between the elements of the configuration is altered; this may be seen most clearly in the doctrine of the Incarnation' (1965, p. 139). Bion draws on Meister Eckhart and John Ruysbroeck, both of whom distinguish the Godhead from God, to differentiate Platonic Forms from the Incarnation. If God is 'a Person independent of the human mind' then phenomena such as 'Good or Beauty' are not *reminders* of a Form (preconceptions) but are *incarnations* of *a part* 'of an independent Person, wholly outside the personality'. The phenomena do not *remind* the individual of the Form but enable the person to achieve *union* with an incarnation of the Godhead, or the thing-in-itself (or Person-in-Himself)' (Bion, 1965, p. 139, italics added).

Bion distinguishes between 'Forms' and 'Incarnation' as representing two different ways of understanding the relationship between ultimate reality and how that reality is apprehended. In the configuration 'Forms' the relationship is between the noumena or thing-in-itself and phenomena. Phenomena for Kant refer to everything that appears in our perception, and noumena are the things-in-themselves of which we cannot know through sensory perception. In the configuration of 'Incarnation' direct contact occurs through relationship to the incarnate Godhead. Phenomena, or that which is manifest, such as through incarnation, also enable one to achieve union with this incarnation of the Godhead, to be O.

Bion also distinguishes incarnation and emanation: 'The religious approach postulates an emanation of the deity and an incarnation of the deity' (1970, p. 88). Again, God and godhead are also differentiated. Meister Eckhart 'expresses his sense that the godhead evolves to a point where it becomes apprehensible by man as the trinity' (Bion, 1970, p. 88), but the godhead in itself is 'formless and infinite'.

Ultimately, the godhead, the thing-in-itself is not known but is become. 'O . . . is an absolute, inhering in ("incarnate" in) everything and unknowable by man' (Bion, 1970, p. 101). We are called to be transformed and changed into the godhead. According to Bion, this was what Eckhart was proposing and why he was condemned. In Meister Eckhart's apophatic anthropology, God and self share the same ground (*grunt*) and this ground of being is unknowable. In *Sermon 2, Intravit Jesus*, Eckhart describes how the self is nameless:

> [The self] is neither this nor that, and yet it is something which is higher above this and that than Heaven is above earth. And therefore I give it finer names than I have ever given it before, and yet whatever fine names, whatever words we use, they are telling lies, and it is far above them. It is free of all names, it is bare of all forms, wholly empty and free, as God in himself is empty and free. It is so utterly one and simple, as God is one and simple, that man cannot in any way look into it.
>
> (in Turner, 1995, p. 141)

## O and Jewish mysticism

On the impossibility of expressing infinity, Bion quotes the Jewish mystic and Kabbalist Isaac Luria (1534–1572) who, when questioned why he had not put his teachings into writing, replied:

> It is impossible because all things are interrelated. I can hardly open my mouth to speak without feeling as though the sea burst its dams and over-flowed. How then shall I express what my soul has received, and how can I put it down in a book?
>
> (Scholem, in Bion, 1970, p. 115)

Bion also uses Luria as an example of the relationship between the mystic and the Establishment. The Establishment expresses suspicion in regard to a true mystic who has direct access to the absolute. Luria avoided difficulty through insisting on his conservatism and by not leaving writings of his own, whereas Meister Eckhart was condemned as heretical for his views on 'identity with the deity – "we are transformed and changed into God"' (Bion, 1970, p. 116).

## The two commandments

What is the relationship between at-one-ment in O, and our relationship to each other, in other words, the relationship between love of the unknown God and love of the unknown other? Bion gives a religious counterpart from Augustine's *City of God* where he teaches that

> only when the individual has regulated his relationship with God, (or more precisely I, for the relationship with God is possible, but not with the God-head because the latter is Darkness and Formlessness, potentially containing all distinctions but yet undeveloped), can he regulate his relationship with his fellow men.
>
> (1965, p. 155)

Love, for Bion, is one of the 'passions' and a term used to 'represent an emotion experienced with intensity and warmth though without any suggestion of vio-lence'. Passion, including love, is the inter-relational or inter-subjective domain of two people present: 'Awareness of passion is not dependent on sense. For senses to be active only one mind is necessary: passion is evidence that two minds are linked and that there cannot possibly be fewer than two minds if passion is pres-ent' (Bion, 1963, pp. 12–13).

Bion alludes to another love, 'vaguely foreshadowed in human speech', which like ultimate reality or O, 'is the further extension to "absolute love" which cannot be described in the terms of sensuous reality or experience' (1992, pp. 371–372).

Let us ground all that I have said thus far with a clinical vignette.

## Case vignette: epiphany

'Jacki' arrives for her first meeting a jot early. She is diminutive, with a strange combination of a very weathered, time-ravaged and gaunt face, and pixie-like vulnerable innocence. As I open the door she looks up at me with piercing blue eyes half hidden by a mop of blond hair bleached by the sun.

Her tentative 'Judith?' is answered by

'Jacki? Come in'.

I usher her into my consulting room. She eyes the blue couch suspiciously and takes a chair instead. I sit down. There is silence for a moment, a pregnant pause before she launches in, like someone drawing a deep breath before plunging into a cold swimming pool.

> I came to see you because my bad temper is getting the better of me and my relationship is on the rocks.

Yet Jacki heaps all the blame on her husband, continually describing him as a life-denying, sullen kill-joy. Returning home after work bubbling away with excitement about her new job as a politician, she immediately feels the smile wiped from her face by his resentment at her merriment. She asks me if I had read the Narnia story *The Last Battle*.

> Josh is so like the Dwarves in the Last Battle. You know, where they all go through the stable to paradise. The dwarfs can't see that they are in paradise because they are so closed-minded. They think they are in a filthy stable. When they are given ambrosia they think they are being given horse pee, when they're given beautiful food they think they are being fed horse shit. They are so careful about being hoodwinked they blind themselves to a heavenly reality before their eyes. When the others are in paradise, they are convinced they are in a stable: they're not stupid, they tell each other, 'We're not going to be taken for a ride'.

After the session I take *The Last Battle* down from my shelf and read this section where Aslan sadly comments:

> You see, they will not let us help them. Their prison is in their own minds, yet they are in that prison; and so afraid of being taken in that they cannot be taken out.
>
> (Lewis, 1978, pp. 147–148)

I wonder whether this relates to Jacki's fears about therapy, that she might be taken for a ride.

Jacki comes in one day and says, 'Actually it's me who is the dwarf'. She ssuspect that casting Josh as one of the dwarfs was 'an off-loading' of a life-attacking force within which she projected on her husband. Via a history of entangled inter-relational dynamics he obligingly acted this out. One way or another, they both co-created the marriage as being like the stable, when the possibilities of paradise, intimacy, clarity and 'becoming in O' were shut outside their defensive, fear-driven minds.

Discovering then taking responsibility for her own dwarf-like fear was a moment of truth, but it also implied needing to step outside her own stable of control to behold a greater and more glorious reality beyond the confines of a constricting psychological prison.

One day Jacki comes in and tells me how during a period of prayer that morning the thought came to her that 'the opposite of love is not hate: it's control'. And then she remembers the dream she'd had the night before:

> I am in a car, sitting in the back seat and the car is driving itself. Perfectly well: it seems it knows where it is going. When I realise there is no one in the driver's seat I panic and say, 'Help, no one is driving the car!' A woman's voice reassures me: 'Don't worry, it knows where it is going, it can drive itself'. I clamber into the front seat and take over the steering wheel. Needless to say, the car immediately veers off the road and goes out of control. I realise I need to trust the car can take me where I need to go and let go of trying to rescue things and control them. It takes us both to a beach where we – this woman and I – get out and walk on the sand. We find all manner of beautiful shells and then we go for a swim. The ocean is deep but clear, the sense of becoming at one with the water and its depths is exquisite.

There are possible transference elements in the dream: analysis being like a process which has its own route, directed by 'the still quiet voice' of the analytic third which reassures us that the car knows where it is going. We don't have to over-direct the process. Jacki later laughingly refers to this as her 'Pelagian heresy' wanting to 'pull herself up by her own bootstraps' and over-control her life, relationships and analysis. The dream points to her developing trust in the car ride of analysis: she was, after all, 'being taken for a ride' but the car knew where it was going and it led to a place where Jacki could play in the sand and swim in the sea, safely. She said she had come to recognise that God's plan (if there was one), might possibly be better than hers, but it was still very hard to trust God.

Following this realisation, she enters a time of deep despair, grief and mourning which was unimaginably painful for her. She whimpers, 'Will it ever get better?' She tells me that she has been through so much but this is the worst harrowing she's ever felt. Before, all the externals might have been 'gruesome' but now the externals are ostensibly much better: she has a good job, three lovely children and she feels more positive towards her husband but internally:

> It feels like the worst dark night of the soul ever, and it does such terrible things to my relationship with God, like if he walked in here I'd just want to punch him in the face and say, 'Fuck you for a joke', then I feel like punching myself.

I wonder if she wants to punch me too, blaming therapy for creating this state of darkness.

I want to offer comfort but I know to do so would be just trying to rescue her from a necessary space of darkness that she is in.

She comes in with a dream:

> I dreamed I fell off a cliff: I realized there was no way I could hold on, do anything, control the outcome. I just suddenly had no choice but to surrender and I just spontaneously cried to God, 'Over to you' and this sense of utter relief in letting go. And then I was enveloped in this sense of infinity, like I was inside the mind of God, a peace that passeth all understanding, and I was floating upwards towards this radiance. I realized there is no limit to joy, felicity, goodness, wellbeing, ecstasy, light. The only limit is my capacity to experience it, open up to it. God has no limits: I do. I could experience infinity to the extent I could bare not to put on the breaks, but open myself into eternity, peace, beatitude even.

She tells me about her meditation session that morning and how at the end of it she realised that she still mistrusts God but an ominous voice within her said: 'But I trust you'. This revelation slowly transforms her life. She begins to behave in a trustworthy manner. Josh begins to trust her, trust that she will no longer fly off the handle into explosive rage. She begins to trust herself. She develops a quiet sense of inner authority, authenticity, as if inhabiting the skin of a lion, closer to her true nature.

## Notes

1  Many analytic writers insist that O is always only a psychoanalytic concept without mystical overtones. Ogden for example warns against any mystical reading:

'In reading late Bion, it is important to bear in mind that O is not a philosophical, metaphysical, mathematical or theological conception; it is a psychoanalytic concept. Bion is exclusively interested in the psychoanalytic experience: he is concerned only with the analyst's task of overcoming what he knows in order to be at one with what is, the O of the analytic experience at any given moment' (2004, p. 86).

Caper (1998) also holds the view that Bion's use of mystical thinkers in his formulations of the domain of O, memory and desire and container-contained was not to be mystical: that they constitute 'a psychoanalytic model of mysticism, not a mystical model of psychoanalysis' (1998, p. 420). Vermote warns that the apparent mysticism of O is seductive and that Bion was not interested in pursuing mysticism (2011).

2  A note on the edition and translation. Bion's citation is from the Allison Peers translation. Allison Peers based his translation of 1935 on the five-volume edition of P. Silverio de Santa Teres, C. D. (Burgos, 1929–31). He revised it in 1951, and it was published posthumously in 1953 as three separate volumes and then in 1964 as one volume in three.

# Inconclusion

We began with Jenny who asked 'What is the meaning of my life?' This is a question that we cannot answer for another, perhaps even for ourselves, but the question remains, awaiting discovery. Many suffer a pervasive sense of dissatisfaction and are looking for something deeper, a sense of purpose. If a patient is asking questions related to the spiritual dimension of life, how do therapists rise to such an occasion? Cultivating a spiritual sensitivity if not a personal practice of meditation and contemplation may be helpful to the life of the therapist, even when sitting with patients not ostensibly interested in spirituality or questions of meaning.

In contemporary society there is a pervasive sense of disillusionment with institutional religion. Yet this still begs questions concerning spiritual dimensions of life. Here we have explored the theme of how spirituality may be differentiated from organised religion. This is not to say that religion is not important, since most mystics encountered in this book were deeply religious as well as mystical. However, there is a concern for discovering one's own authentic truth through personal experience and the freedom to follow one's own calling and path, while recognising the need for authentic sources of revelation and wisdom.

At the heart of this book is the application of the apophatic way to psychotherapy. The apophatic dimension has much to offer psychotherapy because psychotherapy is also concerned with that which is unknowable and ineffable. A core element of the apophatic way is understanding that unknowing is itself a form of apophatic epistemology. As expressed by Dionysius: 'Into the dark beyond all light we pray to come, through not seeing and not knowing, to see and to know that beyond sight and knowledge – itself: neither seeing nor knowing' (Dionysius, *MT* 2. 1026A, in Jones, 2011, p. 25). Apophatic epistemology, the search to know while recognising we do not know, is also an essential dimension for psychotherapy. In sitting with the mystery of another human being, while searching to understand, searching to be understood, we are continually encountering alterity and ineffability, being 'comfortable with uncertainty'. I am not sure 'comfortable' is the right word. It is about being prepared to 'suffer' the anguish of uncertainty, to allow oneself to be submerged in realms of mystery and doubt, laying aside attempts to grasp after false certitudes as defences against the pain of recognising that one does not know. Psychotherapy is not a science where we have exact answers and irrefutable proofs. Being in a process of discovery with another human being is full of enigma, being open to what is being revealed, what forever remains hidden. It is inspired by faith, hope, love and compassion awaiting glimpses of a clear blue sky behind the clouds of confusion, a brush with eternity, a profoundly life changing moment that slips away and has to be rediscovered anew. It is no accident then that Bion and Jung found inspiration in apophatic mystics such as Dionysius, John of the Cross and Meister Eckhart.

We cannot truly appreciate Bion's work without careful consideration of his sources in the apophatic mystics. If, first, we are to uncover the original sources for Bion's advice that the analyst be without memory, desire or understanding in John of the Cross, and if, second, the aim of psychoanalysis is at-one-ment with O, absolute truth, ultimate reality, then the analyst is following in the footsteps of the apophatic mystics. This has radical implications for psychotherapy.

The first part of the book represents the interhuman connections of compassion, love and bearing witness involved in the psychotherapeutic relationship, and the second, the relationship of self to absolute truth, ultimate reality, for some, divinity, the divinity in oneself and the humanity in divinity. For the apophatic mystics, the two areas concerning love and being are one continuum. Lévinas would suggest that to love one's neighbour is to love the neighbour in their enigmatic holiness. Dionysius would suggest that love for God is realisation of the divinity within as well as without. John of the Cross teaches how ultimately the soul realises its inherent divinity and that 'you yourself are his dwelling and his secret inner room and hiding place . . . *Behold*, exclaims the Bridegroom, *the kingdom of God is within you*' (*CB* 1.7, 2017, p. 480). Yet all such attempts to express this fall short of the mark.

Another strand in the book is the continual interplay between the kataphatic and apophatic. The unnameable is approached through names, the inconceivable through concepts, the light unapproachable through darkness and obscurity, the plenitude of the void through images, which then fall away. The apophatic is a way of undoing and going beyond what can be said, yet relying on language to unsay itself. A third way of at-one-ment relates to transcendence of all dualities in a realm beyond knowing.

Alongside interest in spirituality, another 'sign of the times' has been an interest in Eastern religion, particularly Buddhism, Hinduism and Taoism. Many have found renewal through the meditative and contemplative traditions of the East. As well as the apophatic mystics of the Christian and Jewish traditions, another source of inspiration for this book is the ancient tradition of Dzogchen which concerns the discovery of our true nature, which is self-perfected from the beginning, primordially pure, luminous, beyond the falsifications and fabrications of the ordinary grasping mind, beyond dualistic divisions of self/other, beyond psychological confusion, delusion and destructive emotions. Following such re-awakening, the task is to remain in the uninterrupted flow of contemplation, fully present and aware, open to all of life's vicissitudes. It is also inherently about compassion and love that spontaneously arises once one's true condition is revealed and we are released from the constricting fetters of ego-centrism.

All that has been explored in this book are very much my own personal passions: the ethic of analytic hospitality, the role of meditation, contemplation, reverie in psychotherapy, the spiritual practice of the therapist, the ethics of alterity of Lévinas, the inspiration of the apophatic way, particularly Dionysius, John of the Cross, the anonymous author if *The Cloud of Unknowing* and Meister Eckhart, apophatic epistemology and apophatic anthropology, Dzogchen, Bion's work. These are signposts toward the infinite that help me wend my way. In following the apophatic way through darkness and unknowing I have explored themes of personal significance and engaged with the writings of mystics of importance to me. I draw no conclusions. This book is unfinished, at times rough around the edges, repetitive, full of limitations and possible misunderstandings as I have tried to grapple with the big questions of life. All I can dare hope is that there may be some food for consideration, some beacons from beyond this limited scope of work, beaconing you towards discovering your own sources of inspiration that cannot be contained in a book. You, the reader will have your own passions, your own concerns. You will have your own questions concerning, 'What is the meaning of life?'

# Bibliography

Alford, H., ed. (1839). *The Works of John Donne*. Vol. 4. London: John W. Parker.

Allison Peers, E. trans. and ed. (1953). *The Complete Works of Saint John of the Cross, from the critical edition of P. Silverio De Santa Teresa, C. D. Vol I*. New ed., revised. London: Burns Oates & Washbourne Ltd. (Original work published 1935)

Allison Peers, E. trans. and ed. (1964). *The Complete Works of Saint John of the Cross, from the critical edition of P. Silverio De Santa Teresa, C. D. Three Volumes in One*. London: Burns Oates & Washbourne Ltd. (Original work published 1935, revised edition 1953)

Amihai, I. and Kozhevnikov, M. (2014). 'Arousal vs. Relaxation: A Comparison of the Neurophysiological and Cognitive Correlates of Vajrayana and Theravada Meditative Practices'. *PLoS One*, 9(7), e102990.

Amihai, I. and Kozhevnikov, M. (2015). 'The Influence of Buddhist Meditation Traditions on the Autonomic System and Attention'. *BioMed Research International*, 2015: Article ID 731579.

Bambach, C. (2007). *Bordercrossings: Lévinas, Heidegger, and the Ethics of the Other*. Cambridge: Cambridge University Press.

Bar-On, D. (1989). *The Legacy of Silence: Encounters With Children of the Third Reich*. Cambridge, MA: Harvard University Press.

Barron, R., trans. (1994). *Buddhahood Without Meditation: A Visionary Account Known as Refining Apparent Phenomen (nang-jang)*, by Dudjom Lingpa [*Bdud-'joms gling-pa*, b.1835], Junction City: Padma Publications.

Bateson, M. (1979). 'The Epigenesis of Conversational Interaction: A Personal Account of Research Development'. In *Before Speech: The Beginning of Human Communication*, M. Bullowa, ed. London: Cambridge University Press.

Baudinette, S. (2012). *Rethinking Negation: Meister Eckhart's use of Moses Maimonides' Way of Negation*. Honours Dissertation: Centre for Medieval and Renaissance Studies, Department of History, Monash University.

Bion, W. (1959). 'Attacks on Linking'. *International Journal of Psychoanalysis*, 40: 5–6, 308–315.

Bion, W. (1962). *Learning From Experience*. Northvale: Jason Aronson.

Bion, W. (1963). *Elements of Psychoanalysis*. London: Heinemann.

Bion, W. (1965). *Transformations*. London: Karnac.

Bion, W. (1965). 'Memory and Desire'. In *The Complete Works of W. R. Bion. Vol. VI*, C. Mawson and F. Bion, eds. London: Karnac, 2014, pp. 1–17.

Bion, W. (1967). *Second Thoughts*. London: Heinemann.

Bion, W. (1967). 'Notes on Memory and Desire'. In *Cogitations*. London: Karnac, 1992, pp. 380–385.

Bion, W. (1968–1969). 'Further Cogitations (1968–1969)'. In *The Complete Works of W. R. Bion, C.W. XV*, C. Mawson and F. Bion, eds. London: Karnac, 2014, pp. 59–88.

Bion, W. (1970). *Attention and Interpretation*. London: Tavistock.

Bion, W. (1976). 'Penetrating Silence'. In *The Complete Works of W. R. Bion. Vol. XV*, C. Mawson and F. Bion, eds. London: Karnac, 2014, pp. 31–44. (Original work published 1978)

Bion, W. (1976). 'Four Discussions' In *Clinical Seminars and Other Works*. F. Bion, ed., London: Karnac, 1994, pp. 241–292. (Original work published 1978)

Bion, W. (1977). *Seven Servants: Four Works*. New York: Jason Aronson.

Bion, W. (1977). 'Caesura'. In *The Complete Works of W. R. Bion. Vol. X*, C. Mawson and F. Bion, eds. London: Karnac, 2014, pp. 37–49.

Bion, W. (1983). *Learning from Experience*. Northvale, NJ: Jason Aronson (Original work published 1962)

Bion, W. (1990). *Brazilian Lectures: 1973 Sao Paulo. 1974 Rio de Janeiro/Sao Paulo*. Karnac: London.

Bion, W. (1991). *A Memoir of the Future*. London: Karnac.

Bion, W. (1992). *Cogitations*. London: Karnac.

Bion, W. (2014). *The Complete Works of W. R. Bion*, C. Mawson and F. Bion, eds. London: Karnac.

Bollas, C. (1987). *The Shadow of the Object*. London: Free Association Books.

Bond, W., trans. (1967). *Nicholas of Cusa: Selected Spiritual Writings*. New York: Paulist Press.

Boochani, B. (2018). *No Friend but the Mountain: Writing from Manus Prison*. O. Tofighian, trans. Sydney: Pan Macmillian.

Brown, D. G. (1977). 'Drowsiness in the Countertransference'. *International Review of Psycho-Analysis*, 4: 481–492.

Buber, M. (1970). *I and Thou*. W. Kaufmann, trans. New York: Charles. Scribner's Sons. (Original work published 1923)

Buber, M. (1987). *I and Thou*. R. Gregor Smith, trans. Edinburg: T. & T. Clark. (Original work published 1923)

Candea, M. and Da Col, G. (2012). 'The Return to Hospitality'. *Journal of the Royal Anthropological Institute*, 18: S1, S1–19.

Caper, R. (1998). 'The Clinical Thinking of Wilfred Bion. By Joan and Neville Symington'. *International Journal of Psychoanalysis*, 79: 417–420.

Cartledge, P., Millet, P. and Todd, S. (2002). *Nomos: Essays in Athenian Law, Politics, Society*. Cambridge: Cambridge University Press.

Cassian, J. (1997). *The Conferences*, B. Ramsey, trans. New York: Newman Press.

Chesterton, G. (1938). *Autobiography*. London: Hutchinson.

Chrysostom, J. (1982). *On the Incomprehensible Nature of God*, P. Harkins, trans. Washington, DC: The Catholic University of America Press.

Clark, G. (1983). 'A Black Hole in Psyche'. *Harvest*, 29: 67–80.

Clément, O. (1993). *The Roots of Christian Mysticism: Texts From the Patristic Era With Commentary*, T. Berkeley and J. Hummerstone, trans. New York: New City Press.

Colledge, E. and McGinn, B., trans. (1981). *Meister Eckhart: The Essential Sermons, Commentaries, Treatises, and Defense*. The Classics of Western Spirituality Series. New York: Paulist Press.

Colman, W. (2010). 'Mourning and the Symbolic Process'. *Journal of Analytical Psychology*, 55(2): 275–297.

Counsell, M., ed. (1999). *200 Years of Prayer*. Norwich: Canterbury Press.

Cranz, F. E. (2000). *Nicholas of Cusa and the Renaissance*, T. Izbicki and G. Christianson, eds. Aldershot: Ashgate.

Critchley, S. (2002). 'Introduction'. In *The Cambridge Companion to Lévinas*, S. Critchley and R. Bernasconi, eds. Cambridge, England: Cambridge University Press, pp. 1–33.

Critchley, S. and Bernasconi, R., eds. (2002). *The Cambridge Companion to Lévinas*. Cambridge: Cambridge University Press.

The Dalai Lama. (2000). *Dzogchen: Heart Essence of the Great Perfection*, Geshe Thupten Jinpa, Richard Barron, trans. and P. Gaffney, ed. Ithaca: Snow Lion Publications.

Davies, O. (1988). *God Within: The Mystical Tradition of Northern Europe*. London: Darton, Longman and Todd.

Davis, C. (1996). *Lévinas: An Introduction*. Cambridge: Polity Press.

Derrida, J. (1999). *Adieu to Emmanuel Lévinas*, P. Brault and M. Naas, trans. Stanford: Stanford University Press. (Original work published 1997)

Derrida, J. (2000a). 'Hostipitality'. *Angelaki: Journal of the Theoretical Humanities*, 5(3): 3–18.

Derrida, J. (2000b). *Of Hospitality: Anne Dufourmantelle invites Jacques Derrida to Respond*, R. Bowlby, trans. Stanford: Stanford University Press.

Derrida, J. (2001). *On Cosmopolitanism and Forgiveness*, M. Dooley and M. Hughes, trans. London and New York: Routledge.

Derrida, J. (2005). 'The Principle of Hospitality'. *Parallax*, 11(1): 6–9.

Dodds, E. (1928). 'The *Parmenides* of Plato and the Origin of the Neoplatonic "One"'. *Classical Quarterly*, 22: 129–142.

Dowman, K., trans. (1994). *The Flight of the Garuda: Teachings of the Dzokchen Tradition of Tibetan Buddhism*. Boston: Wisdom Publications.

Du Boulay, S. (2005). *The Cave of the Heart: The Life of Swami Abhishiktananda*. New York: Orbis Books.

Dugas, L. and Moutier, F. (1911). *La Dépersonnalisation*. Paris: Felix Alcan.

Eckhart, M. (1981). *The Essential Sermons, Commentaries, Treatises, and Defense*, E. Colledge, B. McGinn, trans. The Classics of Western Spirituality Series. New York: Paulist Press.

Egan, H. (1978). 'Christian Apophatic and Kataphatic Mysticisms'. *Theological Studies*, 39: 399–426.

Eickhoff, F. (1989). 'On the "Borrowed Unconsciousness Sense of Guilt" and the Palimpsestic Structure of a Symptom: Afterthoughts of the Hamburg Congress of the IPA'. *International Review of Psycho-Analysis*, 16(3): 323–329.

Eigen. M. (1993). *The Psychotic Core*. Northvale, NJ: Jason Aronson.

Eigen, M. (1998). *The psychoanalytic mystic*. London: Free Association.

Ellenberger, H. (1970). *The Discovery of the Unconscious*. New York: Basic Books.

Erlandson, S. (2000). *Spiritual But Not Religious: A Call to Religious Revolution in America*. Bloomington: iUniverse.

Fairbairn, W. R. D. (1952). *Psychoanalytic Studies of the Personality*. London: Routledge & Kegan Paul.

Falluomini, C. (2015). *The Gothic Version of the Gospels and Pauline Epistles: Cultural Background, Transmission and Character*. Berlin: Degruyter.

Field, J. (1934). *A Life of One's Own*. London: Virago.

Fliess, R. (1942). 'The Metapsychology of the Analyst'. *Psychoanalytic Quarterly*, 11: 211–227.

Fonagy, P. (1999). 'The Transgenerational Transmission of Holocaust Trauma'. *Attachment & Human Development*, 1(1): 92–114.

Fonagy, P., Gergely, G., Jurist, E. and Target, M. (2002). *Affect Regulation, Mentalization and the Development of the Self.* New York: Other Press.

Fordham, M. (1957). *New Developments in Analytical Psychology.* London: Routledge.

Freud, E. (1961). *Letters of Sigmund Freud.* London: Hogarth.

Freud, S. (1904). 'Freud's Psycho-analytic Procedure'. In *Standard Edition of the Complete Psychological Works of Sigmund Freud.* Vol. 7, J. Strachey, ed. and trans. London: Hogarth Press.

Freud, S. (1905). 'Three Essays on the Theory of Sexuality'. In *Standard Edition of the Complete Psychological Works of Sigmund Freud.* Vol. 7, J. Strachey, ed. and trans. London: Hogarth Press.

Freud, S. (1911). 'Formulations on the Two Principles of Mental Functioning'. In *Standard Edition of the Complete Psychological Works of Sigmund Freud.* Vol. 12, J. Strachey, ed. and trans. London: Hogarth Press.

Freud, S. (1912). 'Recommendations to Physicians Practicing Psychoanalysis'. In *Standard Edition of the Complete Psychological Works of Sigmund Freud.* Vol. 12, J. Strachey, ed. and trans. London: Hogarth Press.

Freud, S. (1913). *The Interpretation of Dreams*, A. Brill, trans. London: George Allen & Unwin. (Original work published 1900)

Freud, S. (1923). 'Two Encyclopaedia Articles'. In *Standard Edition of the Complete Psychological Works of Sigmund Freud.* Vol. 18, J. Strachey, ed. and trans. London: Hogarth Press.

Freud, S. (1925). 'Negation'. In *Standard Edition of the Complete Psychological Works of Sigmund Freud.* Vol. 14, J. Strachey, ed. and trans. London: Hogarth Press.

Freud, S. (1930). *Civilization and Its Discontents: Standard Edition of the Complete Psychological Works of Sigmund Freud.* Vol. 21, J. Strachey, ed. and trans. London: Hogarth Press.

Freyberg, J. (1989). 'The Emerging Self in the Survivor Family'. In *Healing Their Wounds: Psychotherapy With Holocaust Survivors and Their Families*, P. Marcus and A. Rosenberg, eds. New York: Praeger, pp. 85–104.

Froehlich, K. (1987). 'Pseudo-Dionysius and the Reformation of the Sixteenth Century'. In *Pseudo-Dionysius: The Complete Works*. New York: Paulist Press, pp. 33–47.

Fuller, R. (2001). *Spiritual But Not Religious: Understanding Unchurched America.* New York: Oxford University Press.

Germano, D. (1994). 'Architecture and Absence in the Secret Tantric History of the Great Perfection (*rdzogs chen*)'. *The Journal of the International Association of Buddhist Studies*, 17(2): 203–335.

Girón-Negrón, L. (2009). 'Dionysian Thought in Sixteenth-Century Spanish Mystical Theology'. In *Re-thinking Dionysius the Areopagite*, S. Coakley and C. Stang, eds. Chichester: Wiley-Blackwell, pp. 163–177.

Golitzin, A. (1994). '*Et Introibo Ad Altere Dei: The Mystagogy of Dionysius Areopagita, with Special Reference to its Predecessors in the Eastern Christian Tradition.* Thessaloniki: Analecta Vlatadon.

Golitzin, A. (2013). *Mystagogy: A Monastic Reading of Dionysius Areopagita*, B. Bucur, ed. Collegeville: Liturgical Press.

Graf, P. and Schacter, D. (1985). 'Implicit and Explicit Memory for New Associations in Normal and Amnesic Subjects'. *Journal of Experimental Psychology. Learning, Memory, and Cognition*, 11(3): 501–518.

Green, D. (1995). 'The Rise of Germania in the Light of Linguistic Evidence'. In *After Empire: Towards an Ethnology of Europe's Barbarians*, G. Ausenda, ed. San Marino: The Boydell Press, pp. 143–163.

Gregory of Nyssa. (1978). *Life of Moses*, A Malherbe and E. Ferguson, trans. New York: Paulist Press.

Griffiths, B. (1954). *The Golden String*. Glasgow: Collins. (Reprinted 1979).

Griffiths, B. (1992). 'In Jesus' Name'. *Tablet*, 246(7915–16): 498–499.

Grotstein, J. (1990). 'Nothingness, Meaninglessness, Chaos, and the "Black Hole"'. *Contemporary Psychoanalysis*, 26: 257–289.

Grotstein, J. (2007). *A Beam of Intense Darkness: Wilfred Bion's Legacy to Psychoanalysis*. London: Karnac.

Grubrich-Simitis, I. (1984). 'From Concretism to Metaphor: Thoughts on Some Theoretical Aspects of the Psychoanalytic Work With Children of Holocaust Survivors'. *Psychoanalytic Study of the Child*, 39: 301–319.

Guarisco, E. (2015). *Secret Map of the Body: Visions of the Human Energy Structure*. Merigar: Shang Shung Publications.

Guarisco, E., Clemente, A. and Valby, J., trans. (2013). *The Marvelous Primordial State: The Mejung Tantra*. Archidosso: Shang Shung Publications.

Guenther, H. (1996). *The Teachings of Padmasambhava*. New York: Brill Leiden.

Guenther, H. (1975). 'Tantra: Its Origin and Presentation'. In *The Dawn of Tantra*, H. Guenther and C. Trungpa. Berkeley: Shambhala, pp. 6–12.

Guenther, H. (1989). *From Reductionism to Creativity: rDzogs-chen and the New Sciences of Mind*. Boston: Shambhala.

Guenther, H. (1992). *Meditation Differently: Phenomenological-Psychological Aspects of Tibetan Buddhist (Mahamudra and sNyingthig) Practices From Original Tibetan Sources*. Delhi: Motilal Banarsidass.

Hamilton, E. (1960). *The Great Teresa*. London: Burns and Oates.

Harmless, W. (2004). *Desert Christians: An Introduction to the Literature of Early Monasticism*. Oxford. Oxford University Press.

Harmless, W. (2008). *Mystics*. New York: Oxford University Press.

Henderson, D. (2014). *Apophatic Elements in the Theory and Practice of Psychoanalysis: Pseudo-Dionysius and Jung*. London: Routledge.

Hesychios. (1983). 'On Watchfulness and Holiness'. In *The Philokalia Compiled by St Nikodimos of the Holy Mountain and St Makarios of Corinth*. Vol. 1. G. Palmer, P. Sherrard and K. Ware, trans. London: Faber & Faber, pp. 162–198.

Hillman, J. (1989). *A Blue Fire: The Essential James Hillman*, T. Moore, ed. London: Routledge.

Hobson, R. (1974). 'Loneliness'. *Journal of Analytical Psychology*, 19(1): 71–90.

Hobson, R. (1985). *Forms of Feeling*. London: Tavistock.

Hoyt, S. (1912). 'The Etymology of Religion'. *Journal of the American Oriental Society*, 32(2): 126–129.

Humbert, E. (1988). 'The Well-springs of Memory'. *Journal of Analytical Psychology*, 33(3): 3–30.

James, W. (1890). *The Principles of Psychology*. New York: Holt.

James, W. (1902). *Varieties of Religious Experience*. Cambridge, MA: Harvard University Press.

James, W. (1904). 'Does "Consciousness" Exist?' *Journal of Philosophy, Psychology, and Scientific Methods*, 1: 477–491.

John of the Cross. (1934). *The Complete Works of Saint John of the Cross*, E. Allison Peers, trans. London: Burns Oates & Washbourne Ltd.

John of the Cross. (1964). *The Collected Works of St John of the Cross*, K. Kavanaugh and O. Rodriguez, trans. New York: Doubleday.

John of the Cross. (1974). *The Mystical Doctrine of St John of the Cross*, D. Lewis, trans. London: Burns & Oates. (Original work published 1934)

John of the Cross. (1987). *John of the Cross: Selected Writings*, K. Kavanaugh, ed. New York: Paulist Press.

John of the Cross. (1993). *Obras Completas*. 5th ed., J. Rodríguez and F. Salvador, eds. Madrid: Editiorial de Espiritualidad.

John of the Cross. (2007a). *The Ascent of Mount Carmel*, D. Lewis, trans. New York: Cosimo Classics. (Original work published 1906)

John of the Cross. (2007b). *The Living Flame of Love*, D. Lewis, trans. London: Thomas Baker. (Original work published 1912)

John of the Cross. (2008). *The Ascent of Mount Carmel*, E. Allison Peers, trans. New York: Dover. (Original work published 1946)

John of the Cross. (2017). *The Collected Works of St John of the Cross*, K. Kavanaugh and O. Rodriguiez, trans. Washington, DC: ICS Publications.

Johnston, W. (1967). *The Mysticism of the Cloud of Unknowing*. Wheathampstead: Anthony Clark.

Johnston, W. (1973). *The Cloud of Unknowing & The Book of Privy Counseling*. New York: Doubleday.

Johnston, W. (1978). *The Inner Eye of Love: Mysticism and Religion*. London: Fount Paperbacks.

Johnston, W. (1997). *Christian Zen*. New York. Fordham University Press.

Jones, J. (2011). *Pseudo-Dionysius the Areopagite: The Divine Names and The Mystical Theology: Translated From the Greek With an Introductory Study*. Milwaukee, Wisconsin: Marquette University Press. (Original work published 1980)

Jung, C. (1932). 'Psychotherapists or the Clergy'. In *The Collected Works of C. G. Jung*. Vol. 11, R. Hull, trans. London: Routledge & Kegan Paul.

Jung, C. (1933). *Modern Man in Search of a Soul*, W. Dell and C. Baynes, trans. London: Routledge & Kegan Paul.

Jung, C. (1946). 'The Psychology of the Transference'. In *The Collected Works of C. G. Jung*. Vol. 16, G. Adler and R. Hull, trans. London: Routledge & Kegan Paul.

Jung, C. (1954). 'Answer to Job'. In *The Collected Works of C. G. Jung*. Vol. 11, R. Hull, trans. London: Routledge & Kegan Paul.

Jung, C. (1963). *Memories, Dreams and Reflections*, A. Jaffé, ed. and R. Winston and C. Winston, trans. London: Random House.

Jung, C. (1966). 'Two Essays on Analytical Psychology'. In *The Collected Works of C. G. Jung*. Vol. 7, G. Adler and R. Hull, trans. London: Routledge & Kegan Paul. (Original work published 1935)

Jung, C. (1967). 'The Structure of the Unconscious'. In *The Collected Works of C. G. Jung*. Vol. 7, R. Hull, trans. Princeton: Princeton University Press.

Jung, C. (1969). 'On the Nature of the Psyche'. In *The Structure and Dynamics of the Psyche: The Collected Works of C. G. Jung*. Vol. 8, G. Adler and R. Hull, trans. London: Routledge & Kegan Paul.

Jung, C. (1971). 'The Archetypes and the Collective Unconscious'. In *The Collected Works of C. G. Jung*. Vol. 9i, G. Adler and R. Hull, trans. Princeton: Princeton University Press.

Jung, C. (1977). 'Mysterium Coniunctionis: An Inquiry Into the Separation and Synthesis of Psychic Opposites in Alchemy'. In *The Collected Works of C. G. Jung*. Vol. 14, G. Adler and R. Hull, trans. London: Routledge & Kegan Paul.

Karmay, Samten Gyaltsen. (1988). *The Great Perfection (rDzogs-chen): A Philosophical and Meditative Teaching in Tibetan Buddhism*. 2nd ed. Leiden: E.J. Brill.

Kaufmann, W. ed. and trans. (1966). *The Portable Nietzsche*. London: Chatto & Windus.

Kavanaugh, K. and Rodriguez, O., trans. (1964). *The Collected Works of St John of the Cross*. New York: Doubleday.

Kearney, R. (2014). 'The Inescapable Choice: Welcoming or Refusing the Stranger'. *ABC Religion and Ethics*. www.abc.net.au/religion/articles/2014/07/25/4053636.htm (accessed 1 June 2017).

Keats, J. (2002). *Selected Letters of John Keats*, G. Scott, ed. Cambridge, MA: Harvard University Press.

Kenney, J. (2013a). *Contemplation and Classical Christianity: A Study in Augustine*. Oxford: Oxford University Press.

Kenney, J. (2013b). 'Mysticism and Contemplation in Augustine's Confessions'. In *The Wiley-Blackwell Companion to Christian Mysticism*, J. Lamm, ed. London: Wiley-Blackwell, pp. 190–202.

Kestenberg, J. S. (1982). 'A Metapsychological Assessment Based on an Analysis of a Survivor's Child'. In *Generations of the Holocaust*, M. Bergmann and M. Jucovy, eds. New York: Basic Books, pp. 137–158.

Klein, M. (1923). *The Psycho-Analysis of Children*. London: Hogarth.

Kristeva, J. (1991). *Strangers to Ourselves*, L. Roudiez, trans. New York: Harvester.

Laird, M. (2006). *Into the Silent Land: A Guide to the Christian Practice of Contemplation*. Oxford: Oxford University Press.

Lameer, J. (1994). *Al-Fārābī and Aristotelian Syllogistic: Greek Theory and Islamic Practice*. New York: Brill.

Lear, J. (1988). *Aristotle: The Desire to Understand*. Cambridge: Cambridge University Press.

Lear, J. (1990). *Love and Its Place in Nature*. New York: Farrar, Strauss & Giroux.

Leclercq, J. (1987). 'Influence and Noninfluence of Dionysius in the Western Middle Ages'. In *Pseudo-Dionysius: The Complete Works*, C. Luibheid and P. Rorem, trans. Mahway: Paulist Press, pp. 25–33.

Lévinas, E. (1969). *Totality and Infinity*, A. Lingis, trans. Pittsburg: Duquesne University Press. (Original work published 1961)

Lévinas, E. (1985). *Ethics and Infinity*, R. Cohen, trans. Pittsburg: Duquesne University Press. (Original work published 1982)

Lévinas, E. (1987a). 'Philosophy and the Idea of Infinity'. In *Collected Philosophical Papers*, A. Lingis, trans. Dordrecht: Nijhoff.

Lévinas, E. (1987b). *Time and the Other*, R. Cohen, trans. Pittsburg: Duquesne University Press. (Original work published 1982)

Lévinas, E. (1987c). *Time and the Other*, R. Cohen, trans. Pittsburgh: Duquesne University Press. (Original work published 1947)

Lévinas, E. (1990). *Difficult Freedom: Essays on Judaism*, S. Hand, trans. Baltimore: Johns Hopkins University Press. (Original work published 1963)

Lévinas, E. (1994). *Beyond the Verse: Talmudic Readings and Lectures*, G. Mole, trans. Bloomington: Indiana University Press.

Lévinas, E. (1996a). 'Is Ontology Fundamental?'. In *Basic Philosophical Writings*, A. Peperzak, S. Critchley and R. Bernasconi, eds. Bloomington: Indiana University Press, pp. 1–11. (Original work published 1951)

Lévinas, E. (1996b). *Basic Philosophical Writings*, A. Peperzak, R. Bernasconi and S. Critchley, eds. Bloomington: Indiana University Press.

Lévinas, E. (1998). *Otherwise Than Being: Or Beyond Essence*, A. Lingis, trans. Pittsburgh: Duquesne University Press. (Original work published 1961)

Lévinas, E. and Kearney, R. (1986). 'Dialogue With Emmanuel Lévinas'. In *Face to Face With Lévinas*, R. Cohen, ed. Albany: State University of New York Press.

Lewis, C. (1978). *The Last Battle*. New York: Macmillan Publishing Company.

Lieberman, A. (1999). 'Negative Maternal Attributions: Effects of Toddlers' Sense of Self'. *Psychoanalytic Inquiry*, 19(5): 737–754.

Lifton, R. J. (1986). *The Nazi Doctors: Medical Killing and the Psychology of Genocide*. New York: Basic Books.

Lipman, K. (1984). 'Preface'. In *Dzog Chen and Zen*, Namkhai Norbu, ed. Nevada City: Blue Dolphin Publishing, pp. 5–12.

Lipman, K. and Peterson, M., trans. (1987). *You Are the Eyes of the World*, a translation of *The Jewel Ship: A Guide to Meaning of Pure and Total Presence, the Creative Energy of the Universe*, by Longchenpa. Novato: Lotsawa.

Louth, A. (2012). 'Apophatic and Cataphatic Theology'. In *Cambridge Companion to Christian Mysticism*, A. Hollywood and P. Beckman, eds. Cambridge: Cambridge University Press, pp. 137–147.

Luévano, A. (1990). *Endless Transforming Love: An Interpretation of the Mystical Doctrine of Saint John of the Cross According to the Soul's Affective Relation and Dynamic Structures*. Rome: Institutum Carmelitanum.

Luibheid, C. and Rorem, P., trans. (1987). *Pseudo-Dionysius: The Complete Works*. Mahway: Paulist Press.

Macneile Dixson, W. (1958). *The Human Situation*. London: Penguin Books.

Maimonides, M. (1963). *Guide of the Perplexed*, S. Pines, trans. Chicago: University of Chicago Press.

Maimonides, M. (1975). 'Eight Chapters'. In *Ethical Writings of Maimonides*, R. Weiss and C. Butterworth, eds. New York: Dover Publications, pp. 59–104.

Marcel, G. (2010). *Homo Viator: Introduction to the Metaphysic of Hope*, updated ed. South Bend, IN: St. Augustine's Press.

Maslow, A. (1964). *Religions, Values and Peak Experiences*. Columbus: Ohio State University Press.

McGinn, B. (1981). 'Theological Summary'. In *Meister Eckhart, the Essential Sermons, Commentaries, Treatises, and Defense*, E. Colledge and B. McGinn, trans. The Classics of Western Spirituality Series. New York: Paulist Press, pp. 35–36.

McGinn, B. (1991). *The Foundations of Mysticism: Origins to the Fifth Century*. New York: The Crossroad Publishing Company.

McGinn, B. (1994). *The Growth of Mysticism: Gregory the Great Through the 12th Century*. New York: The Crossroad Publishing Company.

McGinn, B. (2001). *The Mystical Thought of Meister Eckhart: The Man From Whom God Hid Nothing*. New York: Crossroad Publishing Company.

McGinn, B. (2012). *The Varieties of Vernacular Mysticism: 1350–1550*. New York: The Crossroad Publishing Company.

McGrath, T. (2000). 'The Transmission of Trauma: An Analysis of the Possible Place of Deferred Action in Passing on the Effects of Trauma'. *Psychoanalytishche Perspectieven*, 41(42): 123–137.

Meares, R. (2000). *Intimacy & Alienation*. London: Routledge.

Meares, R. (2005). *The Metaphor of Play: Origin and Breakdown of Personal Being*, 3rd ed. London: Routledge.

Meister Eckhart. (1981). *The Essential Sermons, Commentaries, Treatises, and Defense*, E. Colledge and B. McGinn, trans. The Classics of Western Spirituality Series. New York: Paulist Press.

Meltzer, D. (1992). *The Claustrum*. London: Clunie Press.

Mendez, H. (2013). *Canticles in Translation: The Treatment of Poetic Language in the Greek, Gothic, Classical Armenian, and Old Church Slavonic Gospels*. PhD. Thesis, University of Georgia.

Merton, T. (1951). *The Ascent to Truth*. New York: Harcourt, Brace & Co.

Merton, T. (1961). *New Seeds of Contemplation*. New York: New Directions.

Merton, T. (1973). *Contemplation in a World of Action*. New York: Doubleday & Co.

Milner, M. (1934). *A Life of One's Own*. London: Routledge. (Reprinted 2011).

Milner, M. (1952). 'Aspects of Symbolism and Comprehension of the Not-Self'. *International Journal of Psychoanalysis*, 33: 181–185.

Milner, M. (1957). *On Not Being Able to Paint*. New York. International Universities Press.

Milner, M. (1987a). *The Suppressed Madness of Sane Men: Forty-four Years of Exploring Psychoanalysis*. London: Tavistock.

Milner, M. (1987b). *Eternity's Sunrise: A Way of Keeping a Diary*. London: Routledge. (Reprinted 2011).

Mingyur, Y. and Swanson, E. (2007). *The Joy of Living: Unlocking the Secret Science of Happiness*. New York: Three Rivers Press.

Mitscherlich, A. and Mitscherlich, M. (1975). *The Inability to Mourn: Principles of Collective Behavior*. New York: Grove.

Modell, A. (2008). 'Implicit or Unconscious? Commentary on Paper by the Boston Change Process Study Group'. *Psychoanalytic Dialogues*, 18: 162–167.

Mondello, G. (2010). *The Metaphysics of Mysticism: Commentary on the Mystical Philosophy of St John of the Cross*. www.johnofthecross.com (accessed 1 June 2017).

Moyn, S. (2005). *Origins of the Other: Emmanuel Lévinas Between Revelation and Ethics*. Ithaca: Cornell University Press.

Nagasawa, T. (2016). 'The Rainbow Body'. In *Sharro: Festschrift for Chögyal Namkhai Norbu*. Garuda Verlag, Switzerland: Garuda Books.

Nagy, G. (2013). *The Ancient Greek Hero in 24 Hours*. Cambridge, MA: Harvard University Press.

Nef, F. (2005). 'Contemplation'. In *Encyclopedia of Christian Theology*, Jean-Yves Lacoste, ed. London: Routledge.

Nicholas of Cusa. (1969). *The Vision of God*, E. Salter, trans. New York: Ungar.

Nicholas of Cusa. (1997). *Selected Spiritual Writings*, L. Bond, trans. New York: Paulist Press.

Nietzsche, F. (1908). *Thus Spake Zarathustra: A Book for All and None*, A. Tille, trans. London: T. Fisher Unwin.

Norbu, N. (1986). *The Crystal and the Way of Light: Sutra, Tantra and Dzogchen*, J. Shane, ed. Harmondsworth: Penguin.

Norbu, N. (1989). 'Foreword', *Self-Liberation Through Seeing With Naked Awareness*, J. Reynolds, trans. Barrytown: Station Hill Press, pp. ix–iv.

Norbu, N. (1996). *Dzogchen: The Self-Perfected State*. Ithaca: Snow Lion Publications.

Norbu, N. (2000). *The Crystal and the Way of Light: Sutra, Tantra and Dzogchen*. New York: Snow Lion Publications.

Norbu, N. (2005). *The Mirror: Advice on Presence and Awareness* (dran pa dang shes bzhin gyi gdams pa me long ma)', A. Clemente, trans. and ed., and A. Lukianowicz, English transl. Arcidosso, Italy: Shang Shung Edizioni.

Norbu, N. and Clemente, A. (1999). *The Supreme Source: The Kunjed Gyalpo: The Fundamental Tantra of Dzogchen Semde*, A. Lukianowicz, trans. Ithica: Snow Lion Publications.

Nouwen, H. (1975). *Reaching Out: Three Movements of the Spiritual Life*. New York: Image Books.

Nyoshul Khenpo. (1995). *Natural Great Perfection: Dzogchen Teachings and Vajra Songs*, Lama Surya Das, trans. Ithaca: Snow Lion.

Ogden, T. (1994). *Subjects of Analysis*. Northvale: Jason Aronson.

Ogden, T. (2001). *Conversations at the Frontier of Dreaming*. London: Karnac.

Ogden, T. (2004). 'An Introduction to the Reading of Bion'. *The International Journal of Psychoanalysis*, 85(2): 285–300.

Ogden, T. (2012). *Creative Readings: Essays on Seminal Analytic Works*. London: Routledge.

O'Gorman, K. (2008). *The Essence of Hospitality From the Texts of Classical Antiquity: The Development of a Hermeneutical Helix to Identify the Origins and Philosophy of the Phenomenon of Hospitality*. PhD Thesis, University of Strathclyde.

Oldmeadow, H. (2008). *A Christian Pilgrim in India: The Spiritual Journey of Swami Abhishiktananda (Henri Le Saux)*. Bloomington: World Wisdom.

Parker, J., trans. (1976). *The Complete Works of Dionysius the Areopagite*. Merrick: Richwood Publishing Co. (Original work published 1897–9)

Perl, E. (2007). *Theophany: The Neoplatonic Philosophy of Dionysius the Areopagite*. New York: State University of New York Press.

Phillips, A. (1988). *Winnicott*. London: Fontana.

Philo. (1981). *On the Contemplative Life, the Giants, and Selections*, D. Winston, trans. Mahwah, NJ: Paulist Press.

Phuntsho, K. (2005). *Mipham's Dialectics and the Debate on Emptiness*. London: Routledge Curzon.

Pickering, J. (2008). *Being in Love: Therapeutic Pathways Through Psychological Obstacles to Love*. London: Routledge.

Pickering, J. (2012). 'Bearing the Unbearable: Ancestral Transmission Through Dreams and Moving Metaphors in the Analytic Field'. *Journal of Analytical Psychology*, 57: 576–596.

Pines, D. (1993). *A Woman's Unconscious Use of Her Body*. London: Virago Press.

Pitt-Rivers, J. (1992). 'Postscript: The Place of Grace in Anthropology'. In *Honor and Grace in Anthropology*, J. Peristiany and J. Pitt-Rivers, eds. Cambridge: Cambridge University Press, pp. 215–246.

Pitt-Rivers, J. (2012). 'The Law of Hospitality'. *HAU: Journal of Ethnographic Theory*, 2(1): 501–517.

Poincaré, H. (1952). *Science and Method*. New York: Dover.

Principe, W. (1983). 'Toward Defining Spirituality'. *Sciences. Religieuses*, 12(2): 127–141.

Proclus. (1963). *The Elements of Theology*, E. Dodds, trans. Oxford: Oxford University Press.

Pseudo-Dionysius. (1987). *The Complete Works*, C. Luibhéid and P. Rorem, trans. New York: Paulist Press.

Quiller-Couch, A., ed. (1953). *The Oxford Book of English Verse: New Edition*. London: Oxford University Press.

Quiller-Couch, A., ed. (1968). *The Oxford Book of Victorian Verse: 1250–1918*. Oxford: Oxford University Press.

Reik, T. (1949). *Listening With the Third Ear: The Inner Experience of a Psychoanalyst*. New York: Grove Press.

Reynolds, J., trans. (1989). *Self-Liberation Through Seeing With Naked Awareness*. Barrytown: Station Hill Press.

Reynolds, J., trans. (1996). *The Golden Letters: The Three Statements of Garab Dorje, the First Teacher of Dzogchen, Attributed to Garab Dorje [dGa'-rab rdo-rje], With a Commentary by Dza Patrul Rinpoche, Entitled the Special Teaching of the Wise and Glorious King*. Ithaca: Snow Lion Publications.

Rhys Davids, T., trans. (1881). *Buddhist Suttas*. Oxford: Clarendon Press.

Robertson Smith, W. (1927). *Lectures on the Religion of the Semites: Fundamental Institutions*. London: A. & C. Black.

Rolt, C., trans. (1987). *Dionysius the Areopagite: The Divine Names and the Mystical Theology*. London: SPCK.

Rorem, P. (1986). 'The Uplifting Spirituality of Pseudo-Dionysius'. In *Christian Spirituality: Origins to the Twelfth Century*, B. McGinn and J. Meyendorff, eds. London: Routledge.

Rorem, P. (1993). *Pseudo-Dionysius: A Commentary on the Texts and an Introduction to Their Influence*. New York and Oxford: Oxford University Press.

Rosenzweig, F. (2005). *The Star of Redemption*, B. Galli, trans. Madison: Wisconsin: The University of Wisconsin Press. (Original work published 1921)

Samuel, G. (1993). *Civilized Shamans*. Washington: Smithsonian Institution Press.

Samuel, G. (2016). 'Mindfulness Within the Full Range of Buddhist and Asian Meditative Practices'. In *Handbook of Mindfulness: Culture, Context, and Social Engagement*, R. E. Purser, D. Forbes and A. Burke, eds. San Francisco: Springer.

Samuels, A. (2003). *Jung and the Post-Jungians*. London: Routledge.

Śāntideva. *Bodhicaryāvatāra*. www.lotsawahouse.org/indian-masters/shantideva/bodhich aryavatara-3 (accessed 1 April 2017).

Scholem, G. (1991). *On the Mystical Shape of the Godhead: Basic Concepts in the Kabbalah*, J. Neugroschel, trans. New York: Schocken Books.

Schott, J. (2008). *Christianity, Empire, and the Making of Religion in Late Antiquity*. Divinations: Rereading Late Ancient Religion. Philadelphia: University of Pennsylvania Press.

Sells, M. (1994). *Mystical Languages of Unsaying*. Chicago: University of Chicago Press.

Sharf, R. (2015). 'Mindfulness and Mindlessness in Early Chán'. In *Meditation and Culture: The Interplay of Practice and Context*, H. Eifring, ed. London and New York: Bloomsbury, pp. 55–76.

Sheldrake, P. (2013). *Spiritualty: A Brief History*. Chichester: Wiley Blackwell.

Shryock, A. (2012). 'Breaking Hospitality Apart: Bad Hosts, Bad Guests and the Problem of Sovereignty'. *Journal of the Royal Anthropological Institute*, 18(s1): S20–S33.

Sierra, M. (2009). *Depersonalization: A New Look at a Neglected Syndrome*. Cambridge: Cambridge University Press.

Sogyal Rinpoche. (2002). *The Tibetan Book of Living and Dying*, P. Gaffney and A Harvey, eds. New York: Harper Collins.

Solovyov, V. (2010). *The Justification of the Good:An Essay on Moral Philosophy*. N. Duggington, Trans. New York: Cosimo Classics. (Original work published 1918)

Sophrony, A. (1973). *The Monk of Mount Athos*, R. Edmonds, trans. London: Mowbrays.

Stang, C. (2009). 'Dionysius, Paul and the Significance of the Pseudonym'. In *Re-thinking Dionysius the Areopagite*, S. Coakley and C. Stang, eds. Chichester: Wiley-Blackwell, pp. 11–25.

Stang, C. (2012). *Apophasis and Pseudonymity in Dionysius the Areopagite: No Longer I.* Oxford: Oxford University Press.

Stang, C. (2013). 'Negative Theology From Gregory of Nyssa to Dionysius the Areopagite'. In *The Wiley-Blackwell Companion to Christian Mysticism*, J. Lamm, ed. London: Wiley-Blackwell, pp. 161–176.

Stein, M. (2008). 'Divinity Expresses the Self ... An Investigation'. *Journal of Analytical Psychology*, 53(3): 305–327.

Stern, D. (2004). *The Present Moment in Psychotherapy and Everyday Life*. New York: Norton.

Stevens, V. (2005). 'Nothingness, No-thing, and Nothing in the Work of Wilfred Bion and in Samuel Beckett's *Murphy*'. *The Psychoanalytic Review*, 92(4): 607–635.

Still, J. (2010). *Derrida and Hospitality*. Edinburgh: Edinburgh University Press.

Strezova, A. (2014). *Hesychasm and Art: The Appearance of New Iconographic Trends in Byzantine and Slavic Lands in the 14th and 15th Centuries*. ANU Press. www.jstor.org/stable/j.ctt13www4f. (accessed 12 October 2017).

Studstill, R. (2005). *The Unity of Mystical Traditions: The Transformation of Consciousness in Tibetan and German Mysticism*. Leiden: Brill.

Symington, N. (1998). *Emotion and Spirit*. London: Karnac.

Symington, N. and Symington, J. (1996). *The Clinical Thinking of Wilfred Bion*. Hove: Routledge.

Tashi Namgyal, D. (2006). *Mahamudra: The Moonlight – Quintessence of Mind and Meditation*. 2nd ed. Somerville: Wisdom Publications.

Taylor, C. (1989). *Sources of the Self*. Cambridge: Cambridge University Press.

Teresa of Ávila. (1976). *The Collected Works of St. Teresa of Ávila*. Vol. 1, K. Kavanaugh and O. Rodriguez, trans. Washington, DC: ICS Publications.

Teresa of Ávila. (1980). *The Collected Works of St. Teresa of Ávila*. Vol. 2. K. Kavanaugh and O. Rodriguez, trans. Washington, DC: ICS Publications.

Teresa of Ávila. (2002). *The Complete Works of St Teresa of Ávila*. Vol. 2. E. Allison Peers, trans. London: Burns and Oates. (Original work published 1944)

Tiso, F. (2016). *Rainbow Body and Resurrection*. Berkeley: North Atlantic Books.

Torres, N. (2013). 'Intuition and Ultimate Reality in Psychoanalysis: Bion's Implicit Use of Bergson and Whitehead's Notions'. In *Bion's Sources: The Shaping of His Paradigms*, N. Torres and R. Hinshelwood, eds. London: Routledge.

Trinkaus, C. (2000). 'Introduction: F. Edward Cranz's Conception of Western Philosophy'. In *Nicholas of Cusa and the Renaissance*, T. Izbicki and C. Christianson, eds. Aldershot: Ashgate.

Trungpa, Chögyam. and Rigdzin. Shikpo. (1968). 'The way of Maha Ati'. In *Collected Works of Chögyam Trungpa*, Vol. 1, C. Gimian ed., Boston: Shambhala, 2003, pp. 461–465.

Trungpa, Chögyam. (1975). 'Laying the Foundation'. In *The Dawn of Tantra*, H. Guenther and C. Trungpa, eds. Berkeley: Shambhala, pp. 6–12.

Trungpa, Chögyam. (2004). *Collected Works of Chögyam Trungpa*. Vol. 5, C. Gimian, ed. Boston: Shambhala.

Tulku Thondup, trans. (1989a). *Buddha Mind: An Anthology of Longchen Rabjam's Writings on Dzogpa Chenpo* [translated selections from the works of Longchenpa (kLong-chen rab-'byams-pa), b.1308]. Buddhayana Series. Ithaca: Snow Lion Publications.

Tulku Thondup, trans. (1989b). *The Practice of Dzogchen by Longchen Rabjam*. Ithaca: Snow Lion Publications.

Tulku Thondup. (1996). *Masters of Meditation and Miracles*. Boston: Shambhala.

Tulving, E. and Schacter, D. (1990). 'Priming and Human Memory Systems'. *Science*, 247: 301–306.

Turner, D. (1995). *The Darkness of God: Negativity in Christian Mysticism*. Cambridge: Cambridge University Press.

Turner, D. (2009). 'Dionysius and Some Late Medieval Mystical Theologians of Northern Europe'. In *Re-thinking Dionysius the Areopagite*, S. Coakley and C. Stang, eds. Chichester: Wiley-Blackwell, pp. 121–137.

Tustin, F. (1988). 'The Black Hole – A Significant Element in Autism'. *Free Associations*, 11: 35–50.

Tyler, P. (2010). *St John of the Cross*. London: Continuum.

Underhill, E. (1922). *A Book of Contemplation the Which is Called The Cloud of Unknowing, in which a Soul is Oned with God*, 2nd ed. London: John Watkins.

Van Schaik, S. (2004). *Approaching the Great Perfection*. Boston: Wisdom Publications.

Vermote, R. (2011). 'Bion's Critical Approach to Psychoanalysis'. In *Bion Today*, C. Mawson, ed. London: Routledge, pp. 349–366.

Waaijman, K. (2005). 'Spirituality: A Multifaceted Phenomenon'. *Studies in Spirituality*, 17: 1–113.

Waldenfels, B. (2002). 'Lévinas and the Face of the Other'. In *Cambridge Companion to Lévinas*, S. Critchley and R. Bernasconi, eds. Cambridge: Cambridge University Press, pp. 63–81.

Walsh, J., ed. (1981). *Cloud of Unknowing*. New York: Paulist Press.

Watson, N. (2011). 'Introduction'. In *The Cambridge Companion to Medieval English Mysticism*, S. Fanous, V. Gillespie, eds. Cambridge: Cambridge University Press, pp. 1–27.

Webb, R. and Sells, M. (1995). 'Lacan and Bion: Psychoanalysis and the Mystical Language Of "Unsaying"'. *Theory Psychology*, 5(2): 195–215.

Wild, J. (1969). 'Introduction'. In *Totality and Infinity*, E. Lévinas, ed. Pittsburg: Duquesne University Press, pp. 11–20.

Winnicott, D. (1949). 'Mind and Its Relation to the Psyche-Soma'. In *Through Paediatrics to Psychoanalysis: Collected Papers*. London: Routledge, 2013, pp. 243–244.

Winnicott, D. (1954). 'Metapsychological and Clinical Aspects of Regression Within the Psychoanalytic Set-up'. In *Through Paediatrics to Psychoanalysis: Collected Papers*. London: Routledge, 2013, pp. 278–294.

Winnicott, D. (1956). 'Primary Maternal Preoccupation'. In *Through Paediatrics to Psychoanalysis: Collected Papers*. London: Routledge, 2013, pp. 300–305.

Winnicott, D. (1965). *The Family and Individual Development*. London: Tavistock.

Winnicott, D. (1969). 'The Use of an Object'. *The International Journal of Psychoanalysis*, 50: 711–716.

Winnicott, D. (1971). *Playing and Reality*. London: Penguin.

Winnicott, D. (1974). 'Fear of Breakdown'. *International Review of Psycho-Analysis*, 1: 103–107.

Winnicott, D. (1986). *Holding and Interpretation: Fragment of an Analysis*. New York: Grove.

Winnicott, D. (1988). *Human Nature*. London: Free Association.

Woolf, V. (1980). *The Diary of Virginia Woolf: 1925–1930*. London: Hogarth Press.

Wordsworth, W. (1961). Recollections of early childhood. In A. Quiller-Crouch, ed., *Oxford Book of English Verse: 1250–1918*. Oxford: Oxford University Press.

Wright, K. (1991). *Vision and Separation: Between Mother and Baby*. London: Free Association Books.

Wynne, P. (2008). *Cicero on the Philosophy of Religion: De Natura Deorum and De Divinatione*. Phd. dissertation. Cornell University.

Yovel, Y., ed. (1999). *Desire and Affect: Spinoza as Psychologist*. New York: Little Room Press.

# Index

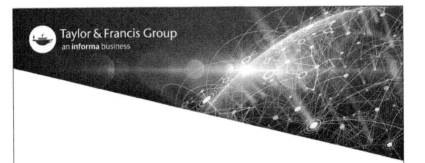